[2

BE

[2.0]

Turning Your Business into an Enduring Great Company

JIM COLLINS *and* BILL LAZIER

PENGUIN / PORTFOLIO

PORTFOLIO / PENGUIN

An imprint of Penguin Random House LLC

penguinrandomhouse.com

First published in hardcover as *Beyond Entrepreneurship* by James C. Collins and
William C. Lazier by Prentice Hall Press in 1992.
Copyright © 1992 by James C. Collins
This edition with new material published by Portfolio / Penguin in 2020 as *BE 2.0*.

Most Portfolio books are available at a discount when purchased in quantity for sales
promotions or corporate use. Special editions, which include personalized covers, excerpts, and
corporate imprints, can be created when purchased in large quantities. For more information,
please call (212) 572-2232 or e-mail specialmarkets@penguinrandomhouse.com. Your local
bookstore can also assist with discounted bulk purchases using the Penguin Random House
corporate Business-to-Business program. For assistance in locating a participating
retailer, e-mail B2B@penguinrandomhouse.com.

ISBN 9780399564239 (hardcover)
ISBN 9780399564246 (ebook)

Printed in the United States of America
1 3 5 7 9 10 8 6 4 2

BOOK DESIGN BY TANYA MAIBORODA

CONTENTS

INTRODUCTION
What is *BE 2.0*?

WHEN BILL LAZIER AND I co-authored the original edition of *Beyond Entrepreneurship*, based on the course we both taught at the Stanford Graduate School of Business, we set out to create a road map for leaders of small to mid-sized enterprises who want to build enduring great companies.

Bill embodied a rare combination of practical experience and academic reflection, and *Beyond Entrepreneurship* encapsulated much of his accumulated wisdom. And while I'd go on to author or co-author multiple *New York Times* and *Wall Street Journal* best sellers on the topic of what makes great companies tick, many leaders have told me that this very first book remains their favorite. When Reed Hastings, co-founder of Netflix, introduced me at a gathering for KIPP Schools in 2014, he surprised me by saying that when he was a young entrepreneur, he'd read *Beyond Entrepreneurship* six times. When Netflix won the Stanford ENCORE Award for the most entrepreneurial company, Hastings gave a piece of advice to aspiring young CEOs: "Memorize the first eighty-six pages of *Beyond Entrepreneurship*." Through *Beyond Entrepreneurship*, Bill became a mentor to entrepreneurs whom he'd never meet, inspiring them to strive to build truly great companies that can long endure.

But why create a re-release of *Beyond Entrepreneurship*, and why now? I decided to re-release *Beyond Entrepreneurship* as *BE 2.0* for three reasons.

First, I'm still fiercely passionate about entrepreneurs and leaders of small to mid-sized companies, whom I've always seen as the readers I most want to reach. This might surprise readers of my later books in which I'd researched companies that had become huge. But the eventual size of those companies obscures the fact that all the companies studied for books like *Built to Last*, *Good to Great*, and *Great by Choice* were once small start-ups, and I researched their entire histories all the way back to their beginnings. I devoted much of my curiosity to understanding why some *early-stage* companies *became* great and lasting, and why others didn't.

Second, I had substantial new material that could be directly useful to today's entrepreneurs and leaders of small to mid-sized companies. This new material, about people decisions, leadership, vision, strategy, luck, and more, found the right home in a re-release of *Beyond Entrepreneurship*. As you move through this book, think of it like a classic old home that has had a major addition. The new material appears in entirely new chapters and "insert essays" spread throughout the book, which are called out with the header "Jim's View from 2020." Nearly half of the text that follows is entirely new to the 2020 edition. I have, however, left the text of the original chapters fully intact as Bill and I wrote them in 1992 (with only a few corrections and minor adjustments). The original text appears throughout with a shaded backdrop.

Third, and most important, this re-release is meant to honor and extend the legacy of my co-author, the greatest mentor in my life, Bill Lazier. Without his shaping hand, I would not be who I am, and my life would not be what it is. When Bill passed away in 2004, I wanted to write something about him and the profound impact he had on people. Immediately following this introduction to *BE 2.0*, I share the story of Bill and what I learned from this wise and generous soul, a man who altered the lives of thousands of young people.

I hope *BE 2.0* helps you create an iconic company. Even more, I hope some of Bill's mentorship carries from these pages to live on through you and those you lead.

Jim Collins
Boulder, Colorado
March 2, 2020

BE
[2.0]

Chapter 1

BILL AND ME

BILL LAZIER WAS THE closest thing to a father I ever had. My own father died when I was twenty-three, and he never took the time to teach me anything about the difference between right and wrong, about core values, about character. I came of age in the late 1970s in the post-Vietnam, post-Watergate era that felt devoid of any grand sense of cause or direction or purpose. By the time I graduated from college in 1980, I'd never had a conversation with any of my classmates about commitment to service as one possible theme for our lives, and we rarely discussed the idea that living to a set of core values should guide our careers. By my early twenties, I had this gnawing feeling that I'd missed something essential, something I couldn't quite put my finger on.

Then I met Bill.

Shortly before my twenty-fifth birthday, during my second year of study at the Stanford Graduate School of Business, I got hit with a lightning bolt of "who luck," the type of luck that comes as a chance meeting with a person who changes your life. The academic dean had offered Bill, a successful entrepreneur and company-builder in his fifties, the opportunity to join the faculty and teach an elective course. Bill had accepted the Stanford position to share his practical wisdom, shifting his energies from building young companies to building young leaders. I'd sought a spot in a different elective course, but the random lottery system that apportioned class assignments put me in Bill's first-ever class offering. I asked my classmates, "Anyone know anything about this Professor Lazier?" Everyone shook their heads no. "Well, I guess I'll just go to the first couple of sessions and see what he's like."

It's a good thing I did. Had the course-sorting mechanism randomly assigned me to a different class, or if I'd dropped the course, it's extremely unlikely that I'd have launched myself down the path I've taken with my life's work. This book would not exist. Nor would any of my other authored or co-authored books, not *Built to Last*, not *Good to Great*, not *How the Mighty Fall*, not *Great by Choice*. None of the research and resulting books that I've had the privilege to write would have happened. And my very character—indeed, my deepest core values—would have been different.

Bill somehow took an interest in me. I think he sensed that I was a high-energy propulsion machine with no clear guiding purpose. He regularly invited my wife, Joanne, and me to his home for dinner with him and his wife, Dorothy. And he kept doing so after graduation, pushing me to think hard about how best to deploy my talents and make a distinctive contribution. He did this in a kind but persistent way, inspiring me to commit to a life of research, writing, and teaching.

Then in 1988, when I had just turned thirty, Bill made a truly gutsy move on my behalf, and my life changed for good. The Stanford Graduate School of Business suddenly and unexpectedly lost a star professor who'd been teaching a popular secondary offering of the course on entrepreneurship and small business that Bill taught. The academic deans asked Bill if he knew anyone who could take over the teaching spot for the coming year while they looked for a "real" replacement. Bill suggested me.

The academic dean expressed skepticism, but Bill fought for me. "I believe in him," said Bill. "And I'll take responsibility to coach him, since he'll be teaching the same course as me, just a different section."

Having no other alternative, the deans relented, hoping that Bill would make sure I didn't mess up too badly.

Imagine you're a young pitcher way down in the minor leagues, and one day the bus carrying the pitchers for a major league team breaks down on the way to Yankee Stadium. The game is about to start, and the managers are scrambling to get someone out on the mound to throw, and you just happen to be standing there. Then someone steps in on your behalf and says, "Hey, kid—grab a glove and ball, and go out there and pitch!" That's the way I felt stepping into the Stanford MBA classroom, filling in for a star professor.

Bill placed upon me a huge burden of responsibility—*he trusted me, he believed in me*—and I didn't want to let him down. He also gave me the lecture about performing best when it counts the most. It's as if we were in the dugout before my chance-of-a-lifetime game, with coach Bill telling me: "This is your shot. If you pitch a near-perfect game, they'll let you pitch again, and this can change your whole life. Now, go out there and throw!"

I threw in the "Yankee Stadium" of Stanford Business School for the next seven seasons.

Life Lessons from a Magnificent Mentor

Bill's greatness lay not in the fact of his success. To be sure, he was successful, by almost any measure. He was a successful entrepreneur whose privately held companies created jobs and generated wealth long after his own life expired. He was a successful teacher and scholar whose reputation earned him an endowed academic chair as the inaugural Nancy and Charles Munger Professor of Business at Stanford Law School (where Bill finished out his teaching career). Bill had such a deep impact on students at the law school that they honored him by naming the outdoor centerpiece of the Munger Graduate Residence the Lazier Courtyard. He was also a successful servant, giving time and money to a variety of social enterprises, including six years as board chair of Grinnell College.

But most of all, Bill was a mentor. Not just to me, but to hundreds of young people. So, before moving on to the more business-focused lessons of this book, I'd like to share a set of life lessons I gleaned from Bill. It's fitting to put these lessons up front in *BE 2.0*, for Bill exemplified that there's no true success without being successful in how you live your life.

Never Stifle a Generous Impulse

One day, two large wooden crates appeared on our front porch, the address labels indicating they'd been shipped by Bill. Upon opening the crates, Joanne and I found a few dozen bottles of spectacularly good wine, French and Italian and Californian. I called Bill and asked what had prompted this much appreciated gift. "Dorothy and I had an inventory problem in our wine cellar, and we needed to make room for some new bottles. We thought you could help us out by taking some of it off our hands."

Bill had mastered the art of getting people to accept his generosity, somehow framing it as though you were actually doing *him* a favor. Bill had a huge wine cellar, and we doubted that he actually had an inventory problem. Jo-anne and I had commented at dinner with him one evening how much we enjoyed his selections of wine. At the time, we couldn't have afforded to stock wine of such quality ourselves. So, Bill simply decided to share, leaving us with the happy problem of how to fit dozens of bottles in a small standing rack in our tiny basement.

Of all the great well-known business leaders, Bill most reminded me of William R. Hewlett, co-founder of the Hewlett-Packard Company (HP). Hewlett believed that a company had a responsibility to everyone it touched and that the people who worked hard to make the company successful de-served to share in the wealth that they helped create. Well ahead of his time, Hewlett embodied these values way back in the 1940s, long before they be-came fashionable in corporate America. HP became one of the first technol-ogy companies to institute significant profit sharing and stock ownership for all long-term employees, and Hewlett became one of the first tech titans to commit to giving a vast chunk of his fortune away. In building his company and living his life, Hewlett adhered to a simple motto that he oft repeated: "Never stifle a generous impulse."

Bill and I were both inspired by Hewlett, and Bill fully embraced Hew-lett's generosity maxim. Bill believed that the American Dream is not just about doing well for yourself; it is even more about the opportunity to do useful work and to freely give of yourself to others. You might give with money. Or with time. Or with service to cause or country. Or by teaching and mento-ring the next generation. Or by putting yourself at risk for something you be-lieve in. In Bill's case, he did *all* these and more. Bill's generosity did not deplete his energy; rather, it had the opposite effect. Because he was so generous and gave so much to other people, it came right back to him, increasing his grati-tude, which he turned right back around into giving, which further increased his energy—round and round the generosity-energy flywheel turned, build-ing ever greater momentum throughout his life.

Know When to Make the Irreversible Leap

Bill started his professional career as a CPA at a prestigious accounting firm. His star rising, Bill knew that he was right on the cusp of being named a partner.

Bill's response to his impending promotion to partnership?

He resigned.

"I always had a big dream to take the entrepreneurial leap to build my own company," he told me of this moment. "And I felt that becoming partner might tie me too much to a comfortable and prestigious position, and that comfort might make it more difficult to make the leap." So, just before they were about to elevate Bill to partner, he jettisoned the comfort and safety that would suffocate his entrepreneurial dream and launched himself out over the chasm.

Keep in mind, this was in an earlier era, when people craved prestige and upper-middle-class security, when entrepreneurship was viewed as a strange and exotic career choice for crazy risk-takers, when recently married professionals with young children rarely exchanged well-trodden paths to success for uncertainty and risk. But to make near-impossible dreams come true, there come moments when you have to go all in, fully committed, with no easy path to retreat. Bill believed that most people fail to achieve their audacious big dreams because they don't fully commit at the crucial moment.

To be clear, Bill didn't advocate making rash, all-in leaps to any random path, blindly chosen. He chose carefully in making bold, irreversible commitments. Still, the point remains: yes, it's risky to throw everything into the pursuit of a low-odds dream, *but if at the critical moment you don't go all in, the odds of achieving the dream go from low to zero.*

For Bill, staying at the accounting firm would have been the paint-by-numbers-kit approach to life, where everything is laid out for you, and as long as you stay within the lines, you're more or less guaranteed to have a nice picture at the end. But there's another choice, the choice that Bill made. You can forgo the certainty of making your life a pretty little painting, one that looks like a whole lot of other people's pretty little paintings, and instead start with a blank canvas where you just might paint a masterpiece.

Later, I had my own gulp moment. About five years into my teaching career, I faced a fundamental life choice. I could take the road well-traveled. I could pursue a traditional academic career, do a PhD followed by years of climbing the professorial-tenure ladder. Or I could forge my own way outside the academy, betting big on my own research and writing.

Over the years, some of my students had asked me about the inherent contradiction in the notion of being a "professor of entrepreneurship." After all, what does the structure and security of academic tenure have to do with the risk and ambiguity of entrepreneurship? So, I thought, "Why not invert the words? Instead of becoming a professor of entrepreneurship, why not become an *entrepreneurial professor?*"

When I told Bill that I wanted to "become a self-employed professor, endow my own chair, and grant myself tenure," he thought that sounded strange and improbable. He believed that I was made to be a teacher, researcher, writer, and professor, and he initially counseled me to build a more traditional and stable academic platform. When I told Bill that I was still going to be a teacher, researcher, writer, and professor—just without the university—he shook his head at the unfounded audacity.

Then I reminded Bill of his own moment of full commitment, when he resigned just before being promoted to partner. "What would have become of your life if you'd listened to those who worried about your decision to abandon partnership for an entrepreneurial path?" I noticed an evanescent smile, and he didn't answer. In retrospect, I think Bill was testing me, probing to see if I believed enough in the "self-employed professor" idea to make the commitment required. He also cared about me enough to challenge my thinking.

Joanne and I did make the irreversible leap, no turning back, in what we call our "Thelma and Louise moment," invoking the classic movie that ends with Thelma and Louise driving a convertible full speed, hands clasped together, hurtling out over a yawning desert canyon. (Although, unlike Thelma and Louise, we actually wanted to land on the other side.) We almost didn't make it, feeling at one point like we were going to smash into the cliffside when our cash reserves ran nearly dry. But if we'd kept open an easy-retreat option back to the comfort of Stanford, my behavior would have been different, less committed. And the odds of success would have dropped from remote to zero.

If you spend your life keeping your options open, that's exactly what you'll do . . . spend your life keeping your options open.

Make the Trust Wager

After leaving Stanford's cloistered cells and collegial culture, I made a number of bad people decisions, having misplaced my trust. I told Bill about the experiences and asked, "Bill, have people ever abused your trust?"

"Sure," he said, "It's just part of life."

"Have you become more distrustful, more self-protective?" I asked, continuing, "These experiences make me want to be much more wary of people."

"Jim, this is one of the big forks in the road of life. On one path, you first assume that someone is trustworthy and you hold that view until you have incontrovertible evidence to the contrary; on the other path, you first assume that someone isn't trustworthy until he or she proves to you that trust is merited. You have to choose which path you want to walk and stick with it."

Knowing that Bill seemed to trust people, I asked, "But what about the fact that people are *not* always trustworthy?"

"I choose to assume the best in people and accept that they sometimes disappoint."

"So, you haven't been burned much?" I challenged.

"Of course, I've been burned!" he snapped. "Quite a few times. But far more often, I find that people rise to what you believe of them. If you trust them, they feel responsible to merit that trust. Have you ever considered the possibility, Jim, that by trusting people you actually help them to be more trustworthy?"

"But some people will just take advantage of that," I pushed back. "And they can hurt you."

Bill then described a situation in which he'd lost "enough money that it hurt" when someone abused his trust. It was nothing catastrophic. ("Never leave yourself open to catastrophe; keep your eyes on the cash flow," he also counseled.) But it stung, especially as it came from someone he'd known for a long time.

Bill put it in terms of upside and downside. Suppose you trust someone, and he or she merits that trust. That's a huge upside. Trustworthy people feel validated and motivated by being trusted. What's the downside if you're wrong? As long as you don't expose yourself to unacceptable loss, you'll feel pain and disappointment. Consider the other side: What's the upside to mistrust? You minimize pain and disappointment. What's the downside to mistrust? This, Bill counseled, is the clincher: if you assume people are not trustworthy, you will demotivate and drive away the very best people. This was Bill's "Trust Wager"—a hardheaded belief that there is more upside and less downside to an opening bid of trust than an opening bid of mistrust.

"So, what do you do, then, if you discover someone truly has abused your trust?" I asked.

"First, you've got to make sure that it's not just a misunderstanding. Or incompetence."

"Incompetence?"

"Sure," Bill said. "There are two types of lost trust. The first is losing confidence in someone's abilities because you discover the person is a well-intentioned incompetent. The second is losing faith in someone's character. You might be able to help someone who is incompetent to become competent, but if you discover someone deliberately and repeatedly took advantage of your trust, you never fully trust them again."

Bill's trust and belief in others acted like a magnet, pulling people up to a higher standard of performance and character simply because they didn't want to let him down. The disappointments never stopped him from believing in people. He bet big on people, over and over again. And when some of those people proved worth the bet, they remained committed and loyal to Bill for the rest of his life.

Build a Meaningful Life by Building Relationships

"You can go at life as a series of transactions, or you can go at life building relationships," Bill once told me. "Transactions can give you success, but only relationships make for a great life."

"How do you know if you have a great relationship?" I asked.

Bill thought about it for a moment, then answered, "If you were to ask each person in the relationship who benefits more from the relationship, both would answer, 'I do.'"

"Isn't that a bit of a selfish way to look at it?" I puzzled.

"No, the whole idea is that each person contributes so much to the relationship that both feel enriched," Bill explained. "Let me ask you, Jim, who do you feel benefits more from our relationship?"

"Oh, that's easy . . . I do! You've given so much to me."

"Ah, that's my point," Bill smiled. "See, I'd answer that I benefit more than you do."

Bill's approach works only when both people invest in the relationship, not primarily for what they'll "get" from it, but for what they can give to it.

Bill was a particularly generous mentor. In the last quarter century of his life, Bill crossed paths with many hundreds of young people who got a slice of his mentorship. I was curious to watch whom Bill chose to mentor, and whom he continued to mentor. Those whom Bill invested in understood that being mentored isn't about "making connections" or "networking" or "getting a mentor to open doors." Mentorship—being a mentor and being mentored—is a *relationship*, not a transaction.

Despite Bill's gracious statement about how much he benefited from our enduring friendship, I always felt that I'd gained so much more from his mentorship than I was able to repay to him. And others touched by Bill's mentorship have told me they felt the same way. But Bill had an unspoken request for all of us. He expected the people he mentored to participate in a virtuous cycle, whereby mentees become mentors of the next generation, who in turn keep the cycle going. And in that way, mentorship becomes not just a two-way relationship, but an expanding web of relationships that extends far beyond the life span of both mentor and mentee.

Start with Values, Always Values

Bill loved teaching the L.L.Bean case. He especially relished engaging with students about its founder, Leon Bean, and how Bean made decisions based more on core values than on maximizing growth and income. In contradiction to a common MBA mindset that more money is the goal, Leon Bean left money on the table in favor of taking care of customers like friends, cultivating a culture to be proud of, and spending time in the outdoors. In Bill's view, entrepreneurial success shouldn't be primarily about what you do but about who you are. Just as a great painting or piece of music reflects the inner values of the artist, so, too, a great company reflects the core values of its entrepreneurial leaders.

Using Bean as a catalytic example, Bill would challenge his students to develop a clear guiding philosophy for life, one not defined by money. One of Bill's favorite case quotes (which you will encounter later in the main text of *Beyond Entrepreneurship*) was Leon Bean's response to people who thought he should grow more rapidly in order to make more money: "I'm already eating three meals a day, and couldn't eat a fourth."

For Bill, money was never the primary scorecard of life. He could have made more money, much more, if he'd spent the last two decades of his life focused on maximizing his business success. He chose instead to teach. Bill taught me a fundamental lesson, both in words and by his example: If you define success by money, you always lose. The real scorecard in life is how well you build meaningful relationships and how well you live to your core values. This means that values come before goals, before strategy, before tactics, before products, before market choices, before financing, before business plans, before every decision. I gleaned from Bill the idea that a company should start not so much with a business plan, but almost with a Declaration of Independence that begins with a statement of values: *We hold these truths to be self-evident.* Values come first, and all else follows—in business, in career, in life.

Bill taught that core values aren't the "soft stuff." Living to core values is the hard stuff.

One core value that Bill instilled in me is the sacred nature of *commitments.* "Be very careful what you commit to," Bill advised. "Because there's no honorable way to fail a commitment freely made."

In 2005, I committed to delivering a closing keynote presentation to a gathering near Fort Lauderdale, Florida, on October 25. I was scheduled to fly in on October 24, the very day that Hurricane Wilma blasted right into southern Florida. Six million people lost power. Airports closed. Hangar doors sheared off. I expected to get a call from those to whom I'd committed, absolving me of my commitment. But the conference had already begun before the hurricane hit, and it was the conference organizer's career-farewell event. He wanted me to come anyway and speak to all the attendees who, after all, were trapped in southern Florida.

What to do?

My team and I debated whether I should cancel. Then I asked a simple question inspired by Bill, "Is it impossible to honor my commitment, I mean truly *impossible*?"

There was, in fact, a remote possibility. I could fly into Orlando, which was still accepting aircraft, and arrive late in the evening. Then I could travel by car, four or five hours through the middle of the night, hoping to avoid hitting downed power lines, trees, and twisted road signs. If the roads were at all passable, I could arrive early in the morning. So, that's what I did, arranging a flight into Orlando about midnight, navigating utterly desolate highways through the night, arriving to no power and people lined up outside supermarkets for water and food, to deliver the closing keynote by gas-powered generator, right on time.

Bill imbued me with the idea that living to core values is often inconvenient, sometimes costly, and always demanding. It is indeed the hard stuff. I remain imperfect in living to all of my core values all the time. But I behave much more consistently with my values because of Bill's teaching and example. He taught me that you must continually self-correct, like a ship at sea being guided by a constellation of stars—sometimes you get a bit off, but you resight on your values and tack back on course. And you do this forever, across the entirety of any life well lived.

Put the Butter on Your Waffles

In 1991, as I began to struggle with drafting the manuscript of what would become *Beyond Entrepreneurship*, I complained to Bill that I felt like I was on a dark journey of despair, trying to make the words work. *Beyond Entrepreneurship* was my first book-sized effort, and I felt terribly inadequate to the task, a feeling reinforced every day when I'd read my text from the day before and think, "I spent six hours to produce something worthy of the wastebasket."

I expected Bill to give me a lecture about the need for discipline to push through the pain, like struggling through the final miles of a marathon. I was starting to understand a truth about the inherent suffering required to get the words right. Writing is like running: If you run your best, it will always hurt. It never gets easier; you only get better.

But instead, I got a lecture on fun. "Well, Jim, if you don't love doing it, you won't stay with it long enough to ever really get good at it." Then he added, "Life is just too short not to enjoy what you're doing. *If we can't make this fun, we should stop doing it!*"

The day after turning in the manuscript for *Beyond Entrepreneurship* to the publisher, Bill suffered a heart attack and had quintuple-bypass surgery. A few months after the surgery, Bill and I met for one of our frequent Saturday-morning waffle-fests at the Peninsula Creamery in Palo Alto, California. When his waffle arrived, Bill put a nice slice of butter right on top.

"Bill!" I exclaimed. "What are you doing? Didn't they tell you to stop eating butter, given your heart?"

Bill calmly poured some warm syrup on the waffle, watching the butter and syrup swirling together in a sugar-fat mixture of yum.

"When I was being wheeled into the operating room," Bill began to explain, "I bet they saw a smile on my face. I realized that if this was to be the end of my life, well, so be it. Dorothy and I had had a fabulous run, a wonderful life. To know that—I mean, to really *feel* it—while heading into the operating room . . . that's the moment I knew I'd had a great life."

"But what does that have to do with butter on the waffles?" I asked.

"I've already had a great life. Everything from here is just a bonus. So, I'm putting butter on my waffles."

Bill never confused a great life with a long life. I walked away reflecting that I couldn't determine the length of my life; all of us are short-lived creatures, vulnerable to being struck down by disease or accident at any time. Forty years, fifty years, sixty years, one hundred years, even one hundred ten years—these are all tiny numbers in the grand sweep of time.

And time *accelerates*. One day while driving to campus with Bill, I asked him if he noticed time going faster as he got older.

"What do you mean?" he asked.

"I'm noticing that weekly garbage days, when I need to put the trash out for pickup, seem to sneak up on me faster and faster," I said, adding, "I know it's still the same seven days it's always been, but it sure feels like a shorter seven days than a decade ago."

"Ah!" laughed Bill. "Wait until you're my age, and you feel like Christmases are coming around as fast as garbage days!"

So, if life is short—even if you live one hundred years—the main question isn't how to extend life as long as possible but how to live a life worth living all the way along, to live a life that you'd feel good about whenever it gets taken away.

The point here isn't really about the butter on the waffles . . . especially if you don't like butter or waffles. The point is a lesson that I wish I better embraced: the sheer value of having fun and enjoying yourself, of loving what you do, of living with the paradoxical assumption that you have decades of life left and that it might come to an end tomorrow.

On December 23, 2004, Bill awoke from a nap and, walking across the room, fell dead from congestive heart failure. Dorothy later told me he had a smile on his face, looking like he died happy with the life he'd led. A couple of hours after Bill died, I received a call with the news. I hung up the phone and turned to Joanne, "Bill's dead." When my father died, I cried only for what I'd never had. But when Bill died, I cried for what I'd lost.

At Bill's memorial service in Stanford's spacious Memorial Church, more than a thousand people gathered, the vast majority of them having been uplifted by his example and his teaching. I sat there and pictured every person like a vector moving through time and space, each with an altered trajectory because Bill had had an impact on their values and choices. If one indicator of a life well led is that you have changed the lives of others—that some people's lives are different and better because of you—it would be hard to have a better life than Bill's.

Chapter 2

GREAT VISION WITHOUT GREAT PEOPLE IS IRRELEVANT

Take our 20 best people away and I tell you that Microsoft would become an unimportant company.

BILL GATES

IN OCTOBER 2007, I received a call from Steve Jobs to discuss his idea to create Apple University as part of his goal to make Apple an enduring great company, one that could continue to deliver superior results and make a distinctive impact long after he was gone. He wanted Apple to soar far above the dispiriting descent that befalls many successful companies as they age beyond their founders, that of becoming just another big company that the world could do without.

Partway into the conversation, I couldn't resist unleashing my curiosity to ask what it was like in the dark days of 1997 when he'd returned to save Apple. Keep in mind, at that time few people thought Apple could survive as an independent company, much less regain greatness. There was no iPod, no iPhone, no iPad, no iTunes. And even if there were glimmers of these world-changing products as nascent ideas, the actual products lay years in the future. (Apple didn't release the iPhone until nearly a decade after Jobs's return.) Microsoft Windows had largely won the personal computer–standards war. One of the greatest start-ups of all time, Apple had fallen to the very edge of capitulation to irrelevance by 1997. So, I asked, "What did you first build upon to emerge from the darkness? What gave you hope?"

I had perhaps the greatest product visionary of our time on the other end of the line, and I expected him to talk about object-oriented operating systems or the remaining potential in the Macintosh computer or perhaps some other "insanely great" product ideas he had on his mind at the time. But no, that's not the answer he gave at all.

Instead, he talked about *people*. Jobs told me he'd found, hidden in the woodwork, some of the right people with whom to build his turnaround—people who still had a burning passion for the change-the-world vision that had marked the company's early days, people who still shared Jobs's passionate dedication to making exquisite products, people who still got excited by making "bicycles for the mind" that could amplify individual creativity. He spoke of them almost like the remnants of the scattered Jedi, hiding away below the radar screen of the Empire, ready to rise again at the right time. Apple's values lived within those people—hidden, dormant, atrophied, but alive—and he began rebuilding first by finding the right passionate believers.

We associate Jobs's spectacular turnaround with the iPod and the iPhone. Not that he ever lost his drive to create the right products, but he'd learned that the only way to build an enduring great company that makes great products is to have the right people working in the right culture. Jobs, the visionary entrepreneur who had led Apple in the early years with a "genius with a thousand helpers" leadership style, became obsessed with building Apple into a company that could be visionary without him. After Jobs's return, Apple became the first American company to cross a $1 trillion market capitalization. And how much of that market capitalization came *after* Jobs stepped down in the final year of his life? More than $600 billion.

As I sat down to upgrade *Beyond Entrepreneurship* into *BE 2.0*, I asked myself, "Is there anything Bill and I left out of the original edition that's so significant that it deserves its own entirely new chapter?" Yes. We should have included a chapter on people decisions, and we should have put it right up front as the very first chapter. Reflecting on more than a quarter century of rigorous research into what makes great companies tick, I've come to see "first who" as the one principle above all others that you must not get wrong. First in importance, *above every other activity*, is the imperative to get the right people on the bus. My research team and I identified the "first who" principle (*first* get the right people on the bus and *then* figure out where to drive it) in *Good to Great*. In this entirely new chapter, I'm not going to repeat what I wrote in that book. Rather, I'm going to expand on the idea, sharing some lessons I've learned about the "first who" principle since *Good to Great*, especially as it pertains to the readers of *BE 2.0*.

You need the right people far more than you need the right business idea, especially since any specific business idea is likely to fail anyway. If you have people who are unsuited to anything except the specific idea or business strategy you have in mind, what happens when that idea fails and you need to move on to the next idea and the next one after that? Alternatively, what if your first idea succeeds, but then you generate an even bigger or better idea that you want to pursue (such as when Apple moved from personal computers to iPods and iPhones)? If you've hired people for only a specific strategy, you've created higher odds of failure right from the start. Even if you're an uber-visionary, perhaps even the next Steve Jobs, the single most important skill for building a great company is making superb people decisions. Without the right people, you simply cannot build a great company, period.

Ed Catmull, co-founder of Pixar Animation Studios and a close colleague of Jobs, believed you can even start with a bad idea and end up with a great result if you have the right people. "Early on, *all* of our movies suck," wrote Catmull in his book *Creativity, Inc.* (which I warmly recommend), adding that "all the movies we now think of as brilliant were, at one time, terrible." Sometimes the Pixar team would even discover that the original story concept had to be jettisoned entirely. *Monsters, Inc.*, for example, began as a story about a man dealing with monsters showing up and following him around, each monster representing an unresolved fear, and it just didn't work. So, the director and his team reworked the story, over and over, iteration after iteration, until they found just the right formula. Catmull built Pixar on the idea that the first question is not "What are the great stories to bet on?" The first question should be "*Who* are the great people to bet on?" Catmull understood that a visionary idea with the wrong people makes a bad film, but great people with the wrong story will change the story to make an excellent film. Despite the fact that nearly every Pixar movie endured episodes of crisis, Catmull's "first who" strategy led to fourteen number one movies in a row.

"History is the study of surprises." This line from history professor Edward T. O'Donnell captures the world in which we live. We're living history, surprise after surprise after surprise. And just when we think we've had all the big surprises for a while, along comes another one. If the first two decades of the twenty-first century have taught us anything, it's that uncertainty is chronic; instability is permanent; disruption is common; and we can neither predict nor govern events. There will be no "new normal"; there will only be a continuous series of "not normal" episodes, defying prediction and unforeseen by most of us until they happen. And that means doubling down on the "first who" principle. If you're going to climb a big, scary mountain that's never been climbed before, your best hedge against unexpected obstacles is making sure you have the right partners on the other end of the rope, people who can adapt to whatever you encounter on the mountain. Even the most visionary among us cannot always predict which ideas will work. And no one can reliably predict what the future will throw at us or even what's coming just around the corner.

Track the Number One Metric

When you have your weekly or monthly or quarterly management team meetings, what's the number one, first-priority metric you look at? Is it sales? Or profitability? Or cash flow? Or something about products or service levels? Or some other metric? Whatever your answer, there's one metric that towers above all others, one metric to track with obsession, one metric upon which the greatness of the entire enterprise hinges. And yet, ironically, for most companies, it's rarely the metric first discussed—if it's discussed at all. However, to build a truly great and lasting company, it must rise to the top.

And what's that metric? *The percentage of key seats on the bus filled with the right people for those seats.* Stop and think: What percentage of your key seats do you have filled with the right people? If your answer is less than 90 percent, you've just identified your number one priority. To build a truly great company, you'll need to strive for having 90 percent of your key seats filled with the right people.

Why not 100 percent of your key seats filled with the right people? At any given moment, there's a very high likelihood that at least some key seats will be temporarily unfilled. It could also be that you've only recently moved someone into a key seat, and you don't yet know how well that person will perform in that seat. And in some cases, the demands of a key seat have grown faster than the capabilities of the person in that seat.

What makes for a key seat? Any seat meeting *any one* of the following three conditions qualifies as key:

1. The person in that seat *has the power to make significant people decisions.*
2. Failure in the seat *could expose the entire enterprise to significant risk or potential catastrophe.*
3. Success in the seat would have a significantly *outsized impact on the company's success.*

The question of whom to put in key seats becomes crucial when you cannot easily get people off your bus. This might be because of family dynamics, quasi-tenured employees, internal politics, or even simple loyalty to some of the people who contributed early on to the company's success. But whatever the constraints—and whatever the reasons—you still have the task to get your key seats filled with the right people.

Know When to Shift from "Develop" to "Replace"

Consider the following scenario: You have a person in a key seat who's doing a good but not great job. You like this person. You really want this person to succeed. You've invested time and energy in this person. But the fact is that you're not yet seeing the A-level performance you need in the seat. When facing this situation, which way do you tilt—toward investing more to *develop* the person or toward acting decisively to *replace* the person? (Note: Replacing the person doesn't necessarily mean kicking him or her off the bus; you might move the person to a different seat.)

There's no single right answer. Looking across the best leaders we've studied, we see about a 50/50 split between those who tilted toward develop and those who tilted toward replace. For example, here are ten of the best corporate leaders in history, five of whom tilted toward developing people and five of whom tilted toward replacing people when they were struggling to deliver superior performance in key seats:

Tilted toward Develop
Anne Mulcahy, Xerox
Bill Hewlett, HP
Herb Kelleher, Southwest Airlines
J. W. Marriott, Marriott
William McKnight, 3M

Tilted toward Replace
Katharine Graham, *The Washington Post*
Andy Grove, Intel
Ken Iverson, Nucor
Peter Lewis, Progressive Insurance
George Rathmann, Amgen

But even those who tilt toward develop have a demarcation line, a point when they confront the brutal fact that they need to replace someone in a key seat. I've asked multitudes of gatherings of executives this question: "Which of the following two categories of mistakes have you more frequently made? Category 1: In retrospect, you waited too long before you acted to move the person out of the key seat. Category 2: In retrospect, you acted too quickly and you should have been more patient. Stop and think: Which mistake do you make more frequently?" In response to this question, the vast majority of hands go up for Category 1, waiting too long before taking decisive action.

To be fair, it's easier to know when you've made a Category 1 mistake than when you've made a Category 2 mistake, especially if the Category 2 mistakes leave the company. Still, the fact remains that every organization struggles with the tension between developing people and replacing people in key seats. And no leader gets it right every single time. Sometimes they invest too long in developing someone and sometimes they act too quickly to replace someone. There's no algorithm to apply, no flow chart to follow, no equation to run to get a perfect hit rate on the decision to develop or replace. The best executives care deeply about their people, and that's why they often wait too long. But they also improve their judgment over time.

Which brings us to a crucial question: *How do you know when you've crossed the demarcation line, when it's time to make the shift from "develop" to "replace" for a key seat?* I've come to believe the best approach is to ask considered questions and let those questions guide you to an answer. I've distilled years of reflection down to seven questions that I offer here to stimulate your thinking when you face the "develop or replace" conundrum. To be clear, these aren't a prescription; you might come up with only one concern and decide to replace, or you might come up with six concerns and decide to develop.

1. *Are you beginning to lose other people by keeping this person in the seat?*
   The best people want to work with the best people, and if they sense chronic tolerance for mediocre performance in key seats, they might begin to vote with their feet. Worse, if you tolerate high-performing people who behave contrary to your stated core values, the true believers will begin to lose heart and become cynical, and some will leave. There's no better way to destroy a great culture than to retain people in key seats who fail to perform or run roughshod over the company's core values.

2. *Do you have a values problem, a will problem, or a skills problem?*
   If someone in a key seat behaves consistently or flagrantly contrary to the core values of the enterprise, the best leaders replace them. If someone passionately embraces the core values of the enterprise and also has the indomitable will to do whatever it takes to master his or her seat, you can be more patient before reaching a decision to replace them in that seat. The hardest call comes with the question of *will*. Does the person lack (or has the person lost) the will to develop to meet the demands of the seat? If not, can you ignite their will? Great leaders never underestimate how much people can grow, but they also know that growth depends on the humility and relentless will to improve. (Credit for the values-will-skills framework goes to the late Dale Gifford of Hewitt Associates, who taught it to me.)

3. *What's the person's relationship to the window and the mirror?*
   The right people in key seats display window-and-mirror maturity. When things go well, the right people point out the window, giving credit to factors other than themselves; they shine a light on other people who contributed to the success and take little credit themselves. And when things go awry, they don't blame circumstances or other people for setbacks and failures; they point in the mirror and say, "I am responsible." People who look in the mirror—who always ask, "What could I have done better? What did I miss?"—will grow. People who always point out the window to explain away problems or affix blame elsewhere will be stunted in their growth.

4. *Does the person see work as a job or a responsibility?*
   The right people in key seats understand that they don't have "jobs"; they have *responsibilities*. They grasp the difference between their task list and their true responsibilities. A great doctor doesn't merely have the "job" of performing procedures but embraces responsibility for the health of the patient. A great coach doesn't merely have the "job" of preparing workouts but embraces responsibility for building his or her players into better people. A great teacher doesn't merely have the "job" of being in the classroom from 8 A.M. to 3 P.M. but embraces responsibility for every child's learning. Every person in a key seat has a broader responsibility than a task list, and the right people never hide behind "I got the tasks done" as an excuse for failing to deliver on the broader responsibility.

5. *Has your confidence in the person gone up or down in the past year?*
   Just as a company's stock price rises or falls as investors gain or lose confidence in the company's growth and performance, confidence in a person

also rises or falls based on his or her growth and performance. The critical variable is the *trajectory* of that confidence over time. When someone says, "Got it!" do you increasingly set your worries aside or do you increasingly feel the need to follow up?

6. *Do you have a bus problem or a seat problem?*

Sometimes you might have a right person on the bus but in the wrong seat. You might have put the person in a seat misaligned with his or her capabilities or temperament. Or perhaps—and this happens frequently in high-growth companies—the demands of a seat might have grown to outstrip the capabilities of the person in that seat.

7. *How would you feel if the person quit?*

If secretly relieved, then you might have already concluded that he or she is a wrong person on the bus. If genuinely distraught, then you might well believe that he or she is still a right person on the bus.

When you've reached the demarcation line and have decided to replace someone in a key seat, keep in mind an essential distinction: *Be rigorous, not ruthless.* Rigor means applying self-honesty and confronting head-on the need to remove someone from a key seat. But being rigorous in decision making doesn't mean being ruthless in how you go about making the change. To be rigorous, not ruthless, requires a blend of courage and compassion. The courage comes in being direct and straightforward, not hiding behind made-up reasons or delegating the hard task to someone else. If you don't have the guts to take personal responsibility for making the decision and delivering the news, then you don't have the right to lead. The compassion comes via tone and respect. Are you handling the change in such a manner that you'd feel comfortable calling this person on his or her birthday next year, and years down the road? And would the person warmly welcome the call?

If You Want to Grow Your People, First Grow Yourself

Anne Bakar didn't expect to become CEO of Telecare, certainly not at age twenty-nine. When her father died from an adverse reaction to a medical treatment, Bakar had thrust upon her responsibility for figuring out what to do with the small psychiatric-services business her father had co-founded. I first met Bakar just as Bill and I were finalizing the manuscript of the original edition of *Beyond Entrepreneurship*. "I loved my father dearly. I want to honor what he built, and I want to make Telecare great and enduring," she said. We gave her a copy of the manuscript and she gathered twenty-four members of her team at the Claremont Hotel in Berkeley to lay the foundations of Telecare as a great company. Bakar and her team latched on to the vision framework laid out in the original vision chapter of *Beyond Entrepreneurship* (the very same vision chapter reproduced in this edition) to capture core values and establish an enduring purpose for the company: *to help people with mental impairments realize their full potential.*

It was a huge ambition for a small company led by a young CEO in the vast world of healthcare and treating mental illness. But Bakar felt passionately about the purpose, inspired by her father's belief that people with mental impairments could make significant recovery. She also had strategic acumen, honed by working at Montgomery Securities, where she had to make investments based on incisive analyses of companies. And she had the courage to place well-chosen big bets, based on empirical validation.

Yet to make Telecare into a great company, Bakar needed to grow into a great leader, to scale her own capabilities right alongside the growth and scale of the company. Anne Bakar 1.0 was smart and strategic, fueled by youthful passion, with just enough leadership instinct to get Telecare moving in the right direction. But that wasn't enough. She had to grow into Anne Bakar 2.0, then Anne Bakar 3.0.

She *learned* how to hire great people and meld them into a cohesive team. She *learned* that culture does not merely support strategy, but that culture *is* strategy. She *learned* how to hire for values and temperament, not just smarts and experience. She *learned* how and when to delegate, and when not to. She *learned* how to hold her unit leaders accountable for keeping the culture vibrant at the front line. She *learned* how to make wise decisions that reduce short-term profits for the sake of long-term greatness. She *learned* how to stay calm and mitigate her impulse to take control from her people when things went wrong. She *learned* how to confront existential threats by moving outside the company to cultivate mentors she could learn from both intellectually and emotionally. "When I confronted organizational crises, I traversed out instead of inward, relentless in seeking out the best advice I could from as many experts as possible," she later reflected. "Although the default impulse may be to retrench when there is uncertainty or chaos, I consciously did the reverse, and that was pivotal to my learning and growth." And her growth didn't stop. As I write these words, Bakar is working on Anne Bakar 3.0, and after 3.0, there will be Anne Bakar 4.0. Bakar's greatest strength is her commitment to grow into the leader Telecare needs, every step of the way.

In 2015, Telecare celebrated its fiftieth anniversary, having grown under Bakar to offering eighty-five programs in eight states and serving tens of thousands of people. Along the way, growth in the value of the employee ESOP (employee stock ownership plan) trounced the S&P 500. And in 2017, Bakar was inducted into the San Francisco Bay Area Business Hall of Fame, a rarified recognition previously conferred upon founders, CEOs, and chairs of companies like Cisco, Salesforce, Intel, Apple, HP, and Charles Schwab.

Most great leaders don't begin as great leaders. Sure, there are a few weird freaks of nature that seem to be born for leadership, who are fascinating to look at, like some sort of exotic bug. They're also largely irrelevant; you simply can't do anything about whether you're born as one of those weird, freaky bugs. And—this is the crucial point—most exceptional leaders grow into their capabilities. Not because they want to "be" a great leader, but because they're trying to be worthy of the people they lead. If you want the people with whom you work to improve their performance, first improve your own. If you want others to expand their capabilities, first expand your own.

What was Dwight Eisenhower doing in early 1936? He was a relatively undistinguished major, serving as an assistant to General Douglas MacArthur in the Philippines. Eight years later he was Supreme Commander of Allied forces. At West Point, he'd shown middling promise. No one said, "Look, there goes the future-great General Eisenhower, and someday they'll name Eisenhower Hall after him." Eisenhower didn't start as *Eisenhower* as we know him today; he *became* that Eisenhower. Of course, it took General George C. Marshall, chief of staff of the Army, to recognize Eisenhower's gifts and help him move more quickly into a position of significant responsibility. As you build and lead your own organization, you might want to be asking, "Who's my hidden Eisenhower?"

Steve Jobs in his twenties couldn't have led Apple's resurgence in the early 2000s. The young Jobs was notorious for temperamental, demeaning outbursts, seen as an immature genius utterly intolerant of anyone who didn't advance his peculiar vision. But he didn't remain stuck in his entrepreneurial immaturity. Young leaders would do well to absorb the book *Becoming Steve Jobs* by Brent Schlender and Rick Tetzeli, which captures Jobs's journey and maturation. Don't confuse Steve Jobs's behavior in his twenties with his leadership effectiveness in his fifties; don't confuse the harsh "genius with a thousand helpers" with the driven, reflective man who sought to build an enduring great company that could outlast him; don't confuse Steve Jobs 1.0 with Steve Jobs 2.0. To understand the message of Steve Jobs's life is to see it not as a success story, but as a *growth* story.

One of the most destructive myths is that a founder-entrepreneur or small-business leader will almost inevitably hit his or her managerial limit and need to be replaced with a "real" CEO to build the company. Steve Jobs 1.0 bought into that myth and it nearly killed Apple; it took Steve Jobs 2.0 to save it. If someone tries to convince you of that myth, ask in response, "Well, if that's true, how do you explain the undeniable, empirical fact that many of the great companies in history were built by a founding entrepreneur?"

Here's a short list (I could make a much longer one) of entrepreneurial founders or co-founders who grew into the very leaders their enterprises needed to scale to greatness: Wendy Kopp (Teach For America), Gordon Moore and Robert Noyce (Intel), George Rathmann (Amgen), Bill Gates (Microsoft), Jeff Bezos (Amazon), Walt Disney (Disney), Bill Hewlett and David Packard (HP), Robert W. Johnson (Johnson & Johnson), J. W. Marriott (Marriott), Herb Kelleher (Southwest Airlines), Sam Walton (Walmart), Ed Catmull (Pixar), Fred Smith (Federal Express), and Phil Knight (Nike). If you're a founding entrepreneur, never let *anyone* talk you into the false belief that founders cannot grow into builders. Our research shows that the average tenure of the shaping architects of enduring great companies is more in the realm of three decades than three years.

The same logic applies to those who, like Anne Bakar at Telecare, inherit leadership by family transition. By sheer statistical odds, perhaps the majority of second- or third-generation family leaders fall short. But again, there are examples that utterly devastate the common wisdom that the children and grandchildren of founders cannot measure up. When Peter Lewis took over Progressive Insurance, his family's business, he was just thirty-two years old. He built Progressive from a small, regional business into one of America's leading automobile insurance companies. J. W. Marriott Jr. began working in his father's small chain of Hot Shoppe restaurants, and led the evolution of his family's business into an iconic hotel and resort company known the world over.

Katharine Graham became one of the greatest CEOs of the twentieth century after unexpectedly inheriting leadership responsibility for her family's company in the wake of her husband's suicide. When *Fortune* magazine gave me the opportunity to pen a cover story on "The 10 Greatest CEOs of All Time," I chose Graham as one of the ten, with the following description:

> On top of the shock and grief, Graham faced another burden. Her father had put the Washington Post Co. in her husband's hands with the idea that he'd pass it along to their children. What would become of it now? Graham laid the issue to rest immediately: The company would not be sold, she informed the board. She would assume stewardship.

"Steward," however, would not describe Graham's approach to her new role. At the time, the *Washington Post* was an undistinguished regional paper; Graham aimed for people to speak of it in the same breath as the *New York Times*. A crucial decision point came in 1971 when she confronted what to do with the Pentagon Papers—a leaked Defense Department study that revealed government deceptions about the Vietnam War. The *Times* had already incurred a court injunction for publishing excerpts. If the *Post* published, it risked prosecution under the Espionage Act. That, in turn, could jeopardize the company's pending public stock offering and lucrative television licenses. "I would be risking the whole company on this decision," Graham wrote in her memoir, *Personal History*. Yet to opt for assured survival at the cost of the company's soul, she concluded, would be worse than not surviving. The *Post* published.

Eventually vindicated by the Supreme Court, it was a remarkable decision for an accidental CEO who suffered from lifelong feelings of insecurity; phrases like "I was terrified" and "I was quaking in my boots" pepper her memoir. That anxiety would soon reach a crescendo as *Post* reporters Bob Woodward and Carl Bernstein doggedly investigated what became known as Watergate. Today we take that story's outcome for granted. But at the time, the *Post* was largely alone in pursuing it. In choosing to publish, Graham built a great paper and, in turn, a great company—one that ranks among the 50 best-performing IPOs of the past quarter-century and earned the investment of Warren Buffett. Graham never awarded herself much credit, insisting that, with Watergate, "I never felt there was much choice." But of course, she did choose. Courage, it's said, is not the absence of fear, but the ability to act in its presence. By that definition, Katharine Graham may be the most courageous CEO on this list.

The old adage "shirtsleeves to shirtsleeves in three generations" might be statistically true, but it isn't a deterministic law of nature. Bill and I loved teaching the L.L.Bean case in our Stanford course. In this case, Leon Gorman, grandson of the founder, was soon to assume leadership of the company, and we pushed our students on the question of whether Leon was the right choice. Gorman was in his early thirties, with a liberal arts degree, a stint in the Navy, and no MBA. Many of our students said no, that the company should instead bring in some "real" management, someone with a Stanford or Harvard MBA and substantial experience building a brand and growing a company.

In his memoir, *L.L.Bean: The Making of an American Icon*, Gorman tells of how, before he became president, he carried a little black notebook with him at all times in which he jotted down notes for how to improve the operation, eventually compiling more than four hundred specific ideas. Upon becoming president, he began to implement the list. Under Gorman, L.L.Bean increased revenues by more than forty times in inflation-adjusted dollars. If that's shirtsleeves to shirtsleeves in three generations, then they must be very nice shirtsleeves indeed.

And so, for those of you entrusted to lead at any level, I have a question: Are you willing to do what it takes to grow into the leader your unit, organization, company, or cause needs? As your company scales from 1X to 2X to 5X to 10X, will you scale your own leadership from 1X to 2X to 5X to 10X? Will you mature your own leadership from version 1.0 into 2.0 and from version 2.0 into 3.0? Will you settle for being just a good leader or—like Anne Bakar and Dwight Eisenhower and Steve Jobs and Katharine Graham and Leon Gorman—will you never stop growing into a great leader? Leadership is a responsibility, not an entitlement; a decision, not an accident; a matter of willful action, not genetics. Whether or not you learn to lead greatly is, in the end, a choice.

Make the Most of "Who Luck"

We most often think of "what luck"—when unexpected and consequential things happen to us. For example, the winning number comes up in a lottery; a storm delays travel for an important meeting; or someone contracts a rare disease. But I've become attuned to a second, more powerful type of luck: "who luck."

Just think of the "who luck" in your own life. It could be the luck of stumbling across a life-altering mentor. It could be the luck of finding a great friend or an ideal life partner or an incredible boss or teammate. It could also take the form of stumbling across someone who'd be a spectacular person on your bus.

I found one of our best research team members by happening to frequent a hamburger restaurant in Boulder. My wife Joanne and I had the same ever-friendly, efficient server a few times in a row, and one evening I began to ask him questions.

"Terrence, are you from Boulder?"

"No, I'm from New Jersey."

"How did you wind up here?"

"I'm in school here at the University of Colorado."

"Are you taking a break from your studies? You seem to be working here every time we come in."

"No, I'm carrying a full load. I'm putting myself through school by working."

"How much are you working?"

"Forty to fifty hours a week."

"While in school?"

"Yep."

"What are you majoring in?"

"I'm doing a double major, economics and finance."

"And how are you doing?"

"All As."

Joanne and I talked on the way home about this remarkable young man we'd met. We were so impressed that, just a few days later, we went back to the same restaurant on a recruiting mission. I wanted that kid on my team.

"You must really like hamburgers," said Terrence, finding his way over to our table.

"We're not here today for the hamburgers," I said. "We came here for you, to encourage you to apply for a position on my summer research team."

Terrence joined the team and worked closely with me for several years before graduating. He became a huge force in our efforts, contributing significantly to three subsequent publications, *Good to Great and the Social Sectors*, *How the Mighty Fall*, and *Great by Choice*. Every one of those works became markedly better because Terrence joined the team.

To practice "first who" means recruiting all the time, keeping yourself highly attuned to stumbling upon great talent wherever you might be. You never know when you're going to get "who luck," but you'll get it, repeatedly. If you look through a "first who" lens in everything you do—if you change every "what" question into a "who" question—you're likely to recognize your "who luck" when it comes.

I've been incredibly lucky so far in my life, but my richest good fortune comes in recognizing and honoring my "who luck" events. I had the good luck to cross paths with Joanne in college and get engaged four days after our first date. I had the good luck to stumble upon Bill Lazier when I happened into his entrepreneurship class the first time he ever taught. I had the good luck of having Jerry Porras reach out to collaborate with me at Stanford on a seminal research project that would become the classic book *Built to Last*. When I look back on my first six decades, I now see them more defined and shaped by "who" than "what," consisting largely of "who luck" incidents—mentors, teachers, friends, colleagues, and partners who have altered and shaped the arc of my life. And now, as I meet the young people like Terrence who cross my path, I hope to be a bit of "who luck" for some of them.

We live in a "what" culture. We ask political candidates, *what* are you going to do about [education or foreign policy or the budget or whatever]? We ask aspiring entrepreneurs, *what's* your great idea? We ask young people, *what* career will you choose? We ask mentors, *what* job should I take? We ask, *what* should we do to solve a pressing problem? Not that these are bad questions, but they're secondary to the question of *who*. Put a right who in charge of foreign policy, and you'll get good policy. Choose a right who for your founding team, and you're more likely to come up with good ideas and make them work. Come upon a right who to be mentored by, and you'll more likely make good career choices. Find a right who to work for, and you'll more likely have a great job experience. Identify the right who to own a problem, and you'll more likely get better solutions than if you try to solve the problem yourself.

Of all the concepts in our research into what makes great companies tick, the shift from a "first what" to a "first who" frame of mind has been the most transformative in how I lead my own life. Accomplishments in themselves bring little meaning or lasting satisfaction, but the *pursuit* of accomplishment arm in arm with the right people can produce tremendous satisfaction. If you're lucky enough to excel at meaningful work you enjoy, you're very fortunate. But if you do meaningful work you enjoy with people you love, you've truly won the lottery.

Focus on Your Unit and Take Care of Your People—Not Your Career

One of my biggest takeaways from the experience of serving a two-year appointment as the Class of 1951 Chair for the Study of Leadership at the United States Military Academy at West Point is the fundamental importance of *unit leadership*. The cellular structure of any truly great organization is the well-led unit, for this is where great things get done. Great leadership at the top doesn't amount to very much without exceptional leadership at the unit level. If you want to build a truly great company or social-sector enterprise, you need to cultivate legions of unit leaders who, in turn, create unit cohesion in pursuit of audacious objectives. If you want to scale your culture, if you want to make the journey from great company to *enduring* great company, you must invest in building a pipeline of the right unit leaders.

The right unit leaders are those who focus first and foremost on their unit of responsibility—those who lead their minibus into a spectacular pocket of greatness—rather than obsessing over their next career move. When young people come to me asking for "career advice," I sometimes tell them, "The best thing you can do for your career is stop focusing on your career." I then tell them about Anne Mulcahy and General Lloyd Austin III.

Anne Mulcahy never sought to become CEO of Xerox, but when the company found itself teetering on the edge of irrelevance in the early 2000s, its stock price down 92 percent and its debt rated as junk, the board struggled with determining who could save the company. Xerox had earlier tried bringing in a "change agent" from outside, and that strategy did not work.

With a wisdom rare in corporate America, the board decided not to seek another savior from outside and decided instead to look for a proven leader from within. Whom will people follow? In whom do people believe? For whom will people double their energies? Whom will people trust? Who has proven results? Who has created pockets of greatness every step of his or her career? And one name came to the fore: Anne Mulcahy. They asked her to shoulder the burden of leading the company, and Mulcahy engineered one of the most unlikely corporate turnarounds in modern history, saving the company from oblivion, recreating robust profitability, rebuilding the balance sheet, and giving the company a shot to regain its position as one of the most storied cases in American business history.

How did many of the greatest CEOs in history become CEO in the first place, especially those who shunned self-promotion? Just as Mulcahy did—with every responsibility they got, each step along their career path, they sought to lead their minibus to exceptional results. As their results grew, they kept getting asked to shoulder the burden of even larger units of responsibility. They paid attention to what was right in front of them, no matter how big or small, leading their minibuses into sparkling pockets of greatness. Mulcahy focused on delivering results in her unit of responsibility, exuding the company's core values, and taking care of her people. People believed in her because she believed in them; people followed her because it was never about her. When the board picked her to lead Xerox out of the darkness, Mulcahy didn't try to change her leadership style. She simply now had leadership responsibility for the whole bus rather than a minibus.

General Lloyd Austin III graduated in the West Point Class of 1975 and rose to the rank of four-star general officer. Toward the end of his illustrious military career, Austin served as vice chief of staff of the Army and then commander of U.S. Central Command, during which time he was responsible for U.S. military efforts in the Middle East from Egypt to Pakistan, including Syria, Iraq, and Afghanistan.

A few years after graduating from West Point, Austin worried about whether he was being promoted fast enough. "Then one day I woke up," he told me, "and decided to stop focusing so much on taking care of my career. Instead, I decided to take care of my people. And that's when everything changed. They would not let me fail!"

During one of my visits with General Austin, he hosted a small dinner for a group of leaders from the business, political, and military-service communities. In the middle of this dinner of assembled dignitaries, General Austin stopped the conversation. "We need to pause to do something important," he said. Three servicemen came out from the kitchen. They'd prepared our meal, and General Austin wanted to make sure we knew about them. He shared a summary of their service and a little bit of personal background on each, and then gave the table a chance to thank them for the exquisite meal. I never saw General Austin pass up an opportunity to shine a light on his people. And I never saw him raise his voice. Calm and quiet, he exuded a palpable command presence infused with personal humility and fierce resolve. General Austin led in a spirit of service—to country, to the accomplishment of mission, to the people he had the honor to lead.

Anne Mulcahy and General Austin exemplify a lesson to learn as early as possible: Take care of your people, not your career. Every responsibility you get, every minibus you drive, every unit you lead—no matter how small— make it a pocket of greatness. If you do that, you're more likely to die of indigestion from having too much opportunity for responsibility than starvation from too little.

Embrace the Jorge Paulo Dilemma

I've had the joy and privilege to observe closely the trajectory of one of the most inspired entrepreneurs and company builders in the world, Brazilian Jorge Paulo Lemann. Lemann and his two partners, Marcel Herrmann Telles and Carlos Alberto Sicupira, started with a tiny brokerage firm and from there built one of the most successful investment banks in Latin America. And while the partners were smart and accomplished at managing money, they discovered they had a peculiar genius for building a culture filled with hungry, fanatic people who thrived on meritocracy. They became so good at building culture that they eventually began to consider buying entire companies outright and then running them based on their cultural operating system with the goal to build and grow them forever. "If we believe in our culture," they said to themselves, "why not bet big on it?"

So, they bought a retail company, Lojas Americanas, and a beer company, Brahma. Their thesis proved correct: If they had the right people with the right cultural DNA, they could deploy those right people into acquired businesses and win big. Lemann and his partners focused on building a "People Machine" to hire and train an ever-larger pool of aggressive, ambitious, young leaders for eventual deployment. Their ultimate "strategy" was to find passionate, driven young people; put them in an intense meritocratic culture; challenge them with audacious goals; and give them a stake in the outcome—what they summarized as Dream-People-Culture. That they didn't know what businesses they might eventually deploy into didn't matter; what mattered, first and foremost, was having enough people with the right cultural DNA to deploy into giant opportunities. And those opportunities just kept coming and getting bigger. Lemann and his partners eventually merged their beer business with Interbrew of Belgium to create InBev.

Each year starting in the early 2000s, the board would come to my management laboratory in Boulder, Colorado, for intense two-day Socratic dialogue sessions driven by one big question: What do we need to do next to build an enduring great company? At one of those meetings, the board began to think seriously about buying Anheuser-Busch, Clydesdales and all.

At one point during a break, Lemann said, "Jim, I sense you are a bit nervous about the magnitude of this thing."

"Yes, I know you thrive on big bets, but this is a huge bet. We need to make sure the board is making a disciplined decision, not one based in hubris."

"I get that, but you don't understand my basic problem," Lemann said, pausing for effect. "I have too many great young leaders, and I've got to give them really big things to do. Never underestimate the power of sustaining momentum."

And that's when I came to fully understand how Lemann, Telles, and Sicupira had created such a powerful momentum machine. From their very earliest days operating as a tiny start-up, they obsessed over finding great people, attracting great people, developing great people. They didn't hire principally to get people with particular skills or to fill an open position or to achieve a specific goal or to pursue a market opportunity. They inverted the entire equation, making a leap of faith that if they filled the machine with fanatically driven people, they'd ignite a virtuous cycle of momentum. First, you get great people. Then you need to give them something big to do. If you pick something big enough, you'll need more great people. Then you have to come up with bigger things to do, which requires getting more great people, which then sends you off in search of even bigger things to do. Repeat, again and again, never stopping, never slowing, never breaking the magic of momentum.

Do you have Jorge Paulo's dilemma? Do you have too many great young and talented leaders, too many ambitious and capable and driven people? If you create this "problem" for your company, you'll be forced to go for the next big dream; otherwise, the best ones will go find something else to do.

If You Need Financial Incentives to Motivate, Then You Have the Wrong People

In our research, we found no systematic pattern linking executive compensation to the process of companies going from good to great. Financial incentives don't—indeed cannot—cause companies to achieve greatness, for the simple reason that *you cannot turn the wrong people into the right people with money.* After all, if someone needs financial incentives to perform at a high level, he or she lacks the intense inner drive, the productive neurosis, required to do great things.

I've had the privilege to study or work with some of the highest-performing enterprises in the world, not just business corporations but also elite military units, successful K–12 schools, championship sports teams, model health-care systems, and social cause organizations. And throughout, I've observed impressive feats of leadership and performance, often with no significant financial incentives in the tool kit.

While I was drafting this chapter, my research team and I were conducting a study on K–12 education, learning from extraordinary school unit leaders (principals) who had improved educational outcomes in the most adverse circumstances. The premise of the study is that having the right unit leader in the building can create the performance culture required to stimulate exceptional teaching. Not one of these school leaders used financial incentives as a key driver in achieving results. *Not one.*

The Cleveland Clinic became one of the most admired health-care institutions in the world by attracting elite physicians who wanted to work with other elite physicians in pursuit of a singular goal: do what's best for the patient. When operating at its best, the Cleveland Clinic turned this "get the right people" obsession into a reinforcing loop of momentum: Start with the right people operating in a collaborative culture that drives patient outcomes, which then feeds into attracting patients from around the world, which then generates reputation and resources to invest in the best research and facilities. All this then attracts even more of the best medical professionals to join the enterprise. And the Cleveland Clinic accomplished all this with a simple salary structure for its physicians—no pay-for-performance incentives based on the number of patients or procedures.

The CEO of the Cleveland Clinic invited me to visit and observe its distinctive culture in action, including the chance to witness an open-heart surgery. It was an exhibition of exquisite choreography in the operating room. When the surgeon put his hand out, without looking up or uttering a word, his surgical assistant would have precisely the right tool ready; the surgeon's hand would open; the tool would be placed in his fingers; his hand would close and then circle back into the chest cavity, all in one seamless motion. The heart-lung-machine operators (cardiovascular perfusionists) timed perfectly the moment to inflate the lungs, right on cue. Every person played his or her part synchronized with the overall procedure, creating the feeling that I was watching a choreographed ballet, beautiful in conception and exquisite in execution. There was absolutely nothing that financial incentives could have done to improve the professionalism in that operating room. After the procedure and throughout my visit, I asked Cleveland Clinic medical professionals what it took to bring them to, of all places, Cleveland, Ohio. The answer was always the same: because they wanted to do the best work with the best people in their field.

Or consider elite military units. Think of the level of responsibility, training, skill, and judgment required to lead a special-forces unit on a dangerous covert operation of national importance. These leaders make a middle-class salary, and there's nothing resembling profit sharing or stock options. When you read *Lone Survivor* by Navy SEAL Marcus Luttrell, you don't see anything in there like, "Well, if you go do these hard and risky missions, there's a big year-end bonus for you." It's not that SEAL culture lacks incentives, but those incentives are largely non-financial.

Far more powerful than any amount of money is respect among fellow SEALs. Dick Couch, who served as a SEAL platoon leader and whose books are highly regarded among members of the SEAL community, summed it up in *The Sherriff of Ramadi*: "In the teams, reputation is everything. A SEAL's reputation follows him from the training commands into the SEAL teams and on into operational deployment. It's a small community and everyone knows everyone else—or has a close friend who does." SEALs routinely risk their own lives to never leave a fellow SEAL behind, not because of anything financial, but because of a sacred promise to each other. Imagine being in a culture in which you know with 100 percent certainty—not 90 percent, not 95 percent, not 99 percent, but absolutely 100 percent—that no matter what happens, you'll never be left behind. You could offer a team of SEALs a million dollars to leave a brother behind, and the nicest response you're likely to get is blank incomprehension followed by outright disgust; you'd likely have a very bad day.

Even at the very top of the U.S. military, multi-star general officers make vastly less than many corporate CEOs—by a factor of five, ten, or even twenty. Whenever I hear corporate board members say, "Well, we need to pay tens of millions to get real leadership talent at the top," I find myself thinking about general officers who are responsible for thousands of lives and manage huge strategic risks while accomplishing difficult national objectives. If it really is about financial incentives, how do we explain the fact that some of the best leaders in the world serve in our military? Or in our schools? Or at the best medical centers? Or in social movements fueled by the energy of thousands of idealistic young people?

To be clear, I'm not saying financial incentives lack impact. Indeed, the evidence from economics makes clear: People *do* respond to incentives (even if they are not the primary source of motivation for the best people). To ignore the influence of incentives is to ignore human nature. And that leads me to a key point: The *wrong* incentives are not merely benign; they can be outright dangerous. If you're trying to build a great company guided by a deeply held set of values, you simply cannot afford to have incentives that reinforce behavior incompatible with your core values, or worse, that reinforce the behavior of the wrong people and drive away the right people. Indeed, the *wrong* incentive system can encourage people to do the wrong things and perhaps even throw a company into crisis.

Consider what happened to Wells Fargo. Dick Cooley and Carl Reichardt led Wells Fargo through a good-to-great inflection in the 1980s and 1990s. Warren Buffett's Berkshire Hathaway bet on Wells Fargo when it was guided by Reichardt's inspired leadership. "With Wells Fargo, we think we have obtained the best managers in the business," Buffett wrote in 1991. He happily watched the value of Berkshire's investment in Wells Fargo grow, which encouraged him to buy more shares along the way.

By 2017, however, Wells Fargo had severely damaged its brand, causing some to wonder if the company had abandoned the principles that had propelled it from good to great in the first place. Contrary to the leadership ethos embodied by Cooley and Reichardt, and the practices that had built customer trust over decades, Wells Fargo (in the words of its own chairman) "violated that trust by opening accounts for certain retail banking customers that they did not request or in some cases even know about." Timothy J. Sloan, who became CEO in the wake of the scandal, wrote in a shareholder letter: "We refunded more than $3.2 million in charges and fees on approximately 130,000 accounts that we could not rule out as being initiated without a customer's authorization."

One hundred thirty thousand is a staggering number. How did this happen, especially in a company that had been truly great in the Cooley-Reichardt era? Part of the answer is that Wells Fargo instituted an aggressive sales culture coupled with an incentive system that pressured people to act contrary to the company's core values. While the report of the independent directors of the board cited multiple contributing factors, it identified the root cause as "the distortion of the Community Bank's sales culture and performance management system, which, when combined with aggressive sales management, created pressure on employees to sell unwanted or unneeded products to customers and, in some cases, to open unauthorized accounts." In an attempt to address the problem, Wells Fargo made key leadership changes and reformed its incentive-compensation system.

No company, no matter how great, is immune to the potential doom loop of misaligned incentives and the wrong people in key seats on the bus. The doom loop begins when you get some of the wrong people on the bus who behave contrary to your company's core values and degrade the culture. Some of these people then become powerful enough to install incentives that are misaligned with the core values. This reinforces the behavior of the wrong people and drives away the right people. The culture becomes increasingly dominated by the wrong people and increasingly inhospitable to the right people. More of the right people get off the bus, and the proportion of wrong people increases to a critical mass. And then one day, you wake up to the horrifying realization that the culture you've carefully cultivated has been destroyed.

The point here is not that a company should have no financial compensation mechanisms. In fact, most of the great companies in our research did employ compensation mechanisms that went beyond traditional salaries. But such compensation mechanisms work *only* so long as they align with a company's values and help accomplish the fundamental function of compensation. And what is that fundamental function? In building a truly great organization, the primary purpose of a compensation system, however structured, is to make sure that you're able to attract and retain the right *people*—self-motivated and self-disciplined people who embrace your core values—not to try to "motivate" the wrong people. It all goes back to the "first who" principle: get the right people on the bus, the wrong people off the bus, and the right people in the key seats.

Of course, the right people should be paid well in their field. And they need to feel that the compensation system is fair. If you're ever wondering whether you might want to share more of the company's financial success with the people who make the company great, keep in mind the Bill Hewlett mantra, "Never stifle a generous impulse."

Build a Culture Where People Depend Upon People

William Manchester became one of the preeminent biographical historians of the twentieth century, known for his books on John F. Kennedy, Douglas MacArthur, and his beloved *Last Lion* series about Winston Churchill. His preamble to *The Last Lion: Volume 2* stands as the best piece of biographical prose I've ever read. But as much as I love his biographies and histories, I found his memoir, *Goodbye, Darkness*, most deeply affecting.

In *Goodbye, Darkness*, Manchester turns his craft on himself to unravel a vexing mystery in his life. He'd been a Marine in the Pacific in the Second World War. On June 2, 1945, while engaged with his unit, Manchester incurred a "million-dollar wound"—bad enough to end his combat deployment with a Purple Heart but minor enough that he'd recover and lead a normal life. Lying in recovery before being shipped home, he decided to defy orders, go AWOL from the field hospital, and return to his unit as it was being deployed behind enemy lines on Okinawa. Just days later, his unit took a direct mortar hit, with Manchester wounded so badly that he'd been thought dead until a medic noticed he was still breathing. This time, he was sent home for good.

Decades after, Manchester had a recurring nightmare of himself as a young sergeant confronting his middle-aged self on top of a hill, "a man divided against his own youth." Unable to force the nightmares back into his unconscious, he decided to write a book weaving three stories into one—the story of the Pacific War, the story of himself as a young Marine in that war, and the story of himself as a middle-aged man returning to visit the islands of the Pacific War. The stories converged on the island of Okinawa at Sugar Loaf Hill, the site of a battle that had cost more than seven thousand Marine casualties in ten days.

But the deeper story was Manchester's desire to unravel the mystery: *Why* had he gone back to his unit, defying orders and going AWOL to risk getting killed, when he could have returned to safe comfort with his honor intact? The answer—which I encourage in the strongest terms that you read in its original context—comes down to what he calls an act of love for his fellow Marines: "They had never let me down, and I couldn't do it to them. I had to be with them, rather than let them die and me live with the knowledge that I might have saved them."

The point here is not that business and organizational life are like war or anything like that. To suggest that building a company—making computers or creating biotech drugs or building out retail stores or running an airline or even building a cause-driven social enterprise—is in the same league as the battle for Sugar Loaf Hill would be a form of sacrilege. No, the point is to highlight the power of creating a culture where people know their comrades are depending on them to come through and they cannot let them down.

The Commandant of the Marine Corps once asked me to give a talk to the top hundred or so general officers. At the lunch beforehand, I asked him, "What's the purpose of boot camp? Why do you retain this somewhat brutal practice?" He told me that people mistakenly think it's all about just finding the strongest physical specimens. The goal, he went on to describe, is not to find the strongest people, but to weed out people who, under duress, default to taking care of only themselves rather than helping those around them.

When Fred Smith first conceived of his idea for a reliable overnight delivery service and wrote it up for a business course at Yale, he got a C on his paper because the professor deemed the idea infeasible. After Yale, Smith made a countercultural move for a Yale graduate in 1966; he enlisted for service in the United States Marine Corps. In combat deployment (where he earned a Silver Star for bravery and two Purple Hearts), Smith gained the central insight that would power Federal Express from an idea into a viable business, from a business into a great company. Like Manchester, he realized that people will do unreasonable things to come through—not for grand ideas or incentives or bosses or hierarchies or even recognition, *but for each other*.

Smith came away from his Vietnam experience with an increased faith that if you start with basic respect for people, and you show trust by putting them in situations where they have to come through because others depend on them, they'll summon whatever it takes to achieve the mission. So, when you have trucks and planes that have to be fully coordinated, where failure to get to a transfer point on time can cascade right on down the line and jeopardize the "absolutely, positively overnight" brand promise, you need more than financial capital, systems, airplanes, and trucks to succeed.

Federal Express has become so embedded in our lives that it's a verb ("Can you FedEx that?"). Yet in the early days the company ran so close to the edge that at one point Smith reputedly made a trip to Las Vegas in desperation, where he won $27,000 to fuel the planes and keep the system alive. The story might be apocryphal, but its endurance in corporate mythology shows how today's giant company was once struggling as a small start-up. But the real source of Federal Express's prevailing against the odds as an early-stage company fighting for its very existence lies not on a Las Vegas gambling table. The secret sauce was Smith's building a culture of trust, respect, and love—a culture of people depending on people. This story is exceptionally well told in the book *Breakthroughs!* by P. Ranganath Nayak and John M. Ketteringham (one of the best casebooks written on innovators who defied the odds), which describes Smith's culture of mutual commitment as the true breakthrough.

When I think back to the time when Bill Lazier went to bat for me with the deans at the Stanford Graduate School of Business, opening up an opportunity for me to teach and setting me on a thirty-year journey to study what makes great companies tick, I see that Bill brought out my best effort because I'd be letting him down if I failed. Yes, a noble purpose combined with audacious goals can do a lot to inspire our efforts. But in the end, we give our best when other people depend upon us to come through, when we cannot let them down.

We live in a world rich in success but impoverished in meaning. A life of relentless work without meaning is brutal and dark. Most of us will never have the depth of love in our daily work that Manchester had with his fellow Marines. But we can move closer to it by building a culture where people depend on people. And in so doing, you will give people something of immeasurable value—work that matters. And *that* is truly great.

Chapter 3

LEADERSHIP STYLE

The key to a leader's impact is sincerity. Before he can inspire with emotion he must be swayed by it himself. Before he can move their tears his own must flow. To convince them he must himself believe.

WINSTON CHURCHILL

WE CALL IT THE *M Syndrome.* M is the initial of a particularly ineffective CEO whom we observed. M is also the first letter of the word *malaise.*

M had an IQ of over 150. M had a Ph.D. and an MBA. M had 20 years of solid industry experience. M was on a first-name basis with the top people in his industry. M worked 80 hours per week. M's market was growing at over 30% per year.

Yet M's company, after early success, floundered and was pulled into a dark downward spiral—into the gloom and malaise of mediocrity. Why? Because M's leadership style was so ineffective—so oppressive—that it hung over the organization like a cold, penetrating mist. It depressed people. It eroded their confidence. It gradually sucked the energy and inspiration out of them. It slowly killed the company, day by day, week by week.

What did M do wrong?

- M preached "respect for people" (because he had read about Hewlett-Packard's belief in respect), yet he never trusted people. M chanted teamwork, but defined team play as blind obedience.

- M was terribly indecisive. Confronted with an important decision, he would analyze it over and over, delaying action. Significant opportunities passed the company by and small problems developed into major crises.
- M had no clear priorities. He constantly hurled lists of 10 to 20 action items at people, telling them "*All* of them are top priority."
- M spent most of his time sealed safely away in his office, behind thick, closed doors. He seldom walked the halls or stopped by to see how people were doing.
- M constantly criticized people, yet never gave any positive reinforcement. A single mistake would haunt an employee forever—M would never give the person a chance to prove that he had learned from the mistake.
- M never effectively communicated the vision of the company. Hence, people felt that there was no vision, that the company was like a ship pounded by violent storms with no sense of direction.
- M spoke and wrote in turgid, technical language. Instead of inspiring people, he left them bored and confused.
- After the company reached a plateau of success (at about $15 million in revenues and 75 employees), M refused to move forward with anything new, bold, or risky. The company stagnated. Ambitious people left.

As in M's case, the primary barrier to greatness in many companies is ineffective leadership. The most advanced technology, the most thoughtful strategy, and the best tactical execution can be totally overshadowed by poor leadership style. This is true for all companies, but is particularly true of small to midsized companies where the top leaders have a dramatic daily impact, and must be the architects of corporate greatness.

Simply put, it's impossible to build a great company if you have a destructive leadership style.

The Multiplier Effect

If you are the top person, your style will set the tone for the entire organization. It is a multiplier effect—for better or worse—the tone you set at the top affects the behavior patterns of people throughout the company. If effective, your style will be a powerful factor in building a great company. If ineffective, or negative, however, it will be like a heavy, wet blanket hanging over the company and weighing it down.

Different Styles

Should everyone have the same leadership style? No, of course not. Your leadership style will be a function of your own unique personality characteristics.

Indeed, there are many effective styles. Some effective leaders are quiet, shy, and reserved; whereas others are outgoing and gregarious. Some are hyperactive and impulsive; others are more methodical. Some are old, wise, and experienced; others are young, brash, and adventurous. Some love to give speeches; others are nervous in front of a crowd. Some are charismatic; others are not. (Do not confuse leadership with charisma. *Charisma does not equal leadership*, and some of the most effective leaders have very little charisma.)

Examine the spectrum of world leaders and notice how much their styles differ: Mahatma Gandhi (frail and soft-spoken), Abraham Lincoln (melancholy and thoughtful), Winston Churchill (the fierce and indomitable bulldog), Margaret Thatcher (stern and tenacious, the "Iron Lady"), Martin Luther King Jr. (impassioned, eloquent). Yet, in spite of the wide range of styles, each of these leaders was highly effective.

Cultivate your own style; don't try to be someone you're not or to take on a style that doesn't fit. Can you imagine Winston Churchill trying to imitate Gandhi's style, wearing a loincloth and speaking in a soft, almost inaudible voice? Conversely, can you imagine Gandhi chewing on big fat cigars and growling, "Our policy is to wage war, by sea, land, and air, with all our might and all the strength God can give us . . . "? These images are absurd. But they're no more absurd than if you try to ape someone else's style.

An effective style grows from within you. It should be entirely yours. No one except you should have a style exactly like yours.

Effective Leadership: Function Plus Style

Effective corporate leadership consists of two parts: leadership *function* and leadership *style*.

The function of leadership—the number-one responsibility of a leader—is to catalyze a clear and shared vision for the company and to secure commitment to and vigorous pursuit of that vision. This is a universal requirement of leadership, and no matter what your style, you must perform this function. (Chapter 2 explains the concept of vision and how to set one.)

In contrast, the style of leadership is unique to each individual. There are many styles that can be used to carry out the function of leadership. But herein lies a thorny paradox. On the one hand, we assert that your style should be peculiar to you, and that many styles can be effective. On the other hand, we have the dreaded M Syndrome, where M's style was the primary barrier to corporate greatness. How can we reconcile this paradox? Does this mean that, although each leader will have his or her own style, some styles are more effective than others?

To resolve the paradox, we have distilled the elements of style we see in the most effective corporate leaders. Although each leader has a unique personal style, there are certain elements that tend to be common across a range of effective styles. See Figure 3.1 that follows.

Effective Corporate Leadership

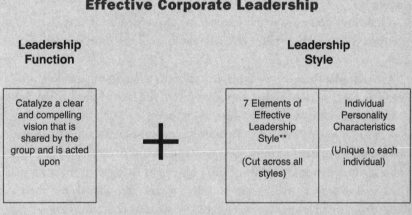

Leadership Function

Catalyze a clear and compelling vision that is shared by the group and is acted upon

Leadership Style

7 Elements of Effective Leadership Style**

(Cut across all styles)

Individual Personality Characteristics

(Unique to each individual)

** Authenticity, Decisiveness, Focus, Personal Touch, Hard/Soft People Skills, Communication, Ever Forward

Figure 3.1

An analogy will help clarify our solution to the paradox. Think for a moment about excellent writers. Each writer has his or her own style; William Faulkner's style is very different from Ernest Hemingway's, and Barbara Tuchman's style differs from that of William Manchester. Although style is personal to each individual writer, there are certain elements that tend to cut across the styles of all great writers: they engage the reader early in the work, capture the imagination with vivid detail, use language well, have good beginnings and endings, and so on.

Just What Exactly Is "Leadership"?

The most significant experience I've had in my ongoing inquiry into the topic of leadership came in 2012 and 2013, when I had the honor and privilege to serve a two-year appointment as the Class of 1951 Chair for the Study of Leadership at the United States Military Academy at West Point. It's one of the world's greatest leadership-development institutions, in the business of building women and men into leaders of character. I traveled to West Point multiple times to engage with cadets and faculty, and to reflect upon the essence of leadership, how leaders can be built and how good leaders can become great leaders.

One of my goals was to gain deeper insight regarding a deceptively simple question, What *is* leadership? We talk about it all the time, but what exactly *is* it?

First, let's be clear: There is no such thing as a "leadership personality." We live in an age of celebrity when people revere the cult of personality, but we confuse personality with leadership, to our peril.

Consider one of the most impactful entrepreneurial leaders of recent decades, a personal hero of mine, Wendy Kopp, founder of Teach For America. For one of my seminars at West Point, I brought Kopp with me for a special guest session with a small group of cadets. One of the first things the cadets noticed was that Kopp was shy, reserved, somewhat uncomfortable being the center of attention. We met in a small seminar room designed for only about thirty people, yet she spoke so softly that cadets strained to hear her over the distant humming of machinery grinding away on a nearby construction project.

She told the story of her anxiety during her senior year of college because she didn't yet know what she wanted to do with her life. As she wandered in this existential funk, she had to complete a senior thesis. She decided to do hers on education, something for which she had a nascent passion, aiming to advance two fundamental premises. First, every single kid, no matter from what family or neighborhood, deserves a shot at a solid education. Second, young people coming out of outstanding colleges could be inspired to self-deploy as teachers for a minimum of two years into some of America's most underserved communities, from the Mississippi Delta to Harlem and the Bronx. She then knew what to do with her life, and she launched Teach For America.

Since its founding, Teach For America has inspired more than half a million young people to apply to the program and has deployed more than sixty thousand corps members into classrooms. When an editor for *Inc.* magazine conducted an interview with me for its thirtieth anniversary issue in 2009, we got to talking about some of the greatest entrepreneurs of all time. In that discussion, I offered Kopp as my hands-down pick for the entrepreneur of the decade.

Wendy Kopp's leadership craft included an instinctive ability to get the right people connected with other right people and then get them all swept up in the noble sense of mission for the kids. Early in her career at Teach For America, Kopp focused on attracting highly capable individuals to the cause and then unleashing them to succeed as classroom teachers and education leaders. As she progressed at Teach For America and now at Teach For All (a network of similar organizations in countries around the world), she embraced a more collective vision of leadership, wherein people at every level of the system—students, parents, teachers, school principals, district administrators, policy officials, businesspeople, health workers—work together toward shared ends. Drawing from the entire ecosystem connected to children, Kopp was able to bring thousands of people, from within and outside of her organization, together in pursuit of a dream, that *all* children *everywhere* will one day have the opportunity to attain an excellent education.

In that seminar room at West Point, Wendy Kopp embodied an essential truth and taught the cadets a profound lesson about leadership: You do not need a powerful, charismatic personality to inspire people to do great things. Nor do you need formalized power. Kopp did not have the power of institutional authority, or the power of hierarchical rank, or the power of exalted title, or the power of voting shares, or the power of government mandates. She didn't even have the power of financial lure, given that most corps members could make a larger salary doing other things with their talents. As James MacGregor Burns taught in his classic text, *Leadership*, we should never confuse brute power with leadership.

True leadership only exists if people follow when they would otherwise have the freedom to *not* follow. Many business leaders think they're leading when in fact they're simply exercising power, and they might discover to their horror that no one would follow them if they had no power. If you rely primarily on rank or title or position or money or incentives or celebrity or any other form of raw power to get things done, quite simply, you've abdicated leadership. Those who issue arbitrary dictates just because they can are the antithesis of leadership. As General Colin Powell, whose book *It Worked for Me* I highly recommend, put it: "In my thirty-five years of service, I don't ever recall telling anyone, 'That's an order.'" Powell learned that it is often far better to exert "command with the most delicate touch."

So, then, if leadership is not personality, power, rank, position, or title, what exactly *is* it? At West Point, influenced directly by the words and reflections of General Eisenhower, I finally crystalized a short definition of leadership that best fits with everything I've studied and observed. That definition is simply this: *Leadership is the art of getting people to want to do what must be done.*

Notice three things about this definition. First, as a leader, it's your responsibility to figure out what must be done. You might do this by your own insight and instinct or, more likely, via dialogue and debate with the right people; but however you do it, you need to get clear. Second, it's not about getting people to do what must be done but about getting them to *want* to do it. Third, it's not a science; it's an *art*.

I love the word "art"—which comes directly from Eisenhower—for it captures what I think Bill and I were groping toward when we originally drafted the leadership chapter in *Beyond Entrepreneurship*: You have to discover and cultivate your own elements of style, a distinctive leadership artistry that makes you effective at getting the right people to work passionately with you in accomplishing what must be done.

Perhaps, like Wendy Kopp, you have a gift for defining a clear and magnetic vision that can be expressed in very few words. Perhaps, like Kopp, you have a gift for getting people to believe in making impossible dreams come true, infusing them with the idea that what other people view as impossible (*All* children! *Everywhere!*) is the only acceptable goal. Perhaps, like Kopp, you have a gift for convening a diverse collection of the right people, quietly setting a tone of collaboration, creating a climate where the truth is heard, and creating space for the best ideas to win. Perhaps, like Kopp, you have a gift for finding smart, practical people who have a passion for turning lofty ideals into scalable systems.

Or perhaps you have an entirely different set of gifts. Perhaps, like Anne Mulcahy, you have the gift of holding a room with a moving speech. Perhaps, like Herb Kelleher of Southwest Airlines, you have the gift of keeping it fun and making your people feel respected and loved. Perhaps, like Katherine Graham, you have the gift of being constitutionally incapable of capitulation, blessed with a stoic determination that seeps into those around you and gives them confidence. Perhaps, like Bill Gates, you have the gift of simplifying a complex world, so that energetic people feel confident and clear about where they are expending their energies.

The key is to figure out your leadership gifts, and then—as Wendy Kopp continues to do—refine them the way a great painter or composer or actor or architect gets better across decades of obsessive attention to his or her craft.

When I look back at the simple framework that Bill and I put in the original edition of *Beyond Entrepreneurship*—the idea of separating leadership function from leadership style—I'm struck by how close to the mark we were to articulating the essence of leadership. In the years since, my skepticism of personality worship has only deepened. All of my subsequent research into what makes great companies tick uncovered convincing evidence that some of the greatest business leaders of all time lacked any obvious charisma. Furthermore, our studies showed that some of the worst episodes of corporate decline and failure happened with colorful charismatic leaders at the helm. (See *How the Mighty Fall*.) Far better to be an uncharismatic leader who gets the right people to confront the brutal facts than to be a magnetic force of personality who leads compliant followers to disaster. If you have charisma, you can still build an enduring great company. But never forget: If your company cannot be great without your personal charisma to inspire, then it is not yet a great company.

Seven Elements of Leadership Style

In this chapter, we've identified the elements of style that are common among effective leaders. They are:

1. Authenticity
2. Decisiveness
3. Focus
4. Personal Touch
5. Hard/Soft People Skills
6. Communication
7. Ever Forward

Leadership Style Element 1: Authenticity

The most important element of leadership effectiveness is authentically living the vision of the company. The values and ambitions of a company are not instilled entirely by what leaders *say*; they're instilled primarily by what leaders *do*.

In a healthy company, there are no inconsistencies between what is said and what is believed deep down—the values come from *within* the leaders and imprint themselves on the organization through day-to-day activity. Think of it as kneading bread—constantly massaging the values into the very essence of the organization.

Granted, effective corporate leaders are aware of the practical benefits of their values. But they would behave consistently with those values in the *absence* of such benefits. And it is precisely this point that makes them so successful and effective.

When Bill Hewlett and Dave Packard started HP, they didn't sit down and ask, "What are the most pragmatic business values?" No. They deeply believed in having respect for people, and they simply acted out this belief in all that they did. It was as natural to them as breathing.

SHOW YOUR CONVICTION

We've observed that effective company leaders convey a ferocious intensity about their values, beliefs, and desires. They're unafraid to show the passion that is associated with these values, at times getting quite emotional.

Jim Gentes, founder of Giro Sport Design, is known to show quite touching emotion when speaking about how Giro's product saved a life or helped an athlete realize a dream.

Phil Knight, CEO of NIKE, is shy; he is *not* a jump-up-and-down cheerleader type. But when speaking to employees about his pride in them during a 1990 company meeting, his emotions were obvious. Knight, founder of one of the most successful companies of our era—a man driven by performance, competition, and winning—showed his tears and could barely finish his talk. It touched the NIKE people to the core because it was *real*.

BE THE BEST ROLE MODEL

Just speaking authentically isn't enough; you also have to *act* authentically. Each decision and action should dovetail with your philosophy, being in itself a statement of your core values.

People in your company are going to be extraordinarily influenced by what you do. As a corporate leader, you are like a parent or teacher, and, as such, people are likely to follow the examples you set.

Don't underestimate the extent to which your actions influence those who work for you. Manners of speech, decision-making style, ways of behaving, and other attributes will rub off. For example, within a few weeks after John F. Kennedy came to office, White House staff members were speaking in Kennedy-like staccato sentences and jabbing the air with their fingers, the way he did.

Such is the nature of how people respond to authority figures. Inevitably, people will begin to emulate you. Even if you have a non-hierarchical environment, you'll still be perceived as an authority figure, and people will respond to you as such.

Therefore, *you've got to be a role model of the culture you want to create.*

Sam Walton, founder and primary leader of Walmart during its rise from a single-store outlet to a successful chain of discount stores, understood the importance of being the consummate Walmart role model. Walton, as portrayed in Vance Trimble's book *Sam Walton*, believed that Walmart's culture should be based largely on frugality—that extreme leanness and efficiency would create unbeatable strength.

Hence, as a role model of this philosophy, Walton wouldn't rent any car more expensive than a subcompact when traveling. When flying on commercial airlines, he flew coach. He ordered cold sandwiches and potato chips for Board of Directors meetings—board members had to bring along their own quarters for Coca-Cola. He obtained his coffee from the vending machine in the lobby, just like everyone else. He drove a beat up old pickup truck, even when hosting English dignitaries (much to their chagrin).

Burton Stacy, of Walton's hometown bank, said, "He [Walton] is not going to be seen in anything better than what his people are allowed . . . Sam Walton is not going to stay in a better hotel . . . nor eat in a better restaurant, nor drive a better car." Jack Stephens, an ex-board member at Walmart, said, "Sam Walton—he lives and breathes efficiency."

Like all effective corporate leaders, Walton is a 100% pure genuine article—nothing artificial, nothing contrived.

In contrast, there is the example of Fortune Systems, a computer venture that failed in the mid-1980s, despite being exceptionally well-capitalized and early in its market. A senior executive said, "We are all a team here, egalitarian in nature, working towards the same goals. We believe in concentrating on the task at hand, not on status symbols."

Yet, in flagrant violation of this sentiment, the senior managers had a separate "executive suite" and the CEO had a private parking space. When we saw this inconsistency, we knew the company was headed for mediocrity at best. It didn't even achieve that.

Like Walton, your stated corporate philosophy must ultimately be a genuine reflection of the values and beliefs you hold *in your own gut*. The values must be so much a part of you—of your own core spirit—that you instinctively respond to situations in a way consistent with your stated philosophy. You shouldn't have to think about it. Likewise, when actions are taken by others that go against those values, it should eat at you on a gut level.

It's also important to carry this authenticity out to the major strategic decision made by the company. Just as you should be an exemplary role model of the values and beliefs through your day-to-day actions, the company itself should be a role model of its philosophy as exemplified by its major decisions.

CASE EXAMPLE: YVON CHOUINARD AND LOST ARROW CORPORATION

At Lost Arrow Corporation (parent company of Patagonia), Yvon Chouinard held a deep conviction about the role his company should play in preserving the natural environment. He backed this up by donating 10% of pre-tax profits every year to environmental causes and sourcing fabrics from companies that used environmentally sound methods, even if those methods were more expensive.

Even more impressive is the long history of managing Lost Arrow in line with this belief. In the early 1970s (decades before being an environmentally conscious company was fashionable), Chouinard set out to use his company to completely change the way rock climbers protect themselves on cliffs; he wanted them to use devices that leave the rock unscarred. He did this by introducing non-damaging protection devices called chocks or nuts.

At the time this was viewed by many as unwise. Few climbers wanted to switch from pitons (metal spikes pounded into the rock, thereby damaging it permanently) and most thought Chouinard was waging an uphill battle. Undaunted, Chouinard introduced the new gear and worked fanatically to get the climbing community to change.

And it worked. By 1975, virtually no one used pitons, and the cliffs were largely preserved for future generations. This action, led by Chouinard, attracted dedicated, loyal employees to the company. They knew that, unlike many companies that simply paid lip service to "concern for the environment," Chouinard *meant* it. And they were inspired by this.

BACK WORDS WITH ACTION

We have no sympathy for managers who don't back their words with actions. Granted, no one is perfect, and we all fail to live 100% up to our ideals. But some company leaders don't even live up to 25% of their ideals. Their talk is rhetoric. Their insincerity is nauseating. They don't deserve to be leaders. And, indeed, they certainly will not build great companies.

Live what you say. Don't just talk about it, *do* it.

What Cause Do You Serve?

During my time serving in the leadership chair at West Point (described in the previous essay), I was surprised to discover that many of the cadets I met seemed happier than my MBA students when I taught at Stanford. I believe a big reason for what I observed is that the ethic of Service—commitment to a cause bigger than oneself—permeates the entire West Point experience. And it's Service with a capital "S." The cadets know that they might even die in rendering that service.

What do Anne Mulcahy, Gordon Moore, Wendy Kopp, and George C. Marshall have in common? They all lead or led in a spirit of service to a cause bigger than themselves. For Mulcahy, the cause was saving the company she loved, Xerox, and creating an inspired future for its people. For Moore, it was building Intel into a catalytic force for revolutionizing the way civilization works through the ever-increasing power of micro-electronics. For Kopp, it is service to the gigantic goal that all children everywhere will have access to an excellent education. For Marshall, it was service to country and defeating tyrannical regimes that marched across their borders to oppress free peoples. These leaders would subjugate their own ambitions and egos in service to their cause.

Consider Marshall, who served as Army chief of staff and a primary architect of the Allied victory in World War II. As one of the highest-ranking military officers in 1944, Marshall could have lobbied to be commander of D-Day, leading the Allied invasion of Europe, guaranteeing himself heroic stature in his lifetime and laying claim to immortal fame. But as military historian and Marshall biographer Professor Mark Stoler teaches in his course *The Skeptic's Guide to American History*, Marshall made clear to President Roosevelt that he'd do whatever was best for the country and the war effort.

Roosevelt said that he couldn't sleep at night without Marshall by his side in Washington. So, Eisenhower got the field role while Marshall continued to serve as architect behind the scenes. It was his fierce resolve for the larger goal and willingness to subvert his personal glory for that goal that marked Marshall as one of history's greatest general officers.

In the research for *Good to Great* (published a decade after Bill and I worked on *Beyond Entrepreneurship*), my research team and I discovered the X factor of good-to-great leadership. It is the principle of Level 5. Level 5 is the highest level in a hierarchy of capability ranging from Level 1 (individual skills) to Level 2 (teamwork skills) to Level 3 (management skills) to Level 4 (leadership skills). At Level 5, a leader applies all the skills from Levels 1 through 4 in service to a cause larger than self, and does so with a paradoxical blend of personal humility and indomitable will. Level 5 leaders are incredibly ambitious. They are fanatic, obsessed, monomaniacal, relentless, exhausting. But their ambition is first and foremost for the cause, for the company, for the purpose, for the work, *not themselves.*

Anne Mulcahy, Gordon Moore, Wendy Kopp, and George Marshall stand as models of Level 5 leadership, as do many of the other leaders in this text, from Anne Bakar and General Lloyd Austin III to Fred Smith and Katharine Graham. So, too, Steve Jobs in his later years, when he grew from Steve Jobs 1.0 to Steve Jobs 2.0 and channeled his creative genius into making Apple a great company that could endure long beyond his own lifetime.

I've been asked many times whether people can become Level 5, and if so, how? Yes, and the best spark to ignite such leadership in yourself is to wrestle with a hard, simple question: *What cause do you serve?* What cause are you willing to sacrifice and suffer for, when you must make decisions that cause pain for yourself and others to advance that cause? What cause will infuse your life with meaning? It might be a grand, highly visible cause or a more private, less-visible cause; what matters is that you lead in service to that cause, rather than in service to yourself.

Leadership Style Element 2: Decisiveness

George C. Marshall pointed out that the greatest gift a leader can have is the ability to decide. Judging from how many executives suffer from chronic indecision, we think Marshall might be right.

Leaders who build great companies seldom suffer from indecision. The ability to decide—to somehow come to a decision, even in the absence of perfect information (and there will *never* be perfect information), is an essential attribute of well-functioning teams and individual leaders.

DON'T LET ANALYSIS PREVENT A DECISION

Analysis allows us to say "maybe," but life (especially in a small to mid-sized company) does not.

Judicious use of analysis is good, as long as you don't fall prey to "analysis paralysis." There are seldom enough facts or data to eliminate all risk or to make a decision based solely on those facts. Furthermore, all business analysis is dramatically affected by your assumptions. Two people looking at the same set of facts will often come to entirely different conclusions about those facts. Why? Because they come at those facts with different assumptions.

For example, you can try this experiment. Ask a group of employees to assess the viability of a potential new product and make a go/no go decision. You provide them with a veritable forest full of facts. Now, they are all excellent employees with exactly the same business training. Yet, about half of them will say "go" and the other half say "no go." Why? To do their analysis, they have to make assumptions, and their assumptions drive their answers.

This is true in most business situations. You can do virtually an endless amount of analysis, but the analysis will seldom be conclusive. And you still have to make a decision.

We're not suggesting that you should be thoughtless about your actions and run off in a blind fury of impulsive activity. Facts, analyses, and probabilities all have their place in decision making. Just remember that the objective is to *make a decision*, not to pulverize it with analysis.

You have to sense when you've done enough analysis and gathered enough facts. Then get on with it. David Starr Jordan, founding president of Stanford University, captured this perfectly in his approach to decision making: "When all the evidence seems to be in, I like to say yes or no at once and take my chances."

FOLLOW YOUR GUT

Jordan's "yes or no" approach still leaves an unanswered question: precisely *how* do you make a final choice based on the imperfect information? Part of the answer lies in being willing to follow your gut instinct—your intuition.

Admittedly, some people are uncomfortable with intuitive decisions. Intuition seems unscientific and irrational, and its use is awkward for those who are not well practiced. Yet the most effective decision makers use a combination of hardheaded analysis *and* intuition.

Paul Cook, founder and guiding force through the development of Raychem Corporation, is a good example. He told an audience during a talk:

> Strangely enough, the company has made two or three big mistakes that it never would have made if I would have followed my intuition faithfully. I would not let that happen anymore. I've learned to trust my intuition faithfully. I really have. It's made a big difference.

Cook is not alone. Paul Galvin (founder of Motorola), William McKnight (builder of 3M), Sam Walton (of Walmart), Kristine McDivitt (CEO for 17 years of Patagonia), and many other corporate executives were comfortable and practiced with their intuition.

There is no such thing as an unintuitive person; everyone has intuition. The difficulty comes in recognizing and using it. What does it take to effectively use your intuition? Here are a few suggestions.

- Go right to the heart of any problem or decision. Don't let a myriad of data, analysis, options, and probabilities overwhelm you and push you into catatonic indecision.
- Clear away the clutter—the long lists of pros and cons—and zero in on the central question. When confronted with a problem, say to yourself, "What's the essence of this? Never mind the details, what's the important thing?" Don't dwell incessantly on all the attributes and complexities of a problem. Pare the situation down to its essential elements.
- A useful technique is to distill a decision down to its core and ask a simple question: Does your gut say "Yes" or "No"?

Over time, you'll develop a finely tuned sense for what your intuition is saying. This "sense" has a special quality to you—you just *know* if something is right. One effective tool for developing this "sense" is to closely observe your internal reactions to the decisions you make.

For example, if you find yourself bogged down in elaborate columns of pros and cons, just randomly pick a decision and observe how you react. If you feel relief, then you probably made the right decision. If, on the other hand, you feel uneasy or tense—a "gnawing" in your stomach—then you probably made the wrong choice. You might try making a decision and living with it for 24 hours without telling anybody. This lets you observe how the decision feels before making it public.

Beware of the influence of fear on your gut instincts. Fear creates self-deception. What passes for an intuitive decision is sometimes a fear-driven decision in disguise. A fear-driven decision is one where, because of the risks involved, you are afraid to do what you know deep down is right. Fear-driven decisions can easily get confused with intuitive decisions because there is a false sense of relief that comes with pacifying the fear. (This false relief doesn't last, however, and the "gnawing" of your intuition eventually returns.)

If you find yourself saying, "I think this is the right thing to do, but I am afraid that . . . ," then you are in danger of making a decision that goes against your gut. To use your intuition effectively, you need the courage to do what you know is right, regardless of the risk.

A famous example of this comes from Harry Truman, one of the most decisive United States presidents, who went with his "gut feel" in making the unpopular decision to fire General MacArthur in 1951. The stakes were enormous, not only for Truman's political stature, but also for the rapidly escalating military conflict in Korea. But Truman fired MacArthur anyway. Years later Truman reflected:

> The only thing I learned from the whole MacArthur deal is that when there is something you know in your *gut* that you have to do, the sooner you get it over with, the better off everybody is.

A BAD DECISION IS OFTEN BETTER THAN NO DECISION

No matter how smart you are, it's impossible to have a 100% hit-rate with decisions. A good number of your decisions will be sub-optimal; that's just the nature of life. If you wait until you're absolutely sure before making a choice, you'll most certainly bog down in a quagmire of indecision.

Doing nothing can *feel* comfortable because it is without immediate risk. But, in the world of a small to mid-sized company that's got to keep moving, it is usually a recipe for disaster. If you've got a pressing problem, *make a decision and get on with it.*

Indecision is often worse than making a wrong decision. Get a jump on the problem; take the offensive rather than letting it back you into a corner where your hand will be forced. If you make a bad decision, so be it. It'll come back soon enough and smack you upside the head and then you can solve it right.

Unfortunately, most of us have a fear of being wrong, which makes it hard to follow this advice. Many of us carry around a strong fear of ridicule, blame, criticism, or being laughed at. In other words, the *psychological* consequences of making a mistake can often seem worse than the actual consequences. We can be reluctant to make a decision for fear that we might—gasp—make a mistake.

You must learn to live with the fact that you will make mistakes—lots of mistakes—and that you will learn from them. Mistakes are in fact a great source of strength; making mistakes is analogous to building muscle in athletic training. Think about it for a minute: how does an athlete get stronger? By pushing to the point of failure. You do, say, three pull-ups and fail on the fourth. The body adapts and gets stronger and the next time you can do four pull-ups, and fail on the fifth. The next time out you can do five pull-ups, and fail on the sixth, and so on.

The process of making decisions, some of which are "failures," and learning from them is "building muscle." If you don't ever make mistakes, you'll forever be stuck at three pull-ups.

Be proud of the fact that you periodically make mistakes. It shows that you're not one of the timid souls who are so terrified of making a mistake that they don't *do* anything worthwhile with their lives. As Paul Garvin, founder and architect of Motorola, said, "Do not fear mistakes. Wisdom is often born of such mistakes."

BE DECISIVE BUT NOT BULLHEADED

Being decisive does *not* mean being inflexible or bullheaded. Yes, you've got to make decisions and commit to courses of action. But you've also got to be willing to make adjustments and adapt to new information or circumstances. If you need to change a decision, do it. It's far better to do that than to either stick doggedly to a bad decision or to never make a decision in the first place. Over the long run, it's far better to be right than consistent.

GROUP DECISION MAKING

How much should you involve others in your decisions? In *Managing for Excellence*, David Bradford and Allan Cohen point out that there is a continuum of decision-making styles. At one end of the continuum is *delegative decision making*, where the leader pushes the decision back to others, saying, "You make the decision."

Next is *pure consensus decision making*, with the decision coming from a group process that the leader facilitates. In a pure consensus style, the group makes the decision. The leader does not impose her solution, but rather seeks a choice that has "general agreement" among the entire group. The leader's skill is in asking questions, making observations, providing input, and catalyzing a decision. Effective consensus leaders guide the group to closure at just the right time—they don't cut off the process prematurely, nor do they let deliberations drag on unproductively.

Consensus does not equal unanimity! Too many managers have interpreted consensus to mean 100% unanimity. Not every person must agree with the decision for there to be consensus; there only needs to be general agreement. General agreement is significantly higher than a 51% majority, but usually falls short of 100% unanimity. It is something that is sensed, rather than quantified. Once a consensus is reached, those who disagreed during the process must agree or get off the ship.

Further along the continuum is *participative decision making*, with the leader asking for ideas, suggestions, evaluations of alternatives, and solutions. However, unlike the pure consensus style, the leader (not the group) ultimately makes the final choice. (An excellent case study of participative decision making is given in *Thirteen Days*, Robert F. Kennedy's book detailing the events of the Cuban Missile Crisis.)

The advantage of participative decision making is that it has the benefit of multiple points of view and vigorous discussion, yet allows an avenue for rapid decision. After an intense thrashing of the issues, the leader can state quickly and resolutely, "This is what we're going to do."

At the far end of the continuum is *autocratic decision making*. In this style, the leader gains only information from others (not suggestions or solutions). The leader does not involve others in the decision-making process or invite group debate of alternatives. The entire decision-making process remains in the leader's hands.

Which style is most effective for long-term health and success? There is no single, clean answer, yet we can offer a few observations.

In general, the most effective leaders tend to make extensive use of participative decision making. The best decisions are made with some degree of participation—no one is brilliant or experienced enough to have all the answers. *No one.*

Bob Miller, CEO of MIPS Computer, a highly effective leader, explained:

> The best decisions come from facilitating ideas and suggestions from a group of great people. Get great people around you, involve them in the decisions, and you'll be right more often than not.

The degree of participation depends largely on the importance of the decision. If you seek wide participation on every single decision, even trivial decisions, people will spend all their time in meetings. However, as the importance of the decision increases, it's generally wise to invite the participation of a wider group.

People are more committed to decisions that they have a hand in shaping than to those that are decreed from above. True, it may take longer to go through a group process (either participative or consensus), but the decision will probably be more quickly and thoroughly acted upon. And it is the action that results from the decision that ultimately matters, not the decision itself. Keep in mind that it can take longer to sway people to accept a decision after it's been made than to involve them in the decision-making process in the first place.

Doesn't a group process invite disagreement among group members—disagreement that can be uncomfortable and difficult to resolve? Yes. And this is good.

To repeat: disagreement during the decision-making process is good. In making important decisions, it's wise to have constructive argument and differing points of view. Disagreement will clarify the issues and produce a more thought-out solution. Without disagreement, you probably don't fully understand the problem.

Referring to the example of the Cuban Missile Crisis, Robert Kennedy wrote about the importance of disagreement in reaching the best decisions:

> The fact that we were able to talk, debate, argue, disagree, and then debate some more was essential in choosing our ultimate course. . . . Opinions, even fact itself, can best be judged by conflict, by debate. There is an important element missing when there is unanimity of viewpoint.

Leaders of great companies also tend to make extensive use of delegative decision making. To build a great company—a company that has effective leaders at all levels—you need to remove yourself from many of the decisions and force people to stand on their own feet. Granted, there are many decisions where you need to be involved, but there are many others where you're not essential. Furthermore, the most innovative companies tend to push decisions as far down in the organization as possible, giving people at all levels the opportunity to move fast, utilize their creativity, apply their intellect, and assume responsibility.

Delegating decisions doesn't mean being detached, nor does it mean standing idly by if the whole ship is going to crash into the rocks. It simply means giving people the power to make decisions that affect their area. It gives people a chance to test themselves and to build their own decision-making "muscle."

Keep in mind that no single style will work in all situations, and that it is helpful to be skilled across a range of methods. We offer the following rough guidelines for group decision making:

1. Whenever appropriate, delegate decisions downwards; give people a chance to build their decision-making "muscle." Be crystal clear about what decisions you have delegated, and hold people accountable for those decisions.
2. On important decisions that require widespread commitment for successful implementation, make the decision as a group, either participative or consensus. Enter the process with your own points of view, but be open to having your ideas influenced by others. Be clear whether the final decision is to be made by consensus or by you.
3. Encourage disagreement during the process.
4. Reserve autocratic decisions for situations where there's no time to invite participation (e.g., when the ship is crashing on the rocks), for trivial decision, for decisions where you want to send a symbolic message to reinforce your values, and for the small set of decisions that you believe should always be made entirely by yourself.
5. Whatever style you use, be up front about it. Pretending to be participative or consensus-oriented in an effort to get "buy-in" to a decision that you've already made is terribly destructive. If you practice this type of deception, people will see it, be unimpressed, and feel manipulated. Such deception creates cynicism and lack of genuine commitment. If you're going to be autocratic, then just be honest about it.

ACCEPT RESPONSIBILITY AND SHARE CREDIT

Be prepared to shoulder full responsibility for poor decisions and, conversely, to share the credit for good decisions. If you do the opposite—if you take all the credit for good decisions but blame others for mistakes—you will quickly lose the respect of your people.

It takes courage when things go awry to say, "It's *my* responsibility." But that's exactly what you should say—at least if you want to garner people's lasting respect and commitment. Some executives try to explain away a bad decision by saying, "The idea was good, but its execution was botched by others." This may be true. But an effective leader will nonetheless shoulder the blame.

When things go well, give your team the glory and the credit. If you're a good leader, you'll have no need to take center stage and credit for your team's effort. Your contribution will be obvious. Just let it be. As the Chinese philosopher Lao-tzu pointed out 2,500 years ago, "True leaders inspire people to do great things and, when the work is done, their people proudly say, 'We did this ourselves.'"

Good Decisions, Right Timeline

During its rise from entrepreneurial start-up to great company, Intel installed a mechanism for decision making called "constructive confrontation." As a member of the Intel team, you carried the burden to argue, debate, and disagree to help solve pressing problems. It didn't matter whether you were a junior engineer or field-marketing person; if you felt the logic and facts pointed to a solution contrary to that proposed by other people in the room, even contrary to the views of the CEO, you were expected to argue for that solution.

Intel's culture of constructive confrontation (sometimes referred to as "disagree and commit") exemplifies a pattern of decision making cultivated by Level 5 leaders in our research. They stimulated dialogue, debate, and disagreement as an indispensable ingredient in making supremely good decisions. They also created a climate where evidence, logic, and facts would trump personality, power, and politics. As a member of a Level 5 team, you have not only the opportunity to engage in the dialogue, you have the *responsibility* to do so. If you fail to advance your argument, if you fail to disagree with the most powerful person in the room, if you fail to bring solid logic and evidence to the debate, if you attack a person rather than the problem, then you're failing in that responsibility.

Cultivating debate, argument, dialogue, and disagreement—all this takes time, resulting in a slower decision-making process than just issuing an executive order. But it also increases the probability of choosing a wise course of action. Sure, you can't afford to spend all of your time in argument, and not all decisions merit exhaustive debate. But on the big decisions that matter most, especially those choices that involve big bets and/or have huge downside if they go wrong, the primary goal must not be to make people comfortable in a haze of happy consensus. The goal must be *to make a good decision and to execute that decision brilliantly.*

Peter Drucker offered a first rule of decision making: do not make a decision unless you have disagreement. In *The Effective Executive*, Drucker wrote the story of General Motors chief executive Alfred P. Sloan in the midst of an important decision. "I take it we are all in complete agreement on the decision here," Sloan reportedly said to his team. Everyone nodded yes. "Then I propose we postpone further discussion of this matter until our next meeting to give ourselves time to develop disagreement and perhaps gain some understanding of what the decision is all about."

Great leaders make clear decisions, but not always fast decisions. Ron Chernow's well-researched masterwork *Washington: A Life* provides exquisite detail of how George Washington—one of the few figures to achieve elite historical stature in both military and political leadership—was slow to decide, firm in decision, and rare to second-guess. His right-hand aide, Alexander Hamilton, said of Washington that he "consulted much, pondered much; resolved slowly, resolved surely." Thomas Jefferson wrote of Washington: "Perhaps the strongest feature in his character was prudence, never acting until every circumstance, every consideration, was maturely weighed; refraining if he saw a doubt but, when once decided, going through with his purpose whatever obstacles opposed." Washington cultivated a culture of open dialogue, practicing his famous self-discipline of silence, encouraging arguments to compete, listening and probing, until he made up his mind to act.

One crucial ingredient in good decisions is knowing the timeline. Sometimes the timeline for a good decision might be months or more, while in other situations, the timeline might be much shorter. In the 1962 Cuban Missile Crisis, President Kennedy had to make decisions that, if unwise, had the downside of full-scale nuclear war. And he had to make those decisions in a timeline measured in days and hours. Still, even with the pressure, he sought clarity and understanding, honed by argument and debate amongst his key advisors and sharpened by his piercing questions.

Ernest R. May and Philip D. Zelikow published the transcripts of President Kennedy and his team deliberating during the Cuban Missile Crisis in *The Kennedy Tapes: Inside the White House during the Cuban Missile Crisis*. Curious to understand the pattern of debate and decision, I asked a member of my research team to systematically analyze the transcripts. As part of that analysis, he calculated President Kennedy's questions-to-statements ratio across the thirteen days of the crisis. The ratio was highest on the first day of the crisis; as the days wore on, President Kennedy's questions-to-statements ratio dropped below where it stood on that day. The high questions-to-statements ratio early indicates that Kennedy wanted to stimulate dialogue and debate and find the best answers rather than issue quick leadership directives.

Robert F. Kennedy described in his classic memoir, *Thirteen Days*, that the president intentionally stayed out of some of the debates, so that his advisors would not be overly influenced by him. When the fate of the world is at stake, the only thing that matters is discovering and eliciting the wisest practical path to diffuse the crisis, and Kennedy provided the space for the best arguments to win. Yet throughout the crisis, as Kennedy reached clarity as to the best next step, he would take action and his team would unify behind the decision (no matter what their prior disagreements had been). The repeating pattern of dialogue, debate, and disagreement—all infused with the best facts available—helped the president make an iterative series of key decisions that saved the world from nuclear annihilation.

Of course, you might find yourself in a situation where you must decide fast and that simply does not allow for extended debate. If you're Ben Sliney, the Federal Aviation Administration's (FAA) national operations manager, on the morning of September 11, 2001, you don't have months, days, or even hours to make momentous decisions; you have *minutes*. Just before 8:30 A.M. on 9/11, Sliney received word that American Airlines 11 out of Boston had been hijacked. Shortly after 8:30, a supervisor interrupted Sliney's morning meeting to relay information that a flight attendant had been stabbed. At 8:46, an aircraft hit the North Tower of the World Trade Center. Sliney's team at the Command Center tried to make sense of reports that a small plane had hit the tower. When images from CNN showed smoke pouring out of a gigantic gash, they quickly realized "that was no small plane." At 9:03, United 175 exploded into the South Tower of the World Trade Center. At that moment, Sliney grasped that America was under a coordinated attack of unknown proportions, and the decision clock started.

"I'm surrounded in an air traffic control facility like this with about forty type-A personalities who are chewing at my arms to get something done," Sliney later recounted. "We were frequently conferring and exchanging information, so there was a lot of urgency . . . to do something positive. . . . I had a tremendous staff that day and a lot of people who would be willing to give me advice unsolicited." Sliney also sought input from headquarters, though he'd received no response before he had to begin making huge decisions. At 9:25, Sliney decided to halt all takeoffs across the country.

Then at 9:37, an American Airlines jetliner slammed into the Pentagon, and Sliney saw clearly what must be done: shut down the entire airspace over the United States, an action utterly unprecedented in US aviation history. At

9:42, thirty-nine minutes after United 175 hit the South Tower, the FAA issued Sliney's directive to land all flights at the nearest airport regardless of destination. People unified behind the decision and executed flawlessly, landing 4,556 airborne flights at airports big and small, all around the country.

In *Great by Choice*, Morten Hansen and I conducted a systematic analysis of the pace of executive decision making, with emphasis on entrepreneurial leaders building great companies in highly turbulent environments. We found that some of the best decisions happened fast and some of the best decisions happened more slowly. We learned that the critical question to ask in any given situation is, "How much time do we have before our risks change?" In some situations, you'll incur no significant increased risk (of either catastrophe or of missing a huge opportunity) by taking more time to decide. In other situations, however, you'll dramatically increase your risks by waiting too long. The key is to know which situation you are in, not to have a bias for "always fast" or "always slow." You need to be good at both. The right decision made in the wrong time frame is a bad decision.

Here, then, is a basic architecture of executive decision making we found in our research:

1. Determine how much time you have to decide, whether minutes, hours, days, months, or even years.
2. Stimulate dialogue and debate—guided by facts and evidence—to determine the best options.
3. Make a decision, firm and unambiguous, once you're clear on what must be done and/or when the decision clock runs out; do not wait for consensus agreement.
4. Unify fully behind the decision and execute with fanatic discipline.

The leaders in our research who built great companies understood that what happens *after* a decision—the level of commitment to and ferocity of implementation—counts at least as much as the decision itself. In a Level 5 leadership culture, wherein members of the team put the success of the company and its cause above their own interests, people unify behind a decision once made. It would be a secular sin to undermine the decision after the fact by saying something like, "Well, that's the decision the CEO made, but I don't think it's a good decision." Across all our research into what makes great companies tick, we found that big decisions almost always happen with disagreement still in the air. But then people commit to making the decision work, even if they had argued aggressively for a different course of action.

Without disagreement, you might not fully understand the problem. Without unified commitment, you'll almost certainly fail to execute. True greatness requires a series of good decisions, supremely well executed, that accumulate one upon another over a long period of time.

Of course, all this depends on having the right people. You need people who can argue and debate out of passionate commitment to the success of the enterprise, who argue for the best decisions to help the organization and its cause, not themselves. You need people who would rather see the team win and their argument lose than to see their argument win and the team lose. You need people who bring facts and evidence to the dialogue, not merely opinions. You need people who accept the responsibility to do everything they can to ensure the success of a decision they disagreed with; and if they cannot live with the decision, they accept the responsibility to self-eject from the bus. You need, in short, Level 5 leaders who can operate on a Level 5 team in a Level 5 culture—that is, if you want to turn your business into a truly great and enduring company.

Leadership Style Element 3: Focus

Do first things first—and second things not at all. The alternative is to get nothing done.

PETER F. DRUCKER

Effective leaders focus their efforts, keeping the number of priorities to a minimum and remaining resolutely fixed on them. You can't do everything; nor can a company on the path to greatness.

TAKE ONE SHOT AT A TIME

Create a short list of key priorities and *keep the list short*. Some leaders have found it useful to have only one priority at any given time. They then concentrate on that single priority until they've dispensed with it.

If you must have more than one priority, then keep it to a maximum of three—any more than three priorities is an admission that you don't really have any priorities.

An illustration of this point was made by Bob Bright, executive director of a Chicago-based sporting events company that owned the Chicago Marathon. During Bright's tenure, the race grew from a regional, second-tier event to a first-class international event and the scene of world records. When asked what the key to his success was, Bright responded with the simple statement, "Never put your rifle on automatic."

We asked him to explain. He told us that he had been in the Marines in Vietnam for eight years. He was in the middle of many battles—he led "bait" teams directly into enemy camps. It was there that he learned one of the most important lessons of his life:

> When you have just a few people, and there is enemy all around you, the best thing is to say, "You take this section from here to here and you take this section from here to here, and *do not* fire on automatic. Take one shot at a time. Don't panic.
>
> Well, the same thing applies to business—and it's really important. Keep yourself focused on one shot at a time. If you don't do that, you're going to end up in a lot of trouble.

This is not meant to equate business with leading a military unit in combat. Still, the basic idea—stay focused, do one thing at a time, don't panic—applies to the hurly-burly of running an entrepreneurial company. Does this mean that you should only have one thing on your "to do" list? Yes and no. Clearly, it is virtually impossible to lead a company and have only one "to do" on your list. But you should be spending the bulk of your time on your number one priority, concentrating your efforts on that priority until it is complete.

MANAGE YOUR TIME, NOT YOUR WORK

The most constrained resource in your company is your time. Virtually every other resource can somehow be acquired or manufactured, but you cannot acquire or manufacture more time for yourself. There are only twenty-four hours in a day.

Kenneth Atchity, president of Atchity Entertainment International, observed that there is a vital difference between managing time and managing work: work is infinite; time is finite. Work expands to fill whatever time is allotted to it. To be productive, therefore, you must manage your time, *not* your work. The key question to ask yourself is not "What am I going to do?" but "How am I going to spend my time?"

It sounds topsy-turvy, but it makes perfect sense if you think about it. The amount of work you have to do, especially if you are the leader of an organization, can expand indefinitely—it's simply not possible to do it all. Atchity hit the point perfectly in his book *A Writer's Time*:

If your work is successful, it generates more work; as a result, the concept of "finishing your work" is a contradiction in terms so blatant and so dangerous that it can lead to nervous breakdowns—because it puts the pressure on the wrong places in your mind and habits.

How often have you felt that you just don't have enough time to get everything done? Probably a lot. We empathize. None of us have (or ever will have) enough time to get everything done. Every night we will go to sleep with work undone. If we lead productive lives, we will die with work undone.

Yet—and this is crucial—there is much more time available than we generally make good use of. If you manage your time wisely, you will probably "discover" many unused wells of productive time in your life.

The first step is to examine where your time actually goes. Periodically keep track of your time and analyze where it is being spent. Is it being spent on your top priorities? Or, is it being distracted and diverted into unimportant activities?

Is your time being spent primarily in activities that reinforce your vision or directly contribute to the pursuit of your strategy? If not, then you're not focused enough.

One sure way to force yourself to focus is to work *less*. J. Willard Marriott, founder of Marriott Corporation, had a useful philosophy that he applied to building his company from a single-unit restaurant to a major corporation: "Work hard. Make every minute on the job count. Work fewer hours—some of us waste half our time."

Winston Churchill, one of the most prolific individuals in history, took time to paint, lay bricks, feed the animals, and socialize. He then spent his work time (which often didn't begin until 11:00 P.M.) only on the most important items.

HARD CHOICES—DECISIVENESS REVISITED

Setting priorities requires making tough choices as to what is really important. One reason so many people have such a difficult time getting focused is that they also have a difficult time making decisions: they balk at choosing which items will be left off their priority list. And you must be willing to take items off the list.

One CEO we worked with drove his management team insane because he was unable to choose priorities. He wanted *everything* done. But, alas, almost nothing got done. He would give people twenty "priorities," which, of course, was an impossible wish-list. One manager justifiably grumbled:

We're supposed to "focus" on twenty items. That's just not possible. But when I go to our CEO and ask, "Which of these are the most important, because I can only do a sub-set of them?" he freezes. He just cannot make hard choices.

This CEO couldn't bring himself to *remove* things from the list, for that would have required a decision. But that is exactly what was needed. The company, not surprisingly, ran into serious difficulties shortly after the above interview.

Leadership Style Element 4: Personal Touch

Leaders who build great companies are "hands on"—always putting their personal touch on the business. There is simply no excuse for being detached, removed, distant, or uninvolved.

BUILD RELATIONSHIPS

Great companies have great relationships: relationships with customers, with suppliers, with investors, with employees, and with the general community. The emphasis in all dealings is on developing and nurturing long-term, constructive relationships.

(Note: This is very different from the half-hearted disingenuous attention given to "employee relations" or "customer relations." In most companies, "employee relations" has the aim of pacifying people, rather than building a relationship with them. We are writing about something quite different here.)

In a great company, employees have a relationship with the firm that goes far beyond the traditional, "I get paid in exchange for work" mentality. Even former employees feel that they still have a relationship with the company well after their employment has ended. Have you ever noticed that employees who have left certain companies still say "we" when talking about that company?

Customers of great companies have a closer tie than the traditional, "I pay you for a product" exchange. They believe that they have a personal relationship with the company. Keep in mind what Leon Bean did with L.L.Bean Corporation, as described in a *Saturday Evening Post* article: " . . . each of his customers seems to share the illusion that L.L.Bean is a personal discovery, and very probably a personal friend."

These close relationships develop because the company's leaders invest their personal time in helping to shape the relationships.

Joanne Ernst is an athlete who had a contractual arrangement with NIKE for seven years. During this time, NIKE leadership invested in building a long-term relationship with Ernst. She even received personal, handwritten notes and Christmas greetings from Chairman Phil Knight.

This personal investment in the relationship created an intense loyalty and commitment to NIKE. And, as a result, Ernst went to great lengths to be a good spokesperson for the company, often going out of her way—far beyond her contractual obligation—to do something "just right." She explained:

> It was never just a pure business transaction. I've always identified with NIKE's spirit—the spirit of competition and the magic of sports. But it's more than that. If I were to do a bad job, I felt that it would be letting down personal friends. That's really the way I felt about it. Even after retiring from sports and ending my formal connection with the company, I still feel part of the NIKE family. I'll always feel that.

Think of every interaction as an opportunity to establish or further develop a long-term, positive relationship. You can only do this with a personal touch. You don't build relationships with employees by writing stale, formal memos; you do it by interacting in a more personal way.

Get out and talk to people. Walk around. Sit in the lunchroom and eat with all levels of people. Get to know the names of as many people as you can. (Some people, like Kristine McDivitt at Patagonia, learn the names of every employee.) Say hello to people by their first names.

Here is an example of what *not* to do. The general manager of a computer company became convinced that he should "do a little of this personal touch stuff." He had read about MBWA (management by walking around) and told his secretary to arrange for meetings with employees in his office. He wanted to schedule some management by walking around so that he didn't really have to go out and walk around!

You may be wondering if that really happened. It did. And, although it's an extreme case, it's by no means isolated. It is also inexcusable. There is simply no justification for not getting out of the office and interacting personally with people on an informal basis.

Larry Ansin, who completely revitalized Joan Fabrics Corporation after taking it over from his father, told us:

> You've got to get out from behind your desk and see for yourself what's going on. Go out and talk to people. Listen to them. Be visible. Don't wall yourself off with a blizzard of corporate memos.

Ansin was much more successful at building a great company than the general manager who "scheduled" management by walking around in his private office.

USE INFORMAL COMMUNICATION

A powerful way to add your personal touch is to use quick, informal communication. One particularly effective method is to keep a stack of personal note paper with you at all times. Use it to jot brief, handwritten notes to people. You'd be amazed what a difference this can make. And it hardly takes any time; sometimes it only takes a minute to jot a personal note and sixty seconds is a small amount of time compared to the impact. It lets people know that you're aware of them and what they're doing, and that you care.

Bill tells of how this particular method made a huge difference to him personally in his relationship with Stanford:

> I was in the middle of a particularly grueling quarter of teaching, and was completely exhausted. I also felt a bit depressed because a number of projects I was working on weren't going all that well. Dejected, I stumbled into my office and shuffled through the stack of mail on my desk. I opened an interoffice mail envelope and, to my surprise and delight, found a short handwritten note from the dean thanking me for my efforts on one of my courses. That one note, which probably took him no more than thirty seconds to write, did a lot to solidify my feelings about Stanford and to boost my morale.

BE ACCESSIBLE AND APPROACHABLE

There is no benefit to stiff formality. Set a tone of being approachable. Go on a first-name basis. Keep the "status barriers" to a minimum. Private parking spaces, ostentatious offices, and flagrant "executives only" privileges should be avoided or downplayed. Executive status symbols put distance between you and the rest of your company.

Figure out how to make yourself accessible. If people feel that there is a moat (complete with alligators in the form of surly secretaries) surrounding your office, you'll certainly begin to lose the personal touch. People at all levels should feel that they can have direct contact with the top executives of the firm.

Does this hold true even as the company grows larger? Does accessibility, direct contact, and personal touch make sense once the firm grows past a certain size?

The answer is yes, and we only have to look at IBM as an example. Even after Thomas J. Watson, Jr. took over from his father (when IBM was already well over a billion dollars), he held fast to the renowned "open door policy." Watson, Jr. wrote in *Father, Son & Company*:

> The open door policy was a practice of Dad's that traced back to the early 1920s. Disgruntled IBM employees were first expected to take up their gripes with their managers. But if they got no satisfaction they had the right to come directly to me. . . . On at least one occasion a single protest led to a substantial change in the way we did business.

As the company grew, Watson's office handled 200–300 cases each year. To keep it manageable, he used personal assistants, who were chosen among IBM's most promising young managers. Even after IBM had grown to over 100,000 employees, Watson would still handle some employee complaints himself " . . . so that word would get around that the head man was still available."

If the Watsons could be accessible and keep a personal touch on the business as IBM grew, then saying "we are too big for that stuff" is a lame excuse indeed.

KNOW WHAT'S GOING ON

Reject the common wisdom that as your company grows you should become detached and removed from what's happening on the firing line. Yes, you need to delegate authority. Yes, you should overcome the compulsive impulse to direct every single decision. True, your time will be stretched and increasingly dominated by "high level" meetings.

However, you should still find time for firsthand exposure to the rhythms and activities of the company. The only way to do this is to see with your own eyes and listen with your own ears. See for yourself what the problems are, what is going well, and how people feel.

For example, Sam Walton constantly sought ways to keep his own fingers on the pulse of the enterprise. Walton would drop in on Walmart sites, unannounced, sometimes as many as ten in a single day. In one instance, Walton awoke at 2:30 A.M., bought a box of doughnuts, took them to a warehouse loading dock, and shared them with the dock workers while asking them how things could be done better. In another instance, he unexpectedly jumped in the cab of a Walmart semi-truck and rode 100 miles to obtain direct personal insight into Walmart's transportation system.

Walton's behavior is not unusual among the most effective corporate leaders. Granted it is time consuming to go out and see for yourself, especially as the company grows. But it is not impossible. The best corporate leaders *make* time for it. They know that people on the shop floor, in the field, or in the lab are just as important to listen to as other executives.

REINFORCE VALUES WITH SYMBOLIC DETAILS

There is a paradox evident in those who build the great companies. On one hand, they concentrate on high-level vision and strategy while, on the other hand, they involve themselves with seemingly trivial details. The acceptance of the paradox lies in understanding that details are not trivial. Details matter. The most effective leaders are obsessed with both vision *and* details. They are fanatical about getting the details right.

How you deal with certain details is actually a very high level statement—a statement about the core values of the company. Involving yourself with certain details can send a very powerful symbolic message.

CASE EXAMPLE: DEBBIE FIELDS

Debbie Fields, founder of Mrs. Fields Cookies, wrote in her book *One Smart Cookie* that she walked into one of her stores unannounced (a very common practice of hers) and noticed " . . . a very unhappy-looking batch of cookies laid out for the customers."

> They were flat and overbaked. A perfect Mrs. Fields Cookie is half an inch in thickness, and these were a quarter of an inch. A perfect Mrs. Fields cookie is three inches in diameter, and these appeared to measure three and one quarter inches. They were also a little more golden brown than they should have been.

The cookies were only off by a quarter of an inch in each direction—a quarter of an inch! But what really hammered home the importance of detail, and reinforced the underlying Mrs. Fields philosophy, was the way she handled the situation.

She could have fired the store manager on the spot, which she didn't do. She could have sent out a corporate memo reemphasizing proper cookie size and color, but she didn't do that either. She did something much more powerful and symbolic.

> I turned to the young man standing next to me and said, "Tell me, what do you think of these cookies?"

"Aw," he said, "they're good enough."

I nodded. I had my answer. One tray at a time, I took the cookies—five of six hundred dollars' worth—and slid them gently into the garbage can. "You know," I said to him, "good enough never is."

Think of reinforcing values as analogous to kneading bread. Your personal involvement with specific details is part of the kneading process. Like Debbie Fields' trashing of six hundred dollars' worth of cookies, your personal touch on a seemingly mundane detail can take on mythic proportions and ingrain itself in people's minds as a vivid symbol of the company's philosophy.

We have a close relationship with Hewlett-Packard Company. Through this relationship we've heard a vast number of stories called "Bill and Dave stories." Each story vividly portrays how Hewlett or Packard dealt with a specific incident in the formative stages of the company.

In one story, according to HP legend, Bill Hewlett, while wandering through a division, noticed a little detail: the stockroom was locked with a chain and padlock. Furious, Hewlett obtained a pair of bolt cutters, destroyed the chain, and left the remnants on the division manager's desk, along with a note: "This isn't how we do things around here. We trust our people. Bill Hewlett."

When asked if this story was true, Hewlett responded simply, "It could be." He then explained that he did a lot of things like the bolt cutter incident in the early days of the company—so many in fact that he couldn't remember them all.

PERSONAL TOUCH VERSUS MICRO-MANAGEMENT

Don't confuse personal touch with micro-management; they are not the same. Micro-management—a horribly destructive behavior—is illustrated in the following description of a certain CEO's management style:

Our CEO tries to control and direct every single little detail. Instead of feeling like you're competent and trusted, you feel that you are being "watched over." He nitpicks everything and it drives us all crazy. Some of our best people have left for other companies because he's so demoralizing. You know the old saying about seeing the forest for the trees? Well this guy is so far down in the trees that he's trying to control the direction and size of *each pine needle*.

This CEO's style is clearly oppressive, but how is it different from personal touch? Are we being consistent? At first we admonish you to "know what's going on" and to "reinforce values with specific details"; then we admonish you to not "micro-manage." How do these fit together?

The difference is simply this: A micro-manager doesn't trust his people, and seeks to *control* every single detail and decision; he believes that ultimately only he will make the right choices. A personal-touch leader, on the other hand, trusts his people to make basically good choices; he respects their abilities.

A micro-manager doesn't respect his people's abilities. A micro-manager makes people feel like they are being suffocated—the way a twenty-year-old would feel if his parents still dictated bedtime. Anyone who has been micro-managed can attest that it has a terribly demoralizing effect.

Micro-managing also limits people's development. Instead of being a guide or role model, a dominant micro-manager seeks to control people and eventually finds himself surrounded by stunted dwarfs who ask, "Why should I learn to think for myself, when he wants to do all the thinking for me?"

Yes, you should be fanatical about getting the details right. Yes, you should shape the group's values with symbolic acts on certain specific details, but not on *every* detail. The symbolic acts are meant to lead the way—to guide, to show, to set an example. They are meant to leave a lasting impression so that you don't need to tightly control people—so that people will behave *of their own accord* consistent with the core philosophy.

You can be hands-on without stifling people; you can have your fingers on the pulse of the organization, yet not suffocate folks. Indeed, a non-controlling personal touch has just the opposite effect of micro-management. Instead of demoralizing people, it elevates and inspires them to perhaps do more than they would otherwise think possible, which leads us right into our next leadership style element.

Don't Confuse Empowerment with Detachment

I'll never forget the first time I saw Jorge Paulo Lemann at work. At the time, back in the early 1990s, most executive offices provided privacy and space in proportion to the supposed importance of the executive. So, when I first visited his offices in São Paulo, I expected to be escorted to Lemann's executive suite. But no such suite existed. Instead, I found a gigantic room, desks jumbled together, a cacophony of activity all about, people gesticulating wildly and so engaged in their work that no one paid me much mind. And right in the middle of the melee sat Jorge Paulo at a simple, non-descript table. His calm countenance evoked the image of a Zen monk sitting down right in the middle of New York City's Times Square, contemplating with equanimity the ocean of activity surging in all directions around him. This, it turned out, was where Lemann spent the majority of his day, watching, listening, conversing, and making himself highly accessible to everyone.

Like all the great creators of culture I've known and studied, Lemann never confused empowerment with detachment. He believed passionately in leading by getting out of the way of his best people. Yet while he didn't micromanage, he was also the antithesis of imperious detachment.

Imperious detachment, or even blissful distraction, appeared as a common thread among many once-great companies as they teetered on the verge of decline. It's as if the executives began to believe that they needed to act like, well, *executives*. Instead of asking questions, they issued directives. Instead of going to see for themselves what the heck was going on, they asked for reports. Instead of getting briefings from those closest to the action, they got information filtered by middle management. Instead of asking, "What are the essential details that I need to grasp?" they said, "I'm staying focused on the Big Picture." Instead of taking notes based on input from people on the front lines, they issued memos for people on the front lines to read.

Winston Churchill sought always to know on-the-ground details as directly as possible. He even created a department entirely separate from the normal chain of command to feed him the brutal facts, so that the unvarnished truth would reach him. One of the few points of angst and disagreement between the King and himself during the Second World War came on the eve of D-Day, when Churchill felt it was his duty to be on-site during the actual attack, watching the action directly from a bombarding ship. King George, horrified by the image of his prime minister ending up on the bottom of the English Channel, appealed to Churchill not to go; and the two of them exchanged multiple dispatches, Churchill arguing to go, the King imploring him not to. In the end, Churchill acquiesced, writing, "I must defer to Your Majesty's wishes, and indeed commands." Even so, just a few days after D-Day, Churchill crossed the Channel to see the action firsthand. He wrote later about reaching a château that had been bombed the night before, "Certainly there were a good many craters around it." Churchill asked General Montgomery, "What is there then to prevent an incursion of German armour breaking up our luncheon?" Montgomery said he didn't think they'd come. Fortunately for history, they did not.

If something is truly a strategic imperative, you need to give it your direct personal attention. Anything not worth your hands-on involvement is, by definition, not a strategic imperative.

In July 1987, George Rathmann awoke to stunning and terrifying news that threatened his young company, Amgen. Rival Genetics Institute had received a patent that circumvented Amgen's proprietary technology for producing EPO (erythropoietin, a hormone released from the kidneys that stimulates red blood cell production). Genetics Institute had gained a patent on so-called natural EPO made from human urine. This "natural" EPO had no commercial viability, as it would require nearly six million gallons of human urine to make enough EPO for one patient for one year. Amgen's technology breakthrough created the only workable path to the end destination of EPO. But the Genetics Institute patent threatened Amgen's ability to fully capitalize on its breakthrough. Summed up an article in *Nature*, "As [Amgen's] genetically-engineered cells are essential to make large quantities of EPO, the situation is perfect for dispute: Genetics Institute has a claim on the final destination and Amgen on the only way of getting there."

Many CEOs involved in a complicated legal battle would delegate to their attorneys to find a way to settle, perhaps arranging a cross-licensing deal to share rewards. But Rathmann took *personal* responsibility as field commander and coordinated the legal effort *himself*. Amgen endured the legal battle with an incensed Rathmann leading the fight. In the end, Amgen won a complete victory in the courts and continued on its odyssey to become one of the first truly great biotech companies.

Rathmann modeled a leadership capability that Kevin Sharer (Amgen CEO from 2000 to 2012) also embraced, even as the company became much larger. Sharer described it as the ability to continually shift between altitudes. On one not-atypical day, as he related in an interview for *Harvard Business Review*, Sharer spent time in the morning with his leadership team on a $100 million investment decision that had vast strategic implications for Amgen's overseas operations. A bit later, he spent time on executive assessments and thinking about succession. Then he spent time with the mock-up for a new boardroom conference table, focused on how the new table might affect group dynamics. Altitude of thirty thousand feet, then three thousand feet, then thirty feet.

So, at what point in an organization's life should an entrepreneurial leader learn to "let go" and cease his or her tortured worrying about getting details right? When should the entrepreneur transition from an intensely hands-on style to a hands-off style? When should the founder shift to focus entirely on vision and strategy, leaving tactics and implementation to others?

These are the wrong questions.

The choice is not between hands-on or hands-off. In our research, the entrepreneurs who led their companies from start-ups into some of the greatest corporations in history generally had *both* a hands-on style *and* an empowering style. No matter how big their companies became, they remained closely connected to their people, hyper-aware of facts on the ground, and directly engaged in strategic imperatives. If you lose your voracious curiosity about tactical details, if you lose passionate interest in people and how they are feeling, if you insulate yourself in the protective cocoon of executive comforts, you may well wake up one day to discover your company has already entered a doom loop of decline and self-destruction.

Even so, the best entrepreneurs in our research didn't let their hands-on leadership slip into soul-crushing micro-management or the pathology of leading as a "genius with a thousand helpers." We observed the "genius with a thousand helpers" model among some of the less successful comparison CEOs in our good-to-great research study. In this model, a brilliant individual—the genius leader—fills key seats with helper-minions who implement his or her great ideas. This "genius with a thousand helpers" model can work exceptionally well in the short term, so long as the genius remains fully engaged (and so long as he or she remains a genius). In the long run, however, this model fails the test of enduring greatness. After all, if everyone depends upon the towering genius to make all the decisions big and small, then the company is likely to succumb to listless, drifting mediocrity when the founder steps away.

Of course, the goal is not just to master the balance of hands-on and empowering leadership. The goal is to become a shaper of culture and builder of people so that the company can be great for decades beyond your own life span. When you've found people who are as fanatic about getting the essential details right as you are, when you've taught them *how* to build and lead a system that delivers consistent tactical excellence, when they strive to far surpass what you yourself achieve during your own tenure, then you've truly set the foundation for an enduring great company.

Leadership Style Element 5: Hard/Soft People Skills

Leaders who build great companies master the paradox of hard and soft. They hold people to incredibly high standards of performance (hard) yet they go to great lengths to build people up—to make them feel good about themselves and about what they are capable of achieving (soft).

THE IMPORTANCE OF FEEDBACK

If we had to pick the single most underused element of effective corporate leadership, it would be feedback—especially *positive* feedback.

It's a fact of human nature that people perform better when they have a positive self-image. Psychologists in a variety of experiments have found that people's performance—*objectively measured*—improves or declines depending on the type of feedback they get. Positive feedback tends to improve performance, whereas negative feedback tends to decrease performance.

Yet, all too often, people get precious little feedback from company leaders—positive *or* negative. This absence of feedback sends a message: We don't care about you. And when people feel you don't care about them they're not going to give their best effort. Why should they?

Great sports coaches—those who have mastered the craft of catalyzing people to perform to their highest possible level—have always known the importance of giving feedback to their athletes and showing that they care.

Tommy Lasorda, manager of the Los Angeles Dodgers for four National League pennants and two World Series championships, said in an interview with *Fortune* magazine:

> Happy people give better performances. I want my players to know that I appreciate what they do for me. See, I believe in hugging my players. I believe in patting them on the back. People say, "God you mean to tell me you've got a guy making a million and half dollars a year and got to motivate him?" I say, absolutely. Everybody needs to be motivated, from the President of the United States on down to the guy who works in the clubhouse.

John Wooden, the most accomplished college basketball coach in history (ten NCAA Championships at UCLA in twelve years), believed in always looking for a way to build his players up and, at the same time, continually challenging them to be better. He held a simple philosophy: "People," he said, "need models, not critics." One of his personal admonitions was, " . . . to end practice on a happy note. I always tried to counterbalance any criticism in practice with a bit of praise."

Another great coach, Bill Walsh (who oversaw three Super Bowl Championship teams at the San Francisco 49ers), emphasized the importance of personal and positive encouragement. Walsh would shake hands and say a positive personal word of encouragement to every player just before each game. He also asked his assistant coaches to acknowledge each player, shake his hand, and offer supportive thoughts.

These coaches are good role models for business executives. They clearly live up to incredibly high standards, and they make dispassionate, objective assessments of people. Yet, they still use positive reinforcement.

Implicit in this, of course, is the assumption that you genuinely care about the people in your organization—that you have compassion, empathy, and respect for them. And, indeed, this is a requirement for effective corporate leadership. An organization run by individuals who don't care about or respect the people working for them is unlikely to attain enduring greatness.

We attribute much of John Wooden's incredible success to his sincere concern for each player. "My love for young people," he wrote, "is the main reason I have stayed in coaching and have refused positions that would have been far more lucrative."

What about negative or critical feedback? You can't run a company and give only positive feedback. Obviously, there are times when critical feedback is necessary. And, certainly, it's essential to give only *honest* feedback. If you fabricate positive feedback just to make someone feel good, it will lose credibility. In addition, there are times when someone's output needs to be critically evaluated, as that person's performance might be falling far short of expectations.

In his book *Building a Champion*, Bill Walsh wrote:

> The stylish, graceful, easy-going, affable, "players' coach" will get you up to 80 percent of the job done. The final 20 percent is attributable to making tough decisions, demanding a high standard of performance, meeting expectations, paying attention to details, and "grabbing and shaking" when necessary.

All that being said, however, we've observed that *poor* leaders err on the side of too much critical feedback and too little positive feedback. In all too many companies, people only get feedback when they do something wrong, rather than all the times that they do something right.

Furthermore, the best leaders are always looking for ways to put people in positions where they'll do well—where they'll perform at levels that merit positive reinforcement. They're always looking for ways to build people up, rather than tearing them down.

Indeed, if you find that you have someone who is not performing well, you might first ask the question, "Do we have this person in the right job?" It's common to find that an employee who languishes in one job, flourishes in a different role. For example, excellent engineers and salespeople often flounder in management roles.

Finally, be aware that when things are going poorly is not necessarily the time to be the most critical. Indeed, harshly berating people who probably already know that things are not going well can be counterproductive. In grim circumstances people often need a little encouragement and support.

CASE EXAMPLE: RUSSELL S. REYNOLDS

An interesting example is how Russ Reynolds, founder of Russell Reynolds Associates, handled a visit to a poorly performing office. The entire office was absolutely terrified of Reynold's pending visit, fearing that he would criticize and perhaps fire people. Everyone was on edge, partly because of the office director's statement that "If you can't deliver, then I'm sure Russ will get rid of you and find someone who can."

At the appointed hour, employees assembled in the main conference room, expecting the worst. Reynolds starting off the meeting just by chatting with people. After about 30 minutes, the office director tried to plunge into a more serious discussion of the problems at hand. Reynolds pulled the discussion back to a lighter, more positive tone. Finally, in exasperation, the office director asked, "Don't you want to get down to business and deal with our problems here?"

"No," responded Reynolds, "I can see that you're doing everything you can. I'm sure if you just keep working at it, something will break and the office will turn around. You're good people here, and I have every confidence in you. Just keep at it."

It was absolutely brilliant. Reynolds knew that people needed to be built up at this point, not torn down. People in the office responded by saying, "Hey, this guy *believes* in us. We *can't* let him down." His belief in them was well-founded; the office rebounded and became a very successful unit.

LEADER AS TEACHER

The most constructive approach to critical feedback follows from the concept of leader as teacher. When you need to provide corrective or negative guidance, think not of yourself as a critic—or even a boss—but as a guide, mentor, and teacher. The process of critique should be an educational experience that contributes to the further development of the individual.

CASE EXAMPLE: H. IRVING GROUSBECK

Irv Grousbeck, co-founder and president of Continental Cablevision, has developed a very effective approach to hard/soft people skills. During a conversation with us, he explained his philosophy and style:

> I've always operated from the model of manager as teacher. I'm interested in how mistakes can be used to improve people's capabilities.
>
> First—and this is important—you don't criticize the person. Instead, you *examine the event*. It's analogous to doing a good job of raising children; you address the issue of a messy closet, rather than criticizing your child for being a messy person.
>
> The same is true in managing. I always ask for the individual's side of the story. I ask him to give me an idea of what happened to make the event turn out the way it did. Then, I'll ask him what options he considered, and I'll present some other options and ask if he considered those. I toss out suggestions in the form of questions.
>
> The whole process is one of education and development. I make it clear that we are sitting on the same side of the table, that there is no problem with him as a person and that there is no problem between him and me. I emphasize that everyone makes mistakes, sometimes illustrating the point by referring to mistakes that I have made.
>
> But I also make it clear that I want the person to learn how the event could have been better handled, so that it can be done better in the future. That way, he is continually developing his capabilities, and the entire company benefits.

Grousbeck has a soft style in providing corrective feedback. Yet, he is resolutely dedicated to a high standard of excellence—both in himself and others. And, more often than not, this standard is attained.

THE ROLE OF HIGH STANDARDS

Do not interpret the importance of building people up and helping them learn from mistakes as meaning that you should permit incompetent, poor, or irresponsible performance. Hand in hand with the need for positive reinforcement is the need for high standards.

Just as giving people positive reinforcement tends to increase their performance, so does the presence of challenge and high expectations. Good teachers have always known that students generally *want* to be challenged, and that they generally respond favorably to high expectations. Think back for a moment about the best teachers you ever had. They are probably the ones that held very stringent standards for the class. The same principle applies to effective corporate leadership.

Like a good teacher, a good leader assumes that people from all walks of life and backgrounds *can* perform at high levels and that, deep down, they want to. A good leader doesn't *demand* high performance (demanding implies that people are basically lazy and are inclined to withhold their best effort—that it must be extracted out of them, like pulling teeth).

No, a good leader offers people the opportunity to test themselves, to grow, and to do their best work.

There is no shortage of people interested in doing something in which they can take pride. But there is a vast shortage of leaders who provide the stimulation of stiff challenge and high standards, combined with the uncompromising belief that seemingly ordinary people can do extraordinary things.

Put people in positions where they're required to rise to a high standard, and let them know that you believe they will do so. Keep in mind the approach Trammell Crow took in building his company: betting on people and having faith in them. In *Trammell Crow* by Robert Sobel, a young developer told of his experience with Crow:

> I remember when he took me into a meeting with the contractors and all the lenders and introduced me to them. He built me up as though I was something that I really wasn't, which I think demonstrated confidence in my abilities. I couldn't believe that he would give someone as young and inexperienced [as I was] that level of responsibility.

This combination of push/pull, yin/yang, hard/soft, high standards/positive reinforcement is the essence of stimulating people to exercise their full capacity. By helping each person to reach his maximum capability, whatever level that might be (and there is a spectrum of abilities across any group of people), you can stimulate the entire company to jump over a very high bar.

Leadership Style Element 6: Communication

We know it sounds trite to underscore the need for communication—and indeed we wish it were trite. The unfortunate fact is that many company leaders are poor communicators. It's not that they can't communicate; it's that they don't.

A great company thrives on communication. Effective leaders stimulate constant communication: up, down, sideways, group, individual, company-wide, written, oral, formal, informal. They work towards having a continual hum of communication throughout the organization.

COMMUNICATE VISION AND STRATEGY

In the next chapter, we hammer home the importance of developing a clear vision and strategy for the company. But just developing it is not enough; you also have to communicate the vision and strategy.

You don't have to be a spectacular orator or eloquent writer to communicate effectively. Don't worry about how to communicate where the company is headed, just say it. And say it a lot. Speak it. Write it. Draw it. Say it again. Never let the vision fall from sight; keep it in front of people at all times. Refer to it constantly.

For example, when Jim Burke was CEO at Johnson & Johnson, he estimated that he spent 40% (yes, that is *forty* percent) of his time communicating the J&J Credo (the company's core values and beliefs).

In watching Doug Stone, former CEO of Personal CAD Systems, move about the company, we noticed that he drew pictures of the company's strategy on flip charts in offices and conference rooms throughout the building. During nearly every meeting he somehow got around to drawing these diagrams, and he left these little drawings all over: on scraps of paper, on people's notepads, on flip charts, on white boards, on bulletin boards, on lunchroom napkins. When asked about this, he said:

> I leave those drawings around on purpose. It's really hard to get an entire organization to understand where it's going, so you've got to keep hammering at the message. I leave those drawings around so that people will continually bump into them and perhaps refer to them during meetings. I guess it's kind of like subliminal suggestion.

USE ANALOGIES AND IMAGES

Use vivid images to convey what the company is trying to do. Use concrete examples to illustrate how the company is actually succeeding in moving towards its vision. Tell stories that illustrate the values and spirit of the organization.

Analogies, parables, and metaphors, graphically described, are a powerful form of communication. Use them.

In 1940, Franklin Roosevelt somehow needed to effectively communicate the concept and necessity of "Lend-Lease" (a program whereby the United States would provide supplies to a beleaguered Britain during the early phases of World War II). He could have gone into all the financial complexities of Lend-Lease, but that would have failed to capture the imagination of the American public. Instead, he resorted to a parable:

Suppose my neighbor's house catches on fire, and I have a length of garden hose. If he can take my garden hose and connect it up with his hydrant, I may help him put out the fire. Now what do I do? I don't say to him before the operation, "Neighbor, my garden hose cost me fifteen dollars; you have to pay me fifteen dollars for it." . . . I don't want fifteen dollars—I want my garden hose back after the fire is over.

One of our favorite business examples is that of Steve Jobs conveying the essence of Apple's vision. In 1980 (before the Macintosh had been created), he said during a talk at Stanford:

[Apple] is based on the principle that one person and one computer is fundamentally different from 10 people and 1 computer. It's like the capital equipment cost of a passenger train: you can buy 1,000 Volkswagens, and, yeah, they're not as comfortable, and they're not quite as fast, but those 1,000 people can go wherever they want, when they want. That's what our industry is all about.

The best analogy . . . is that man on a bicycle is twice as efficient as a condor [the most efficient animal]. Man can make tools that will amplify the inherent ability he has. That's what these computers are all about; they're bicycles.

Get out of the literal. Draw pictures. Tell stories. Use inexact analogies. Be vivid. Don't worry about whether the analogy is logically correct—the point is to communicate effectively, not be logically correct.

ADD PERSONAL TOUCH TO FORMAL COMMUNICATION

Most business writing is dull, turgid, and sterile. It has no life, no spark. There's no personality in it. In an effort to be businesslike or presidential, certain managers eliminate any hope they have of communicating effectively.

Have you ever noticed that a good writer makes you feel that she is having a personal conversation with you? Or that a good speaker draws you in, creating an intimacy between you and him, even though there may be many (perhaps thousands) in the audience? This is the effect you should strive to create.

There are two basic ways to achieving this effect.

- First, reveal yourself. Don't be afraid to share stories from your own experience and observations. Telling something about yourself, your own experience, or your unique view of the world creates intimacy, even though there may not be personal contact between you and the writer or speaker.
- Second, use a direct, personal, and unpretentious style. Use words like we, you, and I rather than depersonalized words like one. Use warm words like friends and comrades. Speak or write directly to the listener as if he's sitting right in front of you. Shorten your sentences. Be vigorous. Use clear language. Use crisp words.

  Don't say: "One can see that there are some dissatisfactions with the methods applied to the labor relations situation." Say: "I can see that you folks are angry about the way you've been treated."

  Don't say: "It's our policy to maximize the value chain and quality vector for our malt beverage products." Say: "We make a great beer."

  Don't say: "The matter at hand is the reduction of financial resources due to litigation-specific economic predation." Say: "Lawsuits are costing us a lot of money."

CALL A DUCK A DUCK—AND DON'T HIDE

It's a big mistake to present unpleasant news in a sugarcoated package and a worse mistake to hide from the responsibility of communicating disagreeable facts. It's far better to be honest and direct.

For example, consider the following memo:

> To: Director of Personnel
> Fr: CEO
> Re: Staff Adjustment
>
> With the decline in our business, it's time to cut expenses. Therefore, we must perform a staff readjustment. Attached is a list of individuals that need to be terminated in the next 60 days. Please discuss the situation with their managers.
>
> Emphasize that this is not a layoff. Rather, tell people that it's simply time to eliminate lower performers.
>
> Since this is the first time in our history that we have had a staff readjustment, please handle the situation with care. I expect you to minimize the disruption.

Think for a minute: what's wrong with this? There are at least four problems with the memo:

1. If something looks like a duck, quacks like a duck, and waddles like a duck, then it's probably a duck. No matter how you phrase it, this staff readjustment is a layoff, and only dullards won't recognize it for what it is.
2. The CEO is hiding. Instead of taking responsibility for announcing an unpleasant decision, he is shunting it off onto the director of personnel.
3. Since the layoff isn't being dealt with in a direct and open way, most people will get their information through rumors. This will magnify their fears and cause them to feel very insecure: "How many will there be? Am I one of them? How long will this go on? Should I start to look for a new job?" In addition, they will be resentful: "Do they think I'm an idiot? Why doesn't our CEO tell us about this? Doesn't he have any respect for us?"
4. The outcome is predictable: some of the very best people—the ones that the company most wants to keep—will choose to leave. Those who remain will expend countless hours of nervous energy worrying about their situation, rather than doing productive work.

People hate being misled. They hate being taken for dullards. They quickly lose respect for leaders who don't deal with them honestly and directly.

What should the CEO have done differently? He should have communicated such a painful decision himself. Here is an example of what a more effective leader might do.

My business friends and partners,

I've always believed in communicating with one another for better or for worse, and being up-front and open with most everything that affects our company. In line with that philosophy, I must address one of the most difficult decisions I've had to make in our entire history.

As you know, we've experienced a dramatic decline in our business. This decline has put us in a situation where we must cut expenses in all areas, including staff. We have therefore decided to have a ten percent layoff.

I know that this must come as a shock; we've never had to do this before. And, God knows, I hope we never have to do it again. But in order to ensure survival of the company, which is at stake, we've concluded that this painful step is necessary.

I want you to know that we've decided to implement the layoff in one wave. You have my word that we fully expect this to be the only layoff; we do not have any other layoffs planned. We'd rather take the bitter medicine in one large dose than drag out the agony and uncertainty over an extended period of time.

No matter how it's presented, the news of a layoff is going to be painful, especially for the unfortunate employees who lose their jobs. However, the more direct approach is likely to produce less disruption and garner greater respect than the first approach.

Calling a duck a duck is not only good communication, it also conveys respect for your people. Always assume that people at all levels have nearly infallible duck detectors, and that they prefer leaders who step forward and shoulder the burden of direct, honest communication.

STIMULATE COMMUNICATION IN OTHERS

Communication shouldn't flow only from top to bottom. It should be taking place at all levels and in all directions. Be aware that your style can inhibit communication in others. Conversely, it can also induce excellent communication. Remember, you set the tone.

Here are a few things you might consider for stimulating communication throughout the organization:

- Ask a lot of questions and leave people time to answer the questions.
- Ask people to come to staff meetings (which should be scheduled at regular intervals) with at least one major point that they think everyone should know.
- Ask people to come to staff meetings with at least one question they would like to ask. Encourage them to ask any questions that are on their

minds. Respond to questions by saying, "Good question. I'm glad you asked that." There's nothing that will shut down communication quicker than if you make people feel stupid for asking questions.

- Ask people in both informal and formal meetings to "speak what is really on your mind."
- When someone disagrees with the group, ensure that the person gets a fair hearing for his disagreement.
- Be spontaneous. Encourage people to get together on the spur of the moment to work on problems. Impromptu informal meetings are some of the best communication vehicles.
- Reduce oppressive, stiff formality. Make people feel comfortable. Loosen your top button and tie. Roll up your sleeves. Kick off your shoes.
- When there are factions or tensions, don't play "go-between." Tell the factions to get together in the same room and discuss the problem themselves, rather than using you as a conduit. People in companies are often like kids in a family—they come running to mom or dad to complain, rather than dealing with a problem directly. Don't encourage this.
- Encourage people to express their feelings as well as their thoughts. We all have strong feelings about things. When feelings are suppressed, real communication cannot take place. Feelings in business? Yes, absolutely. Business, after all, is done by people and people have feelings.
- Don't let one or two personalities dominate all discussion. Draw out the more reticent members of your team by asking them what their views are.
- Thank people for raising key issues, even if those issues are uncomfortable.

Again, it may seem trite to harp on communication. But it's incredibly important, and so many executives are terrible at it. If you're going to err, err on the side of too much communication. You can't overinvest in it.

Leadership Style Element 7: Ever Forward

We would like to emphasize one final element of effective leadership style: an "ever forward" mentality. Leaders of great companies are always moving forward—progressing—as individuals (personal growth) and they pass this ever forward psychology along to the company. They have a high energy level and never become complacent.

HARD WORK

There's no getting around the need for hard work. It's a given. It comes with the territory.

However, there is a big difference between hard work and workaholism. You work hard to get something done. A workaholic, on the other hand, works out of compulsion—fear of some sort. Workaholism is unhealthy and destructive. Hard work is healthy, invigorating, and can be practiced up until the day you die, whereas workaholism leads to burn-out.

We know some effective leaders who work only 40–50 hours a week, but who we nonetheless classify as very hard workers—their level of intensity and concentration when at work is incredibly high. Conversely, we know some workaholics who work 90 hours per week and are basically ineffective. More is not necessarily better.

IMPROVE WITH EACH DAY

Never stop trying to become a more effective leader. You can always be better. There is always a higher standard. Never stop learning or developing your skills. Remain resolutely committed to the constant pursuit of a higher standard. Try, with each day, to be better than the day before.

Pay attention to your weaknesses and shortcomings. Ask for brutal feedback on where you are weak and what you should work on. Ask for candid criticism of your leadership style from those who work with you and for you. Also ask brutally objective outsiders to observe your leadership style and make comment. (This is something we have done for a number of CEOs, and they have found it to be immensely helpful; but it is also painful.) Put objective, honest outsiders on your board of directors.

None of us find it pleasant to have our shortcomings pointed out. It hurts. We therefore tend to avoid getting feedback that we know will expose our shortcomings. But, like distasteful medicine, it's necessary. To be a really exceptional leader, you've got to be committed to continual self-improvement.

KEEP THE ENERGY UP

If you become stale, so will your organization. The moment you cease to be excited and energetic about your work you will simultaneously cease to be effective as a leader. People who build great companies remain energetic their whole tenure. They never "retire on the job." Indeed, some of them never retire at all. They cannot imagine spending their years of wisdom as flaccid, unproductive retirees.

Take care of yourself physically, emotionally, and spiritually. Get enough sleep. Stay healthy. Get some exercise. Have diversions. Read. Converse with interesting people. Expose yourself to new ideas. Spend time in solitary, renewing activities. Set new challenges for yourself. Do whatever is necessary to keep yourself vibrant, stimulated, growing, and alive as a human being.

You've also got to like what you're doing. We've never met an effective small company leader who doesn't basically enjoy his or her work. Doing things you don't enjoy ultimately leads to low energy levels and burn-out.

Finally, one of the best ways to maintain a high energy level is to constantly *change*. Try new things, get involved with new projects, change the way you do things, experiment; do whatever it takes to keep things fresh. Some people think that making changes costs energy. After all, isn't it easier just to keep things the way they are? Ah, but here is the secret: yes, change costs energy but it adds more energy than it uses up.

Have you ever noticed that when you move to a new office or a new house there is an increased level of excitement and energy? You might even complain of the inconvenience of moving, yet the newness of the situation is nonetheless stimulating and invigorating. The same principle applies to work.

OPTIMISM AND TENACITY

Psychological research has shown that the most productive and happy people have a basically optimistic view of the future. We believe the same is true of companies.

Certainly, you should in no way discount the difficulties that must be faced, the setbacks that might be encountered, the pain to be endured, and the possibility of failure. Rose-colored glasses are dangerous indeed. However, you cannot afford to doubt that the company has the ability to make itself and its own future better than it is today. You've got to believe in your company and its future. If you don't, who will?

Optimism, however, is not enough; it must go hand in hand with tenacity and persistence.

When we first met Bob Miller, who took over as CEO of MIPS Computer in 1987 (when the company was heading towards insolvency) and successfully led it out of the "dark days," we were amazed to discover his quiet style. At first, you might even describe him as low-key or soft-spoken. How, we wondered, did he succeed in galvanizing MIPS forward?

After a few minutes, we began to understand. As he talked, we could sense his resolute, firm conviction that MIPS had the potential to shape its industry. Combined with this was a clear and resolute determination that, as long as he was there, he would never give up. Miller described his view of business as like being on a mission, and that he never let obstacles deter him from persistently pressing onward.

KEEP THE COMPANY MOVING "EVER FORWARD"

Paul Galvin, founder of Motorola, continually pointed out that, "Everything will turn out all right if we just keep in motion, moving forward." William McKnight, primary architect of 3M in its early days, emphasized that many of the company's product successes came from stumbling onto something, but that "you can only stumble if you are moving."

Like Galvin and McKnight, corporate leaders who have shaped great companies—people like the Watsons, Leon Gorman and his grandfather Leon Bean, Sam Walton, Bill Hewlett, Akio Morita, William Procter, Walt Disney, and Henry Ford—believed in "ever forward" motion for their companies.

One of the distinguishing characteristics of a great company is that it doesn't stop trying to change, improve, and do new things. A great company never arrives, never believes that it is good enough.

Greatness is not an end point. It's a path—a long, arduous, torturous trail of continual development and improvement. A great company reaches one plateau and then seeks new challenges, new risks, new adventures, new standards. A great company celebrates its successes, savors them, enjoys them—but only as brief stopping points along a never completed journey.

Ever forward. If one thing fails, try another. Fix. Try. Do. Adjust. Move. Act. As Henry Ford said, "You've got to keep doing and going."

TOUCH THE SPIRIT

The essence of leadership, as we have mentioned before, is to catalyze a clear vision that is shared and acted on by the group. But there is one additional element: touching people's spirit.

There is a spiritual side to all of us. For some, it's hidden below case-hardened cynicism, whereas for others it's near the surface. But in all cases it's there to be tapped.

By spiritual we do not necessarily mean religious. We are speaking of the higher side of people; the side that brings a lump to our throats when the underdog prevails; the side that wants to see the good guys win; the side that wants the world to be a better place for our children; the side that compels us to return the extra change when a clerk has given us too much; the side that hopes we would not let our comrades down in battle; the side that causes us to feel outrage at cheating and unfairness; the side that pushes us late into the night to complete an arduous task simply because we gave our word; the side that jumps instinctively into an icy river to save a drowning victim; the side that makes us heroes.

Granted, this is only one side of us. There is another side—the side that Joseph Conrad wrote about in *Heart of Darkness*. It's the side that breaks commitments, lets our comrades down, keeps the extra change, seeks to crush those less fortunate, pursues expediency over excellence, turns a blind eye to our own inconsistencies and weaknesses. All of us have both sides. A leader, however, appeals to the lighter side, stimulating people to take the high road. A leader speaks to the finer qualities we all possess and challenges people to express these qualities. Ultimately, a leader changes people.

Again, we return to our analogy of leader-as-teacher, and we ask you to think about the teachers who have changed your life. Chances are they helped you to see more in yourself than you had seen before. They tapped something inside you that sparked new perceptions of yourself, new expectations of yourself; your ideals for yourself rose to a new level.

Like such a teacher, a leader idealizes people and has resolute conviction that people can rise to this ideal. A leader grabs the spirit in people, pulling it forward and waking it up. A leader changes people's perceptions of themselves, getting them to see *themselves* in the idealized way that *he* sees them.

The leader conveys the message: "We can accomplish our big, hairy goals. I know we can do it, because *I believe in you.*"

Chapter 4

VISION

The basic question is, what vision do you aspire to?
ABRAHAM MASLOW

THE FUNCTION OF LEADERSHIP—THE number one responsibility of a leader—is to catalyze a clear and shared vision for the company and to secure commitment to and vigorous pursuit of that vision. As we discussed earlier, this is a universal requirement of leadership, and no matter what your style, you must perform this function.

Why is vision so important? What exactly is vision? And how do you go about setting one?

Answering these questions is the topic of this chapter. We hope to inspire you to put "catalyze a shared vision" as your number one priority. We will then present the "Collins-Porras Vision Framework"—a useful, concrete framework that removes the fuzziness that surrounds the topic yet, at the same time, preserves the magic or spark that's an essential quality of vision. Throughout this chapter, we will provide specific pointers on the process of catalyzing a shared vision.

Before launching into the benefits of vision, we'd like to provide you a quick snapshot of the overall structure that we will be using throughout this chapter and the rest of the book.

Figure 4-1 shows the basic flow: you begin with vision, move to strategy, and then to tactics. It also shows that vision is composed of three basic parts: core values and beliefs, purpose, and mission.

Diagram of Vision, Strategy, Tactics

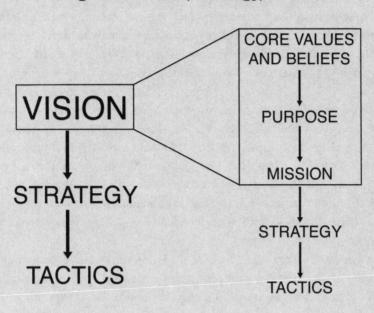

Figure 4-1

We will explain each of these parts later in the chapter, and give many examples. But first we will explain why you should take on the challenging task of setting a vision.

Vision Is Essential to Greatness

Consider any great organization—one that has lasted over the years—and I think you will find that it owes its resiliency to the power of what we call beliefs, and the appeal these beliefs have for its people . . . The basic philosophy, spirit, and drive of an organization have far more to do with its achievements than resources, structure, innovation, and timing.

THOMAS J. WATSON, JR.
FORMER CEO, IBM CORPORATION

Instilling your company with a lasting corporate vision is a challenging task. As one manager told us, "By asking me to do this you're setting the bar at a very high level." And indeed we are. It is *difficult*, we do not deny.

But vision is essential to attaining corporate greatness. Notice that in the above quote Tom Watson didn't say, "Consider any organization . . . "; he said, "Consider any *great* organization . . ."

Vision isn't necessary to make money; you can certainly create a profitable business without it. There are plenty of people who have made a lot of money, yet had no compelling vision. But if you want to do *more* than just make a lot of money—if you want to build an enduring, great company—then you need a vision.

If you examine closely the historical evolution of great companies—companies like IBM, L.L.Bean, Hewlett-Packard, Merck, Herman Miller, 3M, McKinsey & Company, Sony, McDonald's, NIKE, Walmart, Disney, Marriott, Procter & Gamble, Boeing, Johnson & Johnson, Motorola, Federal Express, Russell Reynolds Associates, General Electric, PepsiCo, Pioneer Hi-Bred, among others—you will find that, at some point, *while the company was still relatively small*, key leaders instilled a compelling vision into the organization.

In some cases, like Federal Express, the vision was put in at the founding of the company. In other cases, the company was founded by entrepreneurs to fill a specific need (such as to work for themselves or to bring a specific product to market) and they didn't articulate a broader vision until a few years down the road. Minnesota Mining and Manufacturing Company, for example, was founded simply to mine corundum (a hard substance similar to emeralds) from a small lake in Minnesota. It was only after that initial venture failed and the company groped around for a few years that CEO William McKnight developed a broad, clear vision of 3M Company, and its potential impact on the world.

But, in every case, whether at the founding or a few years down the road, key leaders in great companies catalyze and articulate a shared vision for the entire organization.

Four Great Examples

IBM

Thomas J. Watson, Jr., CEO at IBM from 1956 to 1971, felt that the vision of IBM was the single most important ingredient in IBM's rise from a small company on the brink of bankruptcy in 1914 through the perilous phases of growth to its position as one of the most widely admired and consistently successful corporations in history.

Watson felt this so strongly that he published an entire book on the subject: *A Business and Its Beliefs—The Ideas That Helped Build IBM*, wherein he writes:

> Any organization, in order to survive and achieve success, must have a sound set of beliefs on which it premises all its policies and actions. I believe the most important single factor in corporate success is faithful adherence to those beliefs. Finally, the organization must be prepared to change everything about itself *except* those beliefs.

Watson's father, Tom Watson, Sr., primary architect of IBM, emphasized the importance of vision to IBM. In 1936, he wrote in a letter to his son that the number one asset a leader should develop is "vision."

(You'll notice that terms mission, vision, purpose, values, objectives, beliefs, culture, and philosophy seem to be used interchangeably and somewhat loosely by different authors and managers. Some make extensive use of the word mission. Others use the term vision and still others use purpose, goals, overall aim, objectives, or culture. For the moment, don't get distracted by terminology and spend a lot of time trying to figure out if vision is different from mission is different from values, etc. We will unravel and clarify these with the Collins-Porras Vision Framework presented later in the chapter.)

JOHNSON & JOHNSON
After Robert W. Johnson, Jr. took over from his father as CEO of Johnson & Johnson, he put a great deal of thought into drafting a clear statement of company beliefs. Known thereafter as the "Johnson & Johnson Credo," it became the backdrop for all future planning and decision making in the company.

MCKINSEY & COMPANY
Marvin Bower, chief architect of McKinsey & Company, the world's most successful management consulting firm, placed a great deal of emphasis on the development and communication of a shared vision from the early days of the firm.

In 1937, when McKinsey was a small firm with only two offices (by 1990 it had 48 offices worldwide), Bower dedicated tremendous amounts of time to codify and articulate the McKinsey vision. At the 1953 Annual Firm Conference, Bower unveiled a "Diagram of the Firm's Principal Personality Characteristics," which was used for years as a blueprint for the "McKinsey Approach." Bower later wrote a book on McKinsey, which emphasized McKinsey's vision. The words "our philosophy," "our approach," "we had to think in visionary terms," "we believe," and "our principles" appear extensively throughout the book, and in the chapter titles.

HEWLETT-PACKARD

During the mid-1950s, when the Hewlett-Packard company was only 15 years old and still relatively small, Bill Hewlett and Dave Packard took their management team off-site to the wine country in Sonoma, California, to codify HP's principles and permanent objectives. Referred to thereafter as the "Sonoma Conferences," these meetings solidified the underlying precepts of HP.

You might be thinking, "But my company is small; I'm not sure all this vision talk applies to us. We're not HP, IBM, J&J, or McKinsey. We're just trying to make a go of it."

Good point. But remember, each of the above companies once was a small, struggling enterprise, and, *in every case*, the vision was laid in place *when the company was still small*. It's not that these companies are big and therefore have the luxury of vision; it's that vision helped them become great in the first place. Vision precedes greatness, not vice versa.

A caveat: we don't mean to imply that vision is necessary only if you want to become big. We understand that you might want to remain a small company. If that's what you want, then you still need a vision. Why? Because if you're good, there will be opportunities to grow. The only way to remain small (if that's what you want) is to have a clear vision about what you want the company to be in the first place.

For example, we worked with the owner of a small company that had a serious crisis due to the lack of a clear vision. She tells the story:

> We were nearing the completion of the exhausting development phase of a new product with tremendous market potential. We were then a ten-person company, and this new product

would catapult us to at least three or four times that size. Sounds great, huh?

It was the worst experience of my life! As the product neared completion, we began to run around like chickens with our heads cut off getting ready for the influx of orders. I kept having this feeling in my stomach that something wasn't right; that I really didn't want this.

But we just kept pushing ahead, moving inexorably towards a product launch that would forever change the character of the company. No sane person would turn away from such a great opportunity—growth, profits, wild success, admiration of others, right? Nonetheless, I kept feeling worse and worse, until I reached the end of my rope, completely burned out.

It occurred to me: what we were doing was absolutely contrary to what I wanted for myself, my family, and the company. The problem was that I had never articulated what I wanted our company to be, and we had never talked about it among ourselves. We just kept moving down the day-to-day path of one opportunity after another. Social norms dictated that to grow and become a big overnight success is what we should do. And that's what was driving us. But it wasn't *our* vision for the company, and it wasn't what we wanted out of life. When the stress level finally reached an unbearable peak, we cut the product, and were much happier.

Had we been clear in our minds that our vision was to remain small—a profitable and happy *little* company with a nice lifestyle—we wouldn't have made the decision to do the product, and we never would have gotten ourselves into that horrible mess in the first place.

The Benefits of Vision

Let's now turn our attention to the four primary benefits of corporate vision:

1. Vision forms the basis of extraordinary human effort.
2. Vision provides a context for strategic and tactical decisions.
3. Shared vision creates cohesion, teamwork, and community.
4. Vision lays the groundwork for the company to evolve past dependence on a few key individuals.

A Basis for Extraordinary Human Effort

Human beings respond to values, ideals, dreams, and exhilarating challenges. It's our nature. We will go to phenomenal lengths in an effort to live up to the ideals of our organization, peer group, or society if we share those ideals and consider them worthy. Managers who build their organizations based on a set of worthy values, sound beliefs, and a compelling mission are laying the groundwork for extraordinary human effort.

Most people want to do more than bring home a paycheck. They want work they can believe in and that has meaning. This may not be true of all people, but it's certainly true of the people most likely to be solid contributors to a great company. Tap into the basic human desire for meaningful work and the traditional management problem of "how to motivate employees" largely evaporates. People will be self-motivated when doing work they believe in.

Motivation depends greatly on the extent to which a person can frame her work within a broader overall purpose. This even applies to routine jobs. During a visit to Giro Sport Design, an assembly worker proudly pointed to a bulletin board. Posted there were letters describing serious bicycle crashes, and how Giro helmets saved people from serious brain injury. "Fortunately," wrote one person, "the helmet shattered, instead of my head. Thank you for being in business."

"That's what we do," said the assembly worker. "We're not just making helmets. We're making people's lives better."

A guiding overall aim, when clear and shared, is so powerful that it can even form the backbone of motivation for an entire country. Writing about Israel in 1967, Barbara Tuchman remarked:

> With all its problems, Israel has one commanding advantage: a sense of purpose. Israelis may not have affluence, or television, or enough water, or the quiet life. But they have what affluence tends to smother: a motive.

Creating this motive is your task as a leader. You do this by creating the vision—by creating what Tuchman calls "the exhilarating task" that bonds a group together.

Think of how the British people rallied in a supreme effort to defeat Hitler in World War II. Think of how NASA overcame the odds against putting a man on the moon by the end of the 1960s. Think of how Boeing employees dedicated themselves to the "impossible" task of making the revolutionary 747 Jumbo Jet a commercial reality. Think of how engineers at Apple worked 80-hour weeks to bring out a computer that would change the world.

A Context for Strategic and Tactical Decisions

Corporate vision provides a context within which people at all levels can make decisions. *The importance of this cannot be overemphasized.*

A shared vision is like having a compass and distant destination in the mountains. If you give a group of people a compass and destination point and then turn them loose in the mountains to reach that destination, they will probably figure out a way to get there.

They may encounter obstacles, detours, bad turns, and side canyons along the way. However, with the general directions of the compass, a clear end-goal, and the belief that they are working towards a worthy destination, they will probably reach the target.

In contrast, companies without a shared overall aim have no context, and their people wander aimlessly in the side canyons and take detours to nowhere. Such companies resemble overworked fire departments, with people responding to crises and revenue opportunities as they emerge, rather than proactively making decisions within a coherent conception of what the organization is ultimately trying to do.

> ### CASE EXAMPLE: HOW BOB MILLER SAVED MIPS COMPUTER
>
> MIPS Computer was founded in the mid-1980s to capitalize on significant advances in computer technology. It had over $10 million of venture capital financing, state-of-the-art technology, and the promise of growing market demand for powerful computers. Yet, four years after its founding, it was in turmoil and on the brink of bankruptcy. Why?
>
> MIPS had no clear idea of what precisely it was trying to do. It had no clear idea of what it wanted to become. Instead, the sales department blindly pursued every revenue opportunity, without asking the question: what revenue opportunities make the most sense within the context of what we are trying to achieve?
>
> This, in turn, drove R&D to develop (at great cost) a plethora of unrelated products, without asking the question: how do these products help us attain our vision? MIPS leaders pursued joint ventures that

severely limited the opportunity to distribute overseas, without ever asking the question: how does the overseas market fit with our vision?

Of course, they *couldn't* ask that question, as there was no clear vision. There was no focal point of united effort, and the organization gradually disintegrated into factions. Each faction blamed others for the perilous position of the organization. Morale declined. Good people left for better opportunities. Investors and customers lost confidence and, hence, cash flow went negative.

It took the leadership of a new CEO, Bob Miller, to save the company. Commenting on how he successfully pulled the company out of its malaise to a prominent position in the RISC Technology industry, Miller commented:

> The most important question is: what do you want to be five to ten years from now? The company had never asked or clearly answered that question. That may seem simplistic, but posing that question was the basic solution. Only then could we make good strategic decisions.

Miller's comment leads to a very important point: Strategy is impossible without first setting a vision.

There are thousands of pages in management literature written about strategy. Strategic Management is a required course at most business schools. Large consulting firms build client lists by selling "strategy solutions." There is a good reason for this: sound strategy is essential to attaining greatness.

But think for a minute about the word strategy. What does it really mean? Strategy is *how* one intends to go about attaining a desired end. It is the *means* to an end. Thus, it is wholly impossible to have an effective strategy unless you are clear—absolutely crystal clear—about what the end point is. Strategy is a *path* to attaining your vision. Knowing how to get "there" is impossible if you can't articulate what "there" is.

Most companies (we believe that most organizations do indeed lack clarity of vision) let crises, firefights, and tactical decisions drive the company. We refer to this as "tactics-driving strategy." Vision should drive strategy and strategy, in turn, should drive tactics, not the other way around.

This may seem obvious, and you may be wondering why we're harping on it. We agree. It *is* obvious. However, its practice is also extraordinarily rare. We've noticed that in almost every company with significant organizational problems, one of the root difficulties is the lack of a clear vision. Indeed, it always strikes us as incredible how seriously some organizations suffer from this root problem.

Even in situations of national importance, the phenomenon of tactical success but overall failure due to the lack of a clear overall aim can be played out.

CASE EXAMPLE: THE UNITED STATES WAR IN VIETNAM

You know, you never defeated us on the battlefield.

AN AMERICAN COLONEL, HANOI, 1975

That may be so. But it is also irrelevant.

NORTH VIETNAMESE COLONEL IN RESPONSE

In terms of tactics and logistics, according to Harry G. Summers in the book *On Strategy*, the United States Army was successful in Vietnam. Over a million soldiers a year were transported to and from Vietnam, and they were sustained in the field better than any army in history. In tactical engagements, the army had an extraordinary success rate, with enemy forces thrown back with terrible losses in engagement after engagement. Even so, it was North Vietnam that emerged victorious. How could the United States have succeeded so well, yet failed so miserably?

A wide range of authors on the subject all came to a startlingly simple conclusion: the United States didn't know precisely what it was trying to achieve, and it was therefore impossible to have an effective strategy. A 1974 survey of Army generals who had commanded in Vietnam found that almost 70% of them were uncertain of United States objectives.

"This confusion over objectives," Summers concluded, "had a devastating effect on [United States] ability to conduct the war."

"The principals never defined either the mission or the number of troops," wrote David Halberstam, author of *The Best and the Brightest.* "It seems incredible in retrospect, but it's true. Hence, there was never a clear demonstration of what the strategy would be."

Halberstam might have pointed out that without this clarity of aim, it would have been absolutely impossible to even have a strategy in the first place.

Don't get us wrong. We don't mean to imply that tactical excellence (as the United States had in Vietnam) is unimportant. It's essential, but it should be within the context of a clear overall vision. Vision, then strategy, then tactics.

Cohesion, Teamwork, and Community

As coach John Wooden of the UCLA Bruins pointed out, you have to build up each player to be his best as a guard, center, or forward, but it is even more important to develop the individual player's pride and belief in the whole team and its goals. Coaches like Wooden successfully reconcile the two by having very clear shared goals and an underlying set of principles and values that hold the team together.

Without a shared vision, any organization can easily degenerate into factions. Disparate agendas, turf wars, empire building, and petty politics become prevalent; destructive infighting saps people's energies, rather than working for a common aim and towards the strengthening of the entire organization. It becomes impossible to maintain a strong and positive sense of community.

Companies are usually founded with a clear, vibrant sense of purpose. Yet, as companies mature, they often disintegrate into squabbling factions. Institutional self-enhancement and turf wars smother the spark and spirit of the early sense of purpose.

In one company, we interviewed the top ten managers separately and asked: "What's this company all about? What are you trying to become? What are you trying to achieve?" No two people gave the same answer. As one explained: "We really are a collection of ten individuals with personal agendas, ready to charge in the opposite direction from everyone else. No wonder we have problems."

The company erupted into a devastating series of internal battles, complete with secret pacts among key players to gang up on other players. The company was eventually acquired (for a low price) by a large corporation, leaving one of the VPs to comment:

> We had such potential, and we squandered it. Once we lost a sense of
> unified purpose, we put all our creative energies into fighting among
> ourselves, rather than winning in the market place. It's sad.

Conversely, we've seen companies on the brink of destruction pull together with common purpose and overcome incredible odds. Ramtek Corporation, for example, had filed for Chapter 11 bankruptcy protection. A new CEO, Jim Swanson, took over the company and resurrected it to new life and steered it out of bankruptcy. (Most companies that file Chapter 11 die on the operating table.)

"Our mission," said Swanson, "was to get out of bankruptcy. It was such a challenging task that unified the team to put forth supreme efforts and beat the odds."

Soon after emerging from bankruptcy, Swanson took his team off-site to set a new mission. "We had a big challenge," he said. "We met it. Now we need a new one or else we'll lose that sense of team spirit."

In Chapter 8, "Innovation," we stress the importance of decentralization and autonomy. The problem, of course, is how to unleash individual creativity and, at the same time, move in a unified direction. Vision is the link. If all people in the company have a guiding star on which to sight (a common vision), they can be dispersed in hundreds of independent little boats, rowing in the same direction.

Evolving Past Dependence on a Few Key Individuals

In the early phases of an organization, a company's vision comes directly from its early leaders; it is very much their personal vision. To become great, however, a company must progress past excessive dependence on one or a few key individuals. The vision must become *shared as a community*, and become *identified primarily with the organization*, rather than with certain individuals running the organization. The vision must actually transcend the founders.

To illustrate this point, we like to use the powerful historical example of the founding and subsequent development of the United States. Instead of creating a country that depended on the continued presence of the then living leaders (Washington, Jefferson, Adams, et al.), the founders put in place a set of basic principles that would guide the country for centuries after their death.

In essence, they codified the vision of the country in the Declaration of Independence and the United States Constitution. They thereby ensured that the future of the United States would come close to living up to their beliefs about how the country should run and, just as important, would not require the continued presence of these individuals.

Those fellows in Philadelphia in 1787 were very smart: by instituting the enduring principles of the Constitution, they created the "glue" that would hold the country together even in the absence of a common enemy or the single "great dictator." Students of history will agree that this is very rare indeed.

[Note: We realize that the United States Constitution is not a perfect document. Our purpose here is not to deify the Constitution per se but rather to illustrate the idea of creating an enduring set of principles than from the presence of specific leaders.]

It's interesting to note that when Tom Watson, Jr. took over IBM from his father in 1956, he had the Constitution in mind when he took the top executives off-site to create the "Williamsburg Plan," as he wrote in *Father, Son & Company*:

> I picked Williamsburg [Virginia] because it is a historical place and this meeting was meant to be a kind of constitutional convention for IBM.

In contrast, there is the example of Duncan Syme and Vermont Castings. Syme had a vision: to make the best wood stoves in the world. He believed in this so much that he would personally stand on the production line to ensure that each stove met his exacting standards. During the 1970s, Vermont Castings became the fastest growing company in the wood stove industry, reaching sales of $29 million and margins as high as 60%.

Then, in the early 1980s, Syme stepped away from daily operations and turned the company over to professional managers (day-to-day management, Syme admitted, was not his strength).

But there was a critical problem: Syme's vision went into retirement with Syme. In his absence, the company lowered quality standards, diluted its traditional focus on wood stoves, reduced customer service, and pulled the company away from its original vision. Sales and profit growth flattened, the company lost its ability to bring out innovative products, and many felt the company had lost its greatness.

Syme returned to Vermont Castings in 1986 and got it back on track, reinstalling his vision and regaining the company's position as the premier woodstove maker.

This time, however, he took an entirely different approach, as he explained in *Inc.* magazine. Instead of relying solely on himself to be the guardian of the "Vermont Castings Way," he began a process of institutionalizing his vision. He wrote a "Statement of Vermont Castings Vision and Creed" and began the long process of ensuring that it was expressed in all operational decisions.

Creating a company with a vision (rather than a company with a single visionary leader on whom everything depends) is difficult for some leaders. They like being the "visionary"—the hero or great leader—on whom everything depends. The truly visionary managers are those who make the vision *property of the entire enterprise* and instill it in such a way that it remains strong and intact well after the leader departs from daily operations.

A Vision Framework

The word vision conjures up all kinds of images. We think of outstanding achievement. We think of deeply held values and beliefs that bond the people in a society together. We think or audacious, exhilarating goals that galvanize people. We think of something eternal—the underlying reasons for an organization's existence. We think of something that reaches inside us and pulls out our best efforts.

And therein lies a problem. Vision has a nice feel. We can agree that it's essential to greatness. But what exactly *is* it?

The Collins-Porras Vision Framework

A number of CEOs have told us that they can't seem to get their hands on what vision is. They've heard lots of terms like mission, purpose, values, strategic intent, but no one has given them a satisfactory way of looking at it that will transcend the morass of words and set a coherent vision for the company.

Out of this frustration, the Collins-Porras Vision Framework was developed. Much of the material in this chapter is based on extensive research at Stanford and the article "Organizational Vision and Visionary Organizations" (*California Management Review*, Fall 1991). We need not go into all of the theoretical underpinnings and background research of the framework here. The essence of it is that a good vision consists of:

1. CORE VALUES AND BELIEFS
2. PURPOSE
3. MISSION

We've found that people quickly grasp the concept of core values and beliefs. However, the difference between purpose and mission often causes confusion.

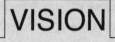

VISION		
CORE VALUES AND BELIEFS	**PURPOSE**	**MISSION**

CORE VALUES AND BELIEFS

A system of guiding principles and tenets; a philosophy of business and life.

Principles that are to be held inviolate.

An extension of the personal core values and beliefs of the leaders of the organization.

PURPOSE

The fundamental reason for the organization's existence.

Grows out of core values.

Like a guiding star always worked towards, but never fully attained.

Should serve to guide the company for 100 years.

MISSION

A bold, compelling, audacious goal.

Has a clear finish line and a specific time frame. Once completed, a new mission is set.

4 TYPES:

1. Targeting
2. Common Enemy
3. Role Model
4. Internal Transformation

Figure 4-2

To quickly grasp the difference between purpose and mission, think of pursuing a guiding star across a mountain range. Your *purpose* is the guiding star, always out there on the horizon, never attainable, but always pulling you forward. Your *mission*, on the other hand, is the specific mountain you are climbing at any moment. While assaulting that mountain, all your focus and energy goes into that specific ascent. But once you reach the top, you sight again on the guiding star (your purpose) and pick yet another mountain to climb (another mission). And, of course, throughout the entire adventure, you remain true to your core values and beliefs.

With these as models, you can set up and codify your own corporate vision from the following examples.

Vision Component 1: Core Values and Beliefs

Core values and beliefs are where vision begins. Core values and beliefs are like an ether that permeates an organization—its decisions, its policies, its actions—throughout all phases of its evolution. Some companies refer to this as their "guiding philosophy."

Core values and beliefs form a system of fundamental motivating principles and tenets—precepts about what is important in both business and life, how business should be conducted, its view of humanity, its role in society, the way the world works, what is to be held inviolate, and so on. You can think of it as analogous to the "philosophy of life" that an individual might have. Core values and beliefs are analogous to a biological organism's "genetic code"— they are in the background, but always present as a shaping force.

The core values and beliefs come from *inside* you. You, as a leader of the company, imprint your personal values and beliefs about life and business through your daily actions.

And therein lies the crucial aspect of core values and beliefs: they must be an *absolutely authentic* extension of the values and beliefs you hold in your own gut. You don't "set" values. The proper question isn't, "What values and beliefs *should* we have?" but rather "What values and beliefs *do we actually hold in our gut?*"

Ultimately, core values and beliefs get instilled by what you *do*, by specific, concrete actions, not by what you say.

For example, L.L.Bean was built on the core values and beliefs espoused by Leon Leonwood Bean. Bean, who founded the company in 1911, had a deeply held personal philosophy summed up simply as, "Sell good merchandise at a reasonable price, treat your customers like you would your friends, and the business will take care of itself."

Nice sentiment. But the foundation of Bean's strength isn't sentiment; it's the actions that reflect the sincerity of the sentiment. He implemented a 100% guarantee of absolute satisfaction via a no-questions-asked policy. (In one instance, the company refunded the full purchase price of a never-worn shirt purchased 32 years earlier.) He decided Bean would never close, keeping the phone-order lines open 24 hours a day, 365 days per year. He demanded that all products be manufactured to exacting standards, and that customers be charged a fair price.

"But that's not values," you might be thinking. "That's just good business." We agree. It is good business.

But the power of Bean's mystique—the reason for its dedicated employees and its fanatically loyal customer base—is the fact that behind its actions are a set of genuine values. Ol' L.L. sincerely believed in treating customers like friends. He wouldn't have done it any other way!

Some Examples

Examples of core values and beliefs from Herman Miller, Telecare Corporation, Merck, Hewlett-Packard, and Johnson & Johnson follow. We believe we can best illustrate core values and beliefs with specific, detailed examples. Some of these examples come from discussions with managers of those companies, documents, or observations of their actions. We're not suggesting that the specific values and beliefs in our examples should be yours. They are illustrations.

Herman Miller, Inc. | Core Values and Beliefs*

We are a research-driven product company; we are not a market-driven company.

We intend to make a contribution to society, through our products, services, and the way we deliver them.

We are dedicated to quality; quality of product, quality of service, quality of relationships, quality of our communications, quality of our promises.

We believe that we should be, for all who are involved, a place of realized potential.

We cannot live our lives isolated from the needs of society.

We are deeply committed to the Scanlon idea, a plan for practicing participative management, including productivity and profit sharing.

Profit, like breathing, is indispensable. While it is not the sole goal of our lives, in the context of our opportunities, profit must be a result of our contribution.

*Abstracted from *Leadership is an Art* by Herman Miller CEO Max De Pree. Published by Doubleday, 1989.

Telecare Corporation | Core Values and Beliefs

We believe in doing a really outstanding job—we simply don't want to do anything without high quality.

We believe in having a long-term commitment to employee development.

We believe that we have a responsibility to society and that our service is vitally needed by individuals, families, and the community.

We believe that we should help patients rehabilitate to their highest level, regardless of impairment.

We believe in hard work and the enjoyment of it.

We believe in growth both for ourselves as individuals and, over the long term, of the organization.

We do not exist to maximize profit, yet we must nonetheless be an efficient, productive, and profitable business, or else we limit our ability to be of service.

Johnson & Johnson | Credo*

We believe that our first responsibility is to our customers.

Our second responsibility is to our employees.

Our third responsibility is to our management.

Our fourth responsibility is to the communities in which we live. We must be a good citizen.

Our fifth and last responsibility is to our stockholders. Business must make a sound profit. When we operate according to our principles, stockholders should realize a fair return.

We are determined with the help of God's grace to fulfill these obligations to the best of our ability.

*Paraphrased from the Johnson & Johnson Credo, by R. W. Johnson, 1943

Hewlett-Packard | Core Values and Beliefs*

In the words of Dave Packard: "The HP Way says, 'Do unto others as you would have them do unto you.' That's really what it's all about."

In the words of Bill Hewlett: "Fundamentally, the HP Way is respect for the individual. If you give him a chance, the individual will do a lot more than you think he can. So you give him the freedom. Respect for the individual—not just employees, but customers and the works."

*From interviews with Bill Hewlett and Dave Packard

Merck & Company | Core Values and Beliefs*

We value above all our ability to serve the patient.

We are committed to the highest standards of ethics and integrity.

We are responsible to our customers, to our employees, and to the societies we serve . . . Our interactions with all segments of society—customers, suppliers, governments and the general public—must reflect the high standards we profess.

We are committed to research that matches science to the needs of humanity.

Since our future as a company rests squarely on the knowledge, imagination, skills, teamwork, and integrity of our employees, we value these qualities most highly.

We expect profit, but profit from work that benefits humanity.

*Abstracted from Merck & Company "Statement of Corporate Purpose," 1989

The Role of Profit

Notice that the companies in our examples tend to view profit as a necessity, rather than the ultimate goal of the business. What do you make of that? How does this fit with the classic business school doctrine that the purpose of a business—the primary responsibility of its managers—is to maximize shareholder wealth?

To become a great company, we ask you to reject the classic business school doctrine. "Maximize shareholder wealth" is a simple theoretical way of looking at business, but it's not supported by the reality of many great companies. Most great companies are formed to meet the goals and express the values of their founders, which is not always the same as maximizing shareholder wealth. For them, profit is simply a strategic necessity rather than the supreme end point.

This may be a jolting concept, we realize. But we're certainly not the only management writers who have come to the same conclusion. Peter F. Drucker, in his classic text, *Management: Task, Responsibilities, Practices*, reached the same conclusion years ago:

> Business cannot be defined or explained in terms of profit . . . The concept of profit maximization is, in fact, meaningless . . . The first test of any business is *not* the maximization of profit, but the achievement of sufficient profit to cover the risks of economic activity.

We don't deny—and neither do the companies we've worked with and studied—that profit is essential. Actually, it's not profit per se that's essential, but the cash flow that it generates. A business cannot exist without adequate cash flow, and to have an eternal, self-generating source of cash, the company must be profitable.

But profitability and cash flow are not what work is ultimately all about. Profit maximization doesn't provide the type of inspirational aim that people throughout the company are willing to put their full energies towards, to commit a part of their spirit to. We are not saying that profit is bad. Yes, absolutely profit is needed, but profit in and of itself does not provide meaning.

Tom Chappell, founder of Tom's of Maine, a highly profitable company, explained in *Inc.* magazine how the pursuit of numbers alone is an endless treadmill:

> Quantitative goals can't invest purpose in a process that has none. The quest simply for *more* of anything is inherently unsatisfying. If there is no point or joy in what you are doing, or if you lose sight of the point, then just measuring your progress can't make it worthwhile or fun. If I can organize people around a purpose, that is the most powerful form of leadership.

Returning to our example of L.L.Bean, we see that Leon Leonwood Bean was motivated primarily by his love of the outdoors, his passion for his products, and a desire to do business in a way that reflected his values. He grew the business slowly, taking 55 years to reach the size of 160 employees. Profit as a percentage of sales in 1966 was only 2.2%, with significant room for improvement (as demonstrated by the fact that profitability improved dramatically after his grandson took over).

Yes, Bean could have had a bigger company, and a more profitable company. But this was not his purpose. As ol' L.L. used to say in expressing satisfaction with his life, "I'm already eating three meals a day, and couldn't eat a fourth."

But if profit maximization is not necessarily the purpose of the business, then what is? This brings us to the next component of a good vision: purpose.

Vision Component 2: Purpose

Purpose, the second primary part of a good vision, is an outgrowth of your core values and beliefs. Purpose is the fundamental reason for your company's existence—its ultimate reason for being. Your company's purpose dovetails with the sense of personal purpose that you and other members of the company hold deep within you, and thereby provides meaning to work.

A crucial aspect of purpose is that it's always worked towards, but never fully achieved, like chasing the earth's horizon or pursuing a guiding star. The enduring aspect of purpose is well illustrated by Steve Jobs, co-founder of Apple and founder of NeXT:

> I don't feel that I'll ever be done. There are lots of hurdles out there, and there's always a hurdle that I'll never reach in my lifetime. The point is to keep working toward it.

To make a personal analogy, purpose plays the role that a sense of life purpose can provide an individual. A person with a purpose will never be at a loss for meaningful work.

Have you ever noticed that extraordinary people—people like Michelangelo, Churchill, Roosevelt, and Maslow—led productive, fulfilled lives right up to their deaths? They had a sense of personal purpose that could never be completed; they would never be done; they could never submit themselves to the oblivion of unproductive retirement. Purpose in a company plays a similar motivating role.

The Statement of Purpose

You should be able to articulate your company's purpose succinctly, in one or two sentences. This is called a "Statement of Purpose." A statement of purpose should quickly and clearly convey why your company exists, how it fills basic human needs and impacts the world.

A good purpose statement is broad, fundamental, inspirational, and enduring. It should serve to guide your organization for at least 100 years.

STATEMENTS OF PURPOSE

MERCK

We are all in the business of preserving and improving human life. All of our actions must be measured by our success in achieving this.

SCHLAGE LOCK COMPANY

To make the world more secure.

GIRO SPORT DESIGN

Giro exists to make people's lives better through innovative, high quality products.

CELTRIX LABORATORIES

To improve the quality of life through innovative human therapeutics.

LOST ARROW / PATAGONIA

To be a role model and tool for social change.

PIONEER HI-BRED INTERNATIONAL

To create agricultural science products that may very well be critical to sustaining mankind in the future.

TELECARE CORPORATION

To help people with mental impairments realize their full potential.

MCKINSEY & COMPANY

To help leading corporations and governments be more successful.

MARY KAY COSMETICS

To be a company that gives unlimited opportunity to women.

KENNEDY-JENKS

Our purpose is to provide solutions that protect the environment and improve the quality of life.

ADVANCED DECISION SYSTEMS

To enhance decision making power.

STANFORD UNIVERSITY

To enhance and disseminate knowledge that improves human kind.

Discovering Purpose: The "Five Whys"

When articulating purpose, don't make the error of simply writing a specific description of your current product lines or customer segments. "We exist to make computers for knowledge workers" is not a good purpose statement. It's neither compelling nor flexible enough to last for 100 years. It's merely descriptive of what a certain company currently does.

A far better purpose would be:

> Our purpose is to make a contribution by creating great tools for the mind that advance humankind.

Does this mean you should avoid mentioning your products or customers in your purpose statement? Yes and no. Yes, you should avoid sterile, descriptive, bland, dull statements like, "We exist to make X products for Y customers."

On the other hand, and if you are clear that you are only going to do that type of product for the next 100 years, then you might produce a purpose statement like Celtrix Laboratories. Celtrix was tempted to state its purpose as "To develop, manufacture, and sell human therapeutics products." Wisely, however, CEO Bruce Pharriss took it a step further and asked, "*Why* do we want to do this? *Why* is this important? *Why* do we want to dedicate a portion of our lives to this?" In response, Celtrix created the following purpose statement:

> To improve the quality of life through innovative human therapeutics.

This process of asking multiple layers of "why" is powerful for getting at purpose. One very powerful "why" question is: "Why should we continue to exist? What would the world lose if we ceased to exist?" [Note: this may seem like an odd question, but it's very effective for quickly getting to the core of purpose: why the company exists.]

Another powerful approach is to start with the statement, "We make X products" and then ask "why" five times. We call this the "five whys" approach. After five whys, you'll find that you're getting down to the fundamental purpose of the business.

Here's an example of how the five whys lead from products to Patagonia's purpose.

> "We make outdoor clothing."
> "Why?"
> "Because it's what we know best and what we like to do."
> "Why is that important?"
> "Because it's the best way to make innovative, high quality products that people will pay well for."
> "Why is that important?"
> "Because that is how we can continue to be financially successful."
> "Why is that important?"
> "Because we need the credibility of being a successful business, and the resources to do business in the way we think it ought to be done."
> "Why is that important?"
> "Because we ultimately exist to be a role model and tool for social change, and the only way we can do that is to be financially viable and successful enough to have the rest of the business community looking to us as a role model."

You Already Have a Purpose

Does every company need a statement of purpose?

In answering this question, let us be clear about one thing: every company *has* a purpose—a reason for being. It's just that most companies have never formally articulated it. Nevertheless, a purpose exists, whether written down or not. Often it's unstated and implicit, but always there, in the woodwork.

For instance, NIKE has existed for years without a formally articulated statement of purpose. Yet, NIKE is driven by a powerful purpose that permeates the entire company: to be a vehicle for competition and victory, both in corporate life and in athletic combat. Although it's not specified in a single-sentence statement, this underlying purpose, which comes from the competitive spirit of founder Phil Knight, is the core driving force of NIKE. (In fact, NIKE's name is that of the Goddess of Victory in Greek mythology.)

Even though you already have a purpose, it's nonetheless a valuable exercise to think through the question: what exactly *is* our purpose? Keeping your answer to a *short and direct* sentence helps to clarify what the business is ultimately all about. And, once clarified, it acts as a test for all decisions: is this action consistent with our purpose?

Purpose Need Not Be Unique

You've undoubtedly noticed that some of the purpose examples we've given could apply to numerous organizations—they don't necessarily differentiate one company from another. That's ok. Purpose is a motivating factor, not a differentiating factor. It's entirely possible for two companies to have the same purpose.

Your mission, on the other hand, will certainly differentiate you from everyone else.

JIM'S VIEW FROM 2020

Purpose Beyond Profits—Don't Confuse Rare with New

"We demand a whole new way of leading to inspire and motivate us," said a twenty-something when I asked a gathering of young people about their views on entrepreneurship and leadership.

"In what way?" I asked.

"For one thing," he said, "we demand that our leaders not only provide direction, but that they also tell us *why*. And it needs to be a 'why' that's much more than maximizing profits for shareholders. We want to be part of something that has a purpose beyond just making money."

I thought about that for a moment, then said, "But the greatest company builders have always done that. You're confusing what's rare with what's new."

When something is rare and exquisite, it can feel "new" when glimpsed for the first time by each successive generation. Greatness is rare, by definition. But the core ingredients of greatness—including the idea of being motivated by a purpose far beyond mere economics—have been exemplified by exceptional company builders for generations. To build an enduring great company *in any era* requires being almost obsessive in pursuit of a purpose. This has always been true. It is still true today. And it will almost certainly remain true forever.

Vision Component 3: Mission

Mission, the third key part of an effective vision, is a clear and compelling overall goal that serves as a focal point of effort.

To quickly grasp the concept of mission, think of the NASA moon mission as articulated by President Kennedy in 1961:

> This nation should dedicate itself to achieving the goal, before this decade is out, of landing a man on the moon and returning him safely to earth.

Unlike purpose, which is never achieved, a mission should be achievable. It translates values and purpose into an energizing, highly focused goal—like the moon mission. It is crisp, clear, bold, exhilarating. It reaches out and grabs people in the gut. It requires little or no explanation; people "get it" right away. Once a mission is fulfilled, you return to purpose to set a new mission.

Remember the analogy of pursuing a guiding star across a mountain range. Your purpose is the guiding star, always out there on the horizon, never attainable, but always pulling you forward. Your mission is the specific mountain you are climbing at any moment. Once you reach the top, you sight again on the guiding star and pick yet another mountain to climb.

A good mission has a finish line—you must be able to know when you've done it, like the moon mission or a mountaintop. A good mission is risky, falling in the gray area where reason says, "This is unreasonable," and intuition says, "But we believe we can do it nonetheless."

We like to use the following phrase to convey the idea of mission:

big, hairy, audacious goal.

Finally—and this is important—a good mission has a *specific time frame* for its achievement.

The moon project was a beautiful example of just such a mission. It was exciting. It was big, hairy, and audacious, yet achievable. It had a clear finish line and it had a time frame.

Reject the Standard Mission Statement

We realize that our definition of mission is different from that used at most companies. Please, reject the standard approach! Most corporate mission statements are terrible. They're all too often nothing more than a description, and a bland one at that, of the operations of the company—a boring stream of words that evokes the response, "True, but who cares?" Managers draft a bunch of words that make sense, but that have all the appeal of snuggling up to a cold, dead fish. They smack of corporate double-speak and are incapable of tapping people's spirit.

Here are some examples of typically ineffective mission statements (from actual companies):

> The Corporation is committed to providing innovative engineering solutions to specialized problems where technology and close attention to customer service can differentiate it from commodity of production or job shop operations.

Just makes you want to go out and conquer the world, doesn't it?

> We provide our customers with retail banking, real estate, finance, and corporate banking products which will meet their credit, investment, security, and liquidity needs.

Now, *that* is really exciting!

> [The company] is in the business of applying micro-electronics and computer technology in two general areas: computer-related hardware; and computer enhancing services, which include computation, information, education, and finance.

This sends a tingle down the spine; we can hardly sit still.

We know we're being a bit sarcastic and harsh. Nevertheless, we've got to get across the point that mission statements like these just don't work. They will not inspire or galvanize your company. As an employee of one of the above companies told us in response to his company's mission statement:

> This is ridiculous. The statement is very long and very boring. By the time I finished reading it, I was totally uninspired and had lost confi-

dence in the people at the top of this organization. I mean, blah—who wants to read this stuff? It's dreary. If they don't show any excitement for what the organization is trying to do, then how can they expect anyone else to get inspired?

Be Compelling and Passionate in Your Mission

Your mission must meet one overriding criterion: it must be *compelling*. The best missions have an element of genuine passion in them.

Don't set a mission like this:

To make and sell athletic shoes on a worldwide basis.

Set a mission like this:

Crush Reebok.

Don't set a mission like this:

To make high-end reduced instruction set micro-processors for a wide range of applications.

Set a mission like this:

Make the MIPS architecture pervasive worldwide by the mid-1990s.

Don't set a mission like this:

To be a producer of automotive products that meet consumer needs and provide an adequate return to shareholders.

Set a mission like Henry Ford's in 1909:

We're going to democratize the automobile.

One of our favorite examples of a good mission statement is Britain's mission in 1940, as articulated by Winston Churchill:

Our whole people and empire have vowed themselves to the single task of cleansing Europe of the Nazi pestilence and saving the world from the new dark ages. We seek to beat the life and soul out of Hitler and Hitlerism. That alone. That all the time. That to the end.

Now *that* is a mission. Granted, Britain's mission in 1940 is hardly the type of goal that could be taken on by a small company. Nevertheless it conveys the idea that a mission should have an element of passion.

Risk, Commitment, and the Zone of Discomfort

But isn't setting such an audacious mission risky? Yes. A good mission should be difficult to achieve. There should be a chance you'll fail, combined with an off-setting belief that you'll make it anyway. That's part of what makes it a real mission.

What about highly conservative companies that have attained greatness? They don't run themselves like "bet the farm" entrepreneurial ventures, do they? Actually, some of the most conservative companies have set highly risky missions. Let's look briefly at three examples: IBM, Boeing, and Procter & Gamble:

- In the early 1960s, IBM bet the company on a big mission: to remake the computer industry with the IBM 360. It was the largest privately financed commercial project ever undertaken, and required more resources than it took to build the first Atomic Bomb. *Fortune* magazine called it "perhaps the riskiest business judgment of recent times." During the 360 introduction, IBM built up nearly 600 million dollars of work in process inventory and almost needed emergency loans to meet payroll.
- Boeing has pushed itself to the limit with risky missions, such as one set in the 1950s: to create a successful commercial jet aircraft. Boeing invested a substantial portion of its net worth in the project which, had it failed, would have jeopardized the company's solvency. The Boeing 707 was the result. A decade later, Boeing made a similar gamble with the 747.
- Procter & Gamble, known as one of the most conservative of all companies, has a history of committing to risky goals. For example, in the early 1900s, P&G established an internal mission: to reach a point where it could provide steady employment for its workers, rather than the hire and fire swings forced by seasonal demands.

These swings were caused by the demands of wholesalers, who ordered in large quantities and then, like a snake digesting a large meal, would lie dormant. To achieve the mission, P&G took the audacious step of setting up a sales force to sell directly to retailers—a move that at the time was thought by industry observers to be insane. But CEO Richard Deupree had a simple philosophy about bold, audacious moves:

> We like to try the impractical and impossible and prove it to be both practical and possible. You do something you think is right. If it clicks, you give it a ride. If you hit, mortgage the farm and go for broke.

Common to each of these companies was 1) a belief that they could fulfill the mission, and 2) a willingness to go for it. This willingness to put it on the line is part of the vision-setting process. Your task is to pick a mission that falls in a zone of discomfort—where it's not a sure bet, yet you believe deep down the company can do it.

You set a mission not by pure analysis, but by analysis plus intuition. You'll never be able to prove ahead of time that an audacious mission is going to be 100% achievable. You have to know in your gut that it can be done, recognizing this simple truth: once committed to a bold challenge, the probabilities of success change.

When Kennedy first proposed the moon mission, he was advised that there was only a 50/50 chance of success. He believed in America's ability to achieve the mission, to somehow turn the odds. He knew that if the country committed to the mission, it would somehow find a way.

Think of it this way. If someone puts you on a difficult mountain climb and leaves you an easy avenue of retreat, the probabilities of success would be at a certain level, say, for the sake of argument, 50%. Now suppose you are on the same mountain and the avenue of escape is removed; if you don't succeed, you die. The probabilities of success change to closer to 100%. Why? Because you are committed. You'll fight, scratch, invent, or somehow figure out a way to the top because you have no other choice.

Be Sincere

Like your values and purpose, your mission has to be sincere and authentic—something that you want to obtain badly enough that you're willing to make personal sacrifices for its attainment. We've seen cases where leaders of a company outline a great-sounding mission that's not an honest reflection of their real aims for the business. This never works and, in fact, is counterproductive.

In one situation, the CEO kept talking about "Our mission . . ." when all he was really working towards was to sell the company and cash out his stock options. Not only did he lose the dedication of most employees, he lost their respect. As one individual put it: "There was no way we could get excited when he wasn't honest with us. I mean, we're not that stupid."

Four Types of Mission

There are four basic types of mission to choose from:

1. Targeting
2. Common Enemy
3. Role Model
4. Internal Transformation.

MISSION TYPE 1: TARGETING

Targeting is just as the name implies: setting a clear, well-defined target and aiming for it. The NASA moon project is a target mission. Ford's aim "To democratize the automobile" and MIPS's aim to make its architecture "pervasive worldwide by the mid-1990s" are also target missions.

Another approach to targeting is to set the goal of taking the company to an entirely new level of overall prestige, success, dominance, or industry position. Here are some examples:

> *Merck*: "To establish Merck as the preeminent drug-maker worldwide in the 1980s." (Set in 1979.)
> *Coors*: "To be number three in the beer industry by the end of the 1980s." (Set in 1980.) "To be number two in the beer industry by the end of the 1990s." (Set in 1990.)
> *Schlage Lock*: "To become the dominant lock supplier in the United States by the year 2000." (Set in 1990.)

Have you ever heard of Tokyo Tsushin Kogyo? Probably not. In 1952, it was a tiny, struggling, seven-year-old company, and its founders were wrestling with the question of how to propel itself along the path to greatness. They decided to set a bold, audacious mission:

> To create a product that becomes pervasive worldwide.

The company then implemented the mission by creating and marketing the first radio small enough to fit in a shirt pocket. Today, the company is known as SONY Corporation.

You've probably noticed that none of our target examples are defined with numbers. Can a quantitative target be an effective mission? Yes, *but with caution*.

For example, Home Depot's mission set in the late 1980s was:

> To go national with $10 billion in sales and 350 locations by 1995.

In 1997, Walmart's founder Sam Walton set the mission:

> To become a $1 billion company by 1980.

This was a mission to more than double the company's size, yet Walmart achieved the mission on schedule with sales of $1.2 billion in 1980.

So why did we say, "Yes, but with caution"?

Because we've found that quantitative missions are often less exciting to people throughout the company than, say, democratizing the automobile or becoming the preeminent company in your industry. Just stating, "Our mission is $50 million in revenues in 1995" won't necessarily excite people. If you use a quantitative mission, be sure to tie it to something meaningful to everyone.

Jack Stack makes an extensive use of quantitative target missions at his company, Springfield Remanufacturing Company. He also makes sure to put the numbers in a larger context, as he explained in an *Inc.* magazine interview:

> Our goals are always based on the security of the company, so the larger meaning is to create jobs and keep people working. Each goal is a must, not a want. We're trying to create a company that will last 30, 40, or 50 years.

Remember, the aim here is not just to create a precise target, but to create one that will galvanize people.

MISSION TYPE 2: COMMON ENEMY

Setting out to defeat a common enemy is a particularly powerful, albeit uncreative, form of mission. It appeals to people's competitive instincts. Picking a common enemy to seek out and destroy—especially if you are the underdog—can create extraordinary unity of purpose. Britain's mission in 1940 (to beat the life and soul out of Hitler) is an excellent historical example. The same type of mission can be set in business.

Pepsi's mission at one point was to "Beat Coke!" A senior executive at Pepsi described the impact of having this mission:

> We always believed, since the early seventies, when Pepsi was widely viewed as the perennial also-ran, that we could do it. All of us started out with that objective, and we never took our eyes off it. . . . It put us on a search-and-destroy mission against a Goliath.

In one of our all-time favorite examples, Honda, when faced with Yamaha's having overtaken them as the number one motorcycle manufacturer in the world, responded with:

Yamaha wo tsubusu!
(We will crush, squash, slaughter Yamaha!)

Soon after Honda established this mission, it so demolished Yamaha that later Yamaha publicly apologized to Honda for having claimed that it would dominate Honda.

NIKE has thrived for years on common enemy missions. First, it set out to beat Adidas in the United States. It did. Then, after the unexpected rise of Reebok, they established the mission of crushing Reebok in the competitive "sneaker wars." (During an interview about the "Sneaker Wars," on ABC's *20/20* aired August 19, 1988, NIKE CEO Phil Knight was asked if he knew the president of Reebok. Knight said yes. The interviewer then asked if he liked the president of Reebok. Knight replied, "No. And I don't want to like him." A board member of NIKE once remarked, "Our idea of a perfect day is to get up in the morning and throw rocks at our competitors.")

Common enemy missions are typically set by companies that are striving to be number one, but have not yet achieved it; they play nicely into a David versus Goliath motivation.

An extremely powerful effect of common enemy missions is that they can convert an organization whose back is against the wall—that is concerned about its very survival—to a "we shall prevail" mode. People don't like to "just survive," they like to win. And a common enemy mission taps into this basic human motivation.

Micron Technology provides an excellent illustration. In 1985, Japanese companies' illegal dumping of their product below cost nearly put the little semi-conductor company out of business. CEO Joseph Parkinson used the existence of an outside foe as a unifying force to pull the company through what he calls "the dark days." Parkinson told us in an interview:

> When things were going bad, I was trying to keep everyone motivated to keep us alive. At first, I wasn't scoring a lot of points, but then it occurred to me to key off the fact that people like to win. I mean, who likes to just survive? So with our backs to the wall, we went on the offensive. Yes, it was a tremendous advantage to have a bitter enemy. But it was more than that. We were sworn to *prevail* over that enemy. And this shift from survival mode to a "we shall prevail" mode—beating the odds as the underdog—is something everyone can get behind, from assembly-line workers to VPs.

A word of caution: in spite of its obvious advantages, there are negative aspects of common enemy missions. It's difficult to spend your entire life at war. What do you do when you've defeated the enemy and become number one? What happens when you are no longer David, and have become Goliath? NIKE, for example, went into a slump after it defeated Adidas. It didn't rebound from that slump until Reebok had slipped by them and became a worthy target of NIKE's competitive wrath.

MISSION TYPE 3: ROLE MODEL

Another useful type of mission is corporate role models. Use organizations that you admire as images of what you want your company to become. Role-model missions are excellent for small to mid-sized companies with bright prospects.

For example, in its early years, Trammell Crow had the mission "To be the IBM of the real estate industry." Jim Gentes at Giro Sport talks about becoming to the cycling industry what NIKE is to athletic shoes and Apple is to computers. Norwest Corporation of Minneapolis aims to be "The Walmart of banking."

And speaking of Walmart, it's interesting to note that Sam Walton used J.C. Penney as his role model, including directly copying Penney's seven principles of business management into the early days of Walmart.

MISSION TYPE 4: INTERNAL TRANSFORMATION

Internal transformation missions are rare. They're usually best in organizations that need a dramatic restructuring.

For example, the United States had an internal transformation mission in the late 1800s: to reconstruct the Union after the Civil War. The Soviet Union's attempt in the late 20th century to become a more free-market economy is another societal example of an internal transformation mission. An excellent corporate example comes from Jack Welch at General Electric:

We are committed to developing the sensitivity, the leanness, the simplicity and the agility of a small company.

For a company the size of GE, this is indeed big, hairy, and audacious.

Since internal transformation missions tend to be most appropriate for large, stagnant organizations, we've encountered very few good examples in small to mid-sized companies.

How Far in the Future?

We've emphasized the importance of having a specific time frame affixed to your mission. How far into the future should a mission stretch? Should it be something that can be fulfilled in six months? A year? Three years? A decade? Fifty years?

There's no definitive answer. Some missions take 30 years or more to fulfill. Others might be fulfilled in a year or less. A good rule of thumb is a 10- to 25-year horizon, perhaps longer if the mission is particularly challenging. Of course, some missions can be fulfilled faster than ten years, and it may be appropriate and effective to have a short time frame.

Whatever time-length mission you set, be sure to recognize when you've fulfilled it and, most important, set a new one. Otherwise, you may fall into one of the most dangerous of traps: the "We've Arrived Syndrome."

JIM'S VIEW FROM 2020

BHAGs, BHAGs Everywhere

When Jerry Porras and I first conceptualized a framework for developing an organizational vision based on our research, we debated what to call the third part of the framework (after core values and purpose). At first, we decided on the more corporate-sounding term "mission." But then one day when teaching the framework in my Stanford course, the term "BHAG" (pronounced

BEE-hag) popped out of my mouth, followed by the phrase "Big Hairy Audacious Goal."

And the BHAG was born.

JIM'S VIEW FROM 2020

VISION – STRATEGY – TACTICS

VISION

CORE VALUES
↓
PURPOSE
↓
BHAG

↓
STRATEGY
↓
TACTICS

VISION

CORE VALUES ⟶	PURPOSE ⟶	BHAG
Enduring principles to live by; a guiding philosophy	The fundamental reason for the organization's existence	Big Hairy Audacious Goal (BHAG is pronounced BEE-hag)
Reflect the personal core values of those who shape the character of the enterprise	Like a guiding star; always pursued, never fully attained	Like a big mountain to climb, a clear finish line to shoot for
Would continue to hold, even when costly to do so; practices and strategies change, but not core values	When pursued with extreme excellence, the company becomes distinctive and irreplaceable in the world	Not a 100% chance of success; requires a leap in capabilities
		Compelling and galvanizing; easy to grasp
Timeless	Should guide the company for at least 100 years	Ideal timeframe: 10 to 25 years

At first, we (Jerry Porras, Bill Lazier, and I) decided we would use BHAG simply as a way to teach what makes for a good mission. We thought it would be easier to get people to engage with a more traditional term than to get leaders to embrace something so big and, well . . . *hairy*.

Within a couple of years, we'd completely inverted our thinking. The more we taught the framework, the more we found people better learned—and grabbed onto—the true spirit of the idea if we went right to its essence. A couple of years after publishing the original edition of *Beyond Entrepreneurship*, I'd fully embraced the big, the hairy, and the audacious. By the time Jerry Porras and I began writing *Built to Last*, we'd pretty much jettisoned the term "mission" and replaced it entirely with "BHAG."

BHAGs started showing up everywhere. Not only did CEOs talk about their BHAGs, but so did government leaders, social-cause entrepreneurs, school principals, sports coaches, military officers, and church leaders.

The *New York Times* even published a feature story about how BHAGs were "sweeping through corner offices around the country." In an interview for that article, the reporter tried to provoke me a bit, relaying that some of the other management thinkers with whom he'd spoken were laying claim to being first to introduce the idea of a BHAG (even if they shunned words like big and hairy and audacious) and that we'd found nothing new.

"What do you say to that?" he challenged.

"I don't think any of us can claim to be the first to have had the idea of a BHAG," I replied. "It certainly goes back long before any of us were alive."

"Well, then, who do you think can claim to be first?" he pushed.

"Hmmm . . . perhaps Moses," I replied.

BHAGs have animated great leaders throughout history, who have used them to stimulate progress and galvanize people. It doesn't really matter whether you call it "mission" or "BHAG" or anything else that works for you. What matters is that you commit to something that meets the tests of a BHAG. Ask yourself the following questions about any BHAG:

- Do you and your people find the BHAG exciting?
- Is the BHAG clear, compelling, and easy to grasp?
- Does the BHAG connect to the purpose of the enterprise?
- Is the BHAG undeniably a goal, not a verbose, hard-to-understand, convoluted, impossible-to-remember mission or vision "statement"?
- Do you have substantially less than a 100 percent chance of achieving the BHAG yet at the same time believe your company can achieve the BHAG if fully committed?
- Would you be able to clearly tell if you've achieved the BHAG?

The best BHAGs make you think big. They force you to engage in both long-term building *and* short-term intensity. The only way to achieve a BHAG is with a relentless sense of urgency, day after day, week after week, month after month, for years. What do you need to do *today*, with monomaniacal focus, and tomorrow and the next day and the day after that to defy the probabilities and ultimately achieve your BHAG? If you're going to put a powerful computer in every pocket, or eradicate malaria, or give every kid a solid K–12 education, or cut crime rates by 80 percent, or render impotent the dark forces of terrorism, or build the most admired company in your industry, or accomplish whatever the goal might be, you cannot possibly achieve the BHAG in mere days or weeks or months. The best corporate BHAGs require 10 to 25 years of relentless intensity to achieve.

For BHAG-driven people, the extended discomfort, the enduring quest, can itself be a form of bliss. When you commit to a BHAG, it lives with you. You wake up in the morning and there, over in the corner—with huge, hairy feet and big, glowing eyes—stands the BHAG. You go to bed at night and there, just as you're about the turn out the light, you once again see the BHAG standing in the corner. "Better get a good night's sleep," the BHAG seems to say, "because tomorrow I own your life again."

Beware the "We've Arrived" Syndrome

It's absolutely essential to recognize when you've fulfilled a mission and therefore need to set a new one.

When a mission has been fulfilled, people will tend to set their own directions and fragment the whole. A classic historical example is that of the World War II allied effort between Russia, England, and the United States. The allies were able to work together remarkably well while they had in common the mission to defeat Hitler. But, alas, once Hitler's fate was assured, the alliance broke apart, plunging the world into the Cold War.

Furthermore, you need new missions to keep the company galvanized towards new challenges. Just as individual people can become lost, adrift, and aimless once they've reached a goal, the same is true of companies. This is what we mean by the "We've Arrived" syndrome.

Jan Carlzon learned this lesson the hard way as CEO of Scandinavian Airlines, after the company reached its first mission. In an interview with *Inc.* magazine, he said:

We had a dream, and we reached it, and we reached it very quickly. But we didn't have another long term objective. So people started to produce their own new objectives. You see, it had all been a little too easy. And we created frustration, because this is a psychological game. Do you know the song Peggy Lee sings, 'Is That All There Is?'

I learned that before you reach an objective you must be ready with a new one, and you must start to communicate it to the organization.

It's not the goal itself that's important. It's the fight to get there.

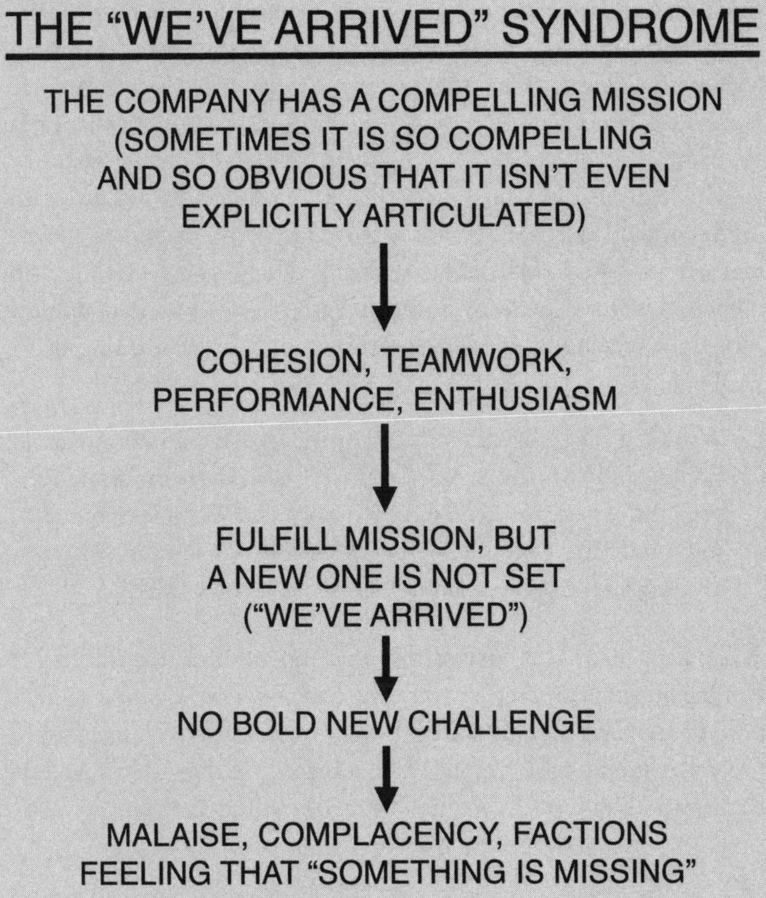

THE "WE'VE ARRIVED" SYNDROME

**THE COMPANY HAS A COMPELLING MISSION
(SOMETIMES IT IS SO COMPELLING
AND SO OBVIOUS THAT IT ISN'T EVEN
EXPLICITLY ARTICULATED)**

↓

**COHESION, TEAMWORK,
PERFORMANCE, ENTHUSIASM**

↓

**FULFILL MISSION, BUT
A NEW ONE IS NOT SET
("WE'VE ARRIVED")**

↓

NO BOLD NEW CHALLENGE

↓

**MALAISE, COMPLACENCY, FACTIONS
FEELING THAT "SOMETHING IS MISSING"**

Figure 4-3

The We've Arrived Syndrome is particularly common in early stage or turnaround companies that are galvanized by the challenge of reaching a point where survival is no longer in question. Because survival in such situations is itself such an overriding goal, the mission to survive often isn't even made explicit—everyone *knows* this is the mission without anyone saying it.

Therein lies the problem. Because it isn't explicit, there isn't the explicit recognition of its fulfillment. No new mission is created to replace the old one. Complacency sets in and factions become prevalent.

CASE EXAMPLE: STRATEGIC SOFTWARE, INC.

Founded in 1976 with no outside venture financing, Strategic Software's founders were dedicated to building a company that would provide excellent software products, financial stability for employees and owners, and a stimulating work environment. For the first seven years, employees and managers worked twelve-hour days in tiny cubicles. "It was us against the world," explained one of the founders. "We were a great team."

Gradually, year by year, the company attained financial success (reaching $25 million in annual revenue with healthy profit margins) and a stable customer base. In 1983, it moved into a prestigious office complex with modern sculptures, perfectly manicured green lawns, water ponds, thick carpets, handcrafted cherry-wood furniture, and its own parking lot.

Then the whole place fell apart. One founder described:

> What was once a great esprit de corps degenerated into intense factions and we lost all sense of team spirit. People began working 9 to 5 and, worse, they acquired a 9 to 5 attitude! We looked around and found that success had brought malaise. We just didn't have that same fighting spirit. From there it was all downhill.

What happened, of course, is that the organization had fulfilled its first big mission (to reach a point where survival was no longer in question). It seemed like there was nothing more to work for. It had arrived. Its leaders should have created a new mission, but they didn't. And the organization stagnated, eventually putting itself up for sale.

The Potential Impact of New Facilities

In the above case example, we made a specific point about the new building. Facilities may not seem like a very important topic; but they are.

We've seen a number of companies, such as the one above, encounter difficulty soon after moving into beautiful new buildings and offices. It's not that the new offices are in themselves bad. But they send a signal: "We've arrived. We're successful. We've made it."

Greg Hadley, an experienced turnaround artist, described the impact of a new building on the psychology of a company that he took over:

> It was like the Taj Mahal. People looked around, and said, "Hey, look at this. We *must* be good. We must already be successful." And then they started paying more attention to their golf game than the business.

Gavilan Computer Company, which burned through tens of millions of dollars of capital in going from start-up to bankrupt, had exquisite corporate offices. As one employee told us, "I felt like I was already working in the FORTUNE 500. It diluted any real sense of urgency. And, you know, it wasn't anywhere near as much fun as some other start-ups I've been with."

Do we mean to imply that you shouldn't have nice places to work? No, of course not; but you should be aware that a beautiful new edifice *symbolizes* having crossed a threshold, having "made it," having completed a mission.

The point of all this is that your company will cross many finish lines in its life, and there will be symbols of these finish lines (a public offering, new buildings, industry awards, or whatever). Your job is to make sure that these symbols lead to continual work towards a compelling mission.

When you reach the top of a mountain peak, begin looking for the next one. Set a new mission. If you just sit there, you'll get cold and die.

Putting It All Together

We've now covered the three basic elements of good vision: core values and beliefs, purpose, and mission. To further illustrate vision, we've included two examples of how these components of vision fit together: Giro Sport Design (a small company) and Merck (a large company).

EXAMPLE OF VISION: GIRO SPORT DESIGN

Core Values and Beliefs

Giro's fundamental, inviolable Values and Beliefs are these:

GREAT PRODUCTS. Every product we introduce must be a unique contribution to the market, not one that is introduced just for the purpose of making money. It must therefore be *innovative*, *high quality*, and the *unquestioned best* in its category.

GREAT CUSTOMER SERVICE. Our service standards are as stiff as our product standards. We should treat our customers as we would our best friends.

GOLDEN RULE. We should treat those with whom we have dealings as we ourselves would like to be treated.

TEAMWORK. No individual should be indispensable. Think we; not I.

BEST EFFORT. Each person should do her very best in each task undertaken. Strive for an A, not a B+.

DETAILS. The little things matter; God is in the details.

INTEGRITY. We are honest. We honor our commitments. We are consistent and fair.

Purpose

Giro exists to make people's lives better through innovative, high-quality products.

Mission (Set in 1990)

Giro's mission is to be a great company. We aim to be the most respected and admired company in the worldwide bicycling industry by the year 2000.

EXAMPLE OF VISION: MERCK

Core Values and Beliefs

We value above all our ability to serve the patient.

We are committed to the highest standards of ethics and integrity.

We are responsible to our customers, to our
employees, and to the societies we serve.

Our interactions with all segments of society—
customers, suppliers, governments, the general public—
must reflect the high standards we profess.

We are committed to research that matches
science to the needs of humanity.

Since our future as a company rests squarely on the knowledge,
imagination, skills, teamwork, and integrity of our employees,
we value these qualities most highly.

We expect profit, but profit from work that benefits humanity.

Purpose

We are in the business of preserving and improving human life.
All of our actions must be measured by our success in achieving this.

Write It Down

It's good practice to codify your vision on paper. Writing it down forces you to think rigorously about what exactly you are trying to do. Even more important, it's a critical step in making it the *organization's* vision, rather than the vision of a single leader.

As Steve Bostic of American Photo Group put it in an interview with *Inc.* magazine:

> You have to get [your vision] on paper. That's key. If people never see the vision—or if it's here today, gone tomorrow—there's no way they can get into it. There are severe limits to what companies that are one man shows can achieve.

Bostic is not alone in this view. R. W. Johnson codified the J&J credo for future generations of J&J leaders. Tom Watson wrote *A Business and Its Beliefs* to codify the basic principles of IBM. Marvin Brower wrote about the McKinsey Vision in a book, *Perspective on McKinsey*. Bill Hannemann at Giro keeps a written version of Giro's vision near him at all times. We even know of one company (Stew Leonard's Dairy) that literally chiseled its enduring principles into stone.

What about flexibility? Don't you want to maintain flexibility to change with times? Does all this "enduring principles" and "100 year purpose" philosophy really make sense? Isn't chiseling your principles in stone a bit limiting?

Change is good, we agree. The question is: what should change, and what should be held tight? The answer lies partially in the hierarchy from values to tactics:

Core Values and Beliefs:	Change seldom, if ever.
Purpose:	Should last for 100 years.
Mission:	Changes whenever one mission is completed and a new one needs to be set (usually every ten to twenty-five years).
Strategy:	Revised annually, then totally recast with each new mission.
Tactics:	In constant flux, to adjust to changing conditions.

A Vivid, Compelling Description:
Paint a Picture with Your Words

It's essential to be able to communicate the vision in vibrant, engaging, and specific words—in words that provoke emotion and generate excitement. Think of it as translating the vision from words into pictures, of creating an image that people can carry around in their heads. We call this "painting a picture with your words."

When you have a mission like, "To be a great company by the year 2000," you need to vividly describe what that means, and then say, "Our mission is to make that picture happen."

Use specific, vivid images. Observe how Jim Gentes describes Giro's aim to become a great company:

> The best riders in the world will be using our products in world-class competition. Winners of the Tour de France, the World Championships, and the Olympic Gold Medal will win while wearing Giro helmets. We will receive unsolicited phone calls and letters from customers who say, "Thank you for being in business; one of your helmets saved my life." Our employees will feel that this is the best place they've ever worked. When you ask people to name the top company in the cycling business, the vast majority will say Giro.

Here's how Henry Ford painted a picture with his words to communicate the mission, "To democratize the automobile":

> I will build a motor car for the great multitude. It will be so low in price that no man making a good salary will be unable to own one—and enjoy with his family the blessing of hours of pleasure in God's great open spaces. The horse will have disappeared from our highways, the automobile will be taken for granted.

Note the specifics: "enjoy with his family the blessing of hours of pleasure in God's great open spaces" and "the horse will have disappeared from our highways." This is what we mean by "painting a picture with your words."

One of our favorite examples of the power of painting pictures with words comes from Churchill, one of the best vision communicators the world has ever known:

Hitler knows that he will have to break us on this island or lose the war.

If we can stand up to him all Europe may be free and the life of the world may move forward into broad, sunlit uplands.

But if we fail, then the whole world, including the United States, including all we have known and cared for,

Will sink into the abyss of a new Dark Age made more sinister, and perhaps more protracted, by the lights of perverted science.

Let us therefore brace ourselves to our duties, and so bear ourselves that if the British Empire and its Commonwealth last for a thousand years

Men will still say:
"*This* was their finest hour."

"But that's Churchill," you say. "I'm not Churchill. I could never communicate like Churchill. And besides, it would be easy to communicate like Churchill if we had a foe like Hitler. But we don't, and never will."

True. Few of us can communicate like Churchill. But we can *learn* from Churchill, and Ford, and others. Churchill wasn't born eloquent. The words did not flow; he worked at it. He labored for hours over his speeches and writings, shaping each phrase with the care Michelangelo might have lavished on the David or Pieta. He paid attention to the details, the specific, vivid images that would stick in people's minds, like "broad sunlit uplands" and "abyss of a new Dark Age."

Although few of us can hope to be as eloquent as Churchill, we can nonetheless use him as a role model for communicating our visions.

Putting It All Together— DPR Construction and Its "Constitutional Convention" for Greatness

The first thing I noticed was the rough hands and crushing grip of each handshake, accentuated by bronzed skin tightened over some rather intimidating forearm musculature. I was sitting down to lunch with some of the founders of DPR Construction, about a year after the company's founding. These were builders, construction people, gruff and curmudgeonly.

Just a few weeks before, two DPR team members had attended a lecture series at Stanford, at which faculty shared their current research and I'd had the privilege to present a pre-publication version of the vision framework that appeared in the original edition of *Beyond Entrepreneurship*. DPR's Peter Salvati called after the session, asking, "Would you meet with us? We'd like to talk with you about your work on building great companies."

When Doug Woods, Peter Nosler, and Ron Davidowski founded DPR, they wanted to defy the traditional construction industry. Enraged by what they saw as hierarchical, shortsighted practices followed by some companies, they declared independence from their former employer. About a year in, the company had fewer than twenty people and just a handful of projects.

"Well, the first thing you need to do is articulate your core values," I said, settling into the lunch conversation.

Silence.

So, I continued, "Then you need to articulate a purpose for being that can guide you like a star on the horizon for decades or centuries."

A cacophony of silence.

Taking a deep breath, then, "And you need a big, hairy goal, a mountain to climb that's almost terrifying in its audacity."

Finally, Woods spoke up, "VALUES?"

He paused.

"PURPOSE?"

He paused again.

"What does all that have to do with the practical realities of building a company?" His message was clear: We're hands-on people, not philosophers. We build stuff. We deal in reality, not academic theory. What the heck are you talking about?

I figured I had nothing to lose by countering, "Think of what you are trying to do as like the founding of the United States, and you—the founding team—are like Jefferson, Franklin, Adams, Washington, and Madison. What would the United States be without the Declaration of Independence and the Constitution? The founders didn't just want to win the war for independence. They wanted to build an enduring great nation that would aspire to embody a set of ideals. And remember, it was those very ideals that Lincoln returned to in the Gettysburg Address and that King later invoked in his 'I Have a Dream' speech."

Woods softened. Yes, Woods wanted to *win*, but not just financially. He and his colleagues wanted to prove in practical fact what a construction company could be, to demonstrate that they could build a more enlightened company *and* win in the market.

And so, the founding team decided to hold a "Constitutional Convention" of sorts, bringing together about twenty DPR people at Thomas Fogarty Winery, high on Skyline Boulevard, looking out on Silicon Valley and the San Francisco Bay. Using the vision framework in the vision chapter of the original edition of *Beyond Entrepreneurship*, they worked for days, not with strategy but with the bigger questions: Why do we exist? What do we want to stand for? What do we want to achieve?"

The critical turning point came in the discussion of DPR's purpose. Somehow, sentiments like "change the world" or "improve people's lives by what we do" just didn't fit or feel appropriate. Finally, one of the founders said simply, "Look, we're builders. That's not just what we do; it's who we *are*. We need to capture that idea in our purpose."

"So, our purpose is to build stuff?" someone asked. "Is that it?"

"Well . . . yeah. To build stuff is pretty accurate."

"But somehow, that's not enough. I'm not sure that makes us anything special."

Back and forth, the dialogue continued.

Then, finally, the phrase "build great things" popped out.

"That's it! We exist not just to build, but *to build great things*—great buildings, a great culture, great client relationships, a great collaborative team, and it all adds up to building a great company." And so, they discovered their purpose: *We exist to build great things*.

The DPR founding team came away from its "Constitutional Convention" with a clearly crafted vision based directly upon the framework in the vision chapter from *Beyond Entrepreneurship*. In addition to the purpose, they articulated four enduring core values (see the following page) and set an audacious goal—to become a truly great construction company by the year 2000—brought to life with a vivid description composed of a dozen tangible images. These were: We will have consistently achieved the lowest possible safety modifier for a general contractor of our size. We have built a major project that has been recognized in an industry magazine. Following a pilot plant project, we are invited back to build a major manufacturing facility without competition. Our friends back East will mention that they have heard about DPR's greatness. Our families will say we work for a great company. We are shortlisted on every project in which we express an interest. For five consecutive years, we never missed an opportunity to be asked back by one of our past clients. We are used by a reputable authority on business as an example of a great company. We receive letters from customers and subcontractors praising DPR and their efforts. We will have minorities and women in senior-level estimator and project manager positions. A national magazine will have written a positive article about DPR and our success. We will routinely receive unsolicited referrals for major projects.

Co-founder Doug Woods later described how big the aspirations felt to the small young company: "To say we wanted to become a truly great construction company by the year 2000 was like a three-year-old saying that I want to graduate from college by the time I'm 10."

DPR did indeed become a truly great construction company, reaching $1 billion in revenues in 1998, and it just kept on building momentum. In 2015, DPR celebrated its twenty-fifth anniversary, with $3 billion in revenue, twenty offices across the country, and three thousand employees. It converted some of the most discerning and creative corporations on the planet into clients, from Pixar to Genentech, from UC Berkeley to the MD Anderson Cancer Center. Along the way, it set its audacious goals even higher, setting a new mission: to be one of the most admired companies—of any type, across all industries—by 2030.

At the twenty-fifth-anniversary gathering, I met the next generation of passionate curmudgeons, younger leaders buying out the founding-era shares in a planned succession, becoming entrepreneurial owners. They showed the same passion for building great things. Their entire attitude conveyed an ethos of being on the balls of their feet, moving forward. Two years later, DPR clicked past $4.5 billion in revenues, and just kept climbing.

As I finalize these words in 2020, DPR is about to celebrate three decades of achievement since its founding. Thirty years of success is a very nice start, but only a start. The drive to build great things never ends.

DPR CONSTRUCTION
COMPLETE VISION EXAMPLE

Core Values

Integrity. We conduct all business with the highest standards of honesty and fairness; we can be trusted.

Enjoyment. We believe work should be fun and intrinsically satisfying; if we are not enjoying ourselves, we are doing something wrong.

Uniqueness. We must be different from and more progressive than all other construction companies; we stand for something.

Ever forward. We believe in continual self-initiated change, improvement, learning, and the advancement of standards for their own sake.

Purpose

We exist to build great things.

First Mission (Big Hairy Audacious Goal)

To become a truly great construction company by the year 2000.

Next Mission (Big Hairy Audacious Goal)

DPR achieved its first audacious mission and established a new mission: to become one of the most admired companies—of any type, across all industries—by 2030.

Clear and Shared

To be effective, a vision must fulfill two key criteria: it must be *clear* (well understood) and *shared* by all the key people in the organization.

This raises a vexing question: should the vision be dictated from the top (from, say, the founder or CEO) or should it be derived from a group process?

The disadvantage of a vision that is dictated from above is that, although usually clear, it may not be widely shared. On the other hand, a vision developed by group process can easily turn out to be an uninspirational "camel"—a "vision by committee" that lacks clarity and spark.

Each company, with the context of its own norms and style, must come to its own conclusion. There is no universally right answer to this dilemma.

We've seen situations where a clear and shared vision is set entirely by group process. To those who are skeptical as to whether a group process can work, we point you again to the founding of the United States of America. Although there certainly were strong leaders present (Washington, Jefferson, Madison, and Adams), the vision of the country was set entirely by a *group* process. In fact, George Washington hardly said a word during the entire Constitutional Convention.

On the other hand, we've seen situations where the vision comes from a single individual. Sam Walton at Walmart and Henry Ford are examples.

So which is better, group process or individual drive? Neither. It depends on the situation and your personal style. The only thing that matters is that you catalyze a clear and shared vision for the company and secure a commitment to vigorous pursuit of that vision. If you do this, you'll be functioning as a leader.

Not Only for Charismatic Visionaries

We'd like to dispel the myth that setting a vision requires that you be somehow blessed with almost mystical or super-human charismatic visionary qualities. To believe this myth, every organization would need a CEO who is a cross between Churchill, Kennedy, and Martin Luther King Jr. Indeed, many managers respond to the notion of vision by thinking, "It's not for me. I don't fit the stereotypical mold of a visionary."

But it is for you, no matter what your style or personal magnetism. Charisma's role in setting vision is vastly overrated. Some of the folks that have instilled extraordinary vision in their companies don't bowl you over with charisma. Phil Knight of NIKE, Kristine McDivitt of Patagonia, Bill Hannemann of Giro, Bob Miller of MIPS, Bill Hewlett of HP, Frank Wells of Disney—even Abraham Lincoln and Harry Truman—don't fit the stereotype of charismatic visionary. You don't have to be a member of some elusive group of people who call themselves visionary. You can just be yourself. As Ted Turner said:

> People don't call themselves visionaries. People get called visionary. All I am is Ted Turner.

The task before you is not to be a single charismatic individual with vision. The task is to build an organization with vision. Individuals die; great companies can live for centuries.

Chapter 5

LUCK FAVORS THE PERSISTENT

You start at the bottom. And even though you see stuff up ahead you know you can't climb, you go and you go and you go until you can touch the obstacle—and more often than not, when you get that close, there's a way past. If you turn back before you can put your nose against it, then you're giving up.

TOM FROST

ON MAY 15, 2007, Tommy Caldwell and I sat together on a ledge on the side of El Capitan in Yosemite Valley. We were on a training day, with Caldwell coaching me on my adventure to climb the three-thousand-foot vertical face via the classic Nose route in a single day, my personal BHAG to celebrate turning fifty.

"I have a question," said Caldwell as we looked out across the vast expanse of granite. "Does a BHAG have to be achievable?"

"Why do you ask?"

"Well, I have this idea for a climb, but I don't know if it's possible." From where we sat, we could see an alabaster-smooth section of the cliff known as the Dawn Wall—so named because it catches the first rays of morning light. Caldwell sat there for a moment, his eyes gazing upon the Dawn Wall shimmering in the sunshine; it almost felt as if El Capitan itself was silently watching, listening. Then he added, "It might be possible, but perhaps not by me. It might be something that has to wait for future generations."

"Tommy," I said, "if you know for certain that you'll achieve it, it's not a BHAG."

Caldwell did in fact commit himself to his BHAG: to "free climb" the Dawn Wall, which (if completed) would be the hardest big-wall free climb in history. (To "free climb" means ascending every inch of the cliff under your own power by clinging by your fingertips; you use ropes only to catch your falls, not to help you ascend.) Some of the holds on the sheer vertical terrain of the Dawn Wall are so small—thinner than the edge of a dime—that they're easier to see by night with a headlamp (when you can get a bit more contrast) than in the glare of daylight.

Over the next seven years, Caldwell struggled to climb the Dawn Wall. He spent the best part of each season attempting to master a sequence of micro-holds spaced across the blank wall like a strange hieroglyphic code that had to be unlocked to reach the top. Repeatedly, as his fingers slipped from razor-thin edges and his feet failed to grip on vertical granite, he took twenty-, forty-, even fifty-foot falls—flying into space more than one hundred stories above the ground—thwacking the wall with an audible "umph" as his rope snapped tight.

But with each attempt, Caldwell got stronger. He innovated, even working with a shoe company to invent an entirely new climbing shoe. Still, he found himself thwarted by the hardest sections in the middle of the wall and reeled from the setbacks. One year he retreated as huge sheets of ice fell from the top of the cliff, like panes of window glass, swooping down and smashing into pieces all around him. In another outing, his partner, Kevin Jorgeson, crunched his ankle in a season-ending injury while attempting to make an eight-foot sideways dynamic jump between holds. In 2013, a wall hook failed, sending a full pack of equipment hurtling on a two-hundred-foot fall before it slammed taut on Caldwell's harness, causing a costochondral separation (involving the rib and sternum, and resulting in excruciating pain simply from breathing). And throughout, he had to find ways to navigate holds without his left index finger, which he'd lost part of in a table-saw accident several years earlier.

Despite all his setbacks and bad luck, he persisted. While other climbers gained recognition for their successes, Caldwell languished on the Dawn Wall. Some people even began to question whether he was squandering the best years of his climbing life (from age twenty-nine to thirty-six) on a quixotic quest.

In the autumn of 2012, I invited Caldwell to be my special guest in one of my leadership seminars for cadets at the United States Military Academy at West Point. Caldwell had been in the midst of preparing for his fifth season on the Dawn Wall, and while we were traveling to West Point, I couldn't resist asking, "Tommy, why do you keep throwing yourself at this climb? You've experienced so much success as a climber, but all this climb seems to do is give you failure upon failure. Why would you go back?"

"I go back because the climb is making me better, it's making me stronger," he replied. *"I'm not failing, I'm growing."* We got into a long conversation about how to think about failure, arriving at the idea that *the opposite side of the coin of success isn't failure but growth.*

"What I find with a lot of people," he continued, "is that they're so focused on success that they don't put themselves in situations where they're likely to grow through the process of failure. But to truly find your ultimate limit, you have to go on a journey of cumulative failure and hopefully come out the other end someday. Even if I never succeed in free climbing the Dawn Wall, it will make me so much stronger, and so much better, that most other climbs will seem easy by comparison."

Two years later, with much of the world enraptured by what the news media began to call "the climb of the century," Caldwell and Jorgeson spent nineteen riveting days on the Dawn Wall from late December 2014 to mid-January 2015. And they got an extraordinary stroke of good luck: a nearly unblemished string of cool, sunny days, providing the perfect conditions for the climb. The top of El Capitan dried off in the sun, gradually eliminating the risk of horrifying, guillotine-like ice sheets slicing down upon them. In January, El Capitan normally has plenty of snow on top, but not in the first two weeks of January 2015. The weather held so dry and sunny that Caldwell could wait extra days on the wall while Jorgeson struggled to complete the hardest middle pitches so that they could finish as a team. They reached the top at a little after 3 P.M. on January 14, 2015—2,801 days after that conversation in 2007 when Caldwell wondered aloud if a Dawn Wall BHAG was achievable.

Had Caldwell not had the good luck to have all the pieces come together at just the right time, with nineteen consecutive days with virtually no bad luck, he might still be languishing to complete the climb. Had there not been the good luck that a Pulitzer Prize–winning journalist for the *New York Times* (the publisher of which just happened to be a rock climber himself) sensed a great story in the making that ended up on the front page multiple times, Caldwell's life trajectory might have been different. And if his partner, Jorgeson, hadn't at first struggled with the middle pitches—creating tremendous drama watched around the world—and then succeeded, their ultimate success would likely have drawn far fewer people to follow the story so intently. When Caldwell and Jorgeson finally succeeded, even President Barack Obama tweeted his congratulations, sending a photo of him standing in front of a painting of Yosemite. But equally true, *had Caldwell not stayed in the game, had he given up, he wouldn't have been in a position to receive all this good luck.*

When he stood atop the Dawn Wall with his arms raised in triumph, I thought to myself, "Tommy Caldwell, meet Steve Jobs." These two individuals each touched my life profoundly, and I draw solace and renewed energy from what for me is a primary teaching from their lives: *Luck favors the persistent.*

I first met Jobs in the late 1980s, when I was teaching my course at the Stanford Graduate School of Business. It was early in my career, and I felt like I needed some assistance to help prove the class valuable to my students. So, I picked up the phone and called Jobs out of the blue: "I'm teaching this course on turning small ventures into great companies, and I'm wondering if you'd do a teaching session with me for my students."

Jobs graciously agreed, and on the appointed day he bounded down into the center of the tiered, theater-style classroom; sat crossed-legged on a table in front of my students; and said, "So, what do you want to talk about?" We then had a nearly two-hour seminar on life, leadership, company building, technology, and the future. He exuded passion for his work, passion for creating, and passion for the idea that putting computers in the hands of millions of creative people would change the world.

Partway through the session, he quipped, "Well, I got booted out of my last company." Just a few years prior, Jobs had lost control of Apple in a bitter boardroom battle, and I'd reached out to him right smack in the dark depths of his "wilderness years" when some people were writing him off, laughing behind his back, seeing him as washed up and increasingly irrelevant. His sister later captured this with a simple vignette she shared in a eulogy, later published in the *New York Times.* When five hundred Silicon Valley leaders gathered for a dinner with the president of the United States, Jobs didn't even garner an invitation. He could have taken his millions from cashed-out Apple stock, retired to leisure-land, and railed about the unfairness of it all. But he didn't.

His new company, NeXT, which he started after Apple, didn't become the Next Big Thing. Still, he got up and went to work—day after day, week after week, month after month, year after year—toiling away without people paying much attention to him, while his archrival Bill Gates took center stage as the chief visionary changing the world.

Then, in 1997—bang!—good luck struck. As I alluded to earlier, in Chapter 2, Jobs's beloved Apple had fallen so far that it faced near extinction. Apple had even engaged in talks with multiple companies about being acquired but failed to reach an agreement with any of its suitors. Apple desperately needed a new operating system, and NeXT just happened to have the very type of operating system Apple needed. So, Jobs got a second chance, bringing himself back to Apple along with the operating system in a package deal. If it weren't for a number of luck events, there would very likely be no iPod, no iPhone, no iPad, no Apple stores, and no Steve Jobs standing at the pinnacle as a global icon. Had Apple achieved spectacular profit growth from 1990 to 1997, there would have been no opportunity for Jobs to return. Had Apple sold itself to another company, there would have been no Apple to reinvigorate. Had Apple not needed the very type of operating system NeXT had developed, there would have been no negotiations leading to Jobs's triumphant return.

So, is Jobs's story just a luck story? And is the rise of Apple as a (bad-to-) good-to-great case primarily a story of good luck? And what about the more general question, "How much of success is explained by luck?"

Some academics and popular writers have argued that extreme success can be better explained by luck and fortunate circumstance than by skill and disciplined adherence to principles; after all, if you ask a stadium full of people to each flip a coin seven times, a few will get seven heads in a row by sheer random chance. It's a provocative line of argument, but when it comes to starting and building an enduring great company, they're simply dead wrong.

In *Great by Choice*, Morten Hansen and I studied some of the most successful entrepreneurs and company builders from the second half of the twentieth century. As part of our analysis, we defined, quantified, and studied the variable of luck. We defined a "luck event" as one that meets three tests: First, *you didn't cause it*; second, it has a *significant potential consequence*, good or bad; and third, it has an *element of surprise*, some aspect of the event is unpredictable before it happens. Using this definition, the evidence showed a lot of luck in the history of these companies. But—and this is the crucial point—we also found comparable amounts of luck in the control set of comparison cases we studied! The big winners did not generally get more good luck, less bad luck, bigger spikes of luck, or better-timed luck than their comparisons. What the best achieved, instead, was a higher *return on luck*. Hansen and I learned that the question is not whether you'll get luck along the way—you certainly will get luck, both good luck and bad. The critical question is what you *do* with the luck that you get. I've come to believe that about 50 percent of great leadership is what you do with the unexpected.

In fact, the evidence suggests that overcoming bad luck and early setbacks might actually *increase* the odds of building an enduring great company.

Together, my research mentor Jerry Porras and I studied eighteen companies that grew from start-up to iconic, becoming what we called "visionary companies" that endured for decades and made an indelible imprint on the world in which we live. To our surprise, we found they were *less* likely to start life with a big-hit success than their more mediocre comparisons. In fact, visionary companies more often had to overcome early failures and defeats, setbacks that helped forge the organizational character that would make them truly exceptional in the long run. That makes sense when you think about it. If you have too much good luck early on—such as hitting the market just right with a "great idea" that rides the wave of the Zeitgeist—it can make you lazy and arrogant. But if you have to overcome failure and bad luck early on, and you mine those experiences for wisdom, you're more likely to develop the capabilities necessary for enduring success. In the long run, it's better to experience failure early and learn how to systematically innovate than to merely have one big megahit.

You can look at life as a search for that one big winning hand, or you can look at life as a *series* of hands well played. If you believe life comes down to a single hand, of course, you can easily lose. But if you see life as a *series* of hands, and if you play each hand the best you can, there's a huge compounding effect. Bad luck can kill you, but good luck cannot make you great. As long as you don't get a catastrophic stroke of bad luck that flat-out ends the game, what really matters is how well you play each hand over the long haul. How will you play this hand and the next—and every hand you're dealt?

Imagine if after having been booted out of Apple in 1985, Jobs had said, "Well, I got a really bad break, a bad hand. Game over." What if he'd lost his work ethic and his passion? What if he'd turned hurt into bitterness, instead of creating and moving forward? I used to think of Jobs as the Beethoven of business—a peculiar creative genius with a compositional body of work (the Macintosh as his third symphony, the iPod as his seventh, and the iPhone/iPad as his ninth). But my view has changed. I've come to see him more as the Winston Churchill of business—a hyper-resilient soul who exemplified the simple mantra, "Never give in, never, never, never, never."

In the 1930s, many viewed Churchill as a relic of a romantic era, irrelevant to the new world order. Heading into his sixties, he could have retired to the countryside, spending the rest of his days painting, laying bricks, feeding his ducks and swans, and grousing that "they just don't get it." But he stayed in the game, writing, serving in Parliament, speaking out about the Nazi threat, challenging the policy of appeasement. And of course, Churchill's finest hours lay years in the future, when Britain stood defiant against the onslaught of Hitler and his Nazi henchmen wreaking pure evil upon the world. Had Churchill failed to persist in his wilderness years, he wouldn't have been perfectly situated to lead when all Europe went dark.

At the end of the Second World War, Churchill found himself thrown out of office when his party lost the election. He felt deeply pained, writing later, "The power to shape the future would be denied me. The knowledge and experience I had gathered, the authority and goodwill I had gained in so many countries, would vanish." As he glowered over his lunch plate, his wife offered that it was perhaps a blessing in disguise, to which Churchill replied, "At the moment it seems quite effectively disguised."

Yet even in his seventies, he stayed in the game. He delivered his famous speech popularizing the term "Iron Curtain," giving a vivid image to the existential threat to freedom posed by the Soviet Union at the onset of the Cold War. He penned his six-volume memoir, *The Second World War* (the best five thousand pages on the art of leadership I've ever read), which won him the Nobel Prize in Literature. He once again became prime minister. Like Steve Jobs, he ceased the relentless drive to be useful only when his body gave out.

Most of us get decked somewhere along the way in life, slammed to the ground, the world looking down on us. And when—not *if*, *when*—that happens, we have a choice. Do we get back up? And when it happens again, do we get back up again? And again, and again, and again, and again? When I'm feeling clobbered by events, pounded by setbacks, or just flat-out exhausted from dealing with my own mistakes, I think of Steve Jobs, Winston Churchill, and Tommy Caldwell. Not persisting in a grim manner, full of endless suffering, but joyfully and gratefully persisting, fueled by passionately pursuing purposeful work. Life is way too long to give up early and way too short to be derailed from what we're passionate about and made to do.

In finishing up this chapter, I'm reminded of a fascinating conversation I had about luck when I had the bad luck of a canceled flight and found myself on a backup flight squeezed into a middle seat. I figured that I might as well make the most of it and see what I could learn from the people sitting next to me. So, I struck up a conversation.

"Where are you from?" I asked the passenger in the aisle seat, a distinguished-looking gentleman who appeared to be in his sixties.

"I live in Denver now."

"Is that where you grew up?"

He laughed, "No, I'm a long way from where I grew up. I grew up in a poor inner-city neighborhood on the east coast."

"What led you to Denver?"

"I own a chain of restaurants."

"How did that happen?"

"Oh, my life has been a story of tremendous luck."

"Like what?"

"It all began with an incredible science teacher. I was sitting in a classroom on the first day of class, not paying attention and not very interested. Then this man came in, set a ladder in the middle of the room, put a pad below the ladder, and walked out. He waited, and then burst back into the room, ran up the ladder, and jumped off with a whooping yell. Then he looked at all of us and said, 'Let's talk about gravity.' He inspired me to get interested in science, and I won a scholarship to a leading science college to study physics."

He went on to describe how this led to taking a job with a blue-chip technology company, then making some excellent investments—"really lucky bets"—and then reinvesting in what would become the chain of restaurants. "I was really in the right place at the right time, and it just kind of took off."

Then the young man sitting in the window seat piped up.

"Well, I can't afford to believe in luck," he said.

"What do you mean?"

"I'm trying to make it into professional baseball, and the odds are really low. But I have to believe that I can make it happen, that I can work and train and put myself in the game. I have to believe that it's up to me. If I believed it was largely luck, I just couldn't endure the struggle. I have to believe in myself."

"You know," said the older man in the aisle seat, "I used to see it just like you. I had to believe it was up to me, that I could do it, that I didn't need luck to make it. I couldn't have done what I've done if I'd started out thinking, 'Well, it's all really a matter of luck.' Now I can see the role of luck in retrospect, but it would have crushed me to believe that the bad luck of where I started would determine where I ended up."

This conversation perfectly illustrates a strange paradox of luck. On the one hand, those who build great companies believe that luck won't determine their ultimate achievement and contribution. They accept full responsibility for creating their own fate. But once they've attained extraordinary success, they write luck back into their own story, recognizing the role it played. If you err on the side of crediting some of your success to luck rather than your own brilliance, you continue to work hard to improve. To ascribe all positive outcomes to your own genius is hubris. After all, what if some good luck covered up your inadequacies that will be exposed when your luck runs out? The key is to be prepared for what you cannot control or predict, and to be strong enough to survive and take full advantage of luck and opportunities when they come.

Those who see life, business, and the pursuit of accomplishment as about finding that one big hit—the one big lucky break—fail to grasp how true greatness happens. No great company, no great career, no great body of work comes about by a single event, a single flip of the coin, a single hand played. Of course, persistence doesn't guarantee success; and the best leaders understand that they may need to change strategies, plans, and methods on the long path to building a great company. But they also understand and live out this simple truth: Luck favors the persistent.

I'd like to close this chapter with an essential caveat about persistence from *Built to Last*. Of all the paragraphs I've authored or co-authored in thirty years, this is one of the most essential for entrepreneurs and leaders of early-stage ventures, reproduced here as a reminder to keep firmly in mind as you build your company:

> The builders of visionary companies were highly persistent, living to the motto: Never, *never*, never give up. But what to persist *with*? The company. *Be prepared to kill, revise, or evolve an idea . . . but never give up on the company.* If you equate the success of your company with the success of a specific idea—as many businesspeople do—then you're more likely to give up on the company if that idea fails; and if that idea happens to succeed, you're more likely to have an emotional love affair with that idea and stick with it too long, when the company should be moving vigorously on to other things. But if you see the ultimate creation as the company, not the execution of a specific idea . . . then you can persist beyond any specific idea—good or bad—and move toward becoming an enduring great institution.

Chapter 6

WHAT MAKES GREAT COMPANIES TICK—THE MAP

In the ever-renewing society what matures is a system or framework within which continuous innovation, renewal and rebirth can occur.

—JOHN W. GARDNER

THIS CHAPTER PULLS TOGETHER decades of research into one road map for building a great company. The origins of The Map trace all the way back to when I first began my research and teaching career at the Stanford Graduate School of Business. One day, as I sat down to craft a new syllabus for the course on entrepreneurship and small-business management, I impulsively typed out a course overview that challenged my students with a lofty aspiration. Instead of focusing solely on the fundamentals of launching a start-up venture and managing a small to mid-sized business, I reframed the entire course around the question of what it would take to build *an enduring great company*.

I fell in love with the question. And I felt energized by the vision of my students doing something noble and audacious with their lives. If they were going to become entrepreneurs, I wanted them to create some of the most successful companies in the world, companies that would make a distinctive and positive impact, companies worthy of admiration, companies that would endure. But I also realized I had a lot of work to do. I just kept looking at the phrase "enduring great company" and thinking to myself, "Wow, I don't know anything about that, but I'm going to figure it out!"

And that sparked a passionate effort to discover and teach what makes great companies tick. Little did I know that it would take a full quarter century of work to satisfy my curiosity.

I wrote my first book on the topic with Bill Lazier, the original edition of *Beyond Entrepreneurship*, which drew from the cases we taught in our course at Stanford and Bill's practical wisdom. From there, guided by the inspired tutelage of my research mentor Jerry Porras, I threw my energies into decades of research, seeking to uncover timeless principles that separate great companies from all the others. Sometimes I partnered with a co-author and sometimes I wrote solo, and I always had research teams composed largely of undergraduate and graduate students from Stanford University and the University of Colorado. Every time we finished one research project and book, there would be another question to answer, another lens to look through, another angle to explore. So, I just kept marching, completing multiple research studies that, in total, drew upon more than six thousand years of combined corporate history. We framed each study and resulting book as the pursuit of an overarching question, such as:

- Why do some start-ups and small businesses grow into visionary companies that change the world and endure for decades, while others fail to achieve such an iconic stature? (*Built to Last*, co-authored with Jerry Porras)
- Why do some companies make the leap from good to great, while other companies in similar circumstances don't? (*Good to Great*)
- Why do some companies attain greatness and then lose it—falling from great to good to mediocre to bad to gone—while others sustain their greatness? (*How the Mighty Fall*)
- Why do some companies thrive in uncertainty, even chaos, and others do not; when hit by big, fast-moving forces that we can neither predict nor control, what distinguishes those who perform exceptionally well from those who underperform or worse? (*Great by Choice*, co-authored with Morten Hansen)

We did not merely study success; we studied the *contrast* between success and failure, ascent and decline, endurance and collapse, greatness and mediocrity. Throughout our research, we employed a rigorous historical matched-pair method that Jerry Porras and I invented, comparing companies that became great to companies in similar circumstances that did not, systematically examining the evolution of the companies from their inception. Our research method rested upon the power of contrast. The critical question is not, "What did the great companies share in common?" The critical question is, "What did the great companies share in common that *distinguished* them from their direct comparisons?" Comparisons are companies that were in the same industry with the same or very similar opportunities and circumstances during the exact same era, but that did not perform as well. We'd systematically analyze the histories of the contrasting cases and ask, "What explains the difference?" (See diagram below, "The Good-to-Great Matched-Pair Research Method," for an illustration of how we applied this methodology in the good-to-great study.)

THE GOOD-TO-GREAT MATCHED-PAIR RESEARCH METHOD

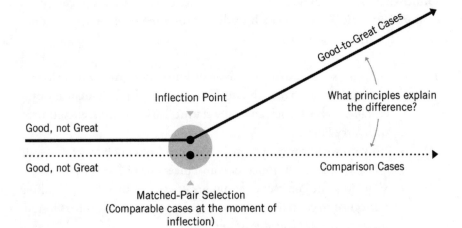

Before we move on, let's address a key point about the great companies in our research. We studied *historical eras* of greatness, not the companies as they are today. Some of the companies in our research stumbled or fell in the subsequent decades after their era of greatness, and you might wonder, "But what about XYZ company? It doesn't seem to be a great company today." Think of our research as comparable to studying a sports dynasty during its best years. Just because the UCLA Bruins basketball dynasty of the 1960s and 1970s under Coach John Wooden (with its ten NCAA championships in twelve years) declined after Wooden retired does not invalidate insights obtained by studying the UCLA basketball program during its dynastic era. In this same vein, a great company can cease to be great, yet this does not erase its era of greatness from the record books. We focused our research lens and based our findings on historical eras of greatness that lasted a minimum of fifteen years (and most lasted substantially longer).

As a reader of *BE 2.0*, you might be puzzling on how the findings apply to smaller companies; after all, many of the companies featured in our research grew into giant corporations. The answer is simple: *All* of the companies we studied were once start-ups and small businesses, and we studied their development from their very beginnings. We learned that it's best to build the foundations of greatness into the architecture of the enterprise as early as possible. To use an analogy, it's better to be parented well, and to enter adulthood as a well-adjusted and healthy individual, than to be parented poorly and have to recover from that fact later in life. Sure, people can—and often do—become successful in life after poor parenting, but that doesn't make poor parenting the best option. So, too, with building companies: You want to parent well. The vast majority of great companies had the foundations of excellence put in place when relatively young and/or small. And while it's possible to transform a massive mediocrity into a great company down the road, it's much better to get the foundations right in the first place.

Each research study added insight and principles. We think of each research project like punching holes and shining a light into a black box, inside which we find enduring principles that distinguish great companies from good ones. Each new study uncovered additional dynamics and allowed us to see previously discovered principles from new angles. We cannot claim that the concepts we uncover "cause" greatness (no one in the social sciences can ever claim causality), but we can claim correlations rooted in the evidence. If you apply our findings with discipline, your chances of building an enduring great company will be higher than if you behave like a comparison case.

After decades of research and multiple books, I began to get questions from people who wanted to engage with the entire body of work in a systematic sequence. The questions were along the following lines: "As a leadership team, where should we begin?" "How do all the ideas across the different books fit together?" "Is there a best order in which to read your work or engage with the concepts?" "Should we proceed book by book or concept by concept?" "Is there a master map of principles across all the books?"

Reflecting on these questions, I realized that, in a sense, I'd actually been doing one giant multi-decade research project that came out in installments, book by book. I decided to cull the most essential concepts across all the research studies, settling upon the twelve most fundamental principles. I then worked to place them in proper sequence, linked together in an overall framework, that would define a path that leaders could follow to create a great company. My goal was to distill my life's work on great companies into a single "map" that could fit on a large whiteboard in my management lab.

Thirty years after starting to crack the code on what makes great companies tick, I presented The Map for the first time to a group of early-stage entrepreneurs from Techstars, a start-up accelerator. I smiled to myself that I'd set out teaching entrepreneurship and small business at Stanford, determined to challenge my students to start and build great companies that could endure, and had come full circle to challenge an entirely new generation of entrepreneurs and small-business leaders. Only this time, I had The Map.

What Makes Great Companies Tick
THE MAP
Developed by Jim Collins

INPUTS				OUTPUTS
STAGE 1 DISCIPLINED PEOPLE	**STAGE 2** DISCIPLINED THOUGHT	**STAGE 3** DISCIPLINED ACTION	**STAGE 4** BUILDING TO LAST	
Cultivate **Level 5 Leadership**	Embrace the **Genius of the AND**	Build momentum by turning **The Flywheel**	Practice **Productive Paranoia** (Avoid the **5 Stages of Decline**)	SUPERIOR RESULTS
First Who, Then What (Get the Right People on the Bus)	**Confront the Brutal Facts** (Live the **Stockdale Paradox**)	Achieve breakthrough with **20 Mile March** discipline	Do more **Clock Building**, less time telling	DISTINCTIVE IMPACT
	Clarify a **Hedgehog Concept**	Renew and extend via **Fire Bullets, then Cannonballs**	**Preserve the Core / Stimulate Progress** (Achieve the next **BHAG**)	LASTING ENDURANCE
		AMPLIFIED BY THE **10X MULTIPLIER** Get a high **Return on Luck**		

In the text that follows, I'll lead you through the essential components of The Map. For each of the principles in The Map, I'll direct you to selected chapters and monographs that tie to that principle. If you (either yourself or your team) want to engage with the full flow of the framework, I'd suggest moving through The Map while doing the directed reading associated with each principle in sequence.

To get started, notice that The Map has both *inputs* and *outputs*.

What Makes Great Companies Tick
THE MAP
Developed by Jim Collins

INPUTS	OUTPUTS

The inputs delineate the *path* to building a great company, composed of a sequence of fundamental principles we derived in our research. The outputs define what a great company *is*, not how you get there. This is an important distinction because people often confuse the two. Is having "the right people on the bus" an input (a means to greatness) or an output (a definition of greatness)? Is achieving superior performance an input (a means to greatness) or an output (a definition of greatness)? In our research, we were very careful to separate inputs from outputs, and the full expression of The Map will make the distinction clear.

Let's turn first to the inputs, beginning with the role of discipline. An overarching theme across our research findings is the role of discipline in separating the great from the mediocre. True discipline requires the independence of mind to reject pressures to conform in ways incompatible with values, performance standards, and long-term aspirations. The only legitimate form of discipline is self-discipline, having the inner will to do whatever it takes to create a great outcome, no matter how difficult. When you have disciplined people, you don't need hierarchy. When you have disciplined thought, you don't need bureaucracy. When you have disciplined action, you don't need excessive controls. When you combine a culture of discipline with an ethic of entrepreneurship, you create a powerful mixture that drives great performance.

To build an enduring great organization—whether in business or the social sectors—you need disciplined people who engage in disciplined thought and take disciplined action. Then you need the discipline to sustain momentum over a long period of time. This forms the backbone of the framework, laid out in four basic stages:

Stage 1: Disciplined People
Stage 2: Disciplined Thought
Stage 3: Disciplined Action
Stage 4: Building to Last

What Makes Great Companies Tick
THE MAP
Developed by Jim Collins

INPUTS				OUTPUTS
STAGE 1 DISCIPLINED PEOPLE	**STAGE 2** DISCIPLINED THOUGHT	**STAGE 3** DISCIPLINED ACTION	**STAGE 4** BUILDING TO LAST	

STAGE 1: DISCIPLINED PEOPLE

Everything starts with people. There are two fundamental principles in Stage 1:

- Cultivate Level 5 leadership.
- First who, then what (get the right people on the bus).

What Makes Great Companies Tick
THE MAP
Developed by Jim Collins

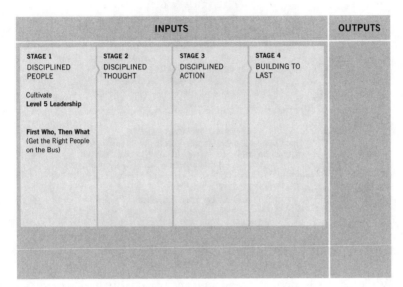

INPUTS				OUTPUTS
STAGE 1 DISCIPLINED PEOPLE	**STAGE 2** DISCIPLINED THOUGHT	**STAGE 3** DISCIPLINED ACTION	**STAGE 4** BUILDING TO LAST	
Cultivate **Level 5 Leadership** **First Who, Then What** (Get the Right People on the Bus)				

Cultivate Level 5 Leadership

Our research showed that having charismatic leadership doesn't explain why some companies become great and others don't. In fact, some of the most disastrous comparison cases had very strong, charismatic leadership in the very era that the companies fell or failed. Rather, our research found that the critical ingredient is Level 5 leadership. The essence of Level 5 leadership is a paradoxical combination of personal humility and indomitable will. The humility expressed at Level 5 isn't a false humbleness; it's a subjugation of personal ego *in service* to a cause beyond oneself. This humility is combined with the fierce resolve to do whatever it takes (no matter how difficult) to best serve that cause. Level 5 leaders are incredibly ambitious, but they channel their ambition into building a great team or organization and accomplishing a shared mission that's ultimately not about them.

LEVEL 5 LEADERSHIP HIERARCHY

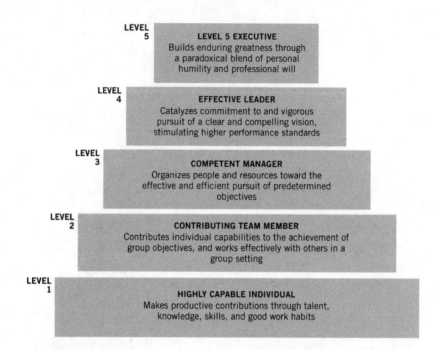

LEVEL 5
LEVEL 5 EXECUTIVE
Builds enduring greatness through a paradoxical blend of personal humility and professional will

LEVEL 4
EFFECTIVE LEADER
Catalyzes commitment to and vigorous pursuit of a clear and compelling vision, stimulating higher performance standards

LEVEL 3
COMPETENT MANAGER
Organizes people and resources toward the effective and efficient pursuit of predetermined objectives

LEVEL 2
CONTRIBUTING TEAM MEMBER
Contributes individual capabilities to the achievement of group objectives, and works effectively with others in a group setting

LEVEL 1
HIGHLY CAPABLE INDIVIDUAL
Makes productive contributions through talent, knowledge, skills, and good work habits

While Level 5 leaders can come in many personality packages, they're often self-effacing, quiet, reserved, and even shy. Every good-to-great transition in our research began with a Level 5 leader who motivated people more with inspired standards than inspiring personality. Every 10x entrepreneurial success in our research had founders and leaders who, while sometimes colorful characters, never confused leadership with personality; they were utterly obsessed with making the company truly great and ensuring it endured beyond themselves. Building a great company requires cultivating Level 5 in yourself and your team. A great company at its best has a Level 5 leadership pipeline and Level 5 unit leaders spread throughout. (Directed reading: *Good to Great*, Chapters 1 and 2; *Great by Choice*, Chapters 1 and 2; *Good to Great and the Social Sectors: A Monograph to Accompany Good to Great*.)

First Who, Then What (Get the Right People on the Bus)

Level 5 leaders who build the greatest and most durable companies think *first* about "who" and *then* about "what." They first get the right people on the bus (and the wrong people off the bus) and then figure out where to drive the bus.

When you're facing chaos, turbulence, disruption, and uncertainty, and you cannot possibly predict what's coming around the corner, your best "strategy" is to have a busload of disciplined people who can adapt and perform brilliantly no matter what comes next. Our research supported what we came to call "Packard's Law" (named in admiration after HP's co-founder): No company can consistently grow faster than its ability to get enough of the right people and still become a great company. If a company consistently grows faster than its ability to get enough of the right people, it will not simply stagnate, it will fall. The number one metric to track isn't revenue or profit or return on capital or cash flow; the number one metric is the percentage of key seats on the bus that are filled with right people for those seats. Everything depends on having the right people. (Directed reading: *Good to Great*, Chapter 3; *BE 2.0*, Chapter 2)

STAGE 2: DISCIPLINED THOUGHT

With the right people in place, you turn to Stage 2, disciplined thought. There are three key principles in Stage 2:

- Embrace the Genius of the AND.
- Confront the brutal facts (live the Stockdale Paradox).
- Clarify a Hedgehog Concept.

What Makes Great Companies Tick
THE MAP
Developed by Jim Collins

INPUTS				OUTPUTS
STAGE 1 DISCIPLINED PEOPLE	**STAGE 2** DISCIPLINED THOUGHT	**STAGE 3** DISCIPLINED ACTION	**STAGE 4** BUILDING TO LAST	
Cultivate **Level 5 Leadership**	Embrace the **Genius of the AND**			
First Who, Then What (Get the Right People on the Bus)	Confront the **Brutal Facts** (Live the **Stockdale Paradox**)			
	Clarify a **Hedgehog Concept**			

Embrace the Genius of the AND

False dichotomies are undisciplined thought. In the words of F. Scott Fitzgerald, "The test of a first-rate intelligence is the ability to hold two opposed ideas in the mind at the same time, and still retain the ability to function." Builders of greatness are comfortable with paradox. They don't oppress themselves with what we call the "Tyranny of the OR," which pushes people to believe that things must be either *A* OR *B*, but not both. Instead, they liberate themselves with the "Genius of the AND." Undisciplined thinkers force debates into stark "Tyranny of the OR" choices; disciplined thinkers expand the conversation to create Genius of the AND solutions. In our research, we found myriad permutations of "Genius of the AND" dualities. For example:

Creativity	*And*	Discipline
Innovation	*And*	Execution
Humility	*And*	Audacity
Freedom	*And*	Responsibility
Cost	*And*	Quality
Short-term	*And*	Long-term
Prudence	*And*	Courage
Analysis	*And*	Action
Idealistic	*And*	Pragmatic
Continuity	*And*	Change
Realistic	*And*	Visionary
Values	*And*	Results
Purpose	*And*	Profit

Of particular note for business corporations, our research showed that visionary companies reject the idea that the sole purpose of a business is to maximize shareholder wealth; visionary companies pursue a core purpose beyond making money AND they generate substantial wealth. (Directed reading: *Built to Last*, Chapter 1, Interlude, and Chapter 3.)

Confront the Brutal Facts (Live the Stockdale Paradox)

Our research found that Level 5 leaders instill the Stockdale Paradox, named after Admiral Jim Stockdale, the highest-ranking officer in the Hanoi Hilton prisoner-of-war camp during the Vietnam War. Stockdale embraced a Genius of the AND in his leadership: You must retain unwavering faith that you can and will prevail in the end, regardless of the difficulties, *and at the same time* you must confront the most brutal facts of your current reality, whatever they might be. You must believe you can survive the camp and will live to see your loved ones again, *and at the same time* you must stoically accept that you will not be out by this Christmas or the next Christmas or even the next Christmas after that. Never fall into the leadership trap of creating false hopes soon to be destroyed by events. Yet equally, never capitulate to despair and lose faith that you will prevail in the end. You need the Stockdale Paradox to go from start-up to great company. You need the Stockdale Paradox to lead a company from good to great. You need the Stockdale Paradox to navigate turbulence and disruption. You need the Stockdale Paradox to reverse decline and engineer a return to success. You need the Stockdale Paradox to continually renew a successful company so that it might endure. Level 5 leaders confront the brutal facts *before* they set vision and strategy, and they create a climate where the truth is heard. Failure to confront the brutal facts is a precursor to catastrophic decline, always. (Directed reading: *Good to Great*, Chapter 4.)

Clarify a Hedgehog Concept

An ancient Greek parable says that the fox knows many things, but the hedgehog knows one big thing. Drawing upon this parable, philosopher Isaiah Berlin famously divided the world into two types of thinkers: foxes and hedgehogs. Foxes embrace the inherent complexity of the world and pursue many ideas, never giving themselves over to a single pursuit or organizing idea. Hedgehogs, in contrast, gravitate toward simplicity and think in terms of a single organizing idea that guides everything. Our research found that those who build great companies tend to be more hedgehog than fox. We also found that they implicitly or explicitly use a Hedgehog Concept for disciplined decision making. A Hedgehog Concept is a simple, crystalline concept that flows from deeply understanding the intersection of the following three circles: (1) what you're deeply passionate about, (2) what you can be the best in the world at, and (3) what best drives your economic engine.

The Hedgehog Concept also reflects the discipline to confront the brutal facts about what you are *not* passionate about, what you *cannot* be the best at, and what does *not* make economic sense. When you become fanatically disciplined in making decisions consistent with the three circles, you begin to generate momentum. This includes the discipline of not only what *to* do, but, equally, what *not* to do and what to *stop* doing. (Directed reading: *Good to Great*, Chapters 5, 6, and 7; *Good to Great and the Social Sectors: A Monograph to Accompany Good to Great.*)

THE THREE CIRCLES
of the Hedgehog Concept

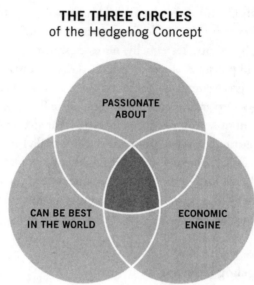

STAGE 3: DISCIPLINED ACTION

In Stage 3, you translate disciplined thought into disciplined action, building momentum to achieve a breakthrough and extend performance. There are three key principles in Stage 3:

- Build momentum by turning the Flywheel.
- Achieve breakthrough with 20 Mile March discipline.
- Renew and extend via fire bullets, then cannonballs.

THE MAP

Developed by Jim Collins

INPUTS				OUTPUTS
STAGE 1 DISCIPLINED PEOPLE	**STAGE 2** DISCIPLINED THOUGHT	**STAGE 3** DISCIPLINED ACTION	**STAGE 4** BUILDING TO LAST	
Cultivate **Level 5 Leadership**	Embrace the **Genius of the AND**	Build momentum by turning **The Flywheel**		
First Who, Then What (Get the Right People on the Bus)	**Confront the Brutal Facts** (Live the **Stockdale Paradox**)	Achieve breakthrough with **20 Mile March** discipline		
	Clarify a **Hedgehog Concept**	Renew and extend via **Fire Bullets then Cannonballs**		

Build Momentum by Turning the Flywheel

Our research showed that no matter how dramatic the end result, building a great enterprise never happens in one fell swoop. There's no single defining action, no grand program, no one killer innovation, no solitary lucky break, no miracle moment. Rather, the process resembles relentlessly pushing a giant, heavy flywheel, turn upon turn, building momentum until a point of breakthrough, and beyond. Pushing with great effort, you get the flywheel to inch forward. You keep pushing, and you get the flywheel to complete one entire turn. You don't stop. You keep pushing. The flywheel moves a bit faster. Two turns . . . then four . . . then eight . . . the flywheel builds momentum . . . sixteen . . . thirty-two . . . moving faster . . . a thousand . . . ten thousand . . . a hundred thousand. Then at some point—breakthrough! The flywheel flies forward with almost unstoppable momentum. Once you fully grasp how to create flywheel momentum *in your particular circumstance*, and apply that understanding with creativity and discipline, you get the power of strategic compounding. Each turn builds upon previous work as you make a series of good decisions, supremely well executed, that compound one upon another. (Directed reading: *Good to Great*, Chapter 8; *Turning the Flywheel: A Monograph to Accompany Good to Great*.)

Achieve Breakthrough with 20 Mile March Discipline

To achieve breakthrough momentum, you need to execute with fanatic discipline on every component of the flywheel. In *Great by Choice*, Morten Hansen and I uncovered a particularly powerful principle of fanatic discipline: the 20 Mile March. To commit to a 20 Mile March means setting forth a standard of performance to hit with relentless consistency. It's like walking across a gigantic country by hitting a minimum march of twenty miles every day. And you stay on the march, no matter what the weather, no matter how tired (or energized) you feel, no matter how unpleasant the surroundings. When you 20 Mile March, you ask, "What do we need to have in place—and what do we need to avoid—so that we can sustain our 20 Mile March without fail?" Our research found that the more turbulent the environment, the more the 20 Mile Marchers win. The 20 Mile March imposes order amidst disorder, discipline amidst chaos, and consistency amidst uncertainty. It is about *consecutive* consistency—meaning, you almost never fail to hit the march. Some companies in our research hit their 20 Mile March for more than forty consecutive years without a miss. Committing to march with *consecutive* consistency achieves a beautiful Genius of the AND: it stimulates the discipline of short-term performance *and* long-term building. You have to hit the march *this* cycle *and every subsequent* cycle for years to decades. (Directed reading: *Great by Choice*, Chapter 3.)

Renew and Extend via Fire Bullets, Then Cannonballs

Over time, a great company renews and extends its flywheel by the principle fire bullets, then cannonballs. Here's the idea: Imagine a hostile ship bearing down on you. You have a limited amount of gunpowder. You take all your gunpowder and use it to fire a big cannonball. The cannonball flies out and splashes in the ocean, missing the oncoming ship. You turn to your stockpile and discover that you're out of gunpowder. You're in trouble. But suppose instead that when you see the ship bearing down, you take a little bit of gunpowder and fire a bullet. It misses by forty degrees. You load another bullet and fire. It misses by thirty degrees. You fire a third bullet, missing by only ten degrees. The next bullet hits—ping!—the hull of the oncoming ship. You have empirical validation, a calibrated line of sight. Now, you take all the remaining gunpowder and fire a big cannonball along the calibrated line of sight, which sinks the enemy ship. Our research showed that calibrated cannonballs correlate with outsized results; uncalibrated cannonballs correlate with disaster. The ability to *scale* innovation—to turn small, proven ideas (bullets) into huge successes (cannonballs)—can provide big bursts of flywheel momentum. Firing bullets then cannonballs is a primary mechanism for expanding the scope of an organization's Hedgehog Concept and extending its flywheel into entirely new arenas. (Directed reading: *Great by Choice*, Chapter 4; *Turning the Flywheel: A Monograph to Accompany Good to Great.*)

STAGE 4: BUILDING TO LAST

If you brilliantly move through all the key principles in Stages 1 through 3, you will likely create a very successful company. In Stage 4, you make your company built to last. There are three key principles in Stage 4:

- Practice productive paranoia (avoid the 5 Stages of Decline).
- Do more clock building, less time telling.
- Preserve the core/stimulate progress (achieve the next BHAG).

What Makes Great Companies Tick
THE MAP
Developed by Jim Collins

INPUTS				OUTPUTS
STAGE 1 DISCIPLINED PEOPLE	**STAGE 2** DISCIPLINED THOUGHT	**STAGE 3** DISCIPLINED ACTION	**STAGE 4** BUILDING TO LAST	
Cultivate **Level 5 Leadership**	Embrace the **Genius of the AND**	Build momentum by turning **The Flywheel**	Practice **Productive Paranoia** (Avoid the 5 Stages of Decline)	
First Who, Then What (Get the Right People on the Bus)	**Confront the Brutal Facts** (Live the **Stockdale Paradox**)	Achieve breakthrough with **20 Mile March** discipline	Do more **Clock Building**, less time telling	
	Clarify a **Hedgehog Concept**	Renew and extend via **Fire Bullets then Cannonballs**	**Preserve the Core / Stimulate Progress** (Achieve the next BHAG)	

Practice Productive Paranoia (Avoid the 5 Stages of Decline)

The first step in being built to last is *don't die*. The only mistakes you can learn from are the ones you survive. Every company is vulnerable to decline. There's no law of nature that the most successful companies will inevitably remain at the top. Any can fall and most eventually do. Entrepreneurs who build great companies differ from less successful comparisons in how they maintain hypervigilance in good times and bad. Leaders who navigate turbulence and stave off decline assume that conditions can unexpectedly change, violently and fast. They obsessively ask, "What if? What if? What if?" By preparing ahead of time, building reserves, preserving a margin of safety, bounding risk, and honing their discipline in good times and bad, they handle disruptions from a position of strength and flexibility. Productive paranoia helps inoculate organizations from falling into the 5 Stages of Decline that can stop the flywheel and destroy an organization. Those stages are (1) Hubris Born of Success, (2) Undisciplined Pursuit of More, (3) Denial of Risk and Peril, (4) Grasping for Salvation, and (5) Capitulation to Irrelevance or Death.

5 STAGES OF DECLINE

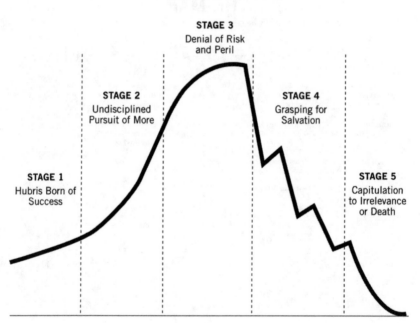

STAGE 3
Denial of Risk
and Peril

STAGE 2
Undisciplined
Pursuit of More

STAGE 4
Grasping for
Salvation

STAGE 1
Hubris Born of
Success

STAGE 5
Capitulation
to Irrelevance
or Death

Our research found that companies going through the first three stages of decline still look strong when viewed from the outside—often experiencing record sales and rapid growth—yet they're already sick on the inside. The more successful your company becomes, the more you need to practice productive paranoia. (Directed reading: *Great by Choice*, Chapter 5; *How the Mighty Fall*.)

Do More Clock Building, Less Time Telling

Leading as a charismatic visionary—a "genius with a thousand helpers" upon whom everything depends—is time telling. Shaping a culture that can thrive far beyond any single leader is clock building. Searching for a single great idea upon which to build success is time telling. Building an organization that can generate many great ideas is clock building. Our research showed that leaders who build enduring great companies make the shift from time telling to clock building. Clock builders create highly replicable recipes, extensive training programs, leadership-development pipelines, and tangible mechanisms to reinforce core values. They get the right people on the bus and then manage the system, not the people. For true clock builders, success comes when the organization proves its greatness not just during one leader's tenure but also when the *next* generation of leadership further increases flywheel momentum. To use an analogy, think of writing the U.S. Constitution as a consummate act of clock building, so that the start-up nation might endure beyond the courage and genius of those who won the War of Independence. Similarly, launching a start-up is like winning the War of Independence, but building a company that can last is like writing the Constitution. (Directed reading: *Built to Last*, Chapter 2; *Great by Choice*, Chapter 6.)

Preserve the Core/Stimulate Progress (Achieve the Next BHAG)

If you accomplish all of the previous principles, you will likely have a successful and enduring company. But there is an even higher standard: to build an institution that is iconic and visionary. Our research uncovered an underlying duality embodied by companies, organizations, and institutions that have become visionary and sustained their greatness. These companies demonstrate a particularly powerful Genius of the AND: preserve the core AND stimulate progress. Think of a yin-yang symbol used in Taoist philosophy. On one side, you have "preserve the core." On the other side, you have "stimulate progress." To preserve the core, visionary organizations have a set of timeless core values and purpose (reason for being) that remain constant over time. To stimulate progress, they have a relentless drive for progress—change, improvement, innovation, and renewal. Enduring great organizations understand the difference between their core values (which almost never change), and operating strategies and cultural practices (which endlessly adapt to a changing world). To be built to last, you must be built to change.

Our research also showed that highly visionary companies often employ BHAGs to stimulate progress. Your core purpose is the guiding star, always out there on the horizon, always pulling you forward. Your BHAG, on the other hand, is the big mountain you're climbing at any moment, a Big Hairy Audacious Goal that you can eventually achieve. While on that mountain, your focus and energy go into that specific ascent. But once you reach the top, you set sight again on the guiding star (your purpose) and pick yet another mountain to climb (another BHAG). And of course, throughout the entire adventure, you remain true to your core values. (Directed reading: *Built to Last*, Chapters 4, 5, and 10; *Good to Great*, Chapter 9; *BE 2.0*, "Vision.")

10X MULTIPLIER—RETURN ON LUCK

Finally, there's an input that amplifies all the other principles in the framework: the principle of return on luck. Throughout all our research, a question gnawed at me: What's the role of luck? Our research showed that the great companies were not generally luckier than the comparisons—they didn't get more good luck, less bad luck, bigger spikes of luck, or better timing of luck. Instead, they got a higher *return* on luck, making more of their luck than others. The critical question is not, "Will you get luck?" but "What will you *do* with the luck that you get?" If you get a high return on a good-luck event, it can add a big boost of momentum to the flywheel. But if you're ill-prepared to absorb a bad-luck event and fail to get a high return on your bad luck, it can stall or imperil the flywheel. About 50 percent of great leadership is what you do with the unexpected.

What Makes Great Companies Tick
THE MAP
Developed by Jim Collins

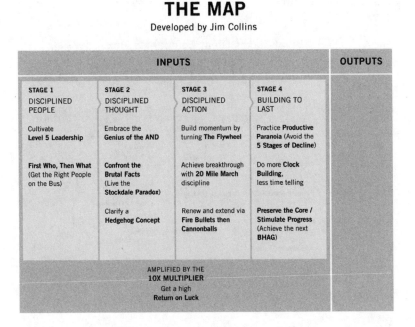

INPUTS				OUTPUTS
STAGE 1 DISCIPLINED PEOPLE	**STAGE 2** DISCIPLINED THOUGHT	**STAGE 3** DISCIPLINED ACTION	**STAGE 4** BUILDING TO LAST	
Cultivate **Level 5 Leadership**	Embrace the **Genius of the AND**	Build momentum by turning **The Flywheel**	Practice **Productive Paranoia** (Avoid the **5 Stages of Decline**)	
First Who, Then What (Get the Right People on the Bus)	**Confront the Brutal Facts** (Live the **Stockdale Paradox**)	Achieve breakthrough with **20 Mile March** discipline	Do more **Clock Building,** less time telling	
	Clarify a **Hedgehog Concept**	Renew and extend via **Fire Bullets then Cannonballs**	**Preserve the Core / Stimulate Progress** (Achieve the next **BHAG**)	
AMPLIFIED BY THE **10X MULTIPLIER** Get a high **Return on Luck**				

Of all the principles in The Map, return on luck is perhaps my favorite. Once you understand that luck can be precisely defined as a discrete event, you see luck events everywhere. (Again, to review from the previous chapter, a "luck event" meets three tests: First, *you didn't cause it*; second, it has a *significant potential consequence*, good or bad; and third, it has an *element of surprise*, some aspect of the event is unpredictable before it happens.) Any framework that didn't account for unpredictable and unforeseen events would be incomplete, and I couldn't be intellectually satisfied until we wrestled with the question of luck. The concept of return on luck accounts for the undeniable fact that luck happens (a lot) yet captures the essential truth that luck itself cannot cause greatness. Catastrophic bad luck can kill a potentially great company, but good luck cannot make a company great. Luck doesn't build great companies that last; people do. (Directed reading: *Great by Choice*, Chapter 7; *BE 2.0*, "Luck Favors the Persistent.")

THE OUTPUTS OF GREATNESS

The previously described principles are the *inputs* to building a great organization. But what are the *outputs* that define a great organization? What are the criteria of greatness? There are three tests: (1) superior results, (2) distinctive impact, (3) lasting endurance.

What Makes Great Companies Tick

THE MAP

Developed by Jim Collins

INPUTS				OUTPUTS
STAGE 1 DISCIPLINED PEOPLE	STAGE 2 DISCIPLINED THOUGHT	STAGE 3 DISCIPLINED ACTION	STAGE 4 BUILDING TO LAST	
Cultivate **Level 5 Leadership**	Embrace the **Genius of the AND**	Build momentum by turning **The Flywheel**	Practice **Productive Paranoia** (Avoid the 5 Stages of Decline)	SUPERIOR RESULTS
First Who, Then What (Get the Right People on the Bus)	**Confront the Brutal Facts** (Live the **Stockdale Paradox**)	Achieve breakthrough with **20 Mile March** discipline	Do more **Clock Building,** less time telling	DISTINCTIVE IMPACT
	Clarify a **Hedgehog Concept**	Renew and extend via **Fire Bullets then Cannonballs**	**Preserve the Core / Stimulate Progress** (Achieve the next **BHAG**)	LASTING ENDURANCE
AMPLIFIED BY THE **10X MULTIPLIER** Get a high **Return on Luck**				

Superior Results

In business, performance is defined by financial results—return on invested capital—and achievement of corporate purpose. In the social sectors, performance is defined by results and efficiency in delivering on the social mission. But whether you're operating in business or the social sectors, you must achieve top-flight results. To use an analogy, if you're a sports team, you must win championships; if you don't find a way to win at your chosen game, you cannot be considered truly great.

Distinctive Impact

A truly great enterprise makes such a unique contribution to the communities it touches and does its work with such unadulterated excellence that, if it were to disappear, it would leave a gaping hole that couldn't be easily filled by any other institution on the planet. If your company went away, who would miss it and why? This does not require being big; think of a small but fabulous local restaurant that would be terribly missed if it disappeared. Big does not equal great, and great does not equal big.

Lasting Endurance

A truly great organization prospers over a long period of time, beyond any great idea, market opportunity, technology cycle, or well-funded program. When clobbered by setbacks, it finds a way to bounce back stronger than before. A great enterprise transcends dependence on any single extraordinary leader; if your organization cannot be great without you, then it is not yet truly great.

AFTER THE MAP—WHAT'S NEXT?

Throughout our research, we studied two sides of a coin. On one side, we studied companies that became great and sustained their greatness for decades. On the other side, we studied companies that failed to become great or that fell from greatness. The Map is informed by both sides of the coin. We learned that while the path to building a great company is narrow, there are many ways to succumb to catastrophic decline and failure.

Fortune asked me to pen a keynote essay for its *Fortune* 500 issue in 2008. In preparing to write the essay, I asked the *Fortune* editors to help me assemble some basic data. Here are a few sobering facts. Of the 500 companies that appeared in the first list in 1955, less than 15 percent held a place on the list in 2008. (The 1955 list included industrial companies only, whereas the 2008 list also included service companies.) Nearly two thousand companies had appeared on the list since its inception, and most were long gone, including many once-celebrated companies. Many of the two thousand simply capitulated their independence along the way, while others died outright. But whether by capitulation or death, the brutal fact is that the vast majority did not endure as great companies.

But there's also a hopeful story to tell. Companies *can* sustain greatness for decades, even if only a few do so. What this means is that you never get to the "end" of The Map. You're never done with the journey. You're never done with the need for disciplined people who engage in disciplined thought and take disciplined action. You're never done renewing the company so that it might be built to last. You're never done preparing for bad luck and capitalizing on good luck, getting a higher return on luck than others. Greatness is an inherently dynamic process, not an end point.

The Map doesn't guarantee a great outcome. But those who adhere to its principles—and who do so with joyful intensity—have much better odds of building a great company that can endure than those who don't. Along the way, perhaps as more of a by-product than a goal, they just might find the daily happiness that comes from doing meaningful work with people they truly like and deeply respect. And it's hard to have a better life than that.

Chapter 7

STRATEGY

Strategy is easy, but tactics—the day-to-day and month-to-month decisions required to manage a business—are hard.

ARTHUR ROCK

"STRATEGY." THE WORD SOUNDS weighty, academic, scientific, ponderous.

To be a strategist, this momentous word implies, we would need the intelligence of a pure mathematician and the skills of a master chess player. High-priced strategy consultants would like us to believe that only the top 5% of academic performers from first-rate graduate schools can be virtuosos of strategic thinking. We're led to envision thoughtful experts of economic theory looking out on the world from lofty offices on the 45th floor of a tall building and applying the mysterious rigors of decision sciences to concoct strategies that dazzle the world with their brilliance.

Well, we've been on the 45th floor, and we can assure you that all these images of strategy are false.

Not that strategy is unimportant. It's very important. And not that strategy consultants are unhelpful. Their objectivity can be useful.

But strategy isn't difficult. Nor is setting strategy a complicated or purely scientific exercise.

The purpose of this chapter is to demystify the topic of strategy and provide a straightforward road map for setting a strategy. We will also address four key strategic issues commonly faced by small to mid-sized companies:

- How fast to grow
- Focus versus diversification
- Whether to go public
- Whether to lead a market or follow

Overview of Strategy

Strategy is simply the basic methodology you intend to apply to attain your company's current mission. "This is how we will achieve our mission." That, in a nutshell, is strategy. There's no mystery to it. It's not a difficult concept.

A good strategy is *not* a thick, turgid plan that lays out every action of the company to the nth degree and requires six months of effort by a strategic planning staff. Business, like life, cannot be entirely planned. Nor should it be. There are far too many uncertainties and unexpected opportunities. Instead, it's better to simply have a clear, thoughtful, and uncomplicated methodology for attaining your mission—a methodology that leaves room for individual initiative, opportunities, changing conditions, experimentation, and innovation.

Four Basic Principles of Setting Effective Strategy

There are four key principles to keep in mind when setting company strategy.

1. The strategy must descend directly from your vision. Remember, it's impossible to set strategy unless you have a crystal clear idea of what you're trying to do in the first place. Vision first, *then* strategy!
2. The strategy must leverage off the strengths and unique capabilities of your company. Do what you're good at.
3. The strategy must be realistic. It must therefore take into account internal constraints and external factors. Confront reality, *even if reality is unpleasant.*
4. Strategy should be set with the participation of those who are going to be on the line to make it happen.

The Process

Setting strategy involves the following basic steps:

First, *review the vision* of the company. If you haven't clarified your vision, do so. In particular, ensure that the current mission is clear. As you recall from Chapter 4, your mission (which is the third component of vision, after core values and beliefs and purpose) is analogous to the specific mountain you are going to climb.

Next, *do an internal assessment* of the company's capabilities. This is analogous to examining capabilities and resources of the expedition team.

Third, *do an external assessment* of the environment, markets, competitors, and trends. This is analogous to studying pictures of the mountain, examining weather reports, assessing new trends in technology that might help you in your ascent, and paying attention to competitors who seek to reach the summit ahead of you.

Finally, taking the internal and external assessments into account, *make key decisions* about how you intend to go about achieving your current mission. This is analogous to mapping out the route you are going to take up the side of the mountain.

Break the strategic decisions down into each of the key components of the business. We find the following categories work well:

- Products (or services); includes product line strategy and manufacturing strategy (or service delivery strategy)
- Customers (or market segments); includes who the customers are that you're serving and how you intend to reach them
- Cash Flow (financial strategy)
- People and Organization
- Infrastructure

Internal Assessment

There are three components of a good internal assessment:

- Strengths and weaknesses
- Resources
- Innovations and new ideas

Diagram of Vision, Strategy, Tactics

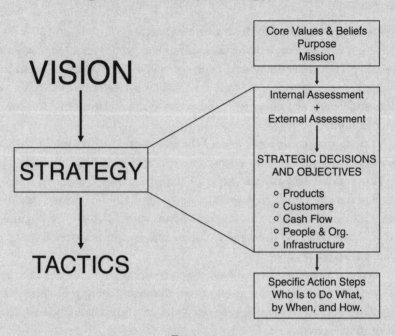

VISION

↓

STRATEGY

↓

TACTICS

Core Values & Beliefs
Purpose
Mission

↓

Internal Assessment
+
External Assessment

↓

STRATEGIC DECISIONS
AND OBJECTIVES

- ○ Products
- ○ Customers
- ○ Cash Flow
- ○ People & Org.
- ○ Infrastructure

Specific Action Steps
Who Is to Do What,
by When, and How.

Figure 7-1

STRENGTHS AND WEAKNESSES

The first thing you need is a clear assessment of what your company is really good at and its blind spots. Remember, strategy should leverage off your strengths.

To get an objective reading on your strengths and weaknesses, we suggest asking a selection of employees and managers to list the top three strengths and the top three weaknesses of the company. To ensure candor, it's sometimes useful to have these submitted anonymously.

It's also valuable to get outside input on this question. Ask trusted advisors, investors, and board members what they see as your strengths and weaknesses. You might even ask a few key customer accounts (which has the additional benefit of developing a closer relationship with your customers).

A particularly useful question is, "What are we better at than anyone else, and what are our unique capabilities that give us a competitive advantage?" The literature of strategic management ascribes a ponderous term to this notion ("Distinctive Competence"), but the idea is really pretty simple. It's also important. Simply put, smart firms stick to doing things they can do better than other firms.

Why should an endurance athlete try to compete in the 100 meter dash? Why should a football linebacker try to become an ice skating champion? Why should an engineering-driven firm try to compete primarily on marketing skills? Why should a company that's great at high-end, well-designed products try to compete in the low-price commodity segment of a market? Why would Walmart try to compete directly with Nordstrom?

This doesn't mean that you shouldn't try to eradicate crippling weaknesses. Any great company is continually working on its weaknesses, always seeking improvement, and your basic strategy should play to your strengths. Do what you're good at.

RESOURCES

Next you want to get a clear picture of your resources. Specific categories of resources to consider might include: cash flow, access to outside capital, scarce materials, production capacity, and people.

INNOVATIONS AND NEW IDEAS

A company can shape its market by innovation as much as a market can shape a company by its demands. Yet innovation is one of the most overlooked aspects of setting strategy.

Make sure that your company is responsive to its own internal creative output. Examine what new innovations and new ideas are bubbling up in product development, research, design, and marketing. List all possible innovations that might come to fruition. Obtain estimates on how quickly the innovation could be made marketable, the level of resources required to complete its development, and the level of marketing required.

The last thing you want to do is kill new ideas and innovations just because they're not planned. In fact, most great ideas are not planned, and if you introduce only products that are planned five years in advance, it's unlikely that you'll produce any breakthrough products.

Innovation is such an important part of corporate greatness that we devote all of Chapter 8 to it. Furthermore, innovation can have a dramatic effect on your strategic options.

The development of the tank, for example, was not part of the allied war strategy at the start of World War I. However, the invention of the tank altered the allied strategy at the end of the war. The generals didn't say, "Our strategy calls for a tank. Build us one." No, the tank was invented by a British War Department skunk-works and presented to the generals who then said, "Hey, we should change our strategy to use this thing."

The same phenomenon occurs in companies, as with HP's entry into pocket calculators, NIKE's "sock-racer" product strategy, Intel's entry into computer add-on boards, and literally hundreds of product strategies developed by 3M. Innovation should be able to influence strategy as much as your strategy should stimulate innovation. Innovation and strategy in a great company are inextricably linked.

External Assessment

There are seven components of a good external assessment:

- Industry/market trends
- Technology trends
- Competitor assessment
- Social and regulatory environment
- Macroeconomy and demographics
- International threats and opportunities
- Overall threats and opportunities

INDUSTRY/MARKET TRENDS

Take a quick snapshot of your industry.

- How are your markets segmented, and in which segments do you compete?
- Roughly, how large are the market segments for your current product line and planned future products?
- Are the market segments for your products (services) growing, stable, or shrinking? How fast? Why?
- What are the dominant trends in your industry? What are the underlying forces behind those trends?
- *Most importantly*, what are your customers telling you about their evolving needs? What are they telling you about how well your company is meeting their needs? How are customer demands changing? Direct input from your customers is an essential part of setting strategy. Get input directly from your customers regularly. They can tell you what's going on in your market because they *are* the market. They can also tell you about your competitors. It's wise to survey your customers at least once per year as an integral part of setting strategy.

- At what stage of evolution is your industry? What does this imply in terms of how the industry might change in the next five years? See nearby diagram, "Stages of Industry Evolution," as a backdrop to this analysis. (Various versions of this chart are common in strategic management and marketing literature. A more detailed version can be found in *Competitive Strategy* by Michael Porter.)

Note: The stages of industry evolution analysis can be an enormously useful tool, but do not assume that all industries evolve the same exact way. See the note at the end of this chapter: "Caveats to Industry Evolution Analysis."

TECHNOLOGY TRENDS

All industries, even "low tech" industries, have a technology component to their evolution, either in products or in process. Every industry is somehow affected by changes in technology. For example, the banking industry, which has not historically been known as "high tech," was nonetheless dramatically changed by computer technology. In back-room processing, effective use of computers became a key strategic advantage for those who mastered their use quickly. In services to customers, adoption of ATMs became an essential part of banking services.

Examine the technology trends in your own industry and ask how you can best use them to your advantage. The question is not whether technology trends will affect your industry, but *how*.

COMPETITOR ASSESSMENT

Never underestimate your competition. One of the biggest mistakes in mapping out a strategy is doing so in ignorance of the competition or, worse, with disdain for the competition.

- Who are your current competitors?
- Who are potential competitors?
- What are their strengths and weaknesses?
- What do you anticipate as being their future moves in the market? What are *their* visions and strategies?
- How do your strengths, weaknesses, and product line stack up against the competition? Where are they vulnerable? Where are you vulnerable?
- Do you have a clear, differentiated position with respect to your competitors? What is it?

Stages of Industry Evolution

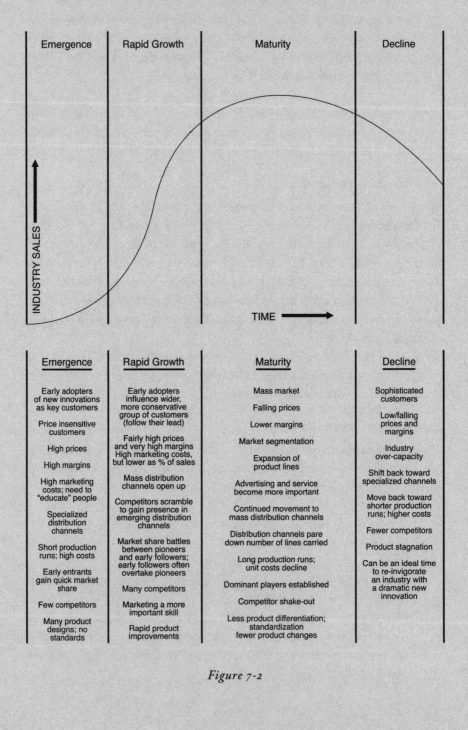

Emergence	Rapid Growth	Maturity	Decline
Early adopters of new innovations as key customers	Early adopters influence wider, more conservative group of customers (follow their lead)	Mass market	Sophisticated customers
Price insensitive customers		Falling prices	Low/falling prices and margins
High prices	Fairly high prices and very high margins High marketing costs, but lower as % of sales	Lower margins	
High margins		Market segmentation	Industry over-capacity
High marketing costs; need to "educate" people	Mass distribution channels open up	Expansion of product lines	Shift back toward specialized channels
Specialized distribution channels	Competitors scramble to gain presence in emerging distribution channels	Advertising and service become more important	Move back toward shorter production runs; higher costs
Short production runs; high costs	Market share battles between pioneers and early followers; early followers often overtake pioneers	Continued movement to mass distribution channels	Fewer competitors
Early entrants gain quick market share		Distribution channels pare down number of lines carried	Product stagnation
Few competitors	Many competitors	Long production runs; unit costs decline	Can be an ideal time to re-invigorate an industry with a dramatic new innovation
Many product designs; no standards	Marketing a more important skill	Dominant players established	
	Rapid product improvements	Competitor shake-out	
		Less product differentiation; standardization fewer product changes	

Figure 7-2

Getting competitor information is fairly easy. Get on the mailing list for your competitor's press releases, publications, and promotional materials. Attend trade shows. Listen to your sales force. Listen to your suppliers. Listen to customers. Listen to technical employees who keep abreast of technology developments. Read trade and business journal articles about your industry and/or your competitors. Read the business section of newspapers in towns where your competitors are located.

Be careful about how you gain competitor information. Under pressure, people can be easily tempted to misrepresent themselves to obtain competitor information on your behalf. This often happens with outside consultants who pose as "students doing a school project on your industry," or who call a competitor saying that they're "doing an internal audit." There are two problems with this. First, it's unethical. Second, it can leave you vulnerable to lawsuits.

For example, in the early 1980s, a prominent strategy consulting firm and one of its clients were sued—successfully—when a young researcher called into a competitor's manufacturing operations, posed as a member of the competitor's finance department, and asked for proprietary cost information.

SOCIAL AND REGULATORY ENVIRONMENT

All companies exist as integral parts of society-at-large, and are affected by powerful social, regulatory, and political forces. Keep abreast of these forces and assess how they might affect your company. Astute anticipation of governmental moves or regulatory-body decisions can create tremendous opportunities. Conversely, ignorance of the same can be disastrous.

MACROECONOMY AND DEMOGRAPHICS

Examine the general macroeconomic climate and assess what impact the overall economy might have on your company.

Pay particular attention to demographic trends. Entire industries can be dramatically affected by demographic changes. For example, the United States's "baby boom" (a gigantic bulge in the birth rate from 1945 to 1960) will continue to have a profound impact on a wide range of industries until at least the year 2020. This is only one of many demographic forces.

For companies doing business in the United States, a subscription to *American Demographics* magazine can be very useful. We also suggest scanning the *Statistical Abstract of The United States* each year to get a macro view of demographic trends.

INTERNATIONAL THREATS AND OPPORTUNITIES

Factor international into your strategic thinking, even if you don't currently sell in foreign markets. International strategy is relevant for all companies; no matter what your size, there will probably be forces pulling you into the international arena. Small companies with good products are often approached by foreign distributors, retailers, resellers, and potential customers.

In an interesting and surprising study, David Birch analyzed the data from 34,000 exporters and found that those companies with between 50 and 500 employees were actually *more* likely to be exporters than larger companies.

When setting strategy, assume that participation in the international arena is a viable possibility and, furthermore, that international opportunities will present themselves unexpectedly. It may not make sense within the context of your vision to take advantage of these opportunities, but you should nonetheless make international an explicit part of your strategy, even if you decide to stay domestic.

Even if you decide not to compete in other countries, it's likely that at least one of your major competitors will be foreign. The days of purely domestic markets are gone forever, and competitor analysis should include a watchful eye on the international landscape.

OVERALL THREATS AND OPPORTUNITIES

In preparing for a strategy session, ask a selected group of employees, managers, and objective outsiders to list the top three external opportunities and top three external threats facing the company. This is a quick and efficient way to tap the insights of a range of people as input to your external assessment.

Throughout the internal and external assessment process, it's absolutely paramount that you do everything possible to see reality—to see things as they really are and not the way you wish they were.

Indeed, one of the things that characterizes great companies is the willingness of their leaders and managers to relentlessly seek the truth, regardless of whether it's good news or bad news. Yet, we have observed that it's all too common for companies to behave just the opposite.

One of us (Jim) worked early in his career for a manager who was horrified at the idea of telling his superiors about problems with a soon-to-be-released product. "Upper management doesn't want to hear bad news," the manager counseled. "Just tell them what they want to hear and they'll be happy. If you give them reality, you'll be viewed as having a negative attitude."

The risk of this approach, of course, is that reality has a funny way of making itself known. You can't submerge it forever, and if you try, it usually comes back to nail you. In the above-mentioned case, the product weaknesses did indeed become apparent, but only *after* the product was on the market. If the company had confronted the problems directly and corrected them *before* going to market, a multimillion dollar catastrophe could have been avoided.

(Incidentally, Jim decided to go against his manager's advice and he raised the issue with senior management. He discovered that his manager was right: they didn't want to hear reality, and they plowed ahead with a doomed product.)

Unfortunately, this is not an isolated incident. Most of us are familiar with situations where people are unwilling or afraid to present unpleasant truths. In many cases, who can blame them? The unspoken rule in all too many companies is: We don't want to see anything negative, even if it is true; we like our rose-colored glasses.

Ignoring facts, explaining away problems, and refusing to see the world as it really is doesn't change reality. It only invites catastrophe.

To illustrate this point, we like to use a vivid example from world history: the decade leading up to World War II. In the 1930s, British, American, and French officials were confronted with an overwhelming series of unpleasant facts: Germany built military arms in violation of the Treaty of Versailles, German forces moved into the Rhineland, Hitler ordered military conscription, Germany devoured Austria and Czechoslovakia.

Yet, amazingly, these facts were not acted upon. Hitler was planning for a major war, but allied officials did not want to see this unpleasant (not to mention politically unpopular) truth. So they behaved much as if the facts did not exist.

In his book *The Gathering Storm*, Winston Churchill described how Neville Chamberlain, Prime Minister of Britain 1937–40, deluded himself:

> His all pervading hope was to go down to history as the great peacemaker, and for this he was prepared to strive continually in the teeth of facts. I begged the government to get these brutal truths into their heads. Had we responded to the facts as they became evident, war could have been averted without the loss of blood.

But these "brutal truths" didn't sink in until it was too late and a devastating war engulfed Europe.

Does this lesson from world history apply to setting business strategy? You bet it does. Whether leading a nation or managing a company, the lesson is the same: ignore reality and it will come back and smack you in the face. It's very important to prevent this from happening in your company.

There are a number of things you can do to ensure that you are not protected from reality.

First, surround yourself with people who tell it like it is. Strange as it seems, this is not an easy task. For one thing, most people know that telling the truth can be politically dangerous and many, like the manager mentioned earlier, are terrified of political fallout.

You need at least a few people around you who aren't afraid of you and who aren't concerned with politics. This is where detached and objective outsiders (consultants and directors) are invaluable. You also need honest people inside—people who are so honest and direct they are almost uncomfortable to have around. You don't have to like them. You just need to listen to them.

Churchill, for example, felt so strongly about this that he created a separate department whose sole responsibility was to root out and present the naked truth about pressing issues. Leaders of great companies never hesitate to reward what Thomas J. Watson, Jr. called "those sharp, scratchy, harsh, almost unpleasant individuals who see and tell you about things as they really are."

Second, personally stay in touch with what's happening. Don't rely solely on status reports or quarterly reviews, and other formal reporting methods for information. Use your company's products. Listen directly to employees at all levels. Talk to customers. Read consumer reports about your products. Personally answer customer complaints. In short, do whatever you can to keep in touch with reality.

Third, never punish people for telling the truth. We all know the story of how Peter the Great responded to the messenger who brought him news of defeat: he executed him.

None of us like to see reality when it's unpleasant or disappointing; all of us are guilty, at least to some degree, of wanting rose-colored glasses. This is no excuse for punishing those who tell us the truth, and the tendency to do so must be vigorously resisted. If people raise a problem or an unpleasant issue, don't chastise them or treat them as if they have a bad attitude. Thank them.

The point here is not that your company should tolerate bellyaching, cynicism, and hopeless despair. None of us has time for that kind of nonsense. The point is that effective strategic decisions can only be made if you are not sheltered from reality, no matter how unpleasant that reality may be.

The Essence of Strategy

In the years since the original edition of *Beyond Entrepreneurship*, I've continued to reflect on the topic of strategy. Drawing upon our research into what makes great companies tick, working with organizations at our management lab in Boulder, and learning from great military leaders and thinkers, I've come to see that sound strategic thinking (once you have clarity of vision) boils down to having insightful, empirically validated answers to three essential questions:

1. Where to place our big bets?
2. How to protect our flanks?
3. How to extend our victories?

WHERE TO PLACE OUR BIG BETS?

The intellectual foundations of strategy trace their roots to history's great military thinkers. In particular, Carl von Clausewitz profoundly influenced the entire field of strategic thinking with his work *On War*. Clausewitz crystalized the thesis of concentrating force into a conflict's center of gravity (where victories would have the greatest impact on military success and achievement of national purpose). "There is no higher and simpler law of strategy than that of *keeping one's forces concentrated*," wrote Clausewitz. (Side note: If you're interested in a smart overview of the history of military strategy, including Clausewitz's work, I recommend U.S. Naval War College Professor Andrew R. Wilson's Teaching Company course *Masters of War: History's Greatest Strategic Thinkers*. I also recommend the essays of retired West Point professor Dr. Michael Hennelly, who has done extensive thinking on the translation of strategic principles into the business world.)

Of course, we should be careful in making a wholesale analogy from military strategy to business strategy. In the military, you develop a strategy to destroy an enemy and force him to capitulate within the context of a clear national/political objective. Whereas in business, you develop a strategy to win customers by creating something of value and making their lives better within the context of a clear corporate vision. That said, this central idea—concentration of force, brilliantly directed into the best opportunities to achieve outsized results—correlates directly with superior strategic outcomes.

Every great company we studied made a few exceptionally good, highly concentrated big bets at pivotal points in their histories. Nucor bet big on mini-mills for manufacturing steel, creating a good-to-great inflection from a nearly failed company with a mish-mash of unrelated businesses into one of the most profitable steel companies in America. Microsoft bet big on Windows, powering its rise from a small computer-languages start-up into one of the most successful software companies in the world. Walt Disney bet big on animated films, then bet big again on Disneyland as the primary inflection from small animated-film company into a major entertainment enterprise. Kroger bet big on superstores, while its chief rival A&P began a long decline to irrelevance and death when it chose to forgo a similar big bet. Apple made a series of big bets throughout its history, from the Apple II and the Macintosh to the iPhone and iPad. Amgen tried a bunch of ideas using recombinant-DNA technology early in its history, and then bet big on EPO (erythropoietin) for low blood cell conditions; the breakout drug catapulted Amgen into becoming one of the first great biotech companies. Southwest Airlines bet big that coupling a simple, low-cost operating model with a loving company culture could give the freedom to fly to people who'd rarely flown before; building on this bet, Southwest Airlines turned itself from a cash-strapped start-up with three aircraft into the most consistently profitable airline in the United States.

Of course, you need *good* big bets. The *wrong* big bets can damage or even cripple a very successful company. So, then, what makes a good big bet distinct from a bad big bet? *Empirical validation*. This is what the principle "Fire Bullets, Then Cannonballs" from *Great by Choice* is all about (described previously, in The Map chapter).

When Robert Noyce and Gordon Moore resigned from Fairchild Semiconductor to launch the start-up semiconductor-chip company Intel, it was one of more than a dozen new semiconductor companies founded at roughly the same time in a nascent Silicon Valley. They didn't have a specific product, but they'd empirically validated "Moore's Law." Moore had calculated that the number of components per integrated circuit that could be produced at minimum cost doubled roughly every year. They decided to bet their new company on the inevitable breakthroughs that would come from this geometric progression.

Next, Noyce and Moore had to place a bet on a specific product line. But on what? They portioned their limited gunpowder into three bullets to fire on three separate ways of designing memory chips. As Leslie Berlin details in her well-researched book *The Man Behind the Microchip*, they didn't know which path would merit the big bet, so they had to explore all three. The team led by Andy Grove and Les Vadasz pursued memory chips built with a MOS (metal-oxide-silicon) technique. Their second chip based on this technology, the 1103, gave Intel a breakthrough: the first semiconductor memory that could compete on price with traditional core memories. Following this, the then tiny company decided to bet big, firing a cannonball on the 1103 and subsequent line of memory chips. The 1103 became the best-selling memory chip in the world, and the subsequent family of chips provided a foundation for Intel's breakout from struggling start-up into successful company. Had Intel not fired multiple bullets to discover which path would work, it might have placed a bad big bet. Fortunately, Intel's founders had the discipline to test and evaluate before placing the big bet.

Any truly successful strategy involves making carefully calibrated big bets. You need empirical validation that the big bet fits with what you are passionate about, what you can be the best at, and what drives your economic engine (your Hedgehog Concept). The best way to know for sure something will work on a large scale is to have proven it first on a small scale. Fire bullets, then cannonballs.

HOW TO PROTECT OUR FLANKS?

The dominant pattern of history isn't stability, but instability; the dominant pattern of business isn't perpetuation of the incumbents, but triumph of the insurgents; the dominant pattern of capitalism isn't equilibrium, but what Joseph Schumpeter famously described as the "perennial gale of creative destruction." In a dangerous, turbulent world full of threats and disruptions, you need to "protect your flanks"—identify and protect against vulnerabilities that, if exposed or exploited, could kill or cripple you.

In May 1940, early in the Second World War, Winston Churchill faced a critical strategic decision. As Nazi Panzer divisions roared across the French countryside supported by Luftwaffe dive bombers, the British deployed to help counter the assault. By May 14, the German armies had breached the French lines, and French officials pleaded with the British to send more squadrons of British Air Force fighters into the battle to save France. The British had resolved to do everything possible to help France repel the Nazi invaders, but at the same time, Churchill had to prepare for the very real possibility that Hitler would defeat France and then turn his deranged fury against England. Churchill and his War Cabinet considered a crux strategic question: How many fighter planes would be needed to defend the Island should France fall? The answer: twenty-five squadrons.

"My colleagues and I were resolved to run all risks for the sake of the battle up to that limit [the twenty-five squadrons]—and those risks were very great—but not to go beyond it, no matter what the consequences might be," wrote Churchill. France did fall, and Hitler turned his sights on invading the Island, which was predicated on gaining dominance in the air. Reichsmarschall Goering felt confident that his Luftwaffe would win the air Battle of Britain and bomb the British into submission. But the twenty-five squadrons proved enough. The British pilots prevailed; Hitler shelved his plans to invade; England stood defiant.

Everything changed on December 7, 1941, with the attack on Pearl Harbor that jolted the United States out of its isolationist posture and into the fight. Churchill later wrote of the moment he learned of the attack: "We then went back into the hall and tried to adjust our thoughts to the supreme world event which had occurred, which was of so startling a nature as to make even those who were near the centre gasp. . . . England would live; Britain would live; the Commonwealth of Nations and the Empire would live. How long the war would last or in what fashion it would end no man could tell, nor did I at this moment care. Once again in our long Island history we should emerge, however mauled or mutilated, safe and victorious. We should not be wiped out. Our history would not come to an end. We might not even have to die as individuals."

But what would have happened without the twenty-five squadrons?

You've got to keep your cause alive long enough for events to play out. If your company gets killed or knocked out of the game, it doesn't matter if luck might later turn your way. This means knowing and having your buffers and reserves—your twenty-five squadrons—in place to absorb setbacks, attacks, bad luck, and even your own blunders so that you have the option to persist. *What are your twenty-five squadrons?*

In our research for *Great by Choice*, Morten Hansen and I systematically analyzed why some start-ups become the 10x winners in highly turbulent, chaotic, and disruptive industries, and why others don't. One of our key findings is that the winners exercise prodigious amounts of productive paranoia. Our research showed that they carried a much higher cash-to-assets ratio than less successful companies as a disciplined habit from early in their development. (Think of a conservative balance sheet as one element of the twenty-five squadrons.) They worried obsessively about unexpected events that could destroy them, and they built buffers so they could survive external shocks. They also shunned uncalibrated risks that could leave them exposed to calamity.

New industries, especially those driven by emerging technologies, often go through a Cambrian-explosion phase, with dozens or hundreds of new companies bursting forth. But then many of those early companies disappear as the industry sorts itself out. Some of them die outright because they mismanage their available cash during heady times and fail to preserve their twenty-five squadrons. If you emerge from the Cambrian explosion and achieve success, you need to become even more paranoid. Your very success can envelop you in a cocoon of comfort that insulates you from perilous changes sneaking up with "little cat feet" (in the words of Andy Grove).

I've puzzled for years over the question of why some companies fail to adapt quickly enough to what Clayton Christensen called "disruptive innovation," while others don't. Reflecting on cases in our research studies, I've concluded that the primary answer is really quite simple—*failure to apply productive paranoia, not just in the short term, but also with a fifteen-plus-year time frame.* When executive teams visit my management lab in Boulder, I often ask them the following three questions:

1. What significant changes in your world (both inside your company and in the external environment) are you highly confident will have happened by fifteen years from now?
2. Which of those changes pose a significant or existential threat to your company?
3. What do you need to begin doing *now*—*with urgency*—to march ahead of those changes?

Morten Hansen and I learned an essential lesson from our research: It's what you do *before* the storm comes that most determines how well you do when the storm comes. Those who fully embrace productive paranoia don't wait until they're caught high on a mountain in a raging storm to secure extra oxygen canisters. Far better to be a paranoid neurotic freak, preparing and marching ahead of potential disruptive shocks that may never come than to get crushed by disruptive shocks because you failed to exercise productive paranoia all the way along, in good times and bad.

It's hard to see the difference between greatness and mediocrity in good times, when almost everyone is thriving. But when the turbulent times come, the difference becomes stark; the companies that exercised productive paranoia far in advance will pull ahead of the weak mediocrities. And even if the ill-prepared survive the disruptive shock, they will likely never close the gap.

The strong and well prepared before the storm continue to pull ahead, never to look back.

HOW TO EXTEND OUR VICTORIES?

At the Battle of Gettysburg, in July 1863, Confederate General Robert E. Lee failed to defeat the Union forces. By the end of the three-day battle, Lee had lost a third of his army, at least twenty-three thousand killed, wounded, or captured. He'd also lost command leaders in comparable proportions, including more than a dozen of his generals. The prospects for Confederate success in the Civil War depended directly upon the success or failure of Lee's Army of Northern Virginia, which in turn depended directly on the leadership genius of Lee himself. As University of Virginia professor Gary Gallagher teaches in his Teaching Company courses Robert E. Lee and His High Command and The American Civil War, if Lee fell, the Confederacy would almost certainly fall.

But what did the Union Army do in the aftermath of its victory at Gettysburg, when it had a perfect opportunity to perhaps crush the Army of Northern Virginia once and for all? It let Lee escape across the Potomac River.

After Lee's escape, Lincoln poured his anguish into a letter he never sent to Major General George Gordon Meade, who led the Union forces at Gettysburg. "Again, my dear general," Lincoln lamented, "I do not believe you appreciate the magnitude of the misfortune involved in Lee's escape. He was within your easy grasp, and to have closed upon him would, in connection with our other late successes, have ended the war. As it is, the war will be prolonged indefinitely. . . . Your golden opportunity is gone, and I am distressed immeasurably because of it." The vast carnage of war continued for nearly another two years before Lee surrendered to General Ulysses S. Grant at Appomattox in April 1865.

Clausewitz insisted on aggressively following up after concentrating force at the decisive point. Any strategy that doesn't account for how to exploit victory is incomplete, inadequate. "What remains true under all imaginable conditions," he wrote, "is that no victory will be effective without pursuit; and no matter how brief the exploitation of victory, it must always go further than an immediate follow-up."

In the years since the original edition of *Beyond Entrepreneurship*, my research colleagues and I have systematically studied some of the most impressive multi-decade episodes of entrepreneurial success in all of corporate history. We examined every major strategic step taken in the rise from small-to-great of companies like 3M, Amgen, Apple, Ford, IBM, Intel, Kroger, Marriott, Merck, Microsoft, Nucor, Progressive Insurance, Southwest Airlines, Stryker, Walmart, Walt Disney, and others. And I've continued my work, learning from sustained growth machines like Amazon and Vanguard. (Again, as a reminder, while the companies we studied did indeed become gigantic corporations, our research studies traced back to when they were tiny, entrepreneurial ventures. Our work is not primarily about big companies; it is much more about what not-yet-great companies do to become great.) Our studies highlight that the most significant results come not just in seizing one moment, but in relentlessly making the most of successful big bets.

Making the most of victories is what the flywheel principle is all about (see the previous chapter on The Map for a brief description of the flywheel concept). I've come to see the flywheel effect as one of the most important strategic principles to come from all of our research into why some companies become great, why some fail to become great, and why some fall from greatness. The big winners are those that take a flywheel from ten turns to a billion turns rather than crank through ten turns, start over with a new flywheel, push it to ten turns, only to divert energy into yet another new flywheel, then another and another. Conversely, we've found that one of the most costly strategic blunders is failing to make the most of victories, failing to fully realize the flywheel effect.

Turning the flywheel doesn't mean doing the same thing, mindlessly repeating what you've done before. It means exploiting, expanding, extending. It means evolving and creating. It doesn't mean Microsoft in its early days sticking with Windows 1 or 2; it means creating Windows 3, Windows 95, Windows 98, Windows XP, Windows 7, Windows 8, Windows 10, and beyond. It doesn't mean Apple repeating the first-generation iPhone over and over; it means a relentless, nonstop evolution and re-creation of the iPhone line. It doesn't mean Southwest Airlines staying in Texas, with the same tired old aircraft on its original triangle loop of Dallas-San Antonio-Houston; it means continually upgrading to the most advanced versions of the 737, moving in concentric circles out across the country, winning market after market. It doesn't mean start-up Amazon selling only books online; it means evolving and expanding the Amazon e-commerce marketplace and its supporting delivery systems to become one of the most ubiquitous and expansive stores in all of human history.

In *How the Mighty Fall*, we studied once-great companies that brought about their own senseless self-destruction. In that research, we found that becoming seduced by the "Next Big Thing"—and thereby neglecting or abandoning the flywheel—is enormously dangerous. To disrespect the potential remaining in your primary flywheel (or worse, to neglect that flywheel out of boredom while you turn your attention to The Next Big Thing in the arrogant belief that its success will continue almost automatically) is hubris. And while you must create robust new extensions to your flywheel (and given enough time, you might even create entirely new flywheels) be sure to keep building momentum with your winning strategies. Never forget, the Next Big Thing is very likely the Big Thing you already have. Make the most of your victories. Keep turning the flywheel.

NEVER FORGET: VISION FIRST

The three elements of strategy described above (big bets, protect flanks, and extend victories) can guide your strategic thinking. But never forget, sound strategy is impossible without clear vision. Muddled strategies flow from muddled vision; clear strategies flow from clear vision. If you want to have a good strategy, you need to first understand with piercing clarity what you are trying to achieve. A good strategy determines how you will achieve your BHAG, guided by your purpose and consistent with your values. Vision *then* strategy *then* tactics.

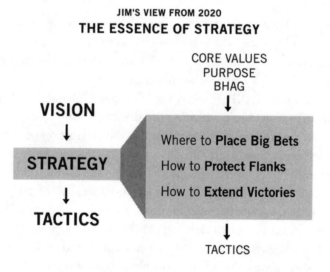

JIM'S VIEW FROM 2020
THE ESSENCE OF STRATEGY

CORE VALUES
PURPOSE
BHAG

VISION

STRATEGY

TACTICS

Where to **Place Big Bets**

How to **Protect Flanks**

How to **Extend Victories**

TACTICS

Think again of your BHAG like a big mountain to climb. Once you've clarified your core values and purpose, you set a BHAG, get the right people on the team, and set a strategy. Then you break the climb down into base camps, which are three- to-five-year targets that move you up the mountain.

Then you set your top priorities for the coming year, the strategic imperatives you must accomplish along the way to your next base camp. Once you hit the base camp, you adjust and clarify your second base camp, then repeat again for your third base camp, and so forth, until you reach the BHAG. Then you set a new BHAG. Repeat, again and again, forever.

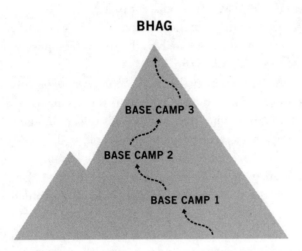

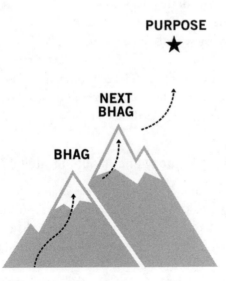

Making Strategic Decisions

Keep in mind the image of a balanced three-legged stool; each leg should be strong in order for the stool to be stable. To make solid strategic decisions, you need *each* of the three legs: vision, internal assessment, and external assessment. Once you have done each of these, strategic decision will, in most cases, be fairly obvious. (See diagram on adjacent page.)

Be sure to pay as much attention to common sense, seasoned judgment, and intuition as to hardheaded analysis. Don't overcomplicate the strategy. Keep it simple and straightforward.

On paper, the basic strategy should fit on *no more than three typed pages*. This may be shocking to those who think of strategic plans as thick, turgid documents. But keep in mind that no one reads thick, turgid documents. Instead think of creating a strategic guide that people at all levels can easily absorb. Specific tactical or implementation plans might be more than three pages, but the basic strategy should be short, clear, and elegant. (In fact, you should be able to capture the essence of the strategy in a few well-worded sentences.)

A useful approach is to take the five primary categories of a business—products (or services), customers (market segments), cash flow, people and organization, and infrastructure—and map out the key elements of your strategy in each of them. An example of the output from such a strategy formulation is included at the end of this chapter.

What about all the boxes, bubbles, grids, and matrices that connote strategic planning? Some of these tools can be useful, but keep in mind that most of these were developed for use in large, multi-business companies. They are, in general, not as relevant in small to mid-sized companies. The best small company strategists don't use complicated matrices or bubble-boxes. Instead, they tend to use good old-fashioned clearheaded thinking.

The Multi-Year Rolling Strategy and Annual Strategic Priorities

It's seldom useful to lay out more than a five-year strategy. Some companies go no further than three years. We suggest having a three- to five-year strategy, revised annually. Think of strategy as dynamic, rather than static—as something that changes and evolves as your internal situation and the external environment changes.

It's also essential to set the top five strategic priorities for the coming year, with a specific person being responsible for each priority.

The Three Legs of Setting Strategy

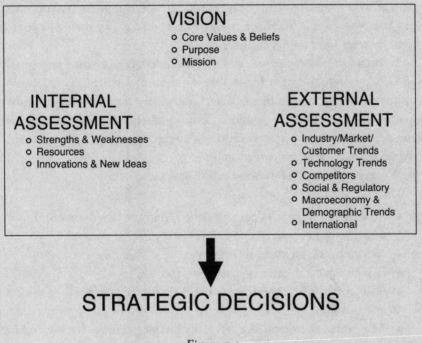

Figure 7-3

Try not to have any more than five strategic priorities for the year. If everything is a priority, then you have no priorities. Even the best companies can only concentrate on a few key issues at a time. (The example given at the end of this chapter also shows such a strategic priority formulation.)

The Annual Strategy Meeting

One of the most effective methods for setting and revisiting strategy is to schedule an off-site strategy meeting once per year. Attendees should include key people from each area of the company. The ideal group size is somewhere between five and ten people. Twenty should be the absolute maximum, although we would strongly encourage you to keep the size under ten.

Some companies have found it useful to hire an outside consultant/facilitator to work with the group during the off-site meeting. Other companies prefer to keep the process entirely internal.

Prior to the meeting, each participant should be asked to prepare by answering a few questions. These questions should be circulated to the participants at least a week prior to the meeting. The content of the questions will vary from year to year, and from company to company, but should be related to the internal and external assessment.

To stimulate people to come to the meeting well prepared, we suggest asking each person to prepare a ten- to twenty-minute presentation on a specific topic. Few things capture people's attention better than knowing that they need to make a public presentation. Certain individuals might take on specific preparation tasks, such as industry/market trends, technology trends, new innovations, and competitor analysis.

We suggest using the following rough agenda:

- Review vision (core values and beliefs, purpose, and mission). Ensure that the vision is agreed upon and crystal clear.
- As a group, do an internal assessment.
- As a group, do an external assessment.
- As a group, decide upon/revise the basic strategy for reaching the current mission.
- As a group, decide on the top five strategic priorities for the coming year.

Someone should have responsibility for summarizing in writing the results of the meeting. This summary can be used as the strategic "guide" and should be distributed to all key people, referred to constantly, and used in setting individual goals and milestones (covered in Chapter 9).

Four Common Key Strategic Issues That Face Small to Mid-Sized Companies

The following four key strategic issues commonly faced by small to mid-sized companies:

- How fast to grow
- Focus versus diversification
- Whether to go public
- Whether to lead a market or follow

How Fast to Grow

In an interview with Bill Hewlett and Dave Packard of HP, they were asked what one piece of advice they would give to people building companies. Hewlett responded:

> Don't grow too fast. You need to grow slow enough to develop good management. Venture capitalists often push these young companies too fast. But if you push too fast, you lose your values.

Growth is one of the most controversial and least understood strategic decisions. Notice that we said decision. How fast you want to grow should be an explicit strategic decision.

Growth is not *de facto* good (or bad for that matter), and rapid growth should not automatically be viewed as a desirable aim. This may sound like heresy to those who believe that a good manager should strive for as much growth as possible. However, the decision to grow rapidly should not be a foregone conclusion and, indeed, there may be reasons *not* to grow rapidly.

The question of growth should, as with all key decisions, tie back to the vision of the company. Do you even want to *be* a big company? Do you want the downsides that rapid growth brings?

Are there downsides to growth? Yes.

For one thing, rapid growth can create a perilous cash flow situation. A common pattern is that a company shells out cash to purchase materials and labor in anticipation of rapid sales increases. It then turns those materials into products and sales but, as you know, cash doesn't come in until months after the initial purchases. If the company doesn't hit its forecasts, cash is tied up in inventory. Cash is like blood or oxygen; without it, you die. And growth eats cash. This is why *roughly half of all bankruptcies occur after a year of record sales*.

There are many other downsides to rapid growth, including the following:

- Rapid growth can hide gross inefficiencies that don't show up until the growth slows.
- Rapid growth stretches a company's infrastructure, often past the breaking point.
- A rapid-growth strategy can pressure your salesforce to commit to prices that severely cut your margins.
- There is tremendous human cost. The stress and strain on people during a rapid growth phase can be extreme.

- Rapid growth leads to increased organizational complexity and reduced communications.
- Large companies tend to be less fun, and rapid growth just brings that about sooner.
- Rapid growth can quickly dilute the culture of your company, making it very difficult to develop management and reinforce your values.

THE WARM BODIES SYNDROME

This dilution of culture comes about largely by what we call the warm bodies syndrome. We've seen companies in a growth frenzy relax their hiring standards: "I don't care who you get. For heaven's sake, just get me a warm body. I need people!"

Warm bodies don't necessarily hold your values. And they might not live up to your standards of excellence. Rapid growth puts pressure on you to be much less discerning in whom you hire; and hiring is one place you want to be extremely careful.

Rapid growth can—and often does—evolve into a growth-for-growth's-sake mentality, which can then undercut the solidity of the company. For example, Osborne Computer priced its computers below cost in an effort to continue its heady growth. Of course, anyone can sell dollar bills for eighty cents—for a while. And Osborne did, right up to the time that it went bankrupt.

CASE EXAMPLE: LIGHTCRAFT

One of us (Bill) was intimately involved with a classic situation where pushing for too much growth was a very poor strategic decision.

Lightcraft, a premier provider of lighting fixtures, competed on superior design, service, and excellent internal management (especially inventory management).

Lightcraft performed very well while it pursued a moderate-growth strategy (10% to 15% annual growth rate). During this time, the company had profit margins far in excess of the industry average, and it was known throughout the industry as an outstanding company with a reputation for consistent tactical excellence.

Then the company was sold to Nu-Tone. The new owners decided to pursue a rapid-growth strategy—50% the first year, which required an entirely different set of management skills than moderate growth. This put a strain on the company. Revenues in the prior year had been

$6 million. Nu-Tone pushed for $9 million in the next year. Bill tells the story best:

> The Nu-Tone salesforce, which replaced Lightcraft's sales reps, began giving discounts that cut deeply into our margins. We had built a big new facility to handle the increase in volume. The building, through an unfortunate set of circumstances, developed structural defects resulting in chunks of concrete falling from the ceiling. Our inventory got out of control—we couldn't manage it as well as we used to, and we had a lot of cash tied up in it. At the rate we were going, we just couldn't provide the same level of customer service. Our whole infrastructure was pressed to the limit, and we began to lose the edge that made us so excellent in the first place.

Lightcraft grew to $7.2 million that year—which would have been high by past standards, but far short of the projected $9 million. Furthermore, since the products had short life cycles, excess inventory built for the $9 million had the possibility of becoming obsolete. The result was a severe deterioration of profitability. Lightcraft slowly lost its reputation and position in the market.

There's an additional downside to rapid growth that deserves special attention: rapid growth tends to create arrogance—a sense of invulnerability—that can lead to disaster. Both corporate and world history are peppered with examples of organizations whose confidence swelled to dangerous proportions, fueled by a string of unbroken successes or rapid expansion, only to blunder into catastrophe. In world history, notable examples include the French Army in 1812 (under Napoleon) and the German Third Reich in 1941 (under Hitler).

The corporate landscape is similarly littered with examples of companies whose rapid growth led them to believe they were unstoppable, only to have that belief dashed to bits. Osborne, Miniscribe, Televideo, Visicorp, Trilogy, and Magnuson Computer are all companies that fell or failed shortly after a period of head-swelling success. In each of these cases, a sense of invulnerability led to poor decisions; arrogance contributed to disaster.

Growth feeds on itself; you may have a great product line in a growing market and be pulled into rapid growth. And once the growth pattern begins, it can be very difficult to slow down. The corresponding exhibit shows how growth feeds on itself.

The Rapid Growth Spiral, and Its Pitfalls

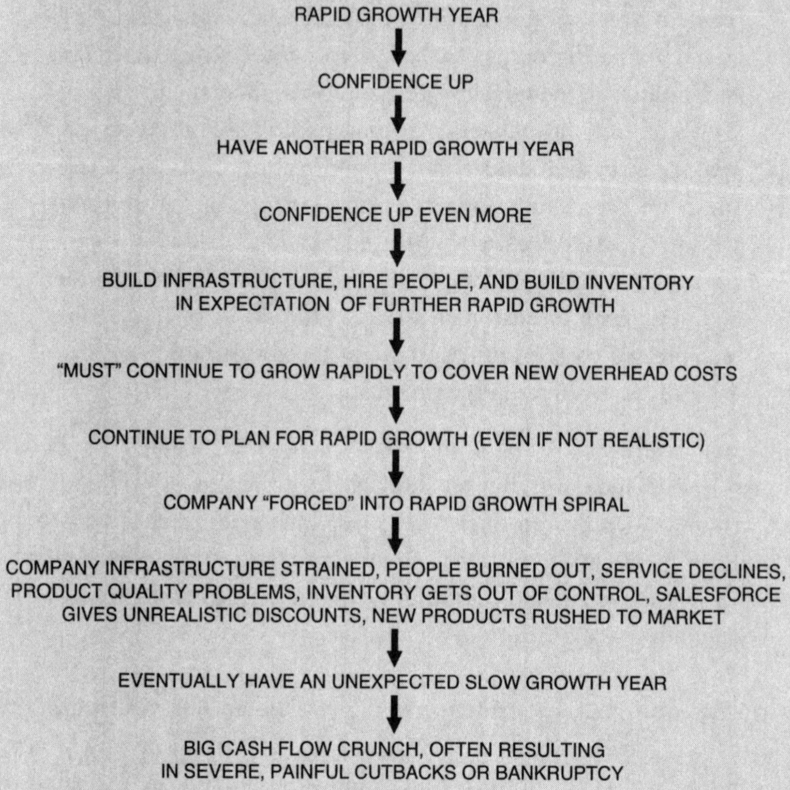

RAPID GROWTH YEAR

↓

CONFIDENCE UP

↓

HAVE ANOTHER RAPID GROWTH YEAR

↓

CONFIDENCE UP EVEN MORE

↓

BUILD INFRASTRUCTURE, HIRE PEOPLE, AND BUILD INVENTORY
IN EXPECTATION OF FURTHER RAPID GROWTH

↓

"MUST" CONTINUE TO GROW RAPIDLY TO COVER NEW OVERHEAD COSTS

↓

CONTINUE TO PLAN FOR RAPID GROWTH (EVEN IF NOT REALISTIC)

↓

COMPANY "FORCED" INTO RAPID GROWTH SPIRAL

↓

COMPANY INFRASTRUCTURE STRAINED, PEOPLE BURNED OUT, SERVICE DECLINES,
PRODUCT QUALITY PROBLEMS, INVENTORY GETS OUT OF CONTROL, SALESFORCE
GIVES UNREALISTIC DISCOUNTS, NEW PRODUCTS RUSHED TO MARKET

↓

EVENTUALLY HAVE AN UNEXPECTED SLOW GROWTH YEAR

↓

BIG CASH FLOW CRUNCH, OFTEN RESULTING
IN SEVERE, PAINFUL CUTBACKS OR BANKRUPTCY

Figure 7-4

CAN SLOW GROWTH WORK?

You're probably wondering whether a slow-growth strategy can work. Sure, there are significant downsides to rapid growth, but doesn't a company need to grow at a rapid clip to remain healthy, exciting, and vibrant? As one senior manager in an executive education program argued, "A company is like a shark; it has to keep swimming, or it dies. You either grow or die."

"Why do you say that?" we asked.

"Because you've got to give people room for advancement. If you're not growing fast, you'll have turnover. People need opportunities to grow into, and there just won't be the opportunities for new challenges. Without fast growth, a company is just not an appealing place to work. You'll also be limited in what you can provide your customers. Besides, who would invest in such a venture?"

He's got a point. Rapid growth makes room for advancement, and we admit there's something exciting about growth.

Nonetheless, there are companies with great people, low turnover (happy people), satisfied customers, superior financial performances, *and* slow-growth strategy.

CASE EXAMPLE: UNIVERSITY NATIONAL BANK AND TRUST

Carl Schmitt, founder and chairman of University National Bank and Trust Company, built his company on an explicit slow-growth strategy. Founded in 1980, Schmitt believed that a slow-growth company can provide superior customer service and quality.

During the 1980s, when most banks were growing at a frenetic pace, Schmitt guided his bank along a methodical slow-growth path, gradually building a reputation for superior service. By the end of the 1980s, his bank boasted a return on assets 45% higher than the average return of other United States Banks, a 1.3% reserve ratio (very healthy), and virtually no non-performing loans. According to George Parker, a board member at University National Bank:

> The return on shareholder's equity at Carl's Bank far exceeds what shareholders could expect to receive by investing in other banks. The bank's slow growth allowed it to get the details right, and generate superior financial performance.

The key to UNB's slow-growth strategy lies in its ability to attract and retain good people. During a 1991 interview with us, Schmitt said:

> Do you know what the average teller turnover is at most banks? 50%. Do you know what we had last year? 0%. We didn't lose a single teller. And we've kept almost all of our top professional talent. People stay with us a long time, and they remain motivated.

How did UNB attract and retain good people without rapid growth? It offered freedom and fun. It hired "refugees" who had exhausted themselves in high-growth environments, and who knew firsthand the costs of growth. Schmitt made UNB a fun place to work. He let all employees—even tellers—have a wide range of decision-making autonomy. As *Inc.* magazine put it, Schmitt set " . . . boundaries for growth while ensuring his employees feel boundless in making day-to-day decisions."

In contrast to University National Bank, however, there are instances where a rapid-growth strategy is the only one that would work. If your mission is to become the dominant player in a rapidly expanding market, it would be unwise to let other competitors zoom too far ahead during the rapid growth phase of the market. For example, Compaq and Apple had no choice but to take a rapid-growth strategy in the exploding personal computer market; no other strategy would have been viable.

So where does all this leave us on the question of growth? Our main message is that growth rate should be part of your strategy formulation process, and that the pros and cons of various growth rates be thoughtfully considered. In general, the healthiest companies *do* grow, but at rates that allow them to put in place the pieces of greatness along the way. The question should not be, "How can we grow the fastest?" No, the question should be, "What growth rate is most consistent with our vision?"

<hr>

JIM'S VIEW FROM 2020

If You Cannot Control Prices, You Must Control Costs

There's a big difference between having a great business and building a great *company*. (By "business" I mean the products and services you offer and the industry in which you operate.) We can find plenty of examples of mediocre or failed companies in great industries. And, conversely, there are a sizeable number of truly great cases in which leaders built great companies in not-so-great industries, such as Southwest Airlines and Nucor (in steel production). Of course, the best combination is to build a great company that is also a great business.

How do you know if you have a truly great business? Warren Buffett has the best answer: *You don't have to hold a prayer meeting to raise prices.*

And what if you're committed to a business wherein you lack pricing power, and you still want to build a great company? Then there's a strategic imperative: *If you cannot control prices, you must control costs.* This is why the leaders of Southwest Airlines and Nucor built their strategies not on being "low price" but on being *low-cost.*

Focus versus Diversification

One of the most effective strategies for a small to mid-sized company is to focus on one particular market or product line and, within that area of focus, be significantly better than the competition. A focused strategy ensures that your limited resources are concentrated to create the maximum advantage. This not only applies to financial resources, but also applies to a resource that is far more valuable: management time and energy.

Larry Ansin, former CEO of the highly successful Joan Fabrics Corporation of Lowell, Massachusetts, told us about his decision to focus:

> If you're diversified into five businesses, as we once were, the businesses that only make up 3% of your sales are going to take 20% of your time, energy, and attention. It's just not worth it. Focus. Do what you do better than anyone else. And the results will probably be very positive, as they were for us once we decided to concentrate all our efforts on one line of business.

Focus keeps you from being just another "also-ran" player. Also rans tend to fall in the worst possible strategic place: too small to take advantage of cost economies of scale, yet not differentiated enough to justify higher prices than the competition. To be stuck in the middle is deadly.

Of course, there are problems with a focused strategy. There is an inherent limit on growth, depending on the size of your target market. There is also the problem of cyclicality—being vulnerable to the ups and downs of any one market. In addition, a focused strategy provides less latitude for being opportunistic.

Nonetheless, we have seldom seen companies suffer because they were too focused, whereas we have seen quite a few companies flounder because they were not focused enough.

CASE EXAMPLE: GFP, INC.

GFP was founded by Clem Atkins in the mid-1970s to bring to market his unique clock designs. His clocks were well received by a specific segment of customers: those who wanted highly functional clocks that were also viewed as works of art.

GFP grew to about $3 million, at which time Atkins decided to diversify into bicycle accessories. "I was interested in cycling, and I thought that my engineering and design skills could produce some excellent new and innovative products," explained Atkins.

And, indeed, the new bicycle products sold well, although Atkins noticed that sales of his clocks were beginning to slip. "All the more reason to diversify," he proclaimed. Atkins then got interested in the newly emerging personal computer market, and decided to produce accessories for personal computer users (special screens, keyboard holders, and other products).

This process of diversification continued—a ski resort, gardening products, recycled paper manufacturing—until the company began to lose money at alarming rates. Sales grew to $5 million and then declined precipitously.

Each of GFP's markets were, in themselves, quite attractive. However, it was too much for GFP to spread itself across that many lines of business. The company never recovered and eventually failed.

Does this mean that a company should *never* diversify? No. Almost all companies eventually diversify. The question is when and how much.

PHASED DIVERSIFICATION

Companies that pursue what we call phased diversification tend to be very successful in their diversifications. Phased diversification is a strategy whereby you focus on one line of business until you have reached your objectives in that market, *then* (and only then) move into a second arena. The nearby diagrams illustrate this concept.

THE LINK BETWEEN VISION AND FOCUS

Your vision should play a role in determining how focused you are.

For example, Celtrix Laboratories, which you'll recall has the purpose "To improve the quality of life through innovative human therapeutics," will produce only products that are innovative and human therapeutics. Joan Fabrics set the mission, "To become the number one player in the upholstery fabrics industry." To pursue this mission, Joan de-diversified entirely out of all unrelated lines of business. To become the number one player in upholstery fabrics, CEO Larry Ansin believed it had to focus on that single line of business.

To become "the most respected and admired company in the worldwide bicycling industry by the year 2000," Giro Sport Design makes a concerted effort to remain focused on that goal. According to President Bill Hannemann:

Our vision statement, and especially the mission part of it, helps us remain focused during strategic decision. Every new product idea is put to the test: Will it help us become the most respected and admired company in the worldwide *bicycling* industry by the year 2000? We also put it against our purpose: Is it innovative, high quality, and the unquestioned best? If it doesn't pass the tests imposed by our vision, then we don't do it. Period.

Whether to Go Public

Most outstanding companies eventually reach a stage where going public (raising cash by selling shares to the general public) is a possibility. For many, the glamour and liquidity (a chance to "cash out") of going public is alluring.

However, it's a common misconception that, once a company reaches a certain size or age, a public offering is always the next natural step. You don't have to go public. It's not preordained.

For example, Minnesota-based Cargill, founded around the time of the American Civil War, grew to 1990 annual revenues of $42 billion (which would have put it ninth on the 1990 Forbes Sales 500 list of public companies) as a private company.

Before leaping into the realm of publicly traded corporations, we would urge you to think strategically about the pros and cons of a public offering. Perhaps no other strategic decision, once executed, has as significant or lasting an impact on a company.

Going public can be a helpful strategic step in working towards your vision, as it provides capital for expansion and investment in new products. It also provides liquidity for shareholders and can help solve some difficult estate-tax problems that occur with the death of a major shareholder.

But there are significant disadvantages to going public:

- It's a drain on management time, both before and after the offering. In the months leading up to an IPO (initial public offering), the top officers of the company are usually overwhelmed by the process. Road shows, "all hands" meetings, writing prospectuses, dealing with press, and other activities can (and usually do) turn into the primary use of management time. After the IPO, time must be spent dealing with the financial community, preparing quarterly and annual reports, and communicating with the press.

Phased Diversification

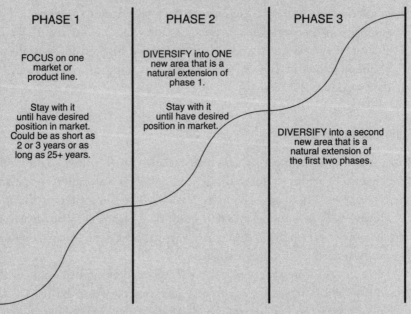

PHASE 1

FOCUS on one market or product line.

Stay with it until have desired position in market. Could be as short as 2 or 3 years or as long as 25+ years.

PHASE 2

DIVERSIFY into ONE new area that is a natural extension of phase 1.

Stay with it until have desired position in market.

PHASE 3

DIVERSIFY into a second new area that is a natural extension of the first two phases.

Examples of Phased Diversification

PHASE 1	PHASE 2	PHASE 3
Running Shoes	Athletic Shoes	Sportswear
Rock-Climbing Hardware	Mountaineering Hardware	Softgoods for Climbers
Electronic Test Equipment	Computers	Integrated Systems
Furniture Upholstery Fabric	Automotive Upholstery Fabric	Airline Upholstery Fabric

Figure 7-5

- It's expensive. Legal fees, accounting fees, printing costs, and filing fees will cost about half a million dollars right off the top. Underwriter's fees (a percentage that is paid to the investment banker who takes your stock to market) can be enormous; 7% of total proceeds is not uncommon. You should assume that the total tab for an IPO will be well over a million dollars for most companies.
- You'll be managing in a fishbowl. You have to disclose financial information. You have to disclose salary information. Every move you make is scrutinized by investment analysts. Competitors can keep a better eye on what you are doing.
- You'll feel pressure to manage for the short term. Every public company feels pressure from the financial community to keep quarterly earnings as high as possible. There's a built-in disincentive to take short-term losses for the sake of long-term health.
- You may lose control of the company. If over 50% of the voting shares are in the hands of outsiders, the company can be bought by anyone who has the resources to acquire the stock.
- There may be a conflict of corporate purpose. Public shareholders view their stock holdings primarily as a *financial* investment. As long as the stock does well, they don't really care what the company is doing. Thus, if your purpose is not strictly to maximize shareholder wealth, you may be at odds with your shareholders. Public shareholders don't generally buy into a vision; they buy into the prospect of a capital gain.

CASE EXAMPLE: TENSOR CORPORATION

Tensor Corporation was founded in 1960 by Jay Monroe, a highly creative and intense man whose main purpose was to have a vehicle for bringing his ideas to market and to have fun. He had a vision for the company where it would make product decisions on aesthetic considerations as much as on short-term return on investment criteria. He felt the company should be able to produce products that might not produce the best short-term financial results, but that would ultimately be better and more interesting contributions to the market.

He made a fateful decision: he took the company public and left himself with less than 50% of the stock. The motivations of the public stockholders (short-term return on investment) came in direct conflict with Monroe's vision. Monroe was eventually faced with losing the company to a corporate raider or changing his vision—a loss either way.

In contrast to the Tensor case, L.L.Bean made the decision to remain a privately held company. A big part of the decision to remain private was a desire to maintain the exceptionally high Bean customer service standards, even if those standards at times affected profitability in the short term. In 1989, being private paid off when Bean decided to take $2 million right off the bottom line in a customer service improvement program.

Commenting on the decision, President Leon Gorman said in a *Wall Street Journal* interview, "It's a good thing we're not a publicly-owned company. We don't have to worry about earnings."

Related to the IPO decision is the strategic decision of outside investors. Certain types of investors, such as most venture capitalists, think primarily in terms of their "cash out" value. If you decide to seek venture capital—or capital from other investors whose primary motivation is to cash out within a few years—be aware that you are simultaneously making the strategic decision to go public or sell out.

In most venture-backed companies, going public (or becoming acquired) is *assumed*, and it's just a matter of *when*. Thus, if going public, for the reasons outlined above, does not fit with your vision for the company, then you probably should *not* seek venture capital or other "cash out" oriented investments.

To Lead a Market or Follow

In general, tremendous benefits accrue to market innovators—first movers or pioneers. Yet, a first-mover advantage is by no means a guarantee of greatness and, indeed, there can be costs to being the market innovator.

The evidence shows that first movers generally acquire a market advantage:

Average Market Share*
Pioneers, Early Followers, and Late Followers

	Consumer Goods	Industrial Goods
Pioneers	29%	29%
Early followers	17%	21%
Late Followers	12%	15%

* Based on a sample of 1,853 businesses. Analyzed by W.T. Robinson and
C. Fornell, *Journal of Marketing Research*, August, 1985.

This doesn't tell the whole story. There are many examples of first movers losing their advantage, usually due to a competitor introducing a better product, performing better marketing, or both. Indeed, early followers often ride the coattails of a pioneer, taking advantage of the fact that the market has already been primed and educated. The following examples, and many more, are provided in *Stanford Business School Research Paper #10084*, "To Pioneer or Follow?: Strategy of Entry Order," by Marvin B. Lieberman and David B. Montgomery.

- Bomar brought out the first hand-held calculators, and stimulated the market with extensive TV advertising. Bomar was then overrun by Texas Instruments and Hewlett-Packard.
- Visicorp, inventor of the market-shaping Visicalc spreadsheet software, was devastated when a well-marketed and vastly superior Lotus 1-2-3 came on the market.
- Docutel, pioneer of the automatic teller machine, lost its market position when competitors introduced ATMs with features not offered by Docutel.
- Osborne Computer, pioneer of the portable computer market, was devastated when competitors introduced superior products, for which it had no answer.
- Ford was dethroned from the number one position in automobiles in the 1920s because it did not adjust quickly enough to the better, more differentiated cars offered by the then struggling General Motors Corporation. Ford never became number one in the auto industry again.
- British Air introduced the first commercial jet, but was overcome by Boeing's superior design in the 707. Boeing has dominated the commercial jet-craft market ever since.

Where does this leave us with respect to a market pioneer strategy versus a market follower strategy? It's clear that there are advantages to being a market leader. You can lock up customers. You can build early market share and gain a dominant trade name. You can get down the learning curve. You can sometimes gain patent protection. You can benefit from high margins, and use the resulting cash flow to fund further product development and marketing.

But—and this is key—taking a market pioneer strategy is not, in itself, enough. Being first will not protect you forever; you also have to *execute* well.

Of course, the ideal position—and the one pursued by many great companies—is to strive for being *both* first *and* best. If you're first and then continually work to improve your product, marketing, and service, you'll be in a very strong position.

This leads us right to the final two key parts of attaining corporate greatness: innovation and tactical excellence.

The thing you *don't* want to do with strategy is to invest all your time trying to plan and not enough time innovating or executing. Clear strategic thinking is essential for being on the right track, but, as Will Rogers said, "Even if you're on the right track, you'll get run over if you just sit there."

No business enterprise can be perfectly planned. Yes, it should have a clear overall vision, and a basic strategic guide for attaining the vision. It's impossible to rigidly plan every action down to the nth detail, and to do so would be an absurd waste of time. There needs to be some level of creative chaos in a great company. Most important, a company can't sit still. People in it have to act, move, do, try, fail, try again, struggle, push, scramble, innovate, and execute the details.

To return to a central theme of this book, it isn't any one thing that makes a company great. It isn't just strategy. It isn't just leadership style. It isn't just vision. It isn't just innovation. It isn't just tactical excellence. It's *all* of these; and it's all of these done consistently well for years.

The following pages contain a strategy formulation example for a small company. This example illustrates the flow from vision, internal assessment, and external assessment to strategy and a set of strategic priorities. The final page of this chapter gives some caveats to the stages of industry evolution analysis.

Strategy Formulation Example

HARDROCK PRODUCTS, INC.

CORPORATE VISION

Core Values and Beliefs

We value high performance for its own sake.

We believe in being your best, maximizing your potential.

We value being in nice physical settings.

We only want to participate in markets where we can be outstanding; if we can't be number one or number two, we don't want to play at all.

We value hard work.

We value having fun, and time away to play.

Purpose

To help outdoors sportspeople realize their full athletic potential, and to be a vehicle for making a living in a sport that we love.

Current Mission

To become the number-one supplier of rock-climbing
hardware in the world by 1997.

INTERNAL ASSESSMENT

Strengths

Leading edge technology and hardware design skills

Knack for creating "core" products with multiple spin-offs

Ability to generate lots of new ideas and innovations

Intimate knowledge of the rock-climbing world

Reputation for reliability, quality, and service

We know how to create great catalogues

Weaknesses

No finance or control skills

Design to production to market coordination is very poor

Cross-functional communication is very poor

Employee training is poor

Great products, but high manufacturing costs

Resources

Strong balance sheet

No debt; capacity to borrow if necessary

Philosophy of keeping close control; no outside investors

Innovations

New bolting technologies invented

New camming technology

Wildcat (code name)

EXTERNAL ASSESSMENT

Industry Trends

Market is approaching maturity with growth of 15% per year

Size is roughly 50,000 climbers U.S., 500,000 worldwide

Market is segmented into sport, traditional, and big wall

Sport-climbing segment is fastest growing

Driving forces of growth:

- New technology making climbing safer
- Climbing competitions and television
  - Baby boom mid-life crises

Technology Trends

Camming devices

Bolting devices

Lighter, stronger raw materials

Competitors

Fragmented; no dominant player

Increasing competition from Europe

Primary direct competitor: Black Diamond

Social and Regulatory Environment

Park services restricting bolting because of effect on rock

Upcoming ISCC safety standards expected by 1993

Product liability insurance cost explosion

Macroeconomy and Demographics

More leisure time

Baby boomers hitting mid-life and are seeking new challenge

International

Market growth in Germany, France, Italy, and Australia

Top Three Opportunities	*Top Three Threats*
1. Sport Climbing	1. Not meeting ISCC standards
2. International markets	2. International competitors
3. Climbing competitions	3. Product liability costs

Overview

To attain our mission of becoming the number one supplier of rock-climbing hardware in the world, we will pursue a strategy of focusing on hardware for rock climbing, with emphasis on the expanding sport-climbing segment. We will compete on superior innovation, design, quality, and service.

Products

We will only make hardware for rock climbing. Until we realize our mission, we will not make products for other sports, nor will we enter the "soft goods" market.

We will compete on superior technology, quality, and service, not on price. We will price at the upper end of the market.

We will develop groupings of "core" products that can be easily tailored to specific needs. This will keep our inventory costs low and our quality high.

We will take advantage of the trends towards sport climbing and speed climbing. We will therefore concentrate our product development efforts on these expanding markets.

We will make all of our products conform to the proposed ISCC safety standards, thus putting us in an excellent position once the safety standards are passed.

We will "over-engineer" our products for safety to protect against product liability lawsuits.

We will concentrate on new product innovation and will introduce two new products per year. We will capitalize on trends in bolting and camming technology.

Product Introductions:

1991: Ultra-light Bolt Drill, Quick Clips
1992: Hardcam, El Cap Pins
1993: Power Cam Unit, Wildcat (code name)

Customers

We will position ourselves, relative to our competition, as *the* supplier of *superior performance* products for the serious rock climber.

We will distribute our products primarily through our own mail order operations and through specialty retail outlets.

We will reach rock climbers through our own catalogue, advertising in specialized rock-climbing magazines, athlete endorsements, and sponsorship of climbing competitions.

We will seek as much "free advertising" as possible by getting the most high-profile climbers to use our gear.

We will seek to develop loyal customers through excellent customer service; 24-hour turnaround on orders; and making the process of ordering from us *enjoyable*.

We will introduce our products in at least three international markets over the next three years:

1991: France
1992: Germany
1993: Italy, Australia

Cash Flow

We will fund the business primarily through operations. We will therefore price our products to provide at least a 50% gross margin.

We will maintain banking relationships, and arrange credit lines (in the event we need them); but we will borrow as little as possible.

We will grow at a controlled rate; maximum of 15% per year.

Sales	Gross Margin	Profit After Tax
1991: 4.5 M	55%	10%
1992: 5.1 M	50%	8%
1993: 5.8 M	50%	10%

People & Organization

We will install a seasoned financial controller.

We will establish design-production-marketing teams responsible for each new product; eliminate the design to production to marketing problems we have had in the past.

We will continue to build our engineering and design staff.

We will continue to hire people who love the outdoors.

We will build up our specialty retail outlet rep force.

We will set up an international division.

We will develop an employee training program.

Infrastructure

We will locate and move into new facilities more conducive to cross-functional communication. We will buy our facilities, rather than rent. We will locate near the mountains.

1991 STRATEGIC PRIORITIES

1. Get Ultra-light Bolt Drill and Quick Clips introduced to market in time for summer season. (Primary responsibility: Joe.)
2. Establish a foothold in Europe; sign up two super-star European climbers for endorsement contracts (one male, one female); set up mail order and hire reps in France; create French catalogue. (Primary responsibility: Beth.)
3. Locate and hire a seasoned financial controller. (Primary responsibility: Bill.)
4. Implement design-to-manufacturing-to-marketing product teams. (Primary responsibility: Sue.)
5. Locate/acquire new facilities; be ready for move by 1992. (Primary responsibility: Bob.)

Caveats to Industry Evolution Analysis

The following comments about the stages of industry evolution analysis come from our own observations and Michael Porter's *Competitive Strategy* (1980, Free Press).

The stages of industry evolution (emergence, rapid growth, maturity, decline) is probably the most common pattern of evolution, but it does not necessarily hold in all industries.

Porter offers four things to keep in mind when using the concept:

1. The duration of the stages varies widely from industry to industry, and it is often not easy to determine which stage the industry is in.
2. Industry growth does not always go through the S-shaped pattern. Industries can skip maturity, passing straight through to decline. Some industries seem to skip the emergence phase altogether.
3. Companies can *affect* the shape of the growth curve through product innovation and repositioning. If a company takes the stages of evolution as given, it becomes an undesirable self-fulfilling prophesy.
4. The nature of competition associated with each stage of evolution is different for different industries. Some industries remain concentrated. Some start fragmented and consolidate. Some remain fragmented.

To these four caveats, we would add a fifth. We believe that many industries are made up of multiple *S* curves. That is, because of product innovations, a single industry may progress through multiple S-shaped curves as new innovations are introduced and moved from emergence to acceptance to decline. Note: this is known as the *Innovation-Adoption Cycle*. The Innovation-Adoption Cycle is well described in Everett M. Roger's ground-breaking book *Diffusion of Innovations* (1983, Free Press). *Diffusion of Innovations* is, in our view, a must read for those interested in how new innovations are adopted by a population.

In sum, the stages of industry analysis is a very useful tool, but it should be used thoughtfully, and not taken blindly as gospel.

Chapter 8

INNOVATION

. . . all progress depends on the unreasonable man.

GEORGE BERNARD SHAW
MAN AND SUPERMAN

THERE'S NO SHORTAGE OF good ideas.

Indeed, the biggest problem in building an innovative organization is *not* stimulating creativity; the problem is how to nurture the creativity that abounds all around us, and how to get that creativity acted upon and turned into innovations. (Think of an innovation as a done idea—an idea that has been implemented.)

That's precisely what this chapter is about. To be an enduring, great company, we believe it must have the ability to innovate continually—to have a constant flow of new ideas, some of which are fully implemented. We say some are implemented (rather than all) because a great company will always have more good ideas than it can fund.

Most companies start with a creative founder. The challenge, however, is to become an innovative company, rather than a company dependent on an innovative founder.

We've identified six basic elements of what it takes to be an innovative company:

1. Receptivity to ideas from everywhere
2. "Being" the customer
3. Experimentation and mistakes
4. People being creative
5. Autonomy and decentralization
6. Rewards

We will guide you through each of these six elements, with specific examples and suggestions, and will conclude with some specific managerial techniques for stimulating creativity and innovation.

Corporate Innovation Element 1: Receptivity to Ideas from Everywhere

Highly innovative companies don't necessarily generate more ideas than their less innovative counterparts (good ideas are in plentiful supply for all companies). But highly innovative companies are more receptive to ideas—and not only to their own ideas but to ideas from everywhere. Furthermore, they do something about the ideas. Not that an innovative company executes every single idea, but it is much more likely to act quickly on a partly baked idea than to spend countless hours deliberating about all the reasons it can't work.

Sadly, however, most of us have been trained to do just the opposite; we're well schooled in criticism, having learned that the way to show how smart we are is to cite all the reasons that something is a stupid idea or doomed to failure.

We've noticed many new MBAs, for example, are adept at finding all the flaws in a business idea, but they're much less practiced at coming up with ways to make the idea work. Many times we've stood facing a self-satisfied person who has just done a marvelous job of demolishing a new product idea during a discussion. Then we ask, "Yes we know it's an imperfect idea. But no idea is perfect. So, now how do you intend to make this idea successful in spite of its flaws?" Some people rise brilliantly to the challenge when they realize the goal is no longer to show how bright they are by shooting holes in ideas. But, alas, others do not. They've been trained too well in the ethos of criticism, and to build a great company, they'll have to overcome this negative training.

Don't get us wrong. We don't mean to imply that every idea is a great idea, or that every new product idea will be a wild success. In fact, quite a few ideas will turn out to be failures. As we shall describe later, even those failures can pay handsome dividends in the long run.

It's essential to keep in mind that many great ideas were at first thought to be stupid ideas. Form 8-1 (below) provides a list of historically significant creations that were thought by so-called experts (we prefer to call them "wet blankets") to be dumb ideas.

We recommend that you circulate a copy of this list to everyone in your company. Put a copy on your own wall or above your desk. Keep it in front of you—and ask others to do the same. It's a helpful reminder about the importance of being receptive to ideas.

The first element in making your company creative and innovative is to seek ideas from everywhere and, most important, to create a climate of receptivity to new ideas. Let us reemphasize: *There is no shortage of good ideas; there is only a lack of receptivity to ideas.*

Ideas from Outside

Don't think that the only ideas worth doing come from within your company. Some of the most creative companies rely extensively on ideas generated outside their walls.

FORM 8-1
Wet Blankets Through History

"This 'telephone' has too many shortcomings to be seriously considered as a means of communication. The device is inherently of no value to us."; Western Union internal memo in response to Bell's telephone, 1876.

"The concept is interesting and well formed, but in order to earn better than a 'C,' the idea must be feasible."; a Yale University management professor in response to Fred Smith's paper proposing reliable overnight delivery service. Smith went on to found Federal Express Corporation.

"We don't tell you how to coach, so don't tell us how to make shoes."; a large sporting shoe manufacturer to Bill Bowerman, inventor of the "waffle" shoe and co-founder of NIKE, Inc.

"So we went to Atari and said, 'Hey, we've got this amazing thing, even built with some of your parts, and what do you think about funding us? Or we'll give it to you. We just want to do it. Pay our salary, we'll come work for you.' And they said, 'No.' So then we went to Hewlett-Packard and they said 'Hey, we don't need you. You haven't got through college yet.'"; Steve Jobs speaking about attempts to get Atari and HP interested in his and Wozniak's personal computer. Jobs and Wozniak founded Apple Computer Company.

"'You should franchise them,' I told them. 'I'll be your guinea pig.' Well, they just went straight up in the air! They couldn't see the philosophy. . . . When they turned us down, that left Bud and me to swim on our own.'"; Sam Walton describing his efforts to get the Ben Franklin chain interested in his discount retailing concept in 1962. Walton went on to found Walmart.

"Who the hell wants to hear actors talk?"; H. M. Warner, Warner Brothers, 1927.

"We don't like their sound and guitar music is on the way out."; Decca Recording Company rejecting The Beatles, 1962.

In 1984, John Henry Patterson was ridiculed by his business friends for paying $6,500 for the rights to the cash register—a product with "limited" or no potential. Patterson went on to found National Cash Register (NCR) Corporation.

"What's all this computer nonsense you're trying to bring into medicine? I've got no confidence at all in computers and I want nothing whatsoever to do with them."; a medical professor in England to Dr. John Alfred Powell, about the CT scanner.

"Drill for oil? You mean drill into the ground to try and find oil? You're crazy."; any number of experienced drillers who Edwin L. Drake tried to enlist in his project to drill for oil in 1859. He later became the first man to strike oil.

"That is good sport. But for the military, the airplane is useless."; Ferdinand Foch, Commander in Chief, allied forces on the western front, World War I.

"The television will never achieve popularity; it takes place in a semi-darkened room and demands continuous attention."; Harvard Professor Chester L. Dawes, 1940.

Apple Computer didn't create the basic ideas behind Macintosh; those ideas had been around for years, developed first on defense research projects and later at Xerox. A group of Apple executives attended a demonstration of mouse and icon technology at Xerox (which was an investor in Apple) and carried the basic ideas over to Apple.

The original McDonald's restaurant was created by the McDonald brothers in San Bernardino, California. Ray Kroc, who founded the company that transformed the McDonald brothers' concept into a chain, simply recognized the potential in what had already been created.

T/Maker Company didn't create the original prototype of *Personal Publisher* (the first desktop publishing package to hit the market); it came from an outside programmer who had initiated the effort on his own.

Johnson & Johnson didn't create Tylenol (a breakthrough non-aspirin pain reliever); the product came from McNeil Laboratories, which was acquired by J&J. Procter and Gamble didn't invent Oxydol or Lava Soap; it obtained them by acquiring William Waltke Soap Company. The 3M Company didn't invent its first landmark product (Wetordry waterproof sandpaper, brought to market in the early 1920s); Francis Oakie, a young Philadelphia ink maker, created the innovation and sold the rights to 3M.

Fight to prevent the NIH syndrome (i.e., If it's Not Invented Here, it can't be any good.) from taking hold at your company. With an open mind, look constantly outside your company for ideas. Let the entire world be part of your R&D lab. Make it possible for the thousands of great ideas swirling around in the world to easily permeate the outer membrane of your company.

Here are some specific activities you might consider:

- Make it everyone's responsibility to be receptive to new ideas submitted to the company from outsiders. Make it the responsibility of a particular individual to respond to ideas submitted by outside individuals. Granted, many ideas won't fit your mission or will be infeasible, but remember that Chester Carlson received icy receptions from over 20 companies to whom he offered his copying technology; frustrated, he founded Xerox.
- Arrange an employee swap with an admired company in another industry, in which one of your employees spends a few weeks at that company and one of theirs spends time at yours. This cross-breeding can stimulate wonderful insights.
- Hire outside designers. Some of the most creative designs come from outside designers (the outer design of the Macintosh computer, for example). Outside designers gain ideas from working with different product categories and different problems across a range of clients, and can therefore bring valuable and stimulating suggestions. (The same principle applies to other types of outside consultants as well.)
- Encourage people to join technical, industry, trade, or other groups where they will come in contact with interesting people and ideas. Offer to pay their membership fees. Join some groups yourself.

- Allow people to travel to events or otherwise spend time out in the world exposing themselves to new ideas. NIKE, for example, allocates a portion of its design budget just for unrestricted travel. NIKE wants its designers to get out of the office and see things, just to spark new ideas.
- Pay for subscriptions to journals and publications that might have interesting new insights, ideas, technologies, and research results. Similarly, start a library and allow employees to purchase books, read them, and place them in the library.
- Invite leading-edge idea people to give a talk or seminar. Encourage outsiders to attend and participate in lively discussion and debate.
- Pay for selected employees to attend education programs, seminars, and university-sponsored events; ask people to present to others in the company (perhaps at a staff meeting) "the most intriguing ideas" they encountered at the event.
- Encourage people to read nonfiction materials *un*related to their work, and to share insights gleaned. Bob Waterman, co-author of *In Search of Excellence*, told us that he gets many ideas via an "eclectic" reading list that ranges from architecture to world history. In fact, research on creativity shows that significant creative contributors have wide interests, a breadth of perspective, and a need for novelty and diversity. *Innovation often comes from seeing the relationship between unconnected ideas and melding them together.*
- Make it easy for customers to feed you thousands (and we do mean thousands) of ideas. At service outlets, make use of a customer suggestion box. Follow the example of Stew Leonard's Dairy (a single-unit, family-owned outlet that does $100 million in annual revenues, located in Norwalk, Connecticut). Stew Leonard's receives an average of 100 comments and suggestions *per day* in its suggestion box. To further stimulate customer ideas, each suggestion is followed up with a thank-you within 24 hours.

Ideas from Inside

Of course, good ideas don't come only from outside; many of the best ideas and innovations bubble up from inside. An organization is a natural incubator for great ideas and innovations.

Right now—the very moment you are reading this chapter—there are many creative ideas, some of them quite good, swirling about inside your company. Just as your company should be receptive to ideas from the outside, it should be receptive to ideas from employees at all levels and all positions. Ideas can emerge from the furthest outposts, as with the Big Mac and the Egg McMuffin (invented by franchises), or from the depths of scientific experimentation, as with the 3M Post-it Notes (created by a single researcher playing around with chemicals and discovering, quite by accident, the unique adhesive that made the product possible).

Remember the customer suggestion box? Well you should also have ways for employees to give suggestions on internal processes. Walmart has a policy called *LTC* (Low Threshold for Change). Store managers regularly seek ideas for improvements and innovations from people working on the floor, and bonuses are sometimes paid for particularly good suggestions.

As a leader of your company, *you* can also be a major source of innovation. Indeed, we've noticed a significant number of new product innovations originating from the top of certain organizations.

- At Giro Sport Design, many new products are the brainchildren of founder Jim Gentes and his design team. At one planning meeting, Gentes introduced over 30 new product possibilities for the company's consideration.
- Honorary Sony Chairman Masaru Ibuka originated the Sony Walkman.
- In its early days, numerous L.L.Bean innovations came directly from L. L. himself.

The point here is *not* that founders and CEOs are necessarily more creative than others, but that their push behind an idea vastly reduces (or completely eliminates) resistance to it. Could the Sony Walkman, which was thought by those in the tape and recording divisions to be a crazy idea, have survived if it had not originated from Honorary Chairman Ibuka? Perhaps; but it certainly would have been less likely.

This returns us again to the central point of this section; the primary challenge you face is not in increasing creativity per se, but in *making your company receptive* to the vast amounts of creativity that already exist. The point is not to build a company that depends on you for its innovation, but to continually work towards an organization that is as receptive to new ideas *as if those ideas had come from you.*

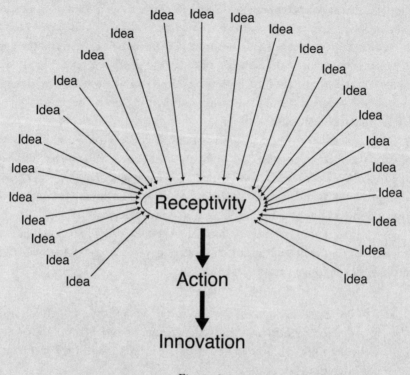

Figure 8-1

Idea-Push or Market-Pull?

Before moving on to the next section, we must address a vexing paradox.

On the one hand, classic business school dogma asserts that you should always define a market need first (via market research and other methods of analyzing customer benefit preferences, price sensitivities, etc.) and *then* develop innovations that meet that need (market-pull or, as it is sometimes called, market focus). This dogma appears sensible. After all, a business should create products or services that meet real customer needs. What better way to ensure this than to define those needs and then target your innovation efforts towards their fulfillment?

Yet, on the other hand, many market-successful innovations did not originate from market-pull, nor were they developed via classic market research techniques. Indeed, *many breakthrough products wouldn't even exist if the companies that created them had relied solely on a market-pull approach to innovation.*

- The fax machine is an American invention; yet, as of 1990, not one fax machine sold on the market is American-made. Why? Because, according to Peter Drucker, market research convinced the Americans that there was no demand for such a gadget.
- The experiment that led to the unique adhesive behind the 3-M Post-it Notes was not driven by pre-defined market demand. Spencer Silver (the scientist) didn't start with the idea in mind that there was a market for his unique adhesive. On the contrary, the adhesive was *a solution looking for a problem*. For over five years, Silver made a pilgrimage around 3M, asking people if they could think of any uses for the adhesive. According to Silver:

    > We had to fight to get [the funding for] a patent, because there was no commercial product readily apparent. . . . It's one of those things you look at and say, 'This has got to be useful.' . . . At times I was angry because this stuff is so obviously unique. I said to myself, 'Why can't you think of a product?'

    > Furthermore, once the Post-it product had been conceived, it failed a four-city market research test! It was only after an intense period of *giving* the product away free—getting people addicted to the little notepads— that the product finally took hold.

- When Fred Smith conceived the idea for Federal Express (overnight nationwide delivery), UPS, Emery Air Freight, and the United States Postal Service had all thought of the idea before. They had rejected it because they had perceived no market need; no customers had ever *asked* for it.
- Debbie Fields, in launching her cookie store chain (Mrs. Fields Cookies), was warned that her ingenious ability to produce hot, soft, luscious cookies would fail; market research reports stated that people like *crispy* cookies, not soft cookies. Her store concept was, according to the market research experts, doomed to failure.
- When David Sarnoff tried to raise investment money to market the radio in the 1920s, he was repeatedly turned down because there was no market demand for the service of sending a message to no one in particular. It was only *after* the product was brought to market that people began to recognize its value; by making the radio available, Sarnoff created a market for its use.

- Windham Hill Record Company was told by distributors and record market experts that there was no market demand for a solo piano album. There was absolutely no indication from the market that such a concept could be successful. Yet the company introduced the innovative George Winston solo piano album anyway, and it sold over 500,000 copies.
- The first microwave oven was built in 1946, based on radar technology imported to the United States from Britain. There was no market demand for a microwave oven. In fact, according to Jack Kammerer, senior vice president of marketing at Amana, who introduced the microwave:

> If this project had been given to a very highly structured company that had spent a year and hundreds of thousands of dollars in market research, they'd have probably thrown it in the wastebasket and never done it. It was only a gut feeling of a couple of individuals that this is the right product for the right time.

Furthermore, certain highly innovative companies are very clear that they consciously foster an idea-push approach to new product innovation. Akio Morita of Sony wrote:

> We seek to lead the public with new products, rather than ask them what they want. Instead of doing a lot of market research, we refine our product and try to create a market for it by educating the public.

This notion of leading a market—of *creating* a market—is essential to breakthrough innovations. With dramatic, new innovations, customers will often not tell you what they want (because they do not know what is possible) until you show them what they can have—as was the case with the 3M Post-it Notes, the radio, and the fax machine.

This is very important to realize, or else your company might bypass tremendous opportunities. As seasoned French design expert Jean Pierre Vitrac put it, "Consumers, when confronted with something new and original, can be tempted by it, contradicting all the criteria previously applied to them."

In a study of sixteen commercial breakthroughs, P. Ranganath Nayak and John M. Ketteringham concluded in their outstanding book *Breakthroughs* that "It is flatly wrong to say that the bulk of successful commercial innovation results from 'market pull' rather than 'technology push.'" In *not one* of the

16 cases did classic market research play a major role in stimulating the original idea behind the breakthrough. According to Nayak and Ketteringham, the original motivation came from the curiosity or problem-solving drive of a single inventor:

> Certainly, the search for a market often followed quickly on the heels of the problem solver's drive. In some cases, it was a parallel phenomenon. *But we found no instance of the market demanding a breakthrough before the inventor had found it lurking in the depths of his semi-consciousness.*

But wait a minute! Surely there is a place for market input into products. We don't want to toss the entire discipline of market research out the window, do we? What about being close to the customer—about listening to consumer input into products? What about great consumer marketing companies, like Procter & Gamble, that attribute much of their success to their ability to identify customer needs and then develop products to meet them?

What about companies like Tensor Corporation, whose Tensor Lamp lost its position in the marketplace because inventor Jay Monroe refused to listen to customer input? What about Visicorp, who failed to respond rapidly enough to customer requests for more powerful features in their best-selling Visicalc Spreadsheet package, and was subsequently destroyed by upstart Lotus Development Corporation? What about Ford's being surpassed by GM in the late 1920s because Henry Ford turned a deaf ear to customers clamoring for more styles and colors, responding with "They can have any color they want, as long as it's black."?

To resolve this dilemma, we must first cut through the clutter and clarify the question.

The question is not whether innovations should meet a genuine human need (to be commercially successful, they had better meet a need). The question is: How should innovation be generated in the first place? What should your company *do* to ensure a continual flow of innovations, including some breakthroughs, that meet genuine human needs?

We will address this question throughout this chapter. But the first step is to recognize that you need both idea-push and market-pull in your company. The classic business school market-pull dogma shouldn't be mindlessly worshipped. Yet, at the same time, there certainly is a place for market input, as ignoring customer input can lead to missed opportunities or disaster. Think of original breakthroughs as coming primarily (although not exclusively) from idea-push, and subsequent incremental innovations coming from customer input. The total amount of innovation is higher by using both approaches, rather than relying exclusively on one.

Reject the extremists. Reject those who say, "*Always* go ask the market what it wants first." Remember, just because customers haven't been asking for the innovation doesn't necessarily mean that they won't be thrilled when it's offered to them. Also reject extremists at the other end of the spectrum who say, "We're so good we *never* need to pay attention to the market; we always know what's best." Be receptive to ideas from everywhere, no matter what their origin.

There is an additional answer to the paradox: what appears to be purely idea-push is often just the opposite. Even though the inventor hasn't done a general market analysis, he is often as close to the customer as he can get: he *is* the customer! This brings us to our second major element of making your company highly innovative.

Corporate Innovation Element 2: Being the Customer

In the end, we make clothes to satisfy us. We wear them.
PATAGONIA CATALOGUE, 1989

One of the best ways to make and keep your company innovative is to have people invent solutions to their own problems or needs. In other words, be your own customer and satisfy yourself. If that is not possible—if you are in a business where you cannot be your own customer—then figure out a way to experience the world as a customer experiences it.

Solve Your Own Problems and Meet Your Own Needs

The idea here is simple. If someone in your company creates an innovation to solve her own problem or meet her own desire, there are probably other people in the world that would benefit from her invention.

Returning to our example of T/Maker and the *Personal Publisher* product, the innovation was stimulated by President and CEO Heidi Roizen's personal need to create a party invitation at her computer. She preferred to use an IBM PC (because she was accustomed to it), yet the lack of IBM graphics software forced her to use a Macintosh. "Too bad it's not possible to do something graphically oriented on an IBM PC," she mused. Out of this personal experience grew the *Personal Publisher* project, which generated the first desktop publishing package to be offered on the IBM PC.

Jim Gentes at Giro comes up with his great ideas not by sitting in an office and staring out the window, but by going out on his bicycle at lunchtime and hammering away against the wind. "On a bike, on the road, is my best laboratory. I'm always trying to figure out ways to make myself go faster with less effort," says Gentes.

Even the original personal computer itself was invented to meet a *personal* need. When asked how he and Steve Wozniak got the idea for the personal computer, Steve Jobs responded:

> Like most great ideas, it came from something right in front of us. We designed this computer because we couldn't afford to buy one; we just wanted to educate ourselves about computers. So *we* were the initial market. Our secondary market was all our friends. Gradually as the number of people that it was neat for expanded, we got more and more excited. We didn't sit in a chair and think, "My god, 10 years from now the survey says that everyone is going to be using personal computers." It didn't happen that way. It was more of a gradual process.

In 1920, the Band-Aid was invented by Earle Dickson, an employee of the fledgling Johnson & Johnson company, whose wife was constantly cutting herself in the kitchen. The accidents occurred frequently enough that he finally decided to make a ready-to-use bandage that she could apply to herself. Laying out a long strip of surgical tape, he placed small pieces of gauze on it at intervals, and to keep the adhesive from sticking, he covered it with a piece of cotton crinoline. Dickinson mentioned his invention to colleagues at work, and thus sparked one of the most successful commercial products in history.

The Woodwork Factor

Think of it as the woodwork factor; by solving your own problem, other people who have the same problem (but who would not be easily identified via classic market research techniques) come out of the woodwork.

The woodwork factor was originally articulated by the team behind the invention of Tagamet, one of the most successful prescription drugs in history. (Tagamet is a drug that heals ulcers without surgery, and changed forever the way people cope with ulcers.) Thomas Collins, the head of Tagamet's United States effort, described:

In my age group, I can remember all sorts of people with ulcers. But they weren't under active treatment. They did whatever they had to. So, from my point of view, I always said, I don't think anybody knows what the hell the size of this market is. This is the woodwork factor. They're all my friends. I had a vision of patients coming out of the woodwork.

Heidi Roizen, Jim Gentes, Steve Jobs, and Earle Dickson also experienced the woodwork factor. In fact, this is what HP meant by its famous next bench syndrome.

Here are some specific things you might do to stimulate people in your company to be the customer and to replicate the woodwork factor:

- Hire customers. NIKE, for instance, has lots of athletes as employees. We visited NIKE during a product development session, and found Marketing Manager Tom Hartge—an avid runner—working with the design team to create shoes that he used on his own runs. NIKE hires elite athletes as product testing consultants who are expected to test the new products under the most severe circumstances and report back with ideas and problems.
- Allow employees to take time to field test products or services. At L.L.Bean, for example, any Bean executive can get an extra week's vacation to do product testing, even if that means a fly-fishing trip in Alaska, going to Ontario for the opening of the duck and goose season, or checking out enormous Danner Yukon cold-weather hunting boots in British Columbia.
- Distribute an annual blank "personal idea journal" to all employees, wherein they are encouraged to make notes about problems and ideas they personally confront in their work and personal lives.
- Communicate the woodwork factor by writing up specific stories in the employee magazine or newsletter about how individuals or teams invented successful products by meeting their own needs. People learn through stories. Make the woodwork theory part of the mythology of the company.

What if you are in a business that makes products or delivers services that you and your employees don't extensively use? Can the woodwork factor work here as well? Yes, but the process is different.

Simulate Being the Customer

If your business is such that you can't literally *be* a customer of your own products, then simulate a way of being the customer. There are two basic approaches.

One approach is to solve the specific problem or fill the specific need of an individual customer—not an individual customer *group*, but a *single, solitary individual customer*. The idea here is the same as above: if you invent a solution to the problem of a single customer, chances are there are other potential customers hidden in the woodwork that would also be interested in the innovation.

For example, baby powder was invented one day in 1890 when a physician wrote Fred Kilmer at Johnson & Johnson Laboratories that one of his patients complained of skin irritation from using a medicated plaster. To solve the problem, Kilmer sent the customer a small container of Italian talc. J&J then decided to include the talc with its plaster products. Soon thereafter hundreds of customers came out of the woodwork, asking for more of the powder, and Johnson's Baby Powder was born.

A second approach is to get so close to the customer that you experience what the customer experiences. Don't work simply to know who your customers are; but to know them. The key is not to assemble reams of market data sheets, which are then analyzed, sorted, and interpreted. No, the key is to directly observe customer experience in the field, in real time. It's much better to actually be there when the customer is wrestling with a certain problem, or attempting to use one of your products or services, than it is to ask him to later recall his experience. We call this the "touch and feel" approach.

CASE EXAMPLE OF TOUCH AND FEEL: BALLARD MEDICAL PRODUCTS

Ballard Medical Products, with sales of about $10 million in 1987, set a strategy to develop and dominate niches that big companies neglected, and to do so by prolific new-product innovation.

The first premise at Ballard, as described in an *Inc.* magazine article, is that customers themselves are an integral part of the product innovation process. The second premise is that salespeople—people actually out dealing directly with customers—are also part of the process. Salespeople are expected to go on-site and interact directly with the customer *as* he goes about his activities. A salesman for Ballard described:

You can't just ask the director of respiratory therapy or the head nurse if there are problems. You've got to walk through yourself . . . and ask the nurses whether *they've* got problems.

The third premise at Ballard is that R&D must respond to product ideas from salespeople. In one instance, the vice president of sales proposed his own product idea, helped design it, and worked with R&D to get it out the door. The entire product innovation cycle—from concept to delivery—was only a few months.

This real-time touch and feel approach to customer input is practiced by the very best product innovators. An even further step you can take is to rotate R&D people into actual sales roles for a period of time or, at minimum, to send them out to the field to interact directly with customers. (Incidentally, we think it's a good idea for you as a leader of the enterprise to spend part of *your* time touching and feeling customer problems.)

NIKE, Herman Miller, Bang and Olufson, BMW, Olivetti, and Patagonia expect their designers to be in close personal contact with the final users of their products. As design manager Paulo Viti of Olivetti puts it:

Of course, this is a somewhat unscientific form of marketing, but it often gets the designers' insight and intuition working much better than boring written reports.

But is it really unscientific? It certainly appears to be. But think for a minute; what's the essence of being scientific? What do scientists do? Do they just read boring written reports assembled by other people? No. They figure out ways to touch and feel the world, so that they can make precise observations about it. They go out and look at things for themselves.

And they experiment.

Corporate Innovation Element 3: Experimentation and Mistakes

What's important is experimentation. I only plan to succeed 10 to 20 percent of the time. I try a lot of different things, and by sheer dumb luck some of them work.

VINOD KHOSLA, CO-FOUNDER, SUN MICROSYSTEMS

By now, we hope you're inspired to be receptive to new ideas from everywhere, to have both idea-push and market-pull, and to be the customer. However, there is probably a nagging question: how do you know if an idea is a good one? Are all of the examples we've given simply examples of luck? What about all the idea-pushes and single-customer solutions that didn't create a wood-work factor? Can you eliminate all risk and determine if an idea is good before acting on it?

Sadly, the nature of innovation is that it is fraught with the unknown. The best way to find out if something is a good idea is to experiment, to give it a try. This, of course, leads to mistakes—ideas that aren't good—but they are part of the process. Innovation requires experimentation and mistakes. You can't have one without the other two, period.

Thomas Edison persisted through over 9,000 iterations before he success-fully invented the light bulb. Finally one of his associates asked, "Why do you persist in this folly? You've failed more than 9,000 times." Edison looked at him incredulously and said, "I haven't even failed once; 9,000 times I've learned what doesn't work." Edison's philosophy of experimentation, mis-takes, and correction, is the heartbeat of innovation.

We've always enjoyed John Cleese's (co-founder of Video Arts) vignette of "Gordon the Guided Missile," which so vividly captures this idea:

> Gordon the guided missile sets off in pursuit of its target. It immedi-ately sends out signals to discover if it is on course to hit the target. And signals come back—'No, you are not on course. So change it up— up a bit and slightly to the left.'
>
> And Gordon changes course and then, rational little fellow that he is, sends out another signal. "Am I on course now?' And back comes the answer, 'No. But if you adjust your present course a bit further to the left you will be.' And the missile adjusts its course again and sends out another request for information. Back comes the answer, 'No Gor-don, you've still got it wrong. Now you must come down a bit and a foot to the right.'
>
> And the guided missile, its rationality and persistence a lesson to us all, goes on and on making mistakes and on and on listening to feed-back and on and on correcting its behavior in the light of that feed-back, until it blows up the Nasty Enemy Thing.
>
> And we then applaud the missile for its skill. And if, then, some critic says, 'Well it certainly made a lot of mistakes on the way,' and we

reply, 'Yes but that didn't matter did it? It got there in the end. All its mistakes were little ones, in the sense that they could be immediately corrected. And as a result of making many hundreds of mistakes, eventually the missile succeeded in avoiding the one mistake which really would have mattered—missing the target.'

Sometimes the mistake-driven innovation process happens quite by accident. For example, the Reebok soft-style "crinkle" shoe leather that fueled demand for its exercise shoes in the 1980s was not planned. It came from a production mistake.

Indeed, many innovations have as their root source some form of just doing it—giving something a try, experimenting, just to see if it will work. Returning to the example of the 3M Post-it Notes, Spencer Silver described the original genesis of the adhesive:

> The key to the Post-it adhesive was doing the experiment. If I had sat down and thought about it, I wouldn't have done the experiment. If I had really seriously cracked the books and gone through the literature, I would have stopped. The literature was full of examples that said you can't do this.
>
> People like myself get excited about looking for new properties in materials. I find that very satisfying, to perturb the structure slightly and just see what happens. I have a hard time talking people into doing that. It's been my experience that people are reluctant to just *try*, to experiment—just to see what will happen.

The idea of using microwave for cooking came about through a simple experiment. Les Vandt, an engineer working on microwave technology, bought some popcorn and held it in front of a microwave power tube. Another engineer commented about the experiment:

> It [the popcorn] began to jump all over hell. It didn't involve the board of directors and all that kind of stuff; just Les Vandt and the bag of popcorn.

One of our favorite examples of innovation via experimentation comes from a small California company, Powerfood, Inc. Powerfood invented a revolutionary energy bar that athletes—runners, climbers, cyclists, swimmers, etc.—

could eat immediately prior to or even *during* exercise to raise their energy levels without upsetting their stomachs. Athletes had suffered for years with the rule, "Don't eat at least three hours before you work out." But with Powerbars, this problem vanished, which has changed the lives of thousands of athletes around the world.

The Powerbar invention illustrates many of the ideas presented thus far. The idea came from Brian Maxwell, an Olympic marathoner who chronically suffered from "hitting the wall" during races due to lack of energy (being the customer, solving his own problem). Maxwell founded the company because the big companies approached with the idea said, "It's impossible to make such a bar, and the market for such a bar is too small, even if we could do it. We're not interested." (Note again the importance of receptivity to ideas from everywhere.) And, finally, the product solution came about via massive experimentation, as described by Maxwell:

> I see Jennifer, Bill, and me in our Berkeley kitchen littered with bags of white powder and bottles of brownish liquids. A balance scale dominates the dining room table and on first glance, visitors conclude that we're the kingpins of some illegal drug empire. Then they notice the baking sheets and pie tins, lined with wax paper and numbered, strewn on every flat surface. Closer inspection reveals sticky-looking patches of strange colored dough in each one. The visitors don't escape without tasting at least four or five and recording their comments on file cards. Those who exercise regularly leave with a baggie of cellophane-wrapped samples to "try before your next workout."

These images of Maxwell and his friends concocting hundreds of experimental samples, Vandt exploding popcorn all over the microwave tubes, Silver mixing chemicals in the lab, and Edison's 9,000 light bulbs are essential to keep in mind when thinking about how to keep your company innovative.

We've even found with our own teaching that our best innovations come from experimentation in the classroom. We just try stuff all the time. Some of the experiments work, and become permanent parts of our course. Others fail and are discarded immediately after the first attempt. We've come up with a number of teaching innovations because we are willing to throw things against the wall and see what sticks. You've got to be willing to do this, even if it means periodically falling on your face (and we've fallen on our faces plenty of times).

Just Do It

We've found the simple phrase "Just Do It" to be immensely helpful in our own efforts to remain creative, and we have tried to pass this along to companies. At one company, we obtained a whole stack of "Just Do It" stickers, notepads, and key chains and had them distributed to people throughout the company. People need reminders that it's ok to "Just Do It"—to act without fifteen layers of approval. In fact, we always try to point out to people that it's far easier to ask for forgiveness than permission. Just Do It.

Don't Make It Big Before You Have To

Successful experimentation requires easy endings. That is, you've got to be willing to try lots of different things, keep those that work, and put a quick, painless death to those that don't.

Keep projects small as long as possible, thus making it easier to say, "Well, *that* didn't work. Let's try something else." If a project becomes too big too quickly, it'll begin to fight for its own life, even though it might be wiser to end the experiment and start a new one: "Hey, we've assigned seventeen people and spent a year on this thing. We *can't* end it."

For example, Novellus Systems, a small semi-conductor equipment company, consistently outmaneuvers competitors 10 times its size by using this "less is more" approach to new product development. The company uses three or four key engineers in the early stage of product design, and adds people only when it is clear the machine will work.

The Role of Product Failures

How far should you take experimentation? Should you take it all the way to the marketplace? It's acceptable to experiment in the lab, but what about the process of bringing products to market, which is much more expensive if the experiment fails?

This is a difficult dilemma, for if you never put out a product unless you have 100% rational certainty that the product will be a success, then you'll never put an innovative product on the market (and you'll be left in the dust by those that do). On the other hand, of course, product failures cost money, time, prestige, and can hurt confidence. There are two basic answers to this dilemma.

First, you can sometimes do small market-test experiments before making a full-blown product introduction. Put it out in a certain geographic area and see how it does. Or thoroughly test the product with a subset of your customers, and learn from their reactions. The idea here is to continue the process of lots of small experiments, mistakes, learning, and correction—just like our friend Gordon the Guided Missile, who self-corrects through thousands of "mistakes," but ultimately hits The Nasty Enemy Thing.

Second, highly innovative companies are not afraid of product failures. Not that they enjoy product failures, but they are willing to risk market failures and then learn from them.

For example, Apple Computer's first two follow-on products to the Apple II (the Apple III and the Lisa) were horrendous failures. But Apple applied all the information learned from those failures to create the incredibly successful Macintosh. Henry Ford introduced numerous products—including some notable failures, such as his original Model B—leading up to the famous Model T. Ford learned from each product introduction (and product failure) in designing the revolutionary Model T. Motorola had a string of valuable product failures from which it learned: the Model 55 radio (1933), the first push-button car radio (1937), a gasoline heater (1947), its first color TV (1957)—these were *all* product failures for Motorola.

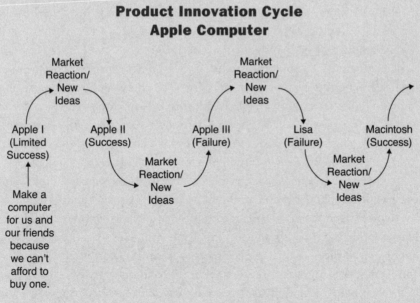

Product Innovation Cycle
Apple Computer

Figure 8-2

Breakthrough Innovation Cycle

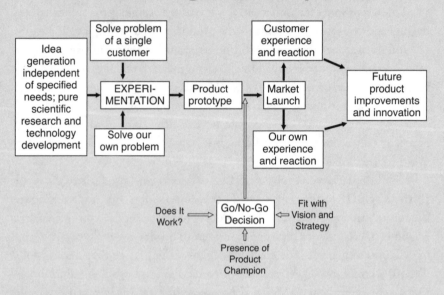

Figure 8-3

Ok, you say, but these are *big* companies; they can afford to have some product failures. What if you're a smaller company? Good point; but look again. In each of the above instances, the product failures occurred early in the company's history, when the company was much more vulnerable. Indeed, one of the reasons they got through the early stages to a place of greatness is partly because they had product failures early on.

The aim is to have multiple product cycles—putting products on the market, learning quickly where they fall short, and continuing to innovate and improve based on market input. (Note: this also applies to new services as well.) The Japanese, less known for breakthroughs than Americans, have mastered the incremental improvement process, which has contributed significantly to their dominance in certain industries, such as cars.

The nearby diagrams show how the breakthrough/incremental-innovation cycle works, and how it played itself out in the early days of Apple Computer.

[Note: Given the management turmoil at Apple since 1985, we found ourselves wondering if we should include Apple examples in this book. Apple has displayed three of the four elements of greatness (performance, impact, and reputation), but we're skeptical about the fourth (longevity). Will Apple be a great company in the year 2040? Given the fact that between 1984—the year the Macintosh was introduced—and 1991 there were no new major breakthrough innovations, and given the dispiriting leadership of Apple's top management (which was criticized for high executive compensation in the years leading up to layoffs in the early 1990s), we're concerned about Apple's long-term prospects for greatness.

Nonetheless, we believe that the phenomenal impact on the world achieved by the company from the late 1970s through the mid-1980s makes it attractive to use a handful of examples from its early history. You'll notice that each of the Apple examples in this book come from before 1985.]

Good Mistakes and Bad Mistakes

Should you be tolerant of all mistakes? Are all mistakes good?

A good mistake comes from an honest effort to try something combined with a diligent attempt to execute it well. A bad mistake is one where an idea fails primarily because of sloppy, inattentive, or indifferent effort. Saying "mistakes are valuable" should not be interpreted as, "we don't have to try to do our best." It's one thing to put the wrong product on the market, it's another to do a sloppy job of putting the product on the market.

The worst mistakes, however, are those that are repeated over and over again. It is the lesson learned from a mistake that makes it valuable, not the mistake itself.

The Popcorn Image

We like to think of an innovative company as having a *popcorn image*. Think of your organization as the popcorn popper, and think of unpopped corn as the seeds of good ideas. An innovative organization has the same feel as popping corn—lots of good ideas placed in a conducive environment, "popping" into experiments all over the place. Next time you go to the movies, observe the popcorn popper in action and keep the image in mind.

During a visit to Patagonia's main facilities (where design, production, research, marketing, and finance all reside), we felt like we were in the middle of just such a popcorn popper. The level of activity—people moving, trying things, talking, walking, designing, drawing, writing, meeting, deciding—was phenomenal. There was no post-lunch lull. There were no dreary, boring meetings. There were no frustrated people sitting around waiting for approval to act. There were no clocks, much less anyone watching those clocks. People moved just as quickly at 4:30 P.M. as they did at 8:00 A.M. People spoke in a rapid-fire "let's make this quick, because I've got a project I'm working on that I want to get back to . . ." style.

Another way is to set aside some uncommitted funds for internally generated ideas. Set aside a certain amount each year as internal venture financing, which can be tapped by people inside the company who want to develop an idea. Someone—or a group—would serve as internal venture capitalist and make decisions about which projects to fund.

Let Persistence Win

A colleague of ours asked Andy Grove, CEO of Intel Corporation, how his company chooses from the large number of new product ideas generated by its entrepreneurial engineers. Grove responded: "No one is ever told to shut up, but you are asked to come up with better arguments. People are allowed to be persistent."

The phrase, "People are allowed to be persistent," is perfect. It captures the notion of a "Darwinian" or free-market style environment where ideas are never killed outright, but where the fittest ideas survive.

In one instance at Intel, a group of middle managers wanted to develop add-on boards for personal computers, but the idea was initially not included in Intel's product strategy. The middle managers received funding from Intel's internal corporate venturing program, and turned the boards into a separate business.

A Company of Experimenters and Tinkerers

To remain innovative, you've got to have people at all levels doing lots of experimenting, tinkering, and doing—creating the popcorn effect. How do you do this? How can you create the environment where this happens? There are three basic answers, which we shall now discuss in detail:

- Employ creative people
- Get out of their way
- Reward them for being innovative

Corporate Innovation Element 4:
People Being Creative

To remain innovative, a company must have people within it who are being creative.

Wait! Before you stop reading because you think this is so completely obvious that it's not worth reading about, please read on. This point is not as obvious as it first appears.

Indeed, most of the literature on corporate innovation has focused primarily or solely on *structural* solutions. Although we agree that there are structural components to remaining innovative (discussed in the next section), innovation ultimately comes because people are being creative within those structures.

Unfortunately, there is a common belief that creative people belong to a special, unique subset of the human race, and that creativity is a trait that belongs *only* to that subset. In other words, the common belief tells us, there are creative people and uncreative people, and uncreative people are forever doomed to remain uncreative.

Garbage.

All people have the capacity to be creative. There is no such thing as an inherently uncreative person; creativity is a capability that resides inside each and every one of us. There is no special breed of person somehow ordained from God with the gift of creativity. Nor is it true that most of us were born deprived of that blessing.

The first step in having people at all levels be innovative is to believe in their inherent creative capability. After all, how can you possibly expect people to innovate if you don't fundamentally believe they can?

Help People Develop Their Creative Capabilities

The second step is to help people develop their personal creativity. Consider the following steps:

- Provide educational training in the creative process. Training sessions and seminars on personal creativity can be very effective in getting people to see that they are creative and how they can be more creative. Some of the most innovative companies, such as NIKE, make extensive use of such training.

  Prior to a creativity seminar at NIKE, we asked, "Why do you want us to come and teach you about innovation? It seems a little odd; teaching NIKE about creativity feels a bit like teaching Jessie Owens about track and field." NIKE training director Pete Schmidt responded:

  > Innovation is the most important aspect of this company
  > and we must preserve it as we grow larger. As we bring in

more and more people, we want them to understand the importance of innovation, and we want to back it up by helping them to be more creative. You can't take it for granted that people will have tapped their full creative talents; we've got to keep stimulating them in that direction.

- Provide educational materials on the creative process. When people are hired, give them a book on personal creativity. Purchase and circulate reading materials on creativity; you might even consider selecting one book per year that the company buys for each person and gives as a gift. Some readings on the creative process that we recommend are:
  - *Creativity in Business* by Michael Ray and Rochelle Myers
  - *Conceptual Blockbusting* by James Adams
  - *The Art of the Problem* by Russell Ackoff
  - *Lateral Thinking* by Edward deBono
  - *A Whack on the Side of the Head* by Richard Van Oech

- Write your own "Innovation Manifesto." Develop your own ideas about corporate innovation. Draw on ideas from this book, your own experiences, and from other authors. Create a one-page innovation statement that every employee gets. It might be a simple list of 10 key points, like
  1. We shall never say, "That is a stupid idea."
  2. We shall experiment first, evaluate later.
  3. We shall take 1,000 ideas from our customers.
  4. We shall produce 25% of our revenues in any year from new products introduced in the past five years.
  5. We shall listen to anyone who has an idea.
  6. We shall never do a "me too" product; every product we do must be innovative in some way.
  7. etc. . . .

Write your own list. It's fun. And valuable.

Hire and Nurture Unusual People

Seek people who have done creative things. Look for people who have done different and interesting activities—people who have started little businesses while in college, people who have had a diverse set of experiences, people who have shown initiative throughout their life, people who don't exactly fit in any pre-defined mold.

THE CASE OF THE MISH-MASH RESUME

Bill Wraith invented some highly innovative financial securities, including something called a *dual issue option*, which involved solving a long-standing finance problem that had been deemed by most finance experts as unsolvable. Who, you ask, is Bill Wraith? Suffice it to say that he's a very creative financial designer.

The fascinating part of this story is how Wraith got the opportunity to create these innovations. His resume read like a completely unfocused collection of items; he'd been a designer, a marketing manager, and a salesman, and he'd jumped from integrated circuits to personal computers to engineering work stations—all before the age of 30. Says Wraith, "Recruiters would look at my resume and think, 'Oh what a mish-mash. Nothing here fits. You're just jumping around with no coherent focus.'" But Wraith had a common thread running through his work: he had a knack for coming up with creative solutions to tough problems.

So he was hired by an investment bank. The bank saw that Bill was very bright and very creative, so they just hired him and turned him loose on tough problems.

Not only do you need to hire a few creative "misfits," you also need to tolerate their sometimes bizarre behavior. Some of the most creative people simply don't fit into typical well-behaved molds. They're often rebels, irritating and somewhat out of control.

Jim worked at McKinsey & Company early in his career. McKinsey is a very conservative organization, full of gray-suited, serious people. Yet, at the same time, McKinsey consistently produced some significant innovative contributions—including the book *In Search of Excellence*. Jim tells the story of encountering co-author Tom Peters in the office:

His office, which was right across the hall from me, was chaotic and covered with all kinds of funny hats: fire hats, World War I helmets, baseball caps, etc. The place did *not* look like a McKinsey office. And then, in the middle of a normal workday, this whirlwind flew by my office in baggy shorts, blown-out tennis shoes, and a t-shirt that had an inscription along the lines of, "Don't ask me any questions, because I really couldn't give a . . ." It was Tom, rushing into his office to pick up a few papers.

Obviously, Peters never entirely fit into the McKinsey mold. Yet the firm tolerated him, letting him run wild while he and Bob Waterman finished the book.

Vinod Khosla, co-founder of Sun Microsystems, spoke on trying to keep Sun innovative:

> You have to balance the "flakes" with the organization. You have to be willing to put up with some unusual people because some of the most creative people are very unusual. I had one engineer (a man) who came to work in a big dress-like gown—sort of like a pregnant lady's dress, something that was real loose and comfortable. And by the way this is not atypical. The point is that these people had the ability to create things we needed to compete.

Do all creative innovations come from weird people? No, of course not. In fact, some of the most creative people we know come in fairly conservative packages. Yet, to have an innovative company, it's also wise to have tolerance for a few unruly crazies. As Max De Pree of Herman Miller puts it, "If you want the best things to happen in corporate life, you have to find ways to be hospitable to the unusual person."

As your company grows, be aware that the type of people attracted to your company will tend to change—there will be more stability conscious types, fewer innovators. Fight this tendency by always hiring a few wild ducks.

Hire Diverse Talents, But Not Divergent Values

Breadth and diversity breed creative insight. People with different experiences and backgrounds working on the same problem will usually produce more creative—and usually better—answers than people with similar experiences. We urge you to hire an eclectic bunch of folks.

At Giro Sport Design, President Bill Hannemann has been adamant about building the senior management team with an incredible diversity of backgrounds—an ex-teacher, an ex-advertising executive, an ex-academic dean, an ex-video game design manager, an ex-Xerox designer. Yet, at the same time, Giro has taken care to screen a very narrow range of core values.

Follow the Giro example; seek diversity in your company. Yet keep the core values tight.

Size/Innovation Evolution Pattern

Small Company
↓
Attract Innovators
↓
Success and Growth
↓
Become Large
↓
Attract Risk Averse and
Stability Conscious People
↓
Install Bureaucracy
↓
Highly Innovative People Leave
↓
Reduced Innovation

Figure 8-4

DIVERSITY OF BACKGROUNDS

DIVERSITY OF CORE VALUES

Hire People Who Don't Know Much

Daniel Boorstin in his landmark work, *The Discoverers* (a detailed history of human discovery and invention), observed that many significant contributions came about because people were naive. In describing Ben Franklin's electricity discoveries, for example, Boorstin explained:

> In fact his (Franklin's) achievement illustrated the triumph of naivete over learning.... His amateur and non-academic frame of mind was his

greatest advantage; like many another discovering American, he saw more because he knew much less about what he was supposed to see.

The same thing happens in business. When people become fat with conventional wisdom, they're dangerous. A lot of being innovative in business is being willing to give something a try because you don't know it flies in the face of conventional wisdom. As Debi Colman, Apple VP of information systems and technology, puts it: "The single biggest roadblock to creativity and innovation I've encountered in business is conventional wisdom."

Returning to our example of Bill Wraith (Mr. Mish-Mash resume), he solved the unsolvable dual issue option pricing problem by purposely *not* learning what other people had done. His boss said, "We have some academic experts on contract you can talk with and you can obtain any journal or publication you want to work on the problem."

"No thanks," said Wraith. "I'd rather look at the problem totally naive. I'm afraid that seeing the blind alleys they took would just get in my way."

So Wraith went off to a dark room for a few days and just thought about the problem on his own. He reached an innovative solution by framing the problem in a way never before conceived. "If I'd known the traditional way to frame the problem, I never would have solved it," says Wraith.

The point here is not that every person you hire should be naive or know nothing about your industry. Knowledge and experience are valuable. But they can also be a liability. The point is to have a balance of experienced, knowledgeable experts *and* naive clean minds. Just because someone doesn't come from your industry or comes from straight from college (or didn't even go to college, for that matter) isn't a reason to turn him away.

Hire Designers

Design talent is one of the most underutilized creative resources in industry. By design talent we mean those who are trained and talented in the craft of design. There are two basic categories of design relevant to most businesses: graphic design and product design. Designers are trained to be highly creative and, most important, to apply that creativity to practical problems.

Think for a minute about great products: BMW cars, the Macintosh computer, Bang and Olufson turntables, Herman Miller furniture. Notice that design is a critical variable in the differentiation of these products—they have extraordinary elegance, beauty, and function.

Design can be a crucial differentiating factor even in mundane industries. For example, Joan Fabrics Corporation attributes much of its success in dominating the furniture upholstery market to the quality of its designs. According to former CEO Larry Ansin:

> Don't underestimate the importance of style—which we achieved through excellent design talent. There's a tendency to think that design is unimportant in traditional, old-line businesses. Not true. We succeeded in large part *because* of our design talent.

Hire designers. Hire graphic designers to help with logos, marketing materials, catalogues, packaging, and the like. Hire product designers to be integrally involved in the product development process, not as simply an adjunct to make the product "pretty," but from the very early conceptions of the product development cycle.

Some companies, such as Braun, Giro Sport Design, Patagonia, and Joan Fabrics, actually hire designers as employees. Whereas others (Herman Miller, Olivetti, Bang and Olufson, and Yamaha, to name a few) make extensive use of outside design consultants and design firms. Whichever path you take, we urge you to "think design" in every aspect of your business, from product development to marketing. Good design should permeate your company— buildings, processes, structures, products, the whole works.

Corporate Innovation Element 5: Autonomy and Decentralization

Freedom, inefficiency, and prosperity are not infrequently found together.
SAMUEL ELIOT MORISON

In 1998, K. C. Jones, then coach of the Boston Celtics, mentioned to a CBS Sports interviewer, "I give the players a lot of leeway on the court, so they can use their imagination and creativity."

"Doesn't that cause problems?" the interviewer asked.

"No," responded Jones. "We've been in the championship four of the past five years, and won it twice."

Jones' approach to coaching illustrates a central truth about creativity: it *requires* autonomy.

Trust, Respect, and Courage

Stanford Business School has a reputation as one of the most innovative educational institutions in the world. We have had the chance to experience how it works firsthand, which is captured in Jim's description of his first year at Stanford:

> I was 30 years old with no track record teaching at the University level. Dean Roberts made me the offer to teach, and then said simply, "Let us know what time slots you want. Good luck." That's all the direction I got. No one asked me what I was going to do in the classroom. No one gave me specific directions. No one even looked at my syllabus. I was given free rein to do pretty much whatever I wanted. Of course, I had seasoned colleagues to consult, and there were some course materials already developed. But I was basically left on my own to just do it.

Two years later, sitting at a luncheon celebrating an honorable mention for his teaching performance, Jim said to Dean Roberts, "You sure took a big risk on me. Why did you do that?"

"That's the way we do things around here," Roberts responded. "I didn't really view it as a risk, but more of an opportunity. See, by letting you go all out we believed that you would do your best work, and produce some good stuff. Of course, it doesn't always work out that way with people, but the innovation and performance we generally get by that approach is worth it."

Given how little Jim knew about what he was doing, we don't fully agree that the proposition was risk-free. But Roberts demonstrated the key element: trust and courage. He was willing to take a chance, and believed that Jim would rise to the occasion.

The basic message is to hire good people, create the environment for them to work, and get out of their way.

This is the magic that Tracy Kidder captured in his wonderful book, *The Soul of a New Machine*, wherein he described the design team's motivations behind the birth of a new computer:

> ... they did the work, both with uncommon spirit and for reasons that, in a most frankly commercial setting, seemed remarkably pure.... more than two dozen people worked on it overtime, without any real hope of material rewards, for over a year and a half; and afterwards, most of them felt glad. That happened because West and the other

managers gave them enough freedom to invent, while at the same time guiding them toward success.

This need for freedom and autonomy is well recognized by companies that remain innovative. Herman Miller allows its designers to work away from central facilities, in whatever environment they find conducive to work. Merck & Company, one of the most innovative pharmaceutical firms, hires the best scientists it can find, lets *them* select targets for basic research (not marketing or corporate), and stays out of their way.

This applies at all levels of human endeavor, from a five-person basketball team to entire societies. Indeed, freedom of action—room to experiment—is the primary factor behind the relative strength of Western economies compared to their centralized, eastern-bloc counterparts. In their book, *How the West Grew Rich*, Nathan Rosenberg and L. E. Birdzell show that the underlying source of the West's economic advancement is the large number of innovations that come about via autonomous experimentation. This experimentation, in turn, comes about because people *can* act, because there are few restrictions holding them back from giving something a try. Just imagine what the United States economy would be like if every new business had to get formal government approval from a ministry of central business control. (Actually, we don't need to imagine; just look at the Soviet economy.)

Yet the tendency of human organization is to move in the opposite direction—to seek control and order, to minimize unexpected surprises. To remain innovative, this tendency must be resisted, and resisted with crushing vigilance.

The oppressive desire to exchange life and soul for sterility and order is like a persistent vine, constantly creeping up the sides of an organization and wrapping itself around its limbs until it can no longer move swiftly and nimbly. Eventually, if left unchecked, the vine will wrap itself around the organization's throat, tighten its vice-grip, and strangle away the company's life spirit.

Indeed, one of the great ironies of corporate evolution is that nearly all new companies begin as highly innovative entities. Yet many of these same companies lose their innovative capabilities as they grow and age—the spirit that was responsible for early development becomes ensnarled in the twisted, suffocating vine of bureaucracy and centralized efforts to control.

DON'T LET THIS HAPPEN TO YOUR COMPANY!

But how? What can be done to prevent this from happening as a company grows larger?

Decentralization: Slicing up the Diamond

The basic solution is decentralization, or as we call it, slicing up the diamond. This is the basic solution pursued by companies that managed to keep an innovative spark alive while becoming much larger, such as Johnson & Johnson and 3M.

The idea is simple: by continually breaking the enterprise into small, semi-autonomous chunks, you can become larger overall, yet retain many of the advantages of being small. People within each small sub-unit can then have a sense of personal ownership, responsibility, autonomy, and accountability that simulates being an entrepreneurial business within the overall corporate umbrella.

George Hatsopoulus, CEO of Thermo Electron Corporation, described in an interview with *Inc.* magazine how this can work:

> You have to find a new structure for U.S. industry that combines the advantages of small companies and the support of large companies. My own answer is to have a bunch of small companies in a family, which gives them financial and management support and strategic direction. But at the same time they are acting as though they are independent companies. Right now [in 1988, with $400 million in revenues] we have 17 business units.

Raychem is another company that has managed to remain highly innovative by continually slicing up the diamond. As the company grew, it continually subdivided, "to keep the company a series of small groups," according to founder Paul Cook:

> If you are going to have literally hundreds of products being developed, . . . that calls for a rather loose, unstructured type of company as compared to a tightly controlled one. We are a *very* tough company to compete against.

When to Decentralize

When should a company decentralize? You should always be heading in that direction—giving people autonomy and room to initiate and act. A good rule of thumb is that when you reach somewhere between 100 and 200 people it's time to think seriously about slicing up the diamond.

Making Decentralization Work

We don't have the space here to cover in immense detail all the specifics of a decentralized structure. Nonetheless, there are some general principles about making a decentralized structure work:

- Link to vision. If your vision (values, purpose, and mission) is clear, people or groups operating autonomously can self-regulate themselves relative to the shared overall vision. They can all sight on the same guiding star, yet be in separate vehicles heading toward that star. *Shared vision is the crucial link in making decentralization work.*
- Overcome lack of centralized control with increased communication and informal coordination. People need to know what other decentralized sub-units are doing so that they can act in concert with them. At Patagonia, for example, product line directors meet at least once per month to coordinate. Another way to gain increased communication and coordination without the burden of increased bureaucracy is to use electronic communications—electronic mail, voice mail, computer networks, tele-conferencing, etc.
- Facilitate the transferring of valuable knowledge between sub-units. Hold internal seminars where members from different sub-units share ideas, present papers, and learn from each other's experiences. Grant prestigious awards to those who contribute a significant idea, invention, or other valuable assistance to another sub-unit.
- Have an open system. People operating autonomously can make good decisions only if they have good information. One of the best ways to achieve this is to make lots of information available to people—even traditionally sensitive information. At NeXT, for example, any employee can get access to any piece of information—even people's salary levels and internal financial information. Although you may not feel comfortable going to this extreme, we urge you to head in this direction. Again, compare centralized, secretive societies like the Soviet Union (and how terribly inefficient they are) with open systems like the United States. The same principle applies to companies.
- Avoid matrix structures. In an attempt to have the best of both worlds, some companies make the mistake of creating matrix organizations. Don't do this. Matrix structures remove the fire of personal ownership, not to mention accountability.

Purpose, Mission, Philosophy

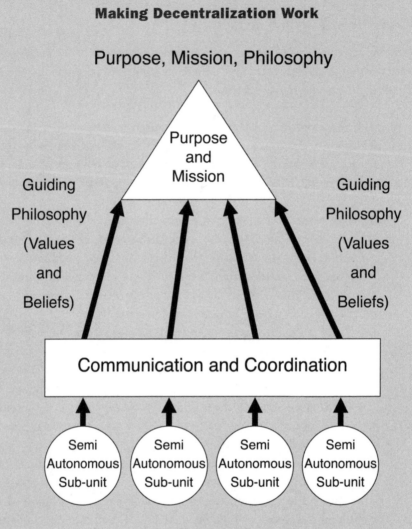

Figure 8-5

You might be wondering, "What about the duplication of effort that can take place in a decentralized environment? Don't you need centralized control to ensure that there's not too much overlap, which would be a waste of resources?"

Good question. But think again of the centralized Soviet-style economy versus the decentralized market-based economy. At first glance, a market-based economy would appear to be less desirable. After all, isn't it inefficient to have 36 separate computer companies all participating in the same industry, each with its own overhead, marketing effort, and product development effort?

Wouldn't it be more attractive to have one National Computer Company and centralize all these functions? Well, of course, we all know that it would be less desirable. There's immense duplication of effort in an industry with 36 companies, but it nonetheless generates more economic wealth and innovation than if there were only one company.

We're not necessarily suggesting that you pit all of your divisions against each other in a complete laissez-faire free-for-all (although both IBM and P&G have made conscious decisions during their evolution to promote spirited internal competition between groups). We ask you to rethink the notion that decentralization, replete with duplication of effort, is less efficient than the alternative.

This brings us to a central truth about organizations: *they are inherently messy*. There are no panaceas, no structures that solve all problems. Any attempts to completely eliminate the mess are doomed to failure. Yes, there are costly inefficiencies in decentralization, but the fire of personal ownership—of being our own little business—elevates human motivation and stimulates innovation in powerful, albeit somewhat chaotic, ways.

"Democracy sure is a chaotic, inefficient system," observed Harry S. Truman, "but it's better than anything else around."

That's precisely the case with decentralization and autonomy; it seems uncontrollable and inefficient. And, in some ways, it is. There is repetition of effort. It can be confusing to customers. There is difficulty in sharing technology. It just seems so unwieldy. However, like freedom and democracy, it's better than the alternative. Much better.

If you want the lightning bolt of innovation to strike again and again, you have to live with the inefficiencies. You've got to make a basic philosophical choice that the inefficiencies and disorder are worth the benefits.

It's impossible to have an organization with all the fire and zeal of decentralization and the complete efficiency of centralized control. Pick decentralization, fully implement it, and live with its difficulties as best you can. If you try to go halfway, it'll be like having a country shift from driving on the right side of the road to driving on the left side of the road, but only implementing it part way.

Corporate Innovation Element 6: Rewards

We listened patiently one day while the CEO of a medium-sized software development company lamented that he couldn't get his people to be more innovative and entrepreneurial. "I really want them to come up with new product ideas and new businesses and to take the initiative to make that happen. But they spend all their time managing their current divisions, and no time developing new things."

"How are they compensated?" we asked.

"Base salary, plus a bonus based on the annual revenues of their division," he responded.

"Would it detract from their current annual revenues to work on something new?" we asked.

"Yes, it would," he conceded. It took only a moment for the inconsistency to sink in.

In another situation, we were asked by an electronics company to examine the question of why many of its most talented engineers and scientists were leaving for other companies. We interviewed the best of those who had left, and received comments like this:

> The only upward path for me was to move into management. But I don't want to be a manager! I'm really happy being a designer, and making creative contributions. It's what I do best, and it's what I love doing. They told me that the only way I could move to a new level of pay (and, I might add, corresponding prestige) was to take a management job. So I left for this start-up where I'll be rewarded handsomely if my contributions are successful in the market, and where I'll be a hero.

These two examples illustrate a simple point: Your reward structure should explicitly recognize the importance of creative contribution.

We don't mean to suggest that people being creative are motivated solely by money, or power, or prestige. In fact, they're often motivated by the desire for interesting work, the challenge of a tough problem, the joy of contribution, or the satisfaction of finding something new. Nonetheless, innovation should be explicitly rewarded. All people, no matter how pure their motivations, are influenced by the reward systems of their organizations. Rewards matter. And if you want to remain innovative, you've got to reward innovation.

Some specific things you might consider:

- Make heroes of creative contributors through awards, honors, and recognition. Establish prestigious awards for extraordinary creative contribution—technical or new business ideas. When possible, give awards to *teams* as well as to individuals. Consider having a new product or business award *and* an internal process innovation award. Write articles in the company newsletter or magazine about people who've done something creative. Even have a "great try" award to recognize people for helpful, heroic failures as well as successes.

- Set measurable innovation goals and evaluate based on those. One of the best is to set the goal that a certain percentage of revenues (25% is a good number) in any given year—both for the company and for any given division—must come from new products or services introduced in the previous five years.

- Have a separate career track for creative contributors who don't want to go into management. Make this career track as potentially lucrative as top management positions. Why should the vice president of finance receive three to four times the compensation of the top creative designer? That makes no sense to us, yet it's exactly what most companies do. In contrast, Herman Miller has one of its top designers on a $100,000 per year retainer for 10 years; other Herman Miller designers have grown wealthy on royalties. Designers are heroes within the Herman Miller culture, and are accorded the same prestige and respect as any corporate vice president.

- Compensate people for specific valuable creative contributions. If someone comes up with an innovative idea about how to reduce production costs and that idea is adopted, why not give a bonus for that contribution? If a team invents a valuable new product, why not reward them specifically for that invention? Perhaps pay royalties or allow them to share in the profits of a new innovation.

- Let people play "pinball." Certain creative people are motivated more than anything else by the desire to pursue their work, the chance to do interesting and challenging things. When an individual or team makes a creative contribution, one of the best rewards is the opportunity to turn their attention to something else new, exciting, and important. Tom West, in Kidder's *Soul of a New Machine*, called this "playing pinball":

> 'You win one game, you get to play another. You win with this machine, you get to build the next.' Pinball was what counted. . . . 'I will do this, I want to do it. I recognize from the beginning it's gonna be a tough job. I'll have to work hard, and if we do a good job, we get to do it again.'

The crucial thing to realize is that truly creative people aren't primarily motivated by the opportunity to rest and take it easy. That's the last thing in the world they want. They want the chance to create, innovate, take on new challenges, learn, and to be valued for their work.

Not Just Products but Processes

We've spent the bulk of this chapter on new product or service innovation, but we also want to emphasize the importance of creativity in all aspects of a business—in marketing, production, organization, the works.

Creative marketing is also important to the success of a company. With the myriad of products and immense noise in the market, you need to invent ways to pierce the customer's screening system and leave a vivid imprint on his mind. This is particularly true for small to mid-sized enterprises that do not have the resources to compete dollar for advertising dollar with large behemoths. We call it *guerilla marketing*—ways of making a huge impact with few resources.

Patagonia avoided the expense of large advertising budgets by creating a spectacular catalogue, complete with authentic adventure photos and riveting text. For years, the catalogue was so beautiful that people looked forward to reading it. Patagonia also struck close relationships with magazine photographers who influence what people wear for photo shoots. You can't place an ad on the cover of *Outside* magazine, no matter what your budget, yet numerous times adventurers have appeared on the cover wearing Patagonia clothing. Patagonia spends only a paltry 1/3% of sales on print advertising.

Bob Moog, CEO of University Games, raises awareness of his game products by hosting a radio game show, wherein the audience calls in to play games over the air. People have fun, remember Moog, and buy games.

Even if you have a good-sized budget for marketing, keep in mind that creativity is still more important than volume.

Think back to the introduction of the Macintosh computer. Those who were watching the Super Bowl on January 25, 1984, will never forget seeing the surrealistic, eerie, grayish image of hundreds of passive people with vacant faces listening to "Big Brother" drone on and on. The famous "1984" commercial reached out from our TV screens and grabbed our full attention. Jolly football fans fell silent, drawn uncontrollably to the spectacle unfolding in their living rooms and bars. The commercial was shown only once, yet left an unforgettable impression. Does anyone remember any other commercials run that day?

Innovative products + Creative marketing = Magic

Don't stop there. Even in supposedly uncreative areas like finance, there is tremendous opportunity for creativity (and we mean legal creativity here). For example, Ben & Jerry's ice cream company circumvented the traditional hassles of full-blown public offerings by doing their own personal-style offering. They avoided expensive Wall Street underwriters by offering stock through the slogan "Get a scoop of the action" (printed on the lids of their ice cream cartons, along with an 800 number). Local folks (mainly customers) snapped up the offering.

Innovation is equally important in day-to-day manufacturing and operations. There is a wonderful example of creativity applied to operations at Federal Express. At one point, packages were getting backed up at its main sorting hub in Memphis, and no control system solved the problem. Then someone noticed that part-time workers were slowing the system down so that they could work (and be paid for) more hours.

Now, think for a moment; what would you do?

The obvious answer would be to set speed standards and enforce the standards with elaborate measurement and reward systems. Federal Express, however, did something simpler and more creative: it simply gave the workers a minimum daily financial guarantee, and announced that those who got done early could leave early. Within forty-five days, the problems were entirely cleared up.

The basic elements of organizational creativity described throughout this chapter—receptivity to ideas, solving your own problems, experimentation and mistakes, having creative people, granting autonomy, and rewarding innovation—apply to all areas of business. Use them. Educate everyone about them. Stimulate innovation everywhere. There's no shortage of good ideas.

Eight Management Techniques for Stimulating Creativity

We've spent most of this chapter describing the traits of companies that remain innovative. We'd now like to discuss things individual managers can do to stimulate creativity.

1. *Encourage; Don't Nitpick.* Keep in mind that there's no shortage of good, workable ideas, but that there's a tremendous shortage of receptivity to ideas. Don't be like one of those "wet blankets" that shot down the radio, the telephone, Federal Express, the personal computer, and NIKE shoes as "dumb ideas."

William McKnight, the man who more than anyone else shaped the innovation capabilities of 3M in its early days, lived by the maxim, "Encourage; don't nitpick." McKnight himself set a precedent of listening to anybody who had an idea. When one of his young inventors would come up with a "screwy idea," McKnight would listen and usually respond by saying, "Sounds interesting. Give it a try. Get to work, and quick."

Don't shoot down an idea by pointing out all its flaws and warts before the idea gets tested. The world is full of critics—critics who never stimulate anything truly great. Don't be one of them.

2. *Be Not Judgmental.* Harshly critical people destroy creativity and initiative. The fear of being criticized or being made to look and feel stupid is the biggest impediment to people experimenting, initiating, trying new things. The problem is not that people are inherently uncreative, it's that people are *afraid* to be creative—afraid of being laughed at, ridiculed, personally attacked, or otherwise psychologically abused. It's the deep-rooted fear we all carry around of the seventh-grade math teacher making an example of us in front of our peers.

The key word, again, is *respect.* Show respect for people's psyches. Don't make people feel stupid or worthless. If someone makes an honest mistake, never attack the person, address the event (review "Hard/Soft People Skills" in Chapter 3).

How you deal with mistakes and failures greatly influences people's creativity. Always ask yourself, "How would *I* want to be dealt with if I made that mistake or had that failure? How could *I* be dealt with so that I'd learn and, at the same time, maintain my desire to try?"

3. *Help Shy People.* Some good ideas never go anywhere because the people who have them are too shy to speak up. In fact, some of the best ideas come from quiet people. Quiet people tend to be excellent observers and thinkers; like cats, they're watchful and attentive, and often intensely curious. Yet they're also often fearful of voicing their ideas.

We have found some of the most insightful comments come from quieter students. When reticent students feel safe to share their points of view, some tremendous ideas emerge. It's not uncommon for a quiet student to finally raise his or her hand and speak with a slight quiver, yet deliver a stunning insight. Other students are left thinking, "Wow, where did that come from?"

To tap this resource—to make it easy for the shy people to contribute—you might need to do more than simply encourage.

Something as simple as a suggestion box, or making it clear that anyone can submit an idea in writing (anonymously if they like), can work. When you get a good idea, share it with everyone, perhaps saying at a staff meeting, "I got a really great idea in the suggestion box that I wanted to share with everyone."

4. *Stimulate Curiosity.* Relentless curiosity, the pure desire to know things, to test them, to see if something will work, fosters creativity. The most creative people ask many questions; it's as if they never outgrew that naive childlike desire to ask why. Create an environment where it's ok to ask questions. Ask questions yourself—not critical questions (again, don't be a wet blanket), but open ended questions in the spirit of inquiry. A favorite question of ours is, "What did you learn from that experience?"

Regis McKenna, whose firm formulated the highly creative marketing campaigns of companies like Apple and Intel, believes that a creative organization is a questioning organization: "I try to get my people to write out at least two pages of questions before they go to any meeting. Actually have the questions written out. You rarely get through the first page. You find that those questions lead to other questions."

Never respond to a question by saying, "That's a dumb question." Don't show disdain for a question. Respond openly, "That's a good question" or "I'm glad you asked that" or "Hmmm, that's intriguing, what do you think?" Do not under any circumstances make people feel stupid for asking questions.

5. *Create Necessity.* Human beings have an amazing ability to innovate their way out of seemingly impossible situations. "Necessity," as the cliché goes, "is the mother of invention." But cliché or not, it's true. In fact, many great ideas have emerged precisely *because* a company lacked the resources to do what it ideally would have liked.

CASE EXAMPLE: GIRO SPORT DESIGN

In 1985, Jim Gentes, founder of Giro Sport Design, knew he had invented a bicycle helmet that could revolutionize the bicycle helmet industry. It was extremely light (only 7.5 ounces), yet passed all safety standards. The helmet, made of expanded polystyrene foam, had no hard plastic shell.

However, Gentes was confronted with a problem. Without a decorative shell, the product was ugly—like riding a bike with a Styrofoam beer cooler on your head. On the other hand, with a standard hard shell, the product lost its weight advantages. Gentes devised a solution: a covering of extremely thin, very light plastic.

A great solution, right? Yes and no. There was one remaining problem: it cost nearly $100,000 for the tooling to make the thin, light shells—an amount far beyond what the then tiny company could afford. Gentes solved the problem by creating colorful LYCRA fabric caps that fit snugly over the helmet. The caps could be removed or washed, or exchanged for other colors. Fashion-conscious riders could thus match the LYCRA helmet covering to their outfits, and teams could get custom covers made to display their team emblem and sponsor names.

The helmet was a tremendous success and did indeed revolutionize the helmet industry, due in large part to the LYCRA coverings. According to Gentes:

> The LYCRA covering was a great idea. It really helped the product and caught everybody's attention. And the irony is that, if we would have had the money for the tooling, we might not have ever invented the LYCRA cover solution.

(As an aside, Giro's LYCRA helmets were so successful that the company was able to fund development of the thin-shell technology and introduce it to the market three years later).

You can replicate the Giro experience in any number of ways. In some instances, you might consciously limit resources. In fact, we believe in running lean even when you have the resources to do otherwise. We've noticed that Silicon Valley companies that've raised too much venture capital money tend to lose the innovative fire necessary for greatness. Gavilan Computers, for example, raised tens of millions in venture funding, yet failed to persist long enough to find a way to win.

Setting stiff, almost impossible, targets also creates necessity. For example, when Motorola was a small, struggling company, founder Paul Galvin would force invention by setting ludicrous targets. In one instance, he told his people to engineer $30 of cost out of a product. They told him it was impossible. He responded that he was sure they could find a way—and that they *had* to find a way. Ten days later, his son Bob (who'd been working on the project) sheepishly reported that they'd accomplished the reduction.

6. *Allow Time Away from the Fray.* Certain highly creative individuals need solitary time to do their best thinking, time away, time to think in silence. Phil Knight, founder of NIKE, believes that people get their best ideas away from the office, at the beach, or running, which is one reason why NIKE has a wide ranging campus with running trails, tennis courts, basketball courts, weight rooms, and aerobics studios. Herman Miller lets its designers choose their venue for creativity—and some choose to do much of their work at home or somewhere else off-site.

   Let people have some "at home" work days. Allow people to sneak off into a quiet room and work undisturbed for a period of time. Follow the example of Claude Rosenberg, founder of Rosenberg Capital Management, who set up two quiet rooms in the office " . . . that I keep trying to get people to use, because I really do believe that your most creative moments will not come in your normal occupation when sitting at your desk." Rosenberg has a corollary to this belief: *require* vacations. "I happen to think vacations should be real breaks from work—I'm really upset with my partners when they go on vacation and they call the office. If you clear your mind, you're probably going to be much more creative."

   At Patagonia, the pattern-making group (part of the design department) has a little sign posted near its area:

   > PLEASE OBSERVE QUIET TIME.
   > Closed from 8:00 to 12:00.

7. *Catalyze Group Problem Solving.* "Quiet time" is not the whole story at Patagonia. In addition to letting people have quiet, solitary incubation and thinking time, it's essential to capture the creativity of multiple minds thrashing about together. Brainstorming and other group activities produce extraordinary ideas.

   Desks at Patagonia are jumbled together in large, open bullpen-style pits (called "Bangladesk"). People are expected to work closely with others—both spontaneously and scheduled—in coming up with new ideas and solutions to problems.

   We've found in our own work, both in business and academics, that the most creative answers come with a combination of time away from the fray *plus* time spent tossing ideas around in group sessions. One plus one is often much greater than two when it comes to generating creative ideas.

A caveat: *The group must not have any wet blankets.* Group creativity sessions can work *only* if there are no members who nitpick ideas to death. Even just one person who prematurely critiques ideas will devastate any chance of a group being creative. Get rid of the nitpickers!

8. *Require Fun.* "As far as I'm concerned, the most important thing is having fun," explains Ted Nierenberg, founder of Dansk International Designs. "If you're not having fun in what you do, lock it up and try something else."

We're serious about fun. Fun leads to creativity. Ask people, "Are you having fun?" Ask yourself. Set enjoyment as an absolute requirement of work; if there's no joy, there will be little creativity. Have you ever noticed that some of the most creative people are a lot like little kids? They like to play, and, to them, work *is* play.

This doesn't preclude hard work. Creativity is hard work, but it should also be fun.

Faith in the Creative Process

We've given you a comprehensive view of corporate innovation, but there's one more element: faith in the creative process.

No one knows exactly how the creative process works. It's often a painful process, fraught with uncertainty. Creative insight comes in unpredictable flashes, usually after extended periods of hard work, frustration, and incubation. We can't say, "Tomorrow at 10 A.M. I will have a great idea." Well, we can say it all we want, but it probably won't happen. It just doesn't work that way. The lightning bolt of creative inspiration usually takes us by surprise, striking while we're in the shower, on the freeway, working in the garden, sweating at the gym, hiking in the hills, swinging a golf club, reading a book, waking up, or in any of a thousand other settings.

The really wild thing about creativity is that, given helpful conditions (spelled out earlier in the chapter), it's *certain* to emerge; we may not know how, when, or in what form, but it *will* come.

To keep a company innovative requires this leap of faith—faith that all people have the capacity to be creative, faith that there are lots of good ideas, faith in the woodwork factor, faith in experimentation, and faith in giving people the freedom to act. Man is by nature an inventor, discoverer, and explorer; we're endowed with a powerful urge to create, and a commensurate ability to do so.

It's exciting to create new things. We feel euphoria with each new "Eureka!" By inventing new products or better ways of doing things we get to feel a small slice of what Columbus must have felt when he discovered the New World or Galileo felt when he invented the telescope.

Indeed, not only does innovation keep a company healthy and prosperous, it satisfies the basic human drive to create and, at the same time, moves humankind forward. What could be more satisfying?

Creativity Is the Easy Part

Think back to when you were five or six years old. Did you play around doing creative things—perhaps drawing pictures or inventing games or building stuff in the backyard or doing other imaginative activities? When I ask groups of people this question, nearly everyone in the room raises his or her hand. When we're kids, we naturally do creative things. That's just the nature of being human. To say, "Be creative" is a bit like saying, "Be sure to breathe." If you're alive, you're creative.

Now, ask yourself a second question: When you were five or six years old, were you relentlessly self-disciplined? When I ask this second question, very few hands go up. Creativity is natural, abundant, ordained, infinitely renewable, encoded, but discipline isn't. The real challenge isn't how to be creative but how to become self-disciplined while keeping vibrant the full force of your natural creativity.

Furthermore, innovation by itself confers only limited competitive advantage. As Gerard Tellis and Peter Golder demonstrated in their book, *Will and Vision*, the pioneering innovators in a new business arena almost never (less than 10 percent of the time) become the big winners. Similarly, across all our rigorous matched-pair research studies, we found no systematic correlation between achieving the highest levels of enduring corporate performance and being first into the game.

The more I've studied great companies, the more I've concluded that the primary strength of American business is not just its robust capacity to innovate. Rather, the real American strength is the ability to *scale* innovation. Although being first can confer an initial advantage, building a well-run company that can innovate repeatedly and execute at scale is a much more significant and sustainable advantage.

Many entrepreneurs default to creative work because it's deeply satisfying, the same way a writer must write, a painter must paint, a composer must compose, a sculptor must sculpt. But to turn your enterprise into an enduring great company requires channeling your energies not just into the fun creative stuff, but equally into building a disciplined organization that can replicate and scale your innovations and deliver them with consistent tactical excellence. In the long run, best beats first.

Chapter 9

TACTICAL EXCELLENCE

God is in the details.
LUDWIG MIES VAN DER ROHE

THINK FOR A MOMENT of building a great company as analogous to creating a new climbing route up the sheer face of El Capitan. All elements discussed thus far are necessary: clarity of goal (shared vision), ability to keep the team going (leadership style), an assault plan (strategy), and creative solutions to a myriad of challenges along the way (innovation). However, there is another crucial element: physically doing the climb. If you don't execute the small details (like tying your knots right) or pay close attention to your hands and feet, you just might end up dead. The same is true of companies.

Think about another analogy. Building a great company is similar to writing a great novel—you need an overall conception (vision), a plot (strategy), and creative ideas to move the plot along. You also must sweat over each sentence, executing the book word-by-word, line-by-line, page-by-page. Hemingway was once asked why he'd rewritten the last page of *A Farewell to Arms* 39 times. He responded simply, "Getting the words right."

This notion of paying attention to the actual tactical execution of your vision and strategy, of "tying your knots right" or "getting the words right," is crucial to corporate greatness. You can have the most inspirational leader, the most profound vision, a brilliant strategy, and a thousand great ideas, but if you don't execute well, you'll never be great. Think of Olympic diver Greg Louganis hitting a consistent string of beautiful dives, and that's what you should be working for. Or think of Hemingway and his 39 revisions.

In fact, many outstanding businesses have been successful *primarily* because of outstanding execution. An *Inc.* magazine survey of its *Inc.* 500 (fastest growing private companies) showed that 88% of CEOs attributed their company's success primarily to extraordinary *execution* of an idea versus only 12% who attributed success primarily to the idea itself.

Jim Gentes, founder of Giro Sport Design, likes to point out that he believes in vision and creativity, but that he just as fervently believes in "getting the helmets right." He's fond of saying, "Hey, I'm not that special. I had an idea, and I just executed that idea really well."

Bill Hannemann, who was hired by Gentes to be president and chief operating officer of Giro, explained that this commitment to tactical excellence convinced him to take the risk of joining Giro when it was a tiny, unproven company with a single product:

> Giro's product was the first of its type on the market. But you always have to ask, "What's being first worth?" If you're not committed to tactical excellence, your first-mover advantage will evaporate. That's what impressed me about Jim; he would never cut corners in the execution of his ideas.

Think about Compaq Computer Corporation, one of the top three personal computer makers (along with IBM and Apple). The astounding thing is that Compaq is a *clone* maker (it copies IBM's architecture); it succeeds because it executed the IBM compatible strategy better even than IBM. (Compaq, by the way, doesn't price lower than IBM, it just makes the same products much better.) It's interesting to note that in 1990 Compaq had the highest pre-tax profit per employee in the computer industry, at $62,579 compared with $53,608 for Apple and $26,955 for IBM.

Think about Walmart. Sam Walton didn't invent discount retailing; in fact, there were many other companies trying to do the same thing in the early sixties, when Walmart was just getting off the ground. As Vance Trimble put it in his historical analysis of Walmart:

> The key ingredient turned out to be Sam's masterful execution of the idea . . . Other retailers were out there trying to do just what he was doing. Only he did it better.

Conversely, there's the example of a West Coast chain of restaurants with a wonderful concept: fast Mexican food that is also good for you (low fat, healthy ingredients). We were excited by this (we love Mexican food, and yet we don't like to eat too much fat, and we're always pressed for time). But, alas, we don't eat there anymore.

Why not? Because of little things. The cashiers had trouble with the computerized order system, thus creating long lines. We got exactly what we ordered only 50% of the time. The food was hot and spicy sometimes, cold and tasteless at others. If you happened to be eating near closing time, they'd put chairs on the tables and glare at you for not eating fast enough. At the time of our writing this, one of the two outlets in our area had closed and the other had much slower traffic than when it first opened.

In short,

Great concept + poor execution = death

Ok, perhaps that's a bit strong. But the best that could be hoped for is bleak mediocrity.

JIM'S VIEW FROM 2020

Deadlines: Freedom in a Framework

I once had a construction project underway, led by a contractor who does exquisite work. But we ran into a problem: The project moved slowly during the summer months, the very time when the project should have been moving much faster (to account for the inevitable slowdowns winter would bring).

So, I said to the contractor, "We need to set a deadline. Why don't you think about it for a week and come back on Friday with a deadline that you could commit to? Then we'll talk."

He came back on Friday and offered, "How about October 31?"

"That's an unacceptable deadline," I responded.

"But it's an extremely aggressive deadline," he pushed back. "I mean, we're going to have to pull out all the stops to hit October 31."

"No, you don't understand my point," I said. "The deadline is *too* aggressive. We both know that there's almost no chance you can hit October 31, which renders it utterly useless as a deadline." I let this sink in. "Why don't you reconsider and come up with a deadline that you can one hundred percent commit to hitting, with perfect work completed absolutely on time, no matter what happens with weather and unexpected problems."

He then offered, "Okay, how about next March 31?"

"At what time on March 31?" I asked.

"You want an exact time?"

"Yes. Otherwise, how will we know with one hundred percent certainty that you hit it?"

"Okay, how about March 31 at 5:00 P.M."

"That sounds much better," I said, knowing that even March 31 would be challenging (but doable). "So, you can one hundred percent commit to that deadline?"

"Yes," he said. "No problem."

The project proceeded along, and one clear-blue, seventy-degree September day I noticed that the crew had accomplished little by 3 P.M.

So, I ambled out and asked the contractor, "How's it coming along with the deadline? You know, one of these days, the weather's going to turn."

"We're working to hit your deadline," he said.

"No, it's not *my* deadline," I replied, then paused. "It's *your* deadline."

The pace quickened. And sure enough, the team hit the deadline, at 4:45 P.M. on March 31, with just fifteen minutes to spare.

Deadlines stimulate progress. But only if they are *commitments*. To hit a deadline means achieving the objective with absolutely A-level work, absolutely complete, absolutely on time, absolutely without complaint, absolutely. If you establish deadlines that everyone knows will slip, then you have no deadlines.

In a culture of discipline, there are only two acceptable ways to miss a deadline. First, the person to whom you have committed initiates a change in the deadline, without your having to ask (explicit, unsolicited absolution). Or second, you're truly incapacitated by something that has happened to you or your loved ones (disease, accident, tragedy), and it would be inhumane to hold you to the deadline.

There's an art to setting deadlines. Some leaders prefer to simply impose a deadline, whereas others prefer to ask for a proposed deadline. I use both approaches, depending on the circumstance, but my primary pattern is to ask for a proposed deadline and then navigate to a realistic date with zero-tolerance for missing (as I did with my contractor). But however you do it, the key is to ensure that people have no ambiguity about their deadlines, that they are committed to meeting them, and that you have a culture where missing deadlines is simply not an option. And that, in turn, means you need people who have the discipline to *refuse* to commit to deadlines that they cannot hit. If deadline slippage becomes routine, then deadlines do more harm than good.

But if you have the right people who view their deadlines as serious commitments, then you can give people tremendous freedom to manage themselves.

A culture of discipline at its best is about *freedom in a framework* of values and responsibilities. It is not about disciplining people; it is about finding *self*-disciplined people who always fulfill their commitments. It is not about expecting mindless obedience to rules or submission to hierarchy; it is about having the right people who crave wide latitude to do their best work.

Never forget a key lesson from our research into what makes great companies tick. All companies have a culture, but few have a culture of discipline, and even fewer build a culture of discipline *while also* sustaining an ethic of entrepreneurship. When you blend these two complementary forces together—a culture of discipline with an ethic of entrepreneurship—you get a magical alchemy of superior performance and sustained results. This is the Genius of the AND that eludes many entrepreneurial companies as they grow up. Deadlines can be a powerful mechanism to achieve the AND, to cultivate a rare blend of freedom *and* structure, creativity *and* discipline, which are distinguishing marks of the truly great. Use deadlines to achieve the AND . . . or use them not at all.

From Vision and Strategy to Tactics

Once you have your vision and strategy, it's necessary to translate them into solid tactical execution.

The first step is to make sure that all key people have a copy of the vision, strategy, and the current year's strategic priorities in front of them at all times. They should be brought to every staff meeting. They should be referred to constantly.

Bill Hannemann of Giro keeps a copy of the strategic priorities with him at all times. Not a staff meeting goes by without his referring to it. "I always try to make sure that our priorities are always being worked on in some specific way," he says.

Milestone Management

Most important, each strategic priority must be broken down into "bite-sized," discrete chunks—milestones. Think back to the analogy of climbing the sheer face of El Capitan. You don't think about all 3,500 feet of rock at once; you break the climb into manageable 100 foot sections (called pitches).

It is the concentration on one pitch at a time that gets you up all 3,500 feet of granite.

Each milestone should have a person responsible for its attainment plus—and THIS IS EXTREMELY IMPORTANT—a specific completion date.

Dates and milestones, however, should not be unilaterally imposed. People are always more committed to objectives and timetables that they have a hand in shaping. We suggest a process whereby individuals and their manager develop the milestone mutually and, whenever possible, the individual picks the date for its completion (one that the manager can live with, of course). We then suggest that the individual (not the manager) put to paper the agreed-upon milestone and date. This process of "signing up" tends to create significant psychological commitment.

Indeed, the transfer of broad vision and strategy to specific milestones owned by specific people who have committed to specific dates is crucial to getting things done.

VISION
↓
STRATEGY

ANNUAL
STRATEGIC
PRIORITIES

<u>SPECIFIC</u> MILESTONES
<u>SPECIFIC</u> DATES
<u>SPECIFIC</u> PEOPLE

Figure 9-1

Of course, getting things done is not enough; things have to get done well. And, to be a great company, they've got to get done *consistently* well, and with continual improvement. This requires building the right environment.

SMaC Mindset

"SMaC" is the essence of consistent tactical excellence. SMaC (pronounced "smack," with a very hard "k" sound at the end . . . *SmmaacK*!) stands for "Specific, Methodical, and Consistent."

You can use SMaC as a way to describe a very disciplined person, such as "Melissa is very SMaC."

You can use SMaC as a verb, such as "Let's SMaC this project."

You can use SMaC as an adjective, such as "Let's build a SMaC system."

You can use SMaC as a noun, such as "SMaC saves lives." (In fact, we have this phrase painted on the wall of our main offices in Boulder, where everyone can see it, as a constant reminder: Be SMaC!)

But SMaC is much more than a catchy and useful word. SMaC is a *mindset*. It's a way of thinking, a way of acting, a way of keeping your wits and executing in chaos, a way of focusing on the right details, a way of getting the right details right.

A former member of my research team who served in the United States Marine Corps once shared a story of a Marine Corps helicopter mechanic that perfectly illustrates the essence of the SMaC mindset. Picture a helicopter mechanic in a war zone. A helicopter has engine trouble and can't take off. Mortars are exploding nearby. Bullets are popping, snapping, whizzing, and zinging about. Amidst chaos and noise and smoke and yelling and confusion, the mechanic opens the engine compartment, works quickly, fixes the problem, and clambers down to the ground. More bullets, more mortars, more noise, more fear. But before the mechanic gives the pilot a thumbs-up, he methodically lays out all his tools on the ground and counts them, literally counts every single one, making sure that in the melee and anxiety, he didn't inadvertently leave a tool in the engine that would crash the helicopter. SMaC!

When Joanne and I had the opportunity to observe an open-heart surgery at the Cleveland Clinic, we witnessed a process that exuded SMaC. Backup systems. Checklists. Communication protocols. And the surgical assistant counting each and every surgical device, just like the helicopter mechanic. SMaC saves lives.

In rock climbing, many crippling or lethal accidents and near misses happen due to being un-SMaC. At age nineteen, I nearly killed myself during the descent off El Capitan due to lack of SMaC. SMaC Mistake #1: My partner and I didn't thoroughly research the location of the rappel sequence (where you descend by sliding down ropes with a friction device) on the East Ledges descent route, and we therefore began our rappel in the wrong place. SMaC Mistake #2: We didn't bring headlamps for a long climb, and we began our descent in the dark. SMaC Mistake #3: I didn't tie a knot in the end of the rope as a fail-safe measure to keep me from rappelling off the end of my rope if it didn't reach an anchor. SMaC Mistake #4: I didn't bring a device to mechanically ascend back up the rope if I became stranded in a blank section of wall. So, I rappelled down the rope in the dark. About twenty feet before reaching the end of the rope, I had a horrifying realization: There were no anchors. I was in the middle of a blank wall, and if I rappelled off the end of my rope, I would plummet hundreds of feet to my death. Fortunately, I had enough residual strength to climb, hand over hand, back up the rope to the ledge, knowing the whole way that letting go would splat me. We shivered on the ledge for the rest of the night until dawn, when we could find our way to the correct descent route in the daylight. Had I died, it wouldn't have been due to a random freak accident but entirely due to my lack of SMaC.

To be truly SMaC involves four basic elements:

1. Specific, replicable processes and mechanisms that create tremendous consistency
2. Checking and cross-checking systems to prevent catastrophic mistakes
3. Rigorous thinking to consider a wide range of contingencies and backups
4. Continuous evolution of SMaC based on understanding the *why* behind SMaC processes

This last element—understanding the *why* so that you can update and change the *what*—is the crucial element that distinguishes an advanced SMaC mindset from mere procedures and bureaucratic policies. If people in your enterprise begin to say to new members, "That's just the way we do things" instead of saying, "This is *why* we do things this way," your enterprise is degenerating from a culture of discipline into a bureaucracy. If mindless adherence to procedure erodes a true SMaC mindset, your enterprise will fail just as surely as if it had no SMaC in the first place.

In my work and teaching with the American military, I learned about the power of AARs, or "After-Action Reviews." The idea is to set aside time after every mission to discuss, review, and learn from what happened. What worked? What did we learn that can be applied to future missions? What didn't work? What did we fail to prepare for? And then integrate the learning from the AAR directly into preparing for what comes next. Done systematically, AARs become part of the training regimen, part of continually developing and refining the SMaC recipes that work best.

We've adopted the AAR model at The Good to Great Project. We do not close out an engagement and call it done until we have had a team AAR, captured the learnings, and integrated any adjustments into our SMaC recipes. Every hour spent in a disciplined AAR pays off in ten hours saved down the road while contributing directly to the consistent tactical excellence that we expect of our system. Over time, I've simplified our AAR process down to three key questions:

> AAR Question 1: What replicable new learning did we gain from what went well?
>
> AAR Question 2: What replicable new learning did we gain from what did not go well?
>
> AAR Question 3: Drawing upon questions 1 and 2, what changes can we make to our SMaC recipe to systematically improve our consistent tactical excellence?

You can think of this as a repeating loop: You feed the learnings from AARs back into systematic training and preparation; you take new actions; you retain SMaC disciplines as you execute those actions; you conduct AARs for learning and improvement; then you go back to the top of the loop. Then repeat, again and again and again, forever, as a habit at the center of your culture of discipline.

Creating an Environment Where People Attain Consistent Tactical Excellence

The bulk of the causes of low quality and low productivity belong to the system [created by management] and thus lie beyond the power of the workforce.
                                        W. EDWARDS DEMING

We ran across a wonderful little article in the *Wall Street Journal*, entitled "How L.L.Bean Restored My Soles—and Warmed My Soul," by A. Richard Barber. In it, he wrote about how Bean employees went to heroic efforts to resole a pair of 30-year-old Feather Weight Lounger Boots in a size Bean no longer carried, and for which there was no standard resoling process.

Barber described how each Bean employee took personal responsibility for his situation, giving him their first names (Maggie, Ann, and Steve) and making themselves personally accountable: "My name is Steve Graham at extension 4445, just so you have someone accountable at our end." He wrote about the "clear, crisp un-world-weary" tones of their voices, and how they were genuinely apologetic about unexpected delays. "It was comforting to know," wrote Barber, "that so many people cared about [my boots]."

Barber concluded the article:

> Thirty years from now I hope I'm speaking to Maggie and Steve and Ann. They gave me a wonderful lift. On this anniversary of our happy encounter, I wish them as happy a holiday as they gave me last year.

Barber's article raises the question: are the people who work at L.L.Bean different from other people? Is there something unusual about Freeport, Maine?

We think not. L.L. Bean doesn't have special access to dedicated, conscientious people—at least not any more than your company does. No, Bean has simply created an environment where people throughout execute well.

This leads us to a central tenet of tactical excellence: if your people aren't executing well, it's not their fault.

It's yours.

Leaders of great companies have faith in the ability of ordinary people to perform extraordinarily well. They know that there are very few lazy, uncaring people and that, given the right environment, most people will deliver outstanding performance. Poor performance is usually the result of poor hiring decisions, poor training, lack of clear expectations, poor leadership, inadequate appreciation, poor job design, or some other failure of the company, not the employee.

There are five basic conditions under which people tend to execute well:

1. *People execute well if they're clear on what they need to do.* How can people possibly do well if they don't have a clear idea of what "doing well" means—if they don't have clear goals, benchmarks, and expectations?
2. *People execute well if they have the right skills for the job.* The right skills come from talents, temperament, and proper training.
3. *People execute well if they're given freedom and support.* No one does a good job with people looking over his shoulder; when people are treated like children, they'll lower themselves to those expectations. Also, people need the tools and support to do their job well. To use an

extreme illustration, imagine how difficult it would be for Federal Express employees to make on-time delivery without reliable trucks.

4. *People execute well if they're appreciated for their efforts.* All people want their efforts to be appreciated. We've consciously chosen the term appreciated rather than rewarded because it more accurately captures that excellent performers value respect and appreciation as much as, and often even more than, money.

5. *People execute well if they see the importance of their work.*

This last condition is so important that we'd like to expand on it.

While waiting for a flight out of San Francisco Airport, we stopped for a shoeshine. We noticed that the shoeshine expert paid great attention to getting our shoes just right, and inspected every angle to ensure the quality of his workmanship.

"Are you guys in a hurry?" he asked. "I'd like to spend a couple extra minutes to let this scuff mark set and then give your shoes an extra coating." We had plenty of time, so we agreed.

While he applied himself to his task, he talked about his work. "It's really important that I get people's shoes done right," he said. "My customers are traveling to important meetings. The last thing they need is for their shoes to look bad. When they go into that meeting, I want their shoes to look wonderful. It's sometimes the details—like poorly shined shoes—that can make people look bad."

And therein lies the essence of tactical excellence: people caring about their work *because they see its importance.*

A powerful example of this is the experience of an airplane parts manufacturer during World War II. The company, according to Peter Drucker (to whom we owe the example), was experiencing terrible problems with its workforce—absenteeism, strikes, slowdowns, and slipshod work.

So what to do? Press people harder? No. Fire the bad apples? No. Increase wages? No. None of these solved the basic problem.

The workers had never been shown the importance of their work! They'd never seen a finished bomber, much less seen where the part they made fitted, or how important that part was to the bomber's performance, or how important the bomber was to the war effort. So the company brought a finished bomber to the factory facilities, along with crew members who told them how important the bombers were to the war effort and how important the part was to the bombers. And, according to Drucker, "the bad morale and unrest disappeared at once."

There's an interesting aspect of the above example: the presence of the crew members. No longer were the workers responsible merely for a part in a bomber, they were responsible for specific people—for George, and John, and Sam—whose lives would depend on the performance of the bomber. The same is true of the shoeshine expert at the airport; he has a sense of direct, personal responsibility for each customer.

People see the importance of their work—and thereby tend to be committed to doing a good job—when they know other people are depending on them.

John Gardner, former secretary of health, education, and welfare and founder of Common Cause, told us a fascinating study on heroism he was involved with. The study asked the question: what motivates people to heroic behavior? The overwhelming answer was not glory, or country, or patriotism, or anything like that. It was primarily a person's belief that comrades were depending on him, and he couldn't let them down.

If you can create an atmosphere where people are dependent on each other—where people think, "I can't let these people down"—you'll get extraordinary performance.

Have you ever wondered how Federal Express managed to grow fast and, at the same time, execute the "absolutely, positively overnight" promise so well? Federal's founders did it by creating an organization where people depend on each other. (As an aside, we think Federal Express is a good example of success due primarily to the quality of execution, rather than the brilliance of the idea. The concept of nationwide overnight delivery was nothing new; other firms had thought of it. Doing it—and doing it well—was the challenge.)

Founder Fred Smith was heavily influenced by his experiences in the Vietnam War, where he was a company commander and reconnaissance flyer. There he observed that the "average person" would do extraordinary things when platoonmates depended on him. He wanted to build a company that would be built on this basic truth.

Smith told Bill Moyers in an interview:

Federal Express is a creature of Vietnam. I don't think I would have done anything like this [without that experience]. People will rise to the occasion if you give them a chance. Give people the challenge and they've got the basic intelligence and outlook to do it.

Art Bass, an early chief operating officer at Federal Express, explained the ethos:

We brought together people who were proud of what they were doing, people who had very few other opportunities in their whole lives to be proud of anything. Whether you were in a truck or a plane or in the hub, you were all alone out there, but everybody was depending on you. You had to come through.

The statement "you had to come through" is perfect. It captures the essence of what you want to create, people depending on other people.

That's exactly how L.L.Bean warmed Richard Barber's soul. Maggie and Steve and Ann at Bean believed they had to come through for Richard. Richard wasn't a consumer. Richard wasn't order number 3365. Richard wasn't that guy with the damned boot problem. He was *Richard*, and he wanted—needed—his boots resoled, and they *couldn't let him down*.

You, as a leader of the company, have a responsibility to make sure that every single person is doing something important and that the person knows *why* her work is important.

Expectations

Picture Denver International Airport when a gigantic summer-afternoon thunderstorm rolls in. Air traffic control halts all traffic. Now consider two different planes on the tarmac, Plane A and Plane B.

Plane A: "Folks, this is the captain. We've been held up by air traffic control for weather. They're telling us we should be on our way in thirty minutes." You settle into your seat. Thirty minutes pass. You're still on the runway. Thirty-five minutes pass. Then forty. The pilot comes back on. "Well, it looks like we're going to be a bit longer. Hopefully, we'll be on our way in another ten or fifteen minutes." Ten more minutes. Then fifteen more minutes. Then, finally, at sixty-five minutes, you hear the engines rev up, and you feel the aircraft position to roar down the runway.

Plane B: "Folks, this is the captain. We've been held up by air traffic control for weather. They're telling us it will be about thirty minutes. But this is Denver, and I've found over the years that sometimes these storms can really last. There might be wind shear and we want to be safe. So, you might want to settle in for a long wait. I don't think we'll be on our way for eighty or ninety minutes." Everyone groans. Then people begin to settle back, taking naps, watching movies, making calls, sending emails, reading books. The clock ticks.

Then at sixty-five minutes, the captain comes back on, "Well, folks, it looks like the weather is clearing up faster than we'd expected, and we're going to be on our way." You hear the engines rev up, and you feel the aircraft position to roar down the runway.

Both Plane A and Plane B took off at sixty-five minutes. But which plane has happier passengers?

The Link to Vision

As described earlier, one of the primary functions of corporate vision is to add meaning, to be a source of motivation for extraordinary human effort. A clear and compelling vision is essential to people seeing the importance of their work. If you haven't yet read Chapter 4 on vision, read it. If you haven't set a vision, do so.

Also, remember that one of the components of a good vision is a set of core values and beliefs, a set of guiding principles and precepts. This underlying set of core values plays an essential role in guiding people's daily behavior and standards. In fact, there is a direct link between values and tactical execution. For example, if one of your core values is "treat customers like human beings" and if it is well inculcated through your organization (as it is at L.L.Bean), people are going to treat customers like human beings.

A Mentality of Continual Improvement

Tactical excellence isn't an end point; it's a path. It's the path of continual improvement.

Think for a moment about the Japanese miracle. "Made in Japan" used to mean "Poor quality." Not anymore. The Japanese have established a worldwide reputation for quality. They are masters of consistent tactical excellence. What happened? How did the Japanese make this extraordinary transformation?

Part of the answer lies in the influence of Dr. W. Edwards Deming, who educated Japanese management in quality control techniques. (Deming's influence on the Japanese was so great that he was awarded the Japanese Second Order of the Sacred Treasure—the first American to ever receive such an honor. The famous Deming Prize, a prestigious and much sought after award for total quality control, is named after Deming.) The central tenet of Deming's work, put forth in his book *Out of the Crisis*, is constant improvement.

Improvement is not a one-time effort. The whole idea is to measure where you are today, evaluate what you can do better, set a plan in place to improve, implement it, measure again, and repeat the process. Infinitely.

The game is to never stand still, to never be good enough. What passes for excellent this year should be mediocre compared to what you're doing five years from now, which should be mediocre compared with 10 years from now, and so on. Forever. There's no end. There's no stopping point. There's no "having made it."

Tactical BHAGs

One of the best methods for achieving great performance is to create unit-level "tactical BHAGs." These break the overall BHAG of the enterprise into smaller goals that then become unit-level BHAGs.

We were looking for a way to stimulate progress in the execution of event commitments at The Good to Great Project. We'd learned over the years that we should have all event logistics largely in place three weeks prior to events. So, we came up with the "T minus 3" mechanism, a full briefing and launch review that would take place no later than three weeks before the event date. This would force us to get ahead in preparing and leave time to make adjustments before the event. We noticed that sometimes we'd fall a bit short of "T minus 3"—hitting the briefing at twenty or sixteen or even fourteen days out. There would always be mitigating factors, such as travel schedules or challenges with getting information from people outside our system. Still, our best tactical results came when we adhered to the "T minus 3" discipline.

So, our team came up with a tactical BHAG: Attain 100 consecutive hits of "T minus 3" success, without a single miss. We called this the 100–0 BHAG (100 successes in a row, with 0 failures). We then put the 100–0 BHAG on the whiteboard for everyone to see, along with the current consecutive count. The key word is *consecutive*; if we missed it even once, the counter would be set back to zero, and we'd start all over again. Every time we completed a "T minus 3," there'd be a celebratory moment of changing the count (e.g., 31–0 turned to 32–0). Everyone knew that if we ever missed once, even by only one day, the counter would be set back to 0–0. Whoever was the person responsible for a specific "T minus 3" felt the building pressure: "I can't be the one to fail and set the counter back to 0–0." But everyone in our system also rallied to pitch in and help, to make sure we never missed. This tactical BHAG compelled people to march ahead, to build time buffers, to minimize all chances of missing. It also increased team camaraderie as we marched.

On March 22, 2018, at 3:03 P.M., our team assembled in the conference room to erase the 99–0 from the whiteboard and replace it with 100–0. One hundred times in a row without a single miss. And at the time of this writing, more than two years later, we've maintained our perfect record. Hitting "T minus 3" has become ingrained as a disciplined habit.

A Six-Part Process

Creating the environment where people throughout achieve consistent tactical excellence involves a six-part, never-ending process.

- Hiring
- Inculturating
- Training
- Goal-setting
- Measuring
- Appreciating.

Creating an Environment for Tactical Excellence
A Six-Part Process

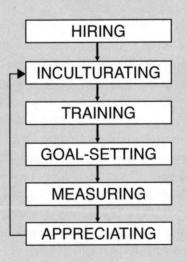

Figure 9-2

1. Hiring

It all starts with hiring decisions. Good people attract good people, who, in turn, attract more good people, and so on. Hiring good people requires a substantial investment of time. We've seen numerous companies get themselves into trouble because they didn't invest properly in the hiring process.

It's more expensive to "un-hire" a poor choice (and then find a new person) than it is to find and hire a good choice in the first place.

What is a good choice? Good shouldn't be defined primarily in terms of education, skills, or specific prior experience (although these will certainly factor into the choice). The *primary* assessment of good should be, "Does this person fit with our values? Is this person willing to buy into what we're all about? Is this person likely to live with our precepts?" As Kristine McDivitt of Patagonia put it:

> I've hired a lot of people who have lacked traditional credentials, and they've worked out great. I've also hired people with awesome credentials who didn't fare so well. I look primarily for a values-fit—especially a love of the outdoors—and an attitude about doing good work. We're fanatical about the quality of what we make, and we want equal fanaticism in the people we hire.

Giro Sport screens rigorously for people who are concerned about quality, innovation, and a solid work ethic. Home Depot looks for home-fix-it do-it-yourselfers who enjoy helping people. Williams-Sonoma, a supplier of cooking devices, searches for people who have a personal interest in fine cooking. Our friends up in Freeport at L.L.Bean seek people who use Bean products and exhibit a generally positive attitude about people; "We look for people who like to help people."

Finding good fits requires looking at a large number of applicants and spending extensive time before making a hiring decision. Stew Leonard's Dairy, for example, hires only one person for every twenty-five applicants. (Roughly half of the company's employees have a relative who also works for the company—a further reinforcement of screening on values.) Marriott, which places great emphasis on finding people who fit, interviewed 40,000 people for 1,200 jobs at a newly minted hotel.

Applicants should never be hired on one interview alone; they should be interviewed by at least two people before an offer is made.

Do reference checks. THIS IS IMPORTANT. If we had to pick one place where companies consistently trip up in the hiring process, it's that they don't do reference checks. Check references with former bosses, subordinates, peers, and others. An employee should never be hired without at least two reference checks, and we recommend five or more.

Finally, avoid hiring outside people for senior positions; hire from within whenever possible. There are two reasons. First, hiring outsiders can devastate morale: "Why should I work hard when they'll just bring in someone above me? I'll never really have a shot at getting promoted." Second, people need to be inculturated into the company, and this is easier if people come in at lower levels and work their way up.

2. Inculturating

Even if you make good hiring decisions, people need to be inculturated into the organization. By "inculturating" we mean instilling and reinforcing the vision, especially the core values. You can't just assume that people fully understand the precepts of your organization when they walk in the door. You need to educate them. And you need to educate them *early*.

In fact, inculturation should begin in the hiring process. Give applicants materials that describe your philosophy; have company representatives talk about the vision during job interviews.

Early in his career, when interviewing for a job with Russell Reynolds Associates, one of us (Jim) was flown out to New York from California to meet personally with founder Russ Reynolds. The entire interview centered on personal and company philosophy. Reynolds sent Jim away with a package of sensitive documents to better understand the company philosophy. No new professional is hired without a personal "philosophy meeting" with Reynolds or another senior officer of the firm.

New hires should be further educated in company values soon after starting work. Some specific steps to consider:

- Give a "starter kit" of written materials to every new hire, and make it clear he or she ought to read it. Obviously, this should include your vision statement, with special emphasis on the core values. Anne Bakar at Telecare Corporation, for example, gives copies of the company's values to all new hires.

    John Mackey, founder and CEO of Whole Foods Market, a chain of health food supermarkets headquartered in Austin, wrote the "Whole

Foods General Information Handbook," which tells the company's history and values. It advises people on how to advance their careers and what to expect from co-workers and supervisors. At a few stores, new hires are given quizzes to show they understand the philosophy.

- Write! Write! Write! Never underestimate the power of the written word. Few company leaders make good use of the most powerful human tool—the pen. Use it. People will read what you write because you're the leader, and they'll be influenced by it. Think of how much weaker the United States would be if the Constitution had never been written down.

  It's a good idea to personally write a letter or article that has a touch of the company's philosophy a few times per year. It can be circulated on its own (to all employees, not an exclusive group) or printed in the employee newsletter or magazine. Leon Gorman, CEO of L.L.Bean, for instance, makes extensive use of the "Bean Scene."

  Use writing as a way to continually reinforce the importance of people's work. Tell stories of how people came through for others who were depending on them. Give examples of how a specific employee made a difference in the life of a customer. Never miss an opportunity to heighten the sense of noble purpose that people at all levels can (and have a right to) feel about their work.

- Write a history of the company that every new employee will receive upon joining. The history should trace the roots of the firm, its phases of evolution, and the origin of its values. Marvin Bower, co-founder and architect of McKinsey & Company, wrote a marvelous book, *Perspective on McKinsey*, which has chapters like:

  > "Years of Shaping Purpose"
  > "The Firm's Early Years"
  > "Building a Distinctive National Firm"
  > "Professionalism: The Firm's Secret Strength"
  > "Developing Our Managing Philosophy and System"

  Three very important points about such a book:

  1. You (if you are a founder, president, or CEO) should write it. The words should come directly from you, not the PR department or an outside writer. Make every new employee feel that you are personally communicating directly with him or her through the pages of your book. Bower's book is an excellent example of this.

2. Write for employees, not the outside world. Write it as a very personal connection between you and employees. Bower's book, for instance, contains the following inscription: "Written privately and printed for readership by only the Personnel of McKinsey & Company, Inc."
3. Don't wait too long. If yours is a young company, you may be wondering if such a history makes sense. We agree that it's awkward to write a history of something that's only a year old. However, by the time the company is five years old, you should be drafting a short corporate history. It needn't be hardbound; it could be reproduced at the copy center. You can then easily update and revise it as the company grows.

- Give a company philosophy talk to all new employees. If possible, do it in person, either in groups or individually. If it is not possible (because of geographic constraints or if your company is too big) then perhaps use video.

  We point you to the example of Jim Miller, president of Miller Business Systems, a 300+ person provider of office services. Miller meets one-on-one with every new employee, during which time he describes the company philosophy and gives the employee a bottle of green liquid labeled "enthusiasm" and an "I believe in myself" mirror. Miller Business Systems won the Office Products Dealer magazine Award of Excellence for customer service in 1987.

- Use a buddy program. Assign each new hire to a buddy who takes him under her wing and personally educates and role models the values, as well as teaches specific skills.

- Send new employees to training seminars that instill values, in addition to teaching specific skills. One of the keys to IBM's successful inculturation of hundreds of thousands of people is that its training programs have always emphasized IBM values and beliefs more than managerial techniques.

3. Training

Even though training programs should have a good dose of inculturation, people also need specific skills training. After all, people can't do a great job unless they know how to.

Train people at all levels, not just managers. Keep in mind that training isn't a perk; it's a tremendous business advantage. Returning to our friends from Freeport, new L.L.Bean front-line employees receive a full week of training on the computerized phone ordering system, telephone skills, and product knowledge. The use of personal names ("this is Steve") doesn't happen randomly; people are taught to do it.

Another example of front-line training comes from Parisan, a retail chain that boasts two times the average national sales volume per square foot. Parisan attributes this success in large part to the fact that front-line employees receive 45 hours of training before they're allowed to deal with customers, plus a 12-hour refresher course after 90 days.

You can use a variety of training methods.

- You can use written materials, such as the Russell Reynolds Associates "Practice Guide," a manual of standards and tactics for the executive search process.
- You can use video and audio. Domino's Pizza, for example, has a VCR in every store on which employees watch videotaped training programs.
- You can use apprenticeship programs, where seasoned successful employees educate new people. This is used at Dansk Designs and at legendary Goldman Sachs.
- You can use outside training courses for teaching specific skills. At Stew Leonard's Dairy, for example, some front-line workers are sent to $600 Dale Carnegie programs. Home Depot offers handyman skill classes each week. Many of the best high-technology firms take advantage of advanced technological training offered at universities.
- You can develop your own courses. NIKE has an entire internal training program with multi-day sessions for mangers. McKinsey started extensive consulting training back in the forties, when it was a tiny firm.
- You can even create your own "university." There's the famous McDonald's Hamburger University; Lenscrafters has three "campuses" for its management training school, known as Precision Lenscrafters University; Apple has an entire group called Apple University. These universities create educational programs attended by company employees.

But whatever you do, don't wait too long. Many smaller companies complain that they don't have the resources to do training. We ask them: how can you possibly expect to develop into a great company without it?

4. Goal-Setting

"How do you get your runners to go so fast?" a second-tier track coach asked the championship track coach.

"They work hard," she responded.

"So do mine," said the second-tier coach. "I make them run all the time. And I tell them I want them to run *fast*. I'm out there yelling and pushing at every practice."

"Not me," said the championship coach. "I never yell at my athletes. I don't even tell them to run fast."

"What do you do?" asked the incredulous second-tier coach.

"It's simple. I sit down with each athlete at the beginning of the season and talk about her ambitions, what I think she's capable of, the team's goals, and where I think she can best help the team. We then mutually develop her goals for the season, and I provide advice to help her reach them."

"So do I," said the second-tier coach.

"Do you? Give me a specific example."

"Well, you know, I just want them to run fast. I want them to win."

"Ah, I see," said the championship coach. "Perhaps you might do better to define the goals more precisely. For example, Jane over there just ran a 5:28 mile at the State meet. Her goal for the season—which she developed with my help—was to break 5:30. I didn't have to yell, push, or anything like that. The 5:30 was pulling her forward every day."

Stop. Think for a minute. Does every employee in your company have specific goals? Did he take the primary role in creating them? Does he believe they're achievable? Does he want to achieve them? Has he translated these goals into quarterly goals, weekly tasks, and daily activities? Do the goals dovetail with the company's vision and strategy? Do the goals fit with his personal ambitions in life?

If so, you can move on to point number 5.

We suspect, however, that you've not skipped to point 5. Most leaders, if they're honest with themselves, can't answer yes to all of the above questions. Yet they ought to be able to.

Goal-setting is one of the most neglected parts of tactical execution. It's hard work, for both the employee and his coach. It takes time, thought, discussion, and negotiation. Yet, on the other hand, once the goals are clear, you can give much more free rein to people; you don't need to look over their shoulders and "direct" their activities.

If goals are set well, the traditional annual review process shouldn't be much of a "review" process at all. The employee should be able to see for himself whether he'd attained his goals—did I run 5:30 or not? He shouldn't need his manager to tell him that.

Does this mean annual performance reviews are superfluous? Not exactly. Instead of the traditional, "here's how you did" review, time should be spent largely on goal-setting. Feedback ("you did well on that project" or "you could have done better; let's figure out how") should be ongoing and continuous throughout the year. The primary purpose of a well-constructed review, on the other hand, is to *set next year's goals*.

Most review processes are ineffective. They're either tied specifically to raises, which tends to suppress serious goal-setting and evaluation, or they're viewed as a piece of administrative trivia.

Toss out the traditional annual review process and replace it with a goal-setting and review process. Consider doing it on a quarterly basis. Yes, quarterly.

Don Lyle, an outstanding manager we've observed in a number of situations and who was an architect of a particularly difficult turnaround at DEI Corporation, uses just such a quarterly goal-setting process. He starts with the long-term company vision and strategy, then breaks that into a set of annual goals. Then he works with his people to break those into their personal annual goals. Then he asks each of them to draw up a list of four or five quarterly goals for each quarter. They discuss them, negotiate, and reach an agreement, which they both sign.

At the end of each quarter, Lyle sits down again with each person to make a mutual assessment on performance versus goals and to update goals for the next quarter. He expects each of his people to do a similar process with their people, who do it with their people, and so on down the line. According to Lyle:

> This process makes sure that we don't let the urgent preempt the important. It keeps us focused on priorities. And it gives people a concrete sense of how they're doing, and this gives them an objective, consistent method for knowing. It's very powerful.
>
> The goals should be specific. For example:
> "Open 35 new customer accounts by July 31."
> "Get our European office up and running by November 30."
> "Have the new bolt-cam product ready for manufacturing by December 31."

"Create a new product introduction process by August 1."

"Write three articles for publication by December 31."

Ideally, the process should merge the individual's personal vision and the company's vision, and then cascade down to quarterly goals, weekly tasks, and daily activities.

Personal Vision ==========>   **Individual Annual Goals**   <==========   Corporate Vision

Quarterly Goals

Weekly Tasks

What am I going to do today?

We recognize that life is chaotic and unpredictable. A perfectly linear process from corporate vision and strategy to individual annual goals, quarterly goals, weekly tasks, and daily activities is improbable. However, that's not a reason to avoid personalized goal-setting. There are lots of things that can affect that runner trying to break 5:30 in the mile. But setting 5:30 as a goal is nonetheless a valuable step.

In a classic study on motivation, Professor Frederick Herzberg found that the number one factor contributing to extreme job satisfaction was personal achievement (number two was recognition). People want to achieve. They want to set goals and reach them. Tap into this natural wellspring of motivation.

5. Measuring

Let's suppose you're a track coach, and your objective is to take the team to a new level of performance. Further suppose that we've taken away your stopwatch and closed the quarter-mile track.

What would you do? You'd probably go out in your car and measure miles on the street and go buy a stopwatch.

Just as a track coach needs to define "fast" and measure speed, a company needs to *define* tactical excellence, *measure* it, and *post* the results.

L.L.Bean measures the percentage of flawless shipments (99.89% in 1987). All packers (not just managers) receive daily updates on percentage of correct orders. Bean has a battery of measurements carefully tracked, ranging from customer wait times to number of defects.

The reason for Bean's extraordinary record is not that it has a standard, or that it has quotas. Rather, the key lies in the fact that Bean tracks its performance, identifies barriers to perfect performance, and continually seeks to improve.

And Bean is not alone in its fetish for measurement.

When Marriott was a small company, founder J. Willard Marriott began a tradition of benchmarking and measuring its tactical execution. (Marriott himself would read and tabulate results from customer comment cards.) That tradition carries forth even today, to the point where it's difficult to stay at a Marriott without being inundated with opportunities to fill out rating forms, which are then collected, collated, dissected, and reassembled into something called the GSI, or Guest Service Index. The Guest Service Index for a given site is analyzed, tracked, and posted at the site for every employee to see. And, most important, the GSI is used as a basis for benchmarking and a guide for continual improvement.

Like Bean and Marriott, great companies have a tradition of defining and measuring tactical excellence. Jim Miller of Miller Business Systems tracks and posts how well the company is doing relative to its standard of completing 95% of customer orders within 24 hours. In 1936, W. R. Hotchkiss, founder of Deluxe Corporation (which prints roughly half of all checks used in the United States), set the goal of continual improvement towards zero printing defects and two-day turnaround. Of course, Deluxe measures, tracks, posts the results, identifies deficiencies, and continually seeks improvement towards perfection.

Have you ever eaten at a Bob Evans Restaurant? The chain of coffee-shop restaurants, founded in the 1940s, has developed a reputation for tactical excellence, culminating in multiple first-place rankings in industry surveys for service, quality, and value.

Bob Evans sets tough standards for itself. A customer should receive water and a pleasant "hello" within 60 seconds of being seated. Hot food should arrive within 10 minutes after ordering. Tables should be ready for the next guest within five minutes. No customer should wait for a table longer than 15 minutes, even at the busiest times. And, you guessed it, Bob Evans constantly measures itself against these standards and tracks its performance. (The Miller Business Systems, Bob Evans, and Deluxe examples are described in the book *The Service Edge* by Ron Zemke and Dick Schaaf, which presents 101 case studies of companies that attain tactical excellence in services.)

People pay attention to that which is measured. Why do people love to participate in sports? Because it's one of the few areas of life where you can objectively see how you're doing, where you can objectively track improvement.

Try an experiment with yourself. Identify a household chore that you really hate to do—taking out the garbage, mowing the lawn, or doing the dishes. Measure yourself on your next chore day. Suppose it takes you 14 minutes to take out the garbage. Now, set a benchmark—say, 10 minutes with zero mistakes. Measure yourself and track your performance. Two things will probably happen. First, you'll probably figure out a way to get better and better. Second, it'll be more fun, like a game.

The same applies to tactical execution. Figure out a way to define tactical excellence, measure it, track it, post it, learn from it, and use it as a way to continually improve. Make it fun. Make it the great game of business.

The link between measurement and continual improvement is captured in "The Shewhart Cycle" (see nearby diagram) originally articulated by Walter A. Shewhart. The Shewhart Cycle is used extensively by the Japanese in their quest for consistent tactical excellence. It's a helpful framework for improvement of any process.

The Shewhart Cycle for Continual Improvement

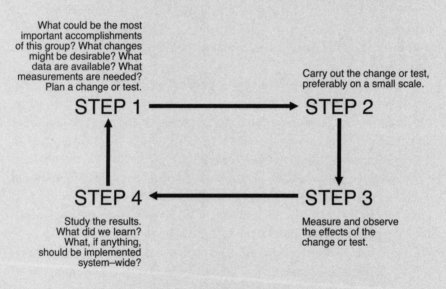

What could be the most important accomplishments of this group? What changes might be desirable? What data are available? What measurements are needed? Plan a change or test.

STEP 1

Carry out the change or test, preferably on a small scale.

STEP 2

STEP 4

Study the results. What did we learn? What, if anything, should be implemented system–wide?

STEP 3

Measure and observe the effects of the change or test.

Figure 9-3

6. Appreciating

Stimulated by Richard Barber's warmed soul (see article referred to earlier in this chapter), we made a phone call to L.L.Bean to place an order—and to ask a question.

"Welcome to L.L.Bean, this is Terri."

After placing our order and having a friendly chat with Terri about the coming of spring (it was early March), we asked, "What makes you folks at Bean take such care with a customer? Why do you, Terri, put so much of yourself into your work?"

At first the question struck her as odd; we might as well have asked her, "Why do you breathe?" But she responded with characteristic cheer:

> It starts with our president. From him on down, I just know that I'm appreciated. They don't take me for granted. It's the little things—the juice and cookies during the Christmas rush, the pat on the back, the thank-yous, the visits from the president. I got this job out of the want ads, just like any other job. But it's not just any other job. They actually care about how I feel. I know I'm important.

If you want mediocrity, take people for granted, show no appreciation, and treat them like peons.

But if you want consistent tactical excellence, make sure people feel respected and appreciated. There's nothing mysterious about it. It's not conceptually difficult. It doesn't require a Ph.D. to figure this out. Simple, honest, genuine appreciation—what could be more obvious and straightforward?

An important question: If we called some of your employees at random and asked them to talk about their relationship with your company, would they give an answer like Terri's at L.L.Bean?

Appreciation should come in all three basic forms: informal, awards and recognition, and financial.

- *Informal appreciation.* Leaders throughout your company should practice the personal touch and hard/soft people skills described in the leadership style chapter. Remember, you set the example; they'll be influenced by your style.

    Informal appreciation should be continuous and timely. People should be shown that they're appreciated throughout the year, not just at review time or at the annual awards ceremony. Do you wait until Valentine's day or a birthday to let your loved one know that he or she is something special? Do you tell your kids they're great only once a year? Of course not. And just like a healthy family, a healthy employee relationship is built on the same day-in and day-out respect and appreciation.

- *Awards and Recognition.* Never underestimate the power of non-financial awards and recognition. Keep in mind that the Herzberg study showed recognition as the second most important factor leading to extreme job satisfaction (behind achievement). Furthermore, what better way to highlight the importance of someone's work than to recognize it publicly, or to give an award?

  Establish awards for customer service heroism, product quality, sales success, or other categories you deem important to being a great company.

  You can have rare, highly prestigious awards, like the "Golden Falcon" award at Federal Express, given for dramatic or heroic achievements. Only a handful of people in any year receive a Golden Falcon, which comes with a personal phone call from the Chief Operating Officer. Combined with these, you can also have awards given more commonly. Federal Express has the "Bravo Zulu," given to hundreds of employees each year for a job well done.

  Award special, well-designed pins or other visible badges of honor. For example, at Lenscrafters, if a customer commends the company's service in a letter and mentions the employee by name, the employee receives a special lapel pin. Next time you watch an Ohio State football game, observe how the players have highly visible "buckeyes" for good plays on their helmets.

  We also encourage you to give public recognition to people. Write about them in the newsletter or company magazine. Comment on them at staff meetings, or at company meetings. Look for opportunities to say, "This person did something excellent. This person's work is important."

- *Financial.* Use financial rewards as a way to further reinforce your appreciation for someone's efforts.

  Make it possible for managers at all levels to grant small bonuses or other financial awards throughout the year. "Throughout the year" is a crucial part of this. People generally expect to receive a raise or bonus on an annual basis. Thus, the traditional annual "compensation increase" does very little, if anything, to express appreciation. In fact, it can often send just the opposite message if people receive less than they expect.

Suppose a dedicated employee is sifting through her mail and finds a note:

> "We're well aware of the tremendous strain on your family during the Christmas rush when you had to work so many extra hours. We appreciate your efforts. Please take your husband and children out for a nice dinner at a restaurant of your choice, and give us the bill. Bravo Zulu."

Or suppose a young engineer picks up his phone and hears the voice of the company president:

> "I just wanted to let you know that you did a great job getting the bugs out of that software in time for the trade show. It really made our product look good. I've had 100 shares of stock options allocated to your account. Keep up the good work."

Or suppose a salesperson who set and exceeded significant goals is told:

> "Congratulations. You set high goals, and made them. I have the honor to tell you that you've earned a spot in the 'Pacesetters' club. You'll receive your own personalized 'Pacesetter' business cards; you and a guest get a night out on the town at our expense; and for the next year, your merchandise discount will be increased from 20% to 33%."

The financial impact of these actions is minimal, yet the psychological impact is enormous. Why? Because these people are getting specific attention that shows personal appreciation for a job well done. The financial rewards are being used in a way to say: *you* did a good job; *you* are appreciated; *your* work is important.

Technology and Information Systems

We've dwelt primarily on the human and motivation side of attaining tactical excellence. And this is proper, as people ultimately get the job done. But we'd like to briefly digress into an additional component of attaining tactical excellence: use of technology and information systems.

We tend to think of computers, information systems, and reams of data as somehow cold, impersonal, and antithetical to the warm, human side of enterprise that we've emphasized in this book. Not true. Information technology is a powerful tool that should be used.

Outstanding companies, like Walmart with its advanced check-out stands and vast databases, are constantly looking for ways to leverage technology and use information systems. L.L.Bean makes extensive use of technological systems to better aid its customers. According to Bean's senior vice president of operations, "I don't see how we can get too much technology out there." Both Bean and Walmart are "people" companies, yet they're heavy users of information technology. Technology and people fit together perfectly, just as a stopwatch is a powerful aid to a track coach.

A Timely Flow of Data

Next time you take an airline flight, glance into the cockpit and notice all the dials, screens, and digital read-outs. The flight crew relies heavily on these instruments, monitoring them constantly while guiding the aircraft safely to its destination.

Keep that image in mind while running your company. Just like the flight crew, you want a constant flow of timely information. What altitude are we flying at? What's our speed? How much fuel do we have? Are our engines doing ok? Are we on schedule? What turbulence might we expect up ahead?

In a small to mid-sized company, you should have a similar body of information. And you should have it fast. You don't want to run out of fuel and, later (after you've crashed), get a delayed report that you're about to run out of fuel. Furthermore, it should be well-summarized and easily accessible. Again, keep in mind the simple digital readout in a cockpit.

The five most critical types of information to track are:

- Cash flow, both current and projected. Cash is like fuel to an airplane; you want to anticipate a fuel shortage long before the panel display flashes: "WARNING! You're almost out of fuel." Related to cash flow is accounts payable and receivable information, with the age of those accounts. Many companies run into serious cash problems because they mismanage their payables and receivables during a period of rapid growth.

- Financial accounting information (balance sheet and income statement) and financial ratios. It's particularly useful to have comparative statements (this period compared with last period, compared with last year). A list of useful ratios is given on page 296.
- Cost information. Many companies make the mistake of continuing unprofitable product lines because they have no idea they're losing money on those lines. Put in place systems for determining costs and profitability by product line (or service line). Know your costs.
- Sales information. Track sales trends in each product or service category, which can be sorted or analyzed along dimensions relevant to your company (geography, price points, by distribution channels, etc.).
- Customer information. Customers are one of your best sources of information; they'll tell you what's good and bad about your products, how you stack up against the competition, why they buy your products, what suggestions they have for improvements and new products, what they use your products for, and just about anything else you ask. They'll even tell you who they are, what they do, how much they make, and where they live. Most important, they'll tell you when you're missing major trends or market needs.

    There are many ways of getting customer information in a systematic, consistent, timely, and continuous way, such as:

    - Customer response cards. Have customers send in warranty response cards that ask information about them, what they bought, and why. Use these to keep continual track of who is buying your products or services and why.
    - Customer service reports. If your company has customer service reps, either in the field or via phone, institute a method by which comments made from customers get tabulated, tracked, and shared throughout the company. Each time a customer calls for service, you can gain information.
    - Customer surveys. If you know who your customers are, you can go back to them and ask questions. People love to tell you what they think of your product or service. People love to share their ideas, suggestions, and frustrations. Do a customer survey regularly, and track how well you're doing in the customers' eyes. The customer is the most important link in the production process—it's ultimately only the customer's satisfaction that really matters.
    - Focus groups. A focus group is a simple technique where you bring together a group of customers in a group setting and have them

respond to questions and products. This can be a rich source of information.

Financial Analysis Ratios

Use these ratios to track the financial health of your company. Track the ratios over time, keeping an eye for negative trends. It's also useful to compare your ratios with the average ratios for your industry. Industry average ratios can be found in the publication "Key Business Ratios" in *Dun's Review* published by Dun & Bradstreet Publications Corporation.

return on assets: profit-after-tax/total-assets
  quick assessment of how efficiently the firm uses its assets.

return on sales: profit-after-tax/net-sales
  quick assessment of profitability of total operations

return on equity: profit-after-tax/stockholder's-equity
  quick assessment of return on stockholder's investment

gross margin: gross-profit/net-sales
  indicates core profitability of product lines

working capital: current-assets less current-liabilities
  indicates basic liquidity of the firm

current ratio: current-assets/current-liabilities
  indicates basic liquidity of the firm

acid test ratio: (current-assets less inventory)/current-liabilities
  removing inventory gives a more clear picture of liquidity

debt to equity: (current-liabilities + long-term debt)/stockholder's equity
  indicates how much the firm relies on debt versus equity for funding

receivables collection period: (avg-receivables-for-the-year x 365)/annual-credit-sales
  indicates how many days it takes for the firm to collect receivables

payables period: (avg-accts-payable x 365)/materials purchases
  indicates how many days it takes for a firm to pay its payables

inventory turnover ratio: COGS/avg-inventory-for-the-year
  indicates how many times the firm turns over its inventory

Form 9-1

Information systems is a gigantic subject—too large for us to deal with it adequately here. Our purpose is not to delve into the myriad of details about these systems, but only to earmark their importance. You probably already have technology and information systems, and perhaps very good ones. We therefore leave you with two questions to consider:

1. Are you using technology to the fullest extent possible? We live in a rapidly advancing technological age, and companies that don't constantly seek ways to use technology to their advantage will be put behind those that do.
2. Is the information *useful*? Don't let the "information experts" determine how your information is packaged. In fact, the problem in many companies isn't the lack of information, it's the poor packaging of that information. Keep working on it until it comes to you in an easily digestible and useful form.

Trust

You'll notice that we've spent no time in this chapter on "control"—on ways of making sure people do the right things, of preventing employees from taking advantage of your company. That's because "control" doesn't work.

Remember the terribly destructive "micro-manager" described in the leadership style chapter, and how he devastated people's morale? (See "Personal Touch" section in the leadership chapter.) Neither you, nor your company, can afford to micro-manage if you want to attain consistent tactical excellence.

People need freedom to act. Motivated, trained, and well-inculturated people don't need to be "controlled." Adults don't need to be treated like children. People tend not to do their best work with someone looking over their shoulders.

Do people in your company—*all* people—have the authority (i.e., without approval from anyone) to make decisions that cost money? They ought to.

Whoa! We bet that got your attention. Are we serious?

Yes. We're very serious. Of course, we don't mean that all people should have the authority to commit the company to million-dollar contracts, or that front-line clerks should be able to authorize the purchase of a new building. But people should have wide discretionary power to take responsibility to make sure something gets done fast, and done right.

It cost L.L.Bean money, in time and labor, to resolve Richard Barber's 30-year-old boots. Bean employees didn't have to get approval to do all the back-flips; they just *did* it. No one sat around and figured the cost versus benefit analysis of spending all that time resoling his boots.

Think about it for a minute. Suppose you had to seek approval for every expense from your banker—every time you wanted to buy a personal computer or install a phone. How well could you run the company? The company would bog down in a morass of paperwork and approval, rather than attaining consistent tactical excellence.

The same principle applies right down on the line. Granted, someone on the front line shouldn't have the same spending authority as you, but the principle is the same. This simple phrase should apply all up and down your organization: "I trust you to do your best to do the right thing."

Rigorous Standards

Trust is only one side of the coin. The other side is rigorous standards.

There are two parts to this: values standards and performance standards.

Values standards are the most rigid. If someone disregards the core values of your company, they should be asked to leave. At first you might see if they just don't understand the values. However, if they understand and then disregard any of your sacred tenets, then they don't belong. It's impossible to inculcate a set of values into an institution if its leadership refuses to weed out people who don't adhere to those values.

Thomas J. Watson of IBM had a simple tenet: If an employee does something unethical, he should be fired—no matter how valuable that person is to the company. Period. No ifs or buts. No penalty box. No second chance. Out. Finished.

Performance standards should be less rigid, but nonetheless very high. Good performers lose respect for companies that tolerate poor performance. There's nothing inconsistent between having a close-knit "family" feeling and weeding out poor performers. Bill Hannemann, president of Giro Sport Design, described how this works at Giro:

> We go to great lengths to build a family environment around here. But we also expect outstanding performance. We try our best to provide job security, but that *doesn't* mean keeping people around who don't perform.

Keep in mind, however, that there may be many causes for poor performance. The person might not have been properly trained. The person might not have been given crystal-clear guidance about what is expected. The person might be in a job that doesn't fit his strengths, but might do well in another position (which might even mean a gentle transition to a position outside the company). Explore these possibilities first.

Unfortunately, however, there are some people who just don't care—and perhaps never will care—about doing a good job. There are some who will consistently miss their milestones, targets, and goals. There are some people who will take personal advantage of every situation. There are some people in whom the dark side wins. Your company should rigorously weed these people out. You can do it with compassion (remember, it was your mistake to hire them in the first place); but it should be done.

Fortunately, these people are rare. And we don't base this claim solely on a personal faith in human nature. A variety of studies on worker motivation reach the same conclusion:

- A 1980 Gallup study conducted for the U.S. Chamber of Commerce concluded that 88% of all working Americans believe it is personally important to them to work hard and do their best on the job. The Gallup study also concluded that a poor work ethic was not responsible for declines in U.S. productivity.
- A study conducted for Connecticut Mutual Insurance Company found that 76% of all Americans frequently feel a sense of dedication to their work.
- A Public Agenda Foundation study asked a wide cross-section of American workers to pick one of the following four descriptions of how they view work:
  1. Work is simply a business transaction; the more I do, the more I get paid.
  2. Work is one of life's unpleasant necessities; I would not work if I did not have to.
  3. I find my work interesting, but I would not let it interfere with the rest of my life.
  4. I have an inner need to do the very best job I can, regardless of pay.

Eighty percent chose "I have an inner need to do the very best job I can, regardless of pay" as the first or second best description of their attitude about work, and the majority (52%) chose it as their first choice. Only 20% chose options one or two as even their second choice.

The vast majority of people (albeit not all people) want to do a good job. They want to be a part of something they can be proud of. They want challenge and an opportunity to show what they're capable of. They'll rise to the occasion when other people are depending on them. They'll do extraordinary work when they're respected.

Make People OPURs

A member of our team at The Good to Great Project was preparing for a vacation and came to me with a detailed plan for how everything associated with her seat would be handled with humming perfection. She had a plan to complete everything that she could get done in advance. She had a plan for what could be handled immediately upon her return, perfectly and solidly on deadline. She had a plan worked out with a colleague who would handle anything that couldn't be handled before or after her trip.

"That's a detailed plan—well done!" I complimented her.

"I understand that I'm the OPUR," she said. "I don't have a job. I have *responsibilities*."

Now here's the twist: she works part time on a flexible schedule and is paid hourly. Yet she has the mindset—the sense of ownership—of an A-player in a full-time professional position. She has fully grasped the idea of being an "OPUR."

OPUR (pronounced OH-purr) stands for *One Person Ultimately Responsible*. For every critical task or objective, there should be a clear OPUR. When you ask, "Who's the OPUR on this?" there should be a clear, unambiguous response from someone, "I'm the OPUR."

The key to maintaining an OPUR culture is that every individual needs to have an OPUR mentality and clear OPUR tasks. But equally, to make the OPUR idea work at its best also requires having a culture in which people willingly step up to "shovel the walks" of their neighbors.

The shovel walks analogy works like this: Imagine you own a home in a town where it snows in the winter and where you're ultimately responsible for your walks being shoveled after a snowstorm. It doesn't matter if you're on vacation, you—as the homeowner—are the OPUR for your sidewalk being shoveled. You don't get to say to the city if your walkway remains icy, "Well, I was on vacation." If you live in a neighborhood where people really do embrace the idea of being *neighbors*, you can ask one of them to shovel your walks for you when you are away. And you do the same for them.

When you blend the OPUR ethic with a good-neighbor policy—accept full responsibility *and* shovel each other's walks—you can have high individual/unit performance and overall group cohesion. This creates a magical combination of being both a high-performance environment *and* a great place to work.

The Final "Secret"—Respect

There's nothing mysterious about building a great company. The builders of outstanding companies that we've had the privilege to observe personally, many of whom we've used as examples throughout this book, are not super-human. They're not smarter than everyone else. Nor do they belong to a rare breed of charismatic entrepreneur.

Many of them are baffled by the question, "What is the secret of your success?" "Secret? There is no secret," is the most common response. They refer back to the basics covered in this book: having a vision, making good strategic decisions, being innovative, and—they always emphasize this—executing well.

If it's not mysterious, then why do only a fraction of companies become extraordinary? None of this is rocket science. It doesn't require hard-to-grasp concepts. Is there something we're missing?

Then we listened closely to what Fred Smith said in his Bill Moyers interview:

> Most people who run companies . . . look down on the people who are working on the factory floor. They have a disdain for the average person, even though that person may be the one who is making them zillions of dollars.

Then the theme behind almost everything we've observed came to the front: respect.

We've always been moved by the story of Jaime Escalante, the high school teacher in Los Angeles on whom the movie "Stand and Deliver" was based. He took a bunch of high school kids from a poor ethnic neighborhood and taught them advanced, college-level calculus. His students consistently passed the advanced placement calculus exam at a rate higher than students in almost any school in the country.

Why did Escalante succeed when most people thought his students had no chance of passing something like the advanced placement calculus exam? During a talk at Stanford he mentioned two simple words: love and respect. He loved his students and he respected them. He respected them enough to demand more of them than anyone else thought possible.

Therein lies the secret, if there is one. Great companies are built on a foundation of respect. They respect their customers, they respect themselves, they respect their relationships. Most important, they respect their people—people at all levels, and from all backgrounds.

They respect their people, and therefore they trust them. They respect their people, and therefore they're open and honest with them. They respect their people, and therefore they give them freedom to act and make decisions. They respect their people, and therefore believe in their inherent creativity, intelligence, and ability to solve problems.

They respect their people, and therefore *expect* high performance. They set high standards and stiff challenges because they believe their people can meet the standard and rise to the challenge. Ultimately, employees in outstanding companies attain consistent tactical excellence because someone believes they *can*.

Out of this respect grows a company that itself is respected—a company that rises to the stature of role model and makes a positive impact on the world, not only through its products, services, and employment, but also as a guide for other companies to follow.

You too can build a company that stands for something, that sets a standard, not only of performance, but also of values. You too can build an organization that rises above the fray and shows by its success that greatness and fundamental human decency and respect go hand in hand. You too can build a company that you can look back on at the end of your life, and say, "I'm proud of what I'm leaving behind, and I respect myself for the way I've gone about doing it. My life has been well spent."

ACKNOWLEDGMENTS

WRITING A BOOK IS not a solo or even a two-person effort. Although it's certainly true this book wouldn't exist without us, it's also true that it wouldn't exist in its present form without the help of many other people.

We are indebted to Paul Feyen and John Willig for seeing the potential in this book long before any of the chapters were written. John, our initial editor, gave us the confidence to write with bold conviction. He gave us helpful insight and guidance at crucial turning points during the writing of the manuscript.

Lee Ann Snedeker, our research assistant and casewriter, deserves the credit for coming up with the title "Beyond Entrepreneurship." Her creative assistance and thoughtful criticism on early drafts were immensely helpful.

Our always cheerful assistants, Karen Stock and Ellen Kitamura, were helpful during many phases of the project. Joan Patton—also known as "Quality Control Central"—did an excellent job of proofing, proofing, and proofing again various production versions of the text.

Janet Brockett applied her extraordinary creative and interpersonal talents to the development of our book cover and icons. Janet was a joy to work with.

We tip our hats to Sybil Grace and the rest of the team at Prentice-Hall who guided the manuscript with professionalism and care through production and out to the market.

We are intellectually indebted to the work of P. Ranganath Nayak and John M. Ketteringham and their book *Breakthroughs!* as a rich source of background material on the development of the 3M Post-it Notes, the microwave oven, Tagamet, Federal Express, and the CT Scanner, which we use as examples in our chapter on innovation.

We are also indebted to Michael Ray and Rochelle Myers, first for being such outstanding teachers, and second, for allowing us to quote extensively from their book *Creativity in Business* and from transcripts of class visitors.

We are thankful for the permission to quote given to us by a wide range of individuals and companies: Bob Miller of MIPS Computer, Bill Hannemann and Jim Gentes of Giro Sport Design, Larry Ansin of Joan Fabrics, Kristine McDivitt of Patagonia, H. Irving Grousbeck of Continental Cablevision, Doug Stone formerly of Personal CAD Systems, Jim Swanson of Ramtek, Anne Bakar of Telecare, Bruce Pharriss of Celtrix Laboratories, David Kennedy of Kennedy-Jenks, Joe Bolin of Schlage Lock Company, Vinod Khosla, co-founder of Sun Microsystems, Pete Schmidt of NIKE, Claude Rosenberg of Rosenberg Capital Management, Debi Coleman of Apple Computer, Mike Kaul of Advanced Decision Systems, Bob Bright formerly of America's Marathon, and Don Lyle of Tandem Computers.

We are particularly thankful to Bill Hewlett from Hewlett-Packard Company, who graciously granted an interview about the early days of Hewlett-Packard to Jim Collins and Jerry Porras, and to Steve Jobs of NeXT Computer for visiting our class and sharing his insights with us and our students. Both of these individuals significantly shaped our thinking, and earned our respect.

We were fortunate enough to have many thoughtful and dedicated readers of our drafts, who critically evaluated our work and provided helpful comments, encouragement, criticism, and suggestions. These include: Art Armstrong, Susan Bandura, Chris Buja, Roger Davisson, Shelly Floyd, Arthur Graham, Irv Grousbeck, Greg Hadley, Bill Hannemann, David Harman, Jim Hutchinson, Chris Jackson, Dirk Long, Bob Miller, Bruce Pharriss, Heidi Roizen, and Richard Wishner.

Finally, perhaps the greatest acknowledgment goes to the hundreds of bright, talented, inquisitive, and inspirational business executives and students who have taken our classes at Stanford's Graduate School of Business. They have shaped our thinking as much as—if not more than—we have shaped theirs. To all of these people who have held us to a high standard and who hold the dream of building an enduring great company, thank you.

J.C.
W.L

ACKNOWLEDGMENTS FOR *BE 2.0*

FOUR PEOPLE SPARKED THE project to create *BE 2.0*. Joanne Ernst, my spouse and life partner of now forty years, first voiced the idea. Joanne always felt that *Beyond Entrepreneurship* could be helpful to a larger number of readers; she also felt that a new edition would give an ideal place to write a substantive homage to Bill Lazier. Inspired by Joanne's idea, I reached out to Bill's widow, Dorothy, to elicit her blessing for a new edition; Dorothy responded enthusiastically and without hesitation. With Joanne and Dorothy urging me to seriously consider doing this project, I approached Adrian Zackheim and Nigel Wilcockson at Penguin Random House (which held the publishing rights to *Beyond Entrepreneurship*) with the idea for *BE 2.0*. I'd worked with both of these exceptional publishing professionals on some of my other books, and they immediately threw their support behind the project. I'm deeply grateful for the warm and persistent urging from Joanne, Dorothy, Adrian, and Nigel to keep pushing through to finish the project.

Members of my team at The Good to Great Project LLC made significant contributions to the effort. Kate DesCombes (aka OPUR Chaos) 20-mile-marched as my senior research assistant on the final push to get the text just right and accurate. Amy Hodgkinson, Sam McMeley, Brandon Reed, Dave Sheanin, and Torrey Udall worked on the early drafts of the book, conducting background research, synthesizing reader feedback, doing fact-checking, and providing helpful feedback. Kate Harris conducted fact-checking and assisted with research on leadership that informed the ideas in the new text. Alexis Bentley and Judi Dunckley reviewed text, cross-checked information, and helped manage the logistics of the critical reader process.

Deborah Knox proved yet again why I am so fortunate to have her detailed and thoughtful editing; I've worked with Deborah as my trusted personal editor on five publishing projects to date, and she makes the words better every time. Janet Brockett contributed her design genius, always creative and distinctive. My agent, Peter Ginsberg, who has worked with me for nearly thirty years, brought his imaginative and open-minded approach to creating publishing partnerships that best serve the cause of the work. Kimberly Meilun at Penguin Random House artfully guided me through the process from final manuscript to finished book.

A bevy of readers contributed their feedback on the entire concept of *BE 2.0*, along with critical commentary on early working drafts. I would like to thank Liat Aaronson, Troy Allen, Kelsy Ausland, Karen Beattie, Joelle Brock,

Tyson Broyles, Tiffanie Burkhalter, Bo Burlingham, Dane Burneson, Dan Burton of Health Catalyst, Christopher Chandler, Shalendra Chhabra (Shalen), Karen Clark Cole, Terrence Cummings (Grande!), Jeff Damir (Stanford GSB 1993) and Lynette Damir of SwaddleDesigns, Steven M. Dastoor, Marty Davidson, Laurel Delaney, David R. Duncan, Soren Eilertsen, Jim Ellis, Andrew Feiler, Jeff Garrison, Randall T. Gerber, Brett Gilliland, Eric Hagen, Brad Halley, Sebastian Huelswitt, Sally A. Hughes of Columbus, Jacob Jaber, Tal Johnson, Kim Jordan, Noha Kikhia, Betina Koski, Lynn M. Krogh, Dana Ladzinski, Dan Markovitz, Clate Mask, Mike Moelter, Anne-Worley Moelter (SFVG), Nick Padlo, Troy E. Porras, Bart Reed, Damien Rizzello, Cynthia Scherr, Greg Schott, William F. Shuster, Adam Stack, Tom Stewart (executive director of the National Center for the Middle Market), Mark Stoleson, Michael Strickland, Bob Swier, Megan Tamte, Mark Toro, William L. Treciak, Elizabeth Zackheim, and Nathaniel (Natty) Zola.

I would also like to thank some of the Level 5 leaders who contributed generously their own stories and who took the time to review sections of the text about them for accuracy: General Lloyd Austin III, Anne Bakar, Tommy Caldwell, Lt. Colonel Michael S. Erwin, Wendy Kopp, Jorge Paulo Lemann, and Peter Salvati of DPR Construction. I would also like to thank the late Steve Jobs for all that he taught me with his example and our conversations over the years.

I would like to end where I began, with Joanne. Throughout the decades of my struggling to get the concepts clear and the words right, she has been my most enduring support and my most trusted intellectual partner. Her blend of unwavering belief and incisive critique is the number one ingredient in the secret sauce of my writing. Writing is not typing; writing is thinking. When my writing lacks clarity, it is most often because my thinking lacks clarity. Easy reading makes for hard writing. Joanne understands all this, and she encourages me to revise and rewrite, revise and rewrite, again and again. More than once, I've shared a hard-fought "final" draft of a chapter, only to have her come back and say, "It's just not there yet. I know you can make it better." And then to leave me with pages of thoughtful commentary about what must be fixed, peppered with an occasional smiley face in the margins when something hits just right. If there is a truer mark of love for one who writes, I know not what it is.

Given that *BE 2.0* has a significantly different structure than the original edition of *Beyond Entrepreneurship*, I felt that the original preface could confuse the reader if it remained at the front of the book. I also recognize that some readers might be curious how Bill and I introduced the original edition. I decided, therefore, to include the original preface for the sake of completeness, but to place it at the end of the book.

PREFACE

When we first met Jim Gentes he was sleeping with his inventory.

Launching a new company out of his cramped, stuffy one bedroom apartment in San Jose, he had turned his bedroom into a warehouse for finished goods. His garage, packed tight with parts and equipment, was staffed with four youths working frantically in 100-degree heat to build bicycle helmets. When Gentes needed more space, he gave a helmet to a neighbor in exchange for use of his neighbor's garage, thus expanding from a single-garage to a double-garage start-up. Fortunately, his neighbors never complained about the daily visits of huge UPS semi-trucks pulling into the tiny driveway to deliver helmet shells and pick up new shipments.

"Headquarters" was the kitchen table, covered with papers, bicycle helmet prototypes, books, and computer printouts from a Macintosh computer that was tilted at a cockeyed angle in the corner. Sitting at that table, surrounded by cycling posters, Gentes, an intense man in his late twenties, told us that he expected to be out of this apartment and into his own building soon, and on his way to being a successful company.

Then he pointed to a stack of books on entrepreneurship and small-business management. "They've been helpful for getting me off the ground," he said. "But they don't tell me what I really want to know."

"What's that?" we asked.

Gentes looked out of the window and waited for 30 or 40 seconds. Then he turned and told us, "I want Giro to be a great company."

And the idea for this book was born.

This book is about how to turn an existing enterprise into an enduring great company. We've written it for people like Jim Gentes—people who want their company to be something special, worthy of admiration and pride. Our focus is on helping them build an extraordinary organization, one that sustains high performance, plays a leadership role in shaping its industry, rises to the status of role model, and remains great for generations. If you're the leader of an enterprise that you want to turn into a great company, this book is for you.

This is *not* a book about how to start a business. We assume that you are (or plan to become) a key contributor to the further development of an existing, operating enterprise—one you started, bought, inherited, or joined.

Although many of the lessons in this book apply to any size company, we've written it primarily for leaders of small to mid-sized enterprises (which could include small enterprises within larger organizations). Why? The foundation of greatness is usually laid while the company is still small and malleable enough to be handcrafted into an entity that fully embodies the values of its leaders.

IBM is great because of the things Tom Watson did long before IBM became the monolith that it is today. NIKE is great because of the things Phil Knight did when NIKE was a scrappy David taking on Goliaths. 3M is great because William McKnight bent the company to his values decades ago. L.L.Bean is great because of Leon Bean's actions when his tiny company operated out of a single building in Freeport, Maine. Patagonia is a candidate for greatness because of the indelible imprint left by Kristine McDivitt during the formative stages of the feisty, renegade company.

If you're the leader of a small to mid-sized enterprise, it's up to you to be the architect of greatness. This book is about being such an architect.

Although we have concentrated on for-profit companies, managers of non-profit organizations will also find much of the material in this book useful. The principles of building a great company generally apply to *any* organization that seeks enduring greatness.

What Is a Great Company?

We define a great company as one that meets the following four criteria:

1. Performance. A great company generates enough cash flow (through highly profitable operations) to be self-sustaining; it also has a solid

track record of meeting other objectives set by its leaders and owners. Although it has ups and downs—and perhaps even some dire times—a great company always recovers and eventually regains high performance.

2. Impact. A great company plays a significant leadership role in shaping its industry. It isn't necessarily the biggest company; it can influence by innovation as well as size.

3. Reputation. A great company is admired and respected by people outside its walls, often being used as a role model.

4. Longevity. A great company has staying power, remaining healthy for decades. The greatest companies are self-renewing institutions whose greatness endures for generations of management, transcending the presence of the individuals who originally shaped the company. When you think of enduring greatness, think of building a company that remains great for 100 years.

A company need not be perfect to be great. No company is perfect; all have their warts. A great company, like a great athlete, trips up now and then, briefly tarnishing its reputation. But a great company is also resilient, and bounces back from its difficult periods—just like a great athlete bounces back from a slump or an injury.

The Shape of This Book: How to Make Your Company Great

Each chapter covers an essential element of attaining corporate greatness, presenting a framework of ideas and methods, supported by specific, vivid examples.

We begin Chapter 1 with *leadership style*. It's impossible to build a great company without an effective leadership style. It all starts with you.

In Chapter 2, we move to the function of effective corporate leadership: catalyzing a *vision*. Every great company has at its foundation a compelling vision. What *is* vision, *why* is it so important, and *how* do you set one? We answer these questions and present a useful framework for setting corporate vision.

In Chapter 3, we de-mystify the topic of *strategy*. Once the vision is clear, you need to make good decisions and have a road map for making the vision happen.

In Chapter 4, we move to an exciting and integral part of greatness: *innovation*. How do you stimulate creativity and keep your company innovative as it evolves? We present a framework and a plethora of specific suggestions and examples.

Finally, we finish Chapter 5 with the importance of *tactical excellence*: how to translate vision and strategy into tactics and, most important, how to create an environment that produces consistent tactical excellence.

In writing this book, we drew heavily from our own practical business experience (we both worked in private industry before returning to Stanford Graduate School of Business to teach), academic research and theory, consulting work, and experience serving as directors for a number of companies. In addition, field research, case writing, and student projects have provided a continual source of examples and insights. The ideas in this book were shaped by our exposure to over 300 specific companies.

By the way, Jim Gentes no longer sleeps with his inventory. Giro has grown over a hundred fold since that meeting at his "headquarters" in 1986, and is well on its way to becoming an enduring, great company. To all of you who share Gentes' dream of corporate greatness, we wish you a similar fate.

James C. Collins and William C. Lazier

NOTES TO CHAPTERS

INTRODUCTION

ix   **Hastings gave a piece of advice to aspiring young CEOs:** Bill Snyder, "Netflix Founder Reed Hastings: Make as Few Decisions as Possible," Stanford Graduate School of Business *Insights*, November 3, 2014, https://www.gsb.stanford.edu/in sights/netflix-founder-reed-hastings-make-few-decisions-possible; "Reed Hastings, Netflix: Stanford GSB 2014 Entrepreneurial Company of the Year," Stanford Graduate School of Business, October 15, 2014, https://www.youtube.com/watch?v=z COolNfs40M.

CHAPTER 1: BILL AND ME

4   **vast chunk of his fortune away:** George Climo, "HP's Profit-sharing Tradition," *Measure*, June, 1979, www.hp.com/hpinfo/abouthp/histnfacts/publications/measure /pdf/1979_06.pdf, 2–5.

4   **Hewlett adhered to a simple motto:** "The Hewlett Family and Foundation History," The William and Flora Hewlett Foundation, https://hewlett.org/about-us /hewlett-family-and-history.

CHAPTER 2: GREAT VISION WITHOUT GREAT PEOPLE IS IRRELEVANT

13   **Take our 20 best people away:** Rich Karlgaard, "ASAP Interview: Bill Gates," *Forbes*, December 7, 1992.

13   **Apple didn't release the iPhone:** "Apple Reinvents the Phone with iPhone," *Apple Newsroom*, January 9, 2007, https://www.apple.com/newsroom/2007/01/09Apple -Reinvents-the-Phone-with-iPhone.

13   **Apple had fallen to the very edge:** Brent Schlender and Rick Tetzeli, *Becoming Steve Jobs: The Evolution of a Reckless Upstart into a Visionary Leader* (New York, NY: Crown Business, 2015) p. 165; Jim Collins and Morten T. Hansen, *Great by Choice: Uncertainty, Chaos, and Luck—Why Some Thrive Despite Them All* (New York, NY: Harper Business, 2011) pp. 91–95.

14   **More than $600 billion:** Tripp Mickle and Amrith Ramkumar, "Apple's Market Cap Hits $1 Trillion," *Wall Street Journal*, August 2, 2018, https://www.wsj.com/articles/ apples-market-cap-hits-1-trillion-1533225150.

15   **Catmull's "first who" strategy:** Ed Catmull, *Creativity, Inc.: Overcoming the Unseen Forces That Stand in the Way of True Inspiration* (New York, NY: Random House, 2014) pp. 90, 112, 127, 315.

15 **This line from history professor Edward T. O'Donnell:** Edward T. O'Donnell, *America in the Gilded Age and Progressive Era Transcript Book* (Chantilly, VA: The Great Courses, 2015) p. 9.

22 **Bakar was inducted:** Telecare Corporation, *Telecare Annual Report* (Alameda, CA: Telecare Corporation, 2014), https://static1.squarespace.com/static/55f9afdfe4b0f-520d4e4ff43/t/5798db9920099eba44dedoaa/1469635483265/Annual+Report_FY13-14_vFinal_Small.pdf, 3, 12; Anne Bakar, Presentation to Haas School of Business, University of California Berkeley, March 16, 2017; "Bay Area Council 2017 Business Hall of Fame—Anne Bakar," Bay Area Council, November 17, 2017, https://www.youtube.com/watch?v=3I4LmlhLL-E.

22 **recognize Eisenhower's gifts and help him:** "Dwight David Eisenhower Chronology," Dwight D. Eisenhower Presidential Library, Museum & Boyhood Home, https://www.eisenhower.archives.gov/all_about_ike/chronologies.html; Chester J. Pach, Jr., "Dwight D. Eisenhower: Life Before the Presidency," Miller Center, University of Virginia, https://millercenter.org/president/eisenhower/life-before-the-presidency; Jean Edward Smith, *Eisenhower in War and Peace* (New York, NY: Random House, 2012) Chapter 6, Chapter 8.

22 **To understand the message of Steve Jobs's life:** Schlender and Tetzeli, *Becoming Steve Jobs*, pp. 76, 392–393.

23 **Our research shows that the average tenure:** Jim Collins and Jerry I. Porras, *Built to Last: Successful Habits of Visionary Companies* (New York, NY: Harper Business, 2002) p. 184.

23 **he built Progressive:** Collins and Hansen, *Great by Choice,* p. 6.

23 **J. W. Marriott Jr. began working:** "J.W. Marriott Jr.," *Marriott International*, https://www.marriott.com/culture-and-values/jw-marriott-jr.mi.

24 **Katharine Graham may be the most courageous CEO:** Jim Collins, "The 10 Greatest CEOs of All Time," *Fortune*, July 21, 2003, 54–68.

25 **L.L.Bean increased revenues:** Leon Gorman, *L.L.Bean: The Making of an American Icon* (Boston, MA: Harvard Business School Press, 2006) pp. 3–5, 29–31; "An Inside Look at an Outdoor Icon," L.L.Bean Company History, https://www.llbean.com/llb/shop/516918?page=company-history, pp. 2–5; Tom Bell, "Leon Gorman, Visionary Who Led L.L. Bean's Growth into a Global Giant, Dies at 80," *Portland Press Herald*, September 3, 2015, https://www.pressherald.com/2015/09/03/l-l-bean-magnate-leon-gorman-dies/.

28 **Xerox had earlier tried tried bringing in a "change agent":** Jim Collins, *How the Mighty Fall: And Why Some Companies Never Give In* (Boulder, CO: Jim Collins, 2009) pp. 113–116; Anthony Bianco and Pamela L. Moore, "Xerox: The Downfall: The Inside Story of a Management Fiasco," *Bloomberg Businessweek*, March 4, 2001, https://www.bloomberg.com/news/articles/2001-03-04/xerox-the-downfall.

28 **Mulcahy engineered one of the most unlikely corporate turnarounds:** Collins, *How the Mighty Fall*, pp. 113–116; Betsy Morris, "The Accidental CEO," *Fortune*, June 23, 2003, https://archive.fortune.com/magazines/fortune/fortune_archive/2003/06/23/344603/index.htm; Kevin Maney, "Mulcahy Traces Steps of Xerox's Comeback," *USA Today*, September 21, 2006, https://www.coursehero.com/file/6128734/Mulcahy-traces-steps-of-Xerox/; Lisa Vollmer, "Anne Mulcahy: The Keys to Turnaround at Xerox," Stanford Graduate School of Business, December 1, 2004, https://www.gsb.stanford.edu/insights/anne-mulcahy-keys-turnaround-xerox; "The Cow in the Ditch:

How Anne Mulcahy Rescued Xerox," *Knowledge@Wharton,* Wharton School of the University of Pennsylvania, November 16, 2005, https://knowledge.wharton.upenn .edu/article/the-cow-in-the-ditch-how-anne-mulcahy-rescued-xerox.

28   **Austin served as:** "Austin Leaves Legacy of Leading from the Front," United States Central Command, April 5, 2016, https://www.centcom.mil/MEDIA/NEWS-AR-TICLES/News-Article-View/Article/885335/austin-leaves-legacy-of-leading-from-the-front; "General Lloyd J. Austin III," U.S. Department of Defense, https://archive.defense.gov/bios/biographydetail.aspx?biographyid=334.

30   **Lemann and his partners:** Cristiane Correa, *Dream Big: How the Brazilian Trio behind 3G Capital—Jorge Paulo Lemann, Marcel Telles and Beto Sicupira—Acquired Anheuser-Busch, Burger King and Heinz* (Rio de Janeiro, Brazil: Primeira Pessoa, 2014) pp. 54–60, 88–90, 131–138, 168–171, 206–223.

31   **In our research, we found no systematic pattern:** Jim Collins, *Good to Great: Why Some Companies Make the Leap . . . and Others Don't* (New York, NY: Harper Business, 2001) pp. 49–52.

31   **And the Cleveland Clinic accomplished all this:** Toby Cosgrove, *The Cleveland Clinic Way: Lessons in Excellence from One of the World's Leading Healthcare Organizations* (New York, NY: McGraw-Hill Education, 2014).

32   **These leaders make:** "Monthly Basic Pay Table: Active Duty Pay January 2019," U.S. Department of Defense, https://militarypay.defense.gov/Pay/Basic-Pay.

32   **Dick Couch, who served as a SEAL Platoon leader:** Dick Couch, *The Sheriff of Ramadi: Navy SEALs and the Winning of al-Anbar* (Annapolis, MD: Naval Institute Press, 2008) p. 52.

33   **multi-star general officers make vastly less:** "Monthly Basic Pay Table: Active Duty Pay January 2019"; Theo Francis and Lakshmi Ketineni, "The WSJ CEO Pay Ranking," *Wall Street Journal,* May 16, 2019, https://www.wsj.com/graphics/ceo-pay-2019.

33   **He happily watched the value:** Collins, *Good to Great,* pp. 42–45; Warren E. Buffett, *1990 Letter to the Shareholders of Berkshire Hathaway Inc.* (Omaha, NE: Berkshire Hathaway Inc., March 1, 1991), https://www.berkshirehathaway.com/letters/1990.html, Marketable Securities; Warren E. Buffett, *1992 Letter to the Shareholders of Berkshire Hathaway Inc.* (Omaha, NE: Berkshire Hathaway Inc., March 1, 1993), https://www .berkshirehathaway.com/letters/1992.html, Common Stock Investments.

33   **Contrary to the leadership ethos embodied by Cooley and Reichardt:** Wells Fargo & Company, *Wells Fargo & Company Annual Report 2016* (San Francisco, CA: Wells Fargo & Company, 2017), https://www08.wellsfargomedia.com/assets/pdf /about/investor-relations/annual-reports/2016-annual-report.pdf, p. 3.

33   **Timothy J. Sloan, who became CEO:** Wells Fargo & Company, *Wells Fargo & Company Annual Report 2016,* p. 5.

34   **In an attempt to address the problem:** Independent Directors of the Board of Wells Fargo & Company, *Sales Practices Investigation Report,* April 10, 2017, https:// www08.wellsfargomedia.com/assets/pdf/about/investor-relations/presenta tions/2017/board-report.pdf, Overview of the Report.

35   **comes down to what he calls an act of love:** William Manchester, *Goodbye, Darkness: A Memoir of the Pacific War* (New York, NY: Little, Brown and Company, 1980) p. 391.

36   **when you have trucks and planes that have to be fully coordinated:** P. Ranganath Nayak and John M. Ketteringham, *Breakthroughs!: How Leadership and Drive Create*

Commercial Innovations That Sweep the World (San Diego, CA: Pfeiffer & Company, 1994) Chapter 13.

36   **Yet in the early days the company:** Roger Frock, *Changing How the World Does Business: FedEx's Incredible Journey to Success—The Inside Story* (San Francisco, CA: Berrett-Koehler Publishers, Inc., 2006) Kindle Edition Chapter 18.

37   **This story is exceptionally well told:** Nayak and Ketteringham, *Breakthroughs!,* Chapter 13.

CHAPTER 3: LEADERSHIP STYLE

38   **"The key to a leader's impact":** William Manchester, *The Last Lion, Alone* (Boston, MA, Little Brown, and Company, 1988) p. 210. Throughout our book, we use Churchill as an example. For an excellent insight into the life and leadership style of Churchill, we refer the reader to Manchester's *The Last Lion* series.

43   **Since its founding, Teach for America:** Laura Baker, "Teach For America by the Numbers," *Education Week*, January 15, 2016, https://www.edweek.org/ew/section /multimedia/teach-for-america-by-the-numbers.html; "The History of Teach For America," Teach For America, https://www.teachforamerica.org/what-we-do/history.

43   **In that discussion, I offered Kopp:** Bo Burlingham, "Jim Collins: How to Thrive in 2009," *Inc.*, April 1, 2009, https://www.inc.com/magazine/20090401/in-times-like -these-you-get-a-chance.html.

43   **As James MacGregor Burns taught in his classic text:** James MacGregor Burns, *Leadership* (New York, NY: Harper Torchbooks, 1978) p. 4.

44   **Powell learned that:** Colin Powell, *It Worked for Me: In Life and Leadership* (New York, NY: HarperCollins, 2012) p. 159.

44   **At West Point, influenced directly:** "Quotes," Dwight D. Eisenhower Presidential Library, Museum & Boyhood Home, November 5, 2019, https://www.eisenhowerli brary.gov/eisenhowers/quotes.

47   **Within a few weeks after John F. Kennedy came to office:** William Manchester, *Portrait of a President: John F. Kennedy in Profile* (Boston, MA: Little Brown, and Company, 1962).

47   **Walton examples:** Vance H. Trimble, *Sam Walton* (New York, NY: Dutton, 1990) pp. 141–155. Vance Trimble's book on Sam Walton is an excellent biographical account of Walton and historical profile of Wal-Mart.

50   **It was his fierce resolve:** Mark A. Stoler, *The Skeptic's Guide to American History Transcript Book* (Chantilly, VA: The Great Courses, 2012) pp. 383–392.

50   **George C. Marshall:** Merle Miller, *Plain Speaking: An Oral Biography of Harry S. Truman* (New York, NY: Berkeley Publishing Group, 1984) p. 406.

51   **"When all the evidence seems to be in":** Michael Ray and Rochelle Myers, *Creativity in Business* (New York, NY: Doubleday, 1986) p. 157.

52   **"Strangely enough":** Ray and Myers, *Creativity in Business*, p. 163.

53   **"The only thing I learned":** Miller, *Plain Speaking*, p. 313.

54   **"Do not fear mistakes":** Harry Mark Petrakis, *The Founder's Touch: The Life of Paul Galvin of Motorola* (New York, NY: McGraw-Hill Book Company, 1965) p. 226.

54   **Continuum of decision-making styles:** An interesting discussion of management decision making styles is described in *Managing for Excellence* by David L. Bradford and Allan Cohen, *Managing for Excellence* (New York, NY: John Wiley & Sons,

1984) p. 185. Although we have adapted and evolved the concepts presented in their book, we were influenced by their description of decision-making styles.

55 **"The best decisions":** C. Krenz, "MIPS Computer Systems," *Stanford Case Study* S-SB-112.

56 **"The fact that":** Robert F. Kennedy, *Thirteen Days* (New York, NY: W. W. Norton & Company, 1969) p. 111.

58 **It didn't matter whether:** Andrew S. Grove, "How to Make Confrontation Work for You," *Fortune*, July 23, 1984.

59 **Sloan reportedly said to his team:** Peter F. Drucker, *The Effective Executive: The Definitive Guide to Getting the Right Things Done* (New York, NY: Harper Business, 2017) Kindle Edition, p. 165.

59 **Washington cultivated a culture:** Ron Chernow, *Washington: A Life* (New York, NY: Penguin Books, 2011), p. 604.

59 **Still, even with the pressure:** Robert F. Kennedy, *Thirteen Days: A Memoir of the Cuban Missile Crisis* (New York, NY: W. W. Norton & Company, 1999).

60 **saved the world from nuclear annihilation:** Kennedy, *Thirteen Days*.

60 **"that was no small plane":** Karen B. Hunter, "The Man in Charge of the Skies Remembers 9/11," *Sandwich Enterprise*, January 11, 2018, https://www.capenews.net /sandwich/news/the-man-in-charge-of-the-skies-remembers/article_89764007 -04bd-5fd6-a0c4-b09c6a15bb1a.html.

60 **Sliney later recounted:** "Aviation Officials Remember September 11, 2001," C-SPAN, September 11, 2010, https://www.c-span.org/video/?295417-1/aviation-officials-re-member-september-11-2001, 56:55–58:22.

61 **landing 4,556 airborne flights:** "Aviation Officials Remember September 11, 2001"; "September 11 Attack Timeline," 9/11 Memorial & Museum, https://timeline.911me morial.org/#Timeline/2.

61 **We learned that the critical question:** Collins and Hansen, *Great by Choice*, pp. 110–113.

62 **"Do first things first":** Peter F. Drucker, *The Effective Executive* (New York, NY: Harper & Row, 1967) p. 24.

63 **"Most people get killed":** Bob Bright, talk given at Stanford Business School, May 1, 1987.

64 **"If your work is successful":** Kenneth Atchity, *A Writer's Time* (New York, NY: W. W. Norton & Company, 1986) pp. 29–31.

64 **Marriott:** Robert O'Brian, *Marriot: The J. Willard Marriott Story* (Salt Lake City, UT, Deseret Book Company, 1987) pp. 265–267.

64 **Churchill:** Manchester, *The Last Lion, Alone,* pp. 3–37.

65 **L.L.Bean:** Arthur Bartlett, "The Discovery of L.L. Bean," *The Saturday Evening Post*, December 14, 1946.

68 **"The open door policy":** Thomas J. Watson, Jr., *Father, Son & Co.* (New York, NY: Bantam Books, 1990) pp. 308–309.

68 **Sam Walton:** Trimble, *Sam Walton*, pp. 141–155.

69 **"They were flat":** Debbi Fields, *One Smart Cookie* (New York, NY: Simon and Schuster, 1987) p. 132.

72 **He even created a department:** Martin Gilbert, *The Churchill War Papers: Never Surrender* (New York, NY: W. W. Norton & Company, 1995) p. xvii.

73   **Fortunately for history:** Winston S. Churchill, *Triumph and Tragedy* (New York, NY: RosettaBooks, 2013) Chapter 1.

73   **This "natural" EPO had no commercial viability:** Edmund L. Andrews, "Mad Scientists," *Business Month*, May 1990.

73   **"Amgen on the only way of getting there":** Alun Anderson, "Growing Pains for Amgen as Epoetin Wins US Approval," *Nature*, June 15, 1989, p. 493.

73   **In the end, Amgen won:** Edmund L. Andrews, "Mad Scientists"; Alun Anderson, "Growing Pains for Amgen as Epoetin Wins US Approval"; Barry Stavro, "Court Upholds Amgen's Patent on Anemia Drug Medicine: The Decision Solidifies Its Position as the Nation's No. 1 Biotech Company and Will Encourage Other Firms to Protect Scientific Discoveries," *Los Angeles Times*, March 7, 1991; Edmund L. Andrews, "Amgen Wins Fight over Drug: Rights to Patent Lost by Genetics Institute," *New York Times*, March 7, 1991; Rhonda L. Rundle and David Stipp, "Amgen Wins Biotech Drug Patent Battle—Genetics Institute's Shares Plunge on Court Ruling as Victor's Stock Surges," *Wall Street Journal*, March 7, 1991; Diane Gershon, "Amgen Scores a Knockout," *Nature*, March 14, 1991; Elizabeth S. Kiesche, "Amgen Wins EPO battle, but Patent War Goes On," *Chemical Week*, March 20, 1991; Paul Hemp, "High Court Refuses Genetics Patent Appeal," *Boston Globe*, October 8, 1991; "High Court Backs Amgen on Drug Patent," *Washington Post*, October 8, 1991; Ann Thayer, "Supreme Court Rejects Erythropoietin Case," *Chemical & Engineering News*, October 14, 1991.

73   **might affect group dynamics:** Paul Hemp, "A Time for Growth: An Interview with Amgen CEO Kevin Sharer," *Harvard Business Review*, July-August 2004, https://hbr.org/2004/07/a-time-for-growth-an-interview-with-amgen-ceo-kevin-sharer.

75   **Psychologists:** Thomas J. Peters and Robert H. Waterman, *In Search of Excellence* (New York, NY: Warner Books, Inc., 1982) pp. 55–60.

75   **Psychologists:** Russell A. Jones, *Self-Fulfilling Prophecies: Social, Psychological and Physiological Effects of Expectancies* (Hillsdale, NJ: Lawrence Erlbaum Associates, 1977) p. 167.

75   **"Happy people":** "The Business Secrets of Tommy Lasorda," *Fortune*, July 3, 1989, pp. 129–135.

75   **"End practice on a happy note":** John Wooden, *They Call Me Coach* (Chicago, IL: Contemporary Books, 1988) p. 108.

75   **San Francisco 49ers:** Bill Walsh, *Building a Champion* (New York, NY: St. Martin's Press, 1990) p. 147.

76   **Wooden:** Wooden, *They Call Me Coach*, p. 60.

76   **"The stylish":** Walsh, *Building a Champion*, p. 97.

79   **"I remember when he took":** Robert Sobel, *Trammell Crow: Master Builder* (New York, NY: John Wiley & Sons, 1990) p. 234.

80   **Jim Burke:** Warren Bennis, *On Becoming a Leader* (Reading, MA: Addison-Wesley Publishing Company, 1989) p. 192.

81   **"Suppose my neighbor's house":** William Manchester, *The Glory and the Dream* (New York, NY: Bantam Books, 1990) pp. 229–230

81   **"[Apple] is based on":** Steven P. Jobs, talk given at Stanford Business School, May 1980.

88   **Paul Galvin, founder of Motorola:** Petrakis, *Founder's Touch*, p. viii.

88 **William McKnight:** Mildred Comfort, *William L. McKnight, Industrialist* (Minneapolis, MN: T. S. Denison & Company, Inc., 1962) p. 179.

88 **Henry Ford:** Robert Lacey, *FORD: The Men and the Machine* (New York, NY: Ballantine Books, 1989) p. 141.

CHAPTER 4: VISION

90 **"The basic question":** Edward Hoffman, *The Right to Be Human: A Biography of Abraham Maslow* (Los Angeles, CA: Jeremy P. Tarcher, Inc., 1988) p. 280.

91 **"Consider any great organization":** Thomas J. Watson, Jr., *A Business and Its Beliefs* (New York, NY: McGraw-Hill Book Company, Inc., 1963) pp. 4–5. This short book is a landmark contribution, and we'd recommend it highly.

92 **3M:** Minnesota Mining and Manufacturing Company, *Our Story So Far: Notes from the First 75 Years of 3M Company* (St. Paul, MN: Minnesota Mining and Manufacturing Company, 1977).

93 **"Any organization in order to survive":** Watson, *A Business and Its Beliefs*, pp. 4–5.

93 **Watson's father:** Thomas J. Watson, Jr., *Father, Son & Co.* (New York, NY: Bantam Books, 1990) p. 51.

93 **Johnson & Johnson Credo:** Lawrence G. Foster, *A Company That Cares: One Hundred Year Illustrated History of Johnson & Johnson* (New Brunswick, NJ: Johnson & Johnson Company, 1986) p. 108.

94 **McKinsey:** Marvin Bower, *Perspective on McKinsey* (New York, NY: McKinsey & Company, Inc., 1979). This is not a book in general circulation; it was written and privately printed for readership by only personnel of McKinsey & Company. Jim worked at McKinsey early in his career where he read and was impressed by the book.

96 **"With all its problems, Israel":** Barbara W. Tuchman, *Practicing History* (New York, NY: Ballantine Books, 1982) p. 134.

98 **Miller's comment leads:** C. Krenz, "MIPS Computer Systems," *Stanford Case Study* S-SB-112.

99 **"You know, you never defeated us":** Harry G. Summers, Jr., *On Strategy: A Critical Analysis of the Vietnam War* (New York, NY: Bantam Doubleday Dell Publishing Group, Inc., 1982) p. 21.

99 **In terms of tactics and logistics:** Summers, *On Strategy*, pp. 21–22.

99 **"This confusion over objectives":** Summers, *On Strategy*, p. 149.

99 **"The principals never defined":** William Manchester, *The Glory and the Dream* (New York, NY: Bantam Books, 1990) p. 1054.

102 **"I picked Williamsburg":** Watson, *Father, Son & Co.*, pp. 285–289.

102 **Vermont Castings:** C. Hartman, "Keeper of the Flame," *Inc.*, March 1989, pp. 66–76.

103 **Collins-Porras framework:** J. Collins and J. Porras, "Organizational Vision and Visionary Organizations," *California Management Review*, Fall 1991.

105 **"Sell good merchandise":** Arthur Bartlett, "The Discovery of L.L. Bean," *The Saturday Evening Post,* December 14, 1946.

105 **L.L.Bean actions:** "L. L. Bean, Inc. (B)," *Harvard Business School Case* 9-676-014.

106 **Herman Miller:** Max De Pree, *Leadership Is an Art* (New York, NY: Doubleday Dell Publishing Group, Inc., 1989) pp. 4–80.

106 **Telecare Corporation:** Interview with Anne Bakar, CEO.

107 **Johnson & Johnson Credo:** Foster, *A Company That Cares*, p. 108.

107 **Dave Packard:** "Interview with Bill Hewlett and Dave Packard," *HP Lab Notes Journal*, March 6, 1989.

107 **Bill Hewlett:** Interview with Jim Collins and Jerry Porras, November, 1990.

107 **Merck & Company:** Merck & Company, "Statement of Corporate Purpose," 1989.

108 **"Business cannot be defined":** Peter F. Drucker, *Management: Tasks, Responsibilities, Practices* (New York, NY: Harper & Row, 1974) pp. 59–61.

108 **"Quantitative goals can't invest":** T. Richman, "Identity Crisis," *Inc.,* October 1989, p. 100.

109 **L.L.Bean:** "L.L. Bean, Inc. (B)," *Harvard Business School Case* 9-676-014.

109 **"I don't feel that I'll ever be done":** Steve Jobs, talk given at Stanford Business School, March 1989.

110 **Merck:** Merck & Company, "Statement of Corporate Purpose," 1989.

110 **Schlage Lock Company:** Schlage Corporate Vision Statement, 1990.

110 **Celtrix:** Bruce Pharriss, Interview with authors, July 1991.

110 **Lost Arrow/Patagonia:** J. Collins, "Lost Arrow Corporation (C)," *Stanford Business School Case* S-SB-117C.

110 **Pioneer Hi-Bred:** Ron Zemke and Dick Schaaf, *The Service Edge: 101 Companies That Profit from Customer Care* (Markham, Ontario: Penguin Books, 1989) p. 462.

110 **Telecare Corporation:** Anne Bakar, Interview with authors, July 1991.

111 **Mary Kay Cosmetics:** Mary Kay Ash, *Mary Kay on People Management* (Newport Beach, CA: Books on Tape, Inc., 1984), cassette 1, side 1.

111 **Kennedy-Jenks:** David Kennedy, Interview with authors, July 1991.

111 **Advanced Decision Systems:** Mike Kaul, Interview with authors, July 1991.

114 **"This nation should":** Daniel J. Boorstin, *The Americans: The Democratic Experience* (New York, NY: Vintage Books, 1974) p. 596.

115 **Examples of ineffective mission statements:** F. David, "How Companies Define Their Mission," *Long Range Planning,* Volume 22, #1, February, 1989, pp. 90–92.

116 **"Make the MIPS architecture":** C. Krenz, "MIPS Computer Systems," *Stanford Case Study* S-SB-112-TN.

116 **democratize the automobile:** Boorstin, *The Americans: The Democratic Experience*, p. 548.

116 **"Our whole people":** Winston S. Churchill, *Blood, Sweat, and Tears* (New York, NY: G. P. Putnam's Sons, 1941) p. 403.

117 **IBM 360:** Watson, *Father, Son, & Co.*, pp. 346–351.

117 **Boeing:** Harold Mansfield, *Vision: Saga of the Sky* (New York, NY: Madison Publishing Associates, 1986) pp. 329–339.

118 **To achieve the mission, P&G:** Oscar Schisgall, *Eyes on Tomorrow: The Evolution of Procter & Gamble* (Chicago, IL: J. G. Ferguson Publishing Company, 1981) pp. 87–98.

118 **"We like to try the impractical":** Schisgall, *Eyes on Tomorrow*, p. 200.

118 **50/50 chance of success:** Boorstin, *The Americans: The Democratic Experience*, p. 595.

119 **Merck mission:** P. Gibson, "Being Good Isn't Enough Anymore," *Forbes*, November 26, 1979, p. 40.

119 **Coors Mission:** C. Poole, "Shirtsleeves to Shirtsleeves," *Forbes,* March 4, 1991, p. 56.

119 **Tokyo Tsushin Kogyo:** Akio Morita, *Made in Japan* (New York, NY: Dutton, 1986) pp. 63–74.

120 **Home Depot:** C. Hawkins, "Will Home Depot Be 'The Wal-Mart of the '90s'?," *Business Week*, March 19, 1990, p. 124.

120 **Wal-Mart:** Vance H. Trimble, *Sam Walton* (New York, NY: Dutton, 1990) p. 168.

120 **"Our goals are always based":** "Being the Boss," *Inc.*, October 1989, p. 49.

121 **"We always believed":** John Schulley, *Odyssey* (New York, NY: Harper & Row Publishers, 1987) pp 4–5.

121 **"Yamaha wo tsubusu!":** G. Stalk, Jr., "Time—The Next Source of Competitive Advantage," *Harvard Business Review,* July-August, 1988, p. 44.

121 **Phil Knight:** "Sneaker Wars," *ABC's 20/20*, August 19, 1988.

122 **Parkinson:** J. Collins, "Passion Can Provide a Propelling Purpose," *San Jose Mercury News*, August 7, 1988, p. PC 1.

122 **Trammell Crow:** N. Aldrich, "The Real Art of the Deal," *Inc.*, November 1988, p. 82.

122 **Norwest:** S. Weiner, "The Wal-Mart of Baking," *Forbes*, March 4, 1991, p. 65.

122 **Walmart:** Trimble, *Sam Walton*, pp. 33–34.

123 **"We are committed":** The General Electric Story (Schenectady, NY: General Electric Company, 1989) p. 128.

125 **sweeping through corner offices around the country:** Adam Bryant, "When Management Shoots for the Moon," *New York Times*, September 27, 1998, https://www.nytimes.com/1998/09/27/business/business-when-management-shoots-for-the-moon.html.

127 **"We had a dream":** "The Art of Loving," *Inc.*, May, 1989, p. 46.

131 **"You have to get [your vision] on paper":** "Thriving on Order," *Inc.*, December 1989, p. 47.

132 **"I will build a motor car":** Robert Lacey, *FORD: The Men and the Machine* (New York, NY: Ballantine Books, 1986) p. 93.

133 **"Hitler knows that he will have to break us":** William Manchester, *The Last Lion, Alone* (Boston, MA: Little, Brown, and Company, 1988) p. 686.

136 **Co-founder Doug Woods:** "Our History," DPR Construction, https://www.dpr.com/company/history.

136 **In 2015, DPR celebrated:** "Our History," DPR Construction.

136 **DPR clicked past $4.5 billion:** "Our History," DPR Construction.

138 **"People don't call themselves visionaries":** V. Woodruff, "Giving the Globe a Nudge: Ted Turner," *Vis a Vis*, August 1988, p. 58.

CHAPTER 5: LUCK FAVORS THE PERSISTENT

139 **You start at the bottom:** Sam Scott, "Sheer Focus," *Stanford Magazine*, July/August 2014, https://stanfordmag.org/contents/sheer-focus.

141 **President Barack Obama tweeted:** Barack Obama, Obama White House Twitter, January 14, 2015, https://twitter.com/obamawhitehouse/status/555521113166336001?lang=en.

142 **Jobs didn't even garner an invitation:** Mona Simpson, "A Sister's Eulogy for Steve Jobs," *New York Times*, October 30, 2011, https://www.nytimes.com/2011/10/30/opinion/mona-simpsons-eulogy-for-steve-jobs.html.

145 **"At the moment it seems quite effectively disguised":** Winston S. Churchill, *Triumph and Tragedy* (New York, NY: RosettaBooks, 2013) Chapter 40.

147 **But if you see the ultimate creation as the company:** Jim Collins and Jerry I. Porras, *Built to Last: Successful Habits of Visionary Companies* (New York, NY: Harper Business, 2002) p. 28.

CHAPTER 6: WHAT MAKES GREAT COMPANIES TICK—THE MAP

148 **In the ever-renewing society:** John W. Gardner, *Self-Renewal: The Individual and the Innovative Society* (New York, NY: W. W. Norton & Company, 1995) p. 5.

150 **Just because the UCLA Bruins:** "John Wooden—A Coaching Legend: October 14, 1910–June 4, 2010," UCLA Athletics, https://uclabruins.com/sports/2013/4/17/208183994.aspx.

158 **In the words of F. Scott Fitzgerald:** F. Scott Fitzgerald, "The Crack-Up," *Esquire*, February 1, 1936, http://classic.esquire.com/the-crack-up.

CHAPTER 7: STRATEGY

171 **"Strategy is easy":** A. Rock, "Strategy vs. Tactics from a Venture Capitalist," *Harvard Business Review*, November-December 1987, p. 63.

175 **The development of the tank:** William Manchester, *The Last Lion: Visions of Glory* (New York, NY: Dell Publishing, 1983) pp. 510–512.

177 **Stages of industry evolution:** Michael Porter, *Competitive Strategy* (New York, NY: The Free Press, 1980) pp. 158–162.

180 **David Birch:** D. Birch, "Trading Places," *Inc.*, April 1988, p. 42.

181 **"His all pervading hope":** Winston S. Churchill, *The Gathering Storm* (Boston, MA: Houghton-Mifflin Company, 1948) p. 222.

182 **created a separate department:** Churchill, *The Gathering Storm*, p. 468.

182 **"Sharp, scratchy, harsh, almost unpleasant individuals":** T. Watson, "The Greatest Capitalist in History," *Fortune*, August 31, 1987, p. 24.

183 **"There is no higher and simpler law":** Carl von Clausewitz, *On War* (Princeton, NJ: Princeton University Press, 1976) p. 204.

184 **profitable airline in the United States:** "Southwest Airlines Reports 47th Consecutive Year of Profitability," *Southwest Airlines*, January 23, 2020, http://investors.southwest.com/news-and-events/news-releases/2020/01-23-2020-112908345.

184 **When Robert Noyce and Gordon Moore:** Leslie Berlin, *The Man behind the Microchip: Robert Noyce and the Invention of Silicon Valley* (New York, NY: Oxford University Press, 2005) p. 159.

184 **Moore had calculated:** Gordon E. Moore, "Cramming More Components onto Integrated Circuits," *Proceedings of the IEEE* 86, no. 1 (January 1998): 82–85. (This is a reprint from the original publication: Gordon E. Moore, "Cramming More Components onto Integrated Circuits," *Electronics* 38, no. 8 [April 19, 1965]: 114–117).

185 **The 1103 became the best-selling memory chip:** Berlin, *The Man Behind the Microchip*, Chapter 7, Chapter 8, Chapter 9.

185 **"perennial gale of creative destruction":** Joseph A. Schumpeter, *Capitalism, Socialism and Democracy* (New York, NY: Harper Perennial, 2008) p. 84.

185 **The answer: twenty-five squadrons:** Winston S. Churchill, *Their Finest Hour* (New York, NY: RosettaBooks, 2013) Chapter 2.

186 **"no matter what the consequences might be":** Churchill, *Their Finest Hour*, Chapter 2.

186 **"We might not even have to die as individuals":** Winston S. Churchill, *The Grand Alliance* (New York, NY: RosettaBooks, 2013) Chapter 32.

187 **in the words of Andy Grove:** Andrew S. Grove, *Only the Paranoid Survive: How to Exploit the Crisis Points That Challenge Every Company* (New York, NY: RosettaBooks, 2004) Chapter 6.

188 **As University of Virginia professor Gary Gallagher teaches:** Gary W. Gallagher, *Robert E. Lee and His High Command Transcript Book* (Chantilly, VA: The Great Courses, 2004); Gary W. Gallagher, *The American Civil War Transcript Book* (Chantilly, VA: The Great Courses, 2000).

188 **Abraham Lincoln papers:** Series 1. General Correspondence. 1833–1916: Abraham Lincoln to George G. Meade, Tuesday, July 14, 1863 (Meade's failure to pursue Lee)," *Library of Congress*, https://www.loc.gov/resource/mal.2480600/?sp=1&st=text.

188 **What remains true under all imaginable conditions:** Von Clausewitz, *On War*, p. 263.

195 **"Don't grow too fast":** Interview on HP-TV video, viewed by the authors.

196 **Osborne Computer priced:** K. Baron, "Spectacular Failures," *Peninsula*, July 1989, p. 40.

197 **rapid growth tends to create arrogance:** Baron, "Spectacular Failures," pp. 40–50.

199 **University National Bank Case Example:** "Small Business: Second Thoughts on Growth," *Inc.*, March 1991, pp. 60–66, and K. Moriarty, "University National Bank and Trust Company," *Stanford Business School* Case S-SB-125.

200 **Warren Buffett has the best answer:** Andrew Frye and Dakin Campbell, "Buffett Says Pricing Power More Important Than Good Management," *Bloomberg*, February 17, 2011, https://www.bloomberg.com/news/articles/2011-02-18/buffett-says-pricing-power-more-important-than-good-management?sref=30J96vqe.

201 **"If you're diversified":** Larry Ansin, talk given at Stanford Business School, October 1990.

203 **Cargill:** M. Berss, "End of an Era," *Forbes*, April 29, 1991, p. 41.

205 **Tensor:** T. Gearreald, "Tensor Corporation," *Harvard Business School Case* #9-370-041.

206 **"It's a good thing we're not a publicly owned company":** J. Pereira, "L.L. Bean Scales Back Expansion Goals to Ensure Pride in Its Service is Valid," *Wall Street Journal*, July 31, 1989.

216 **Porter's caveats:** Porter, *Competitive Strategy*, pp. 158–162.

CHAPTER 8: INNOVATION

217 **" . . . all progress depends":** Jorgen Palshoj, "Design Management at Bang and Olufsen," in *Design Management*, ed. Mark Oakley (Oxford, England: Basil Blackwood, 1990) p. 42.

219 **"This 'telephone'":** M. Miller "Sometimes the Biggest Mistake Is Saying No to a Future Success," *Wall Street Journal*, December 15, 1986, p. 30.

219   "The concept is interesting and well formed": P. Ranganath Nayak and John M. Ketteringham, *Breakthroughs!* (New York, NY: Rawson Associates, 1986) p. 318.

219   "We don't tell you how to coach": Nayak and Ketteringham, *Breakthroughs!*, p. 238.

219   "So we went to Atari and said": Steve Jobs, talk given at Stanford Business School, May 1980.

221   "You should franchise them": Vance H. Trimble, *Sam Walton* (New York, NY: Dutton, 1990) p. 99.

220   "We don't like their sound": Miller, "Sometimes the Biggest Mistake Is Saying No to a Future Success," p. 30.

220   National Cash Register: Daniel J. Boorstin, *The Americans: The Democratic Experience* (New York, NY: Vintage Books, 1974) pp. 201–202.

220   "What's all this computer nonsense": Nayak and Ketteringham, *Breakthroughs!*, p. 158.

220   "Drill for oil?": Boorstin, *The Americans: The Democratic Experience*, p. 46.

220   "the airplane is useless": Basil H. Liddell Hart, *The Real War* (Newport Beach, CA: Books on Tape, *Inc.,* 1989), cassette 3, side 1.

220   "The television will never achieve popularity": William Manchester, *The Glory and the Dream* (New York, NY: Bantam Books, 1990) p. 240.

220   ideas behind Macintosh: T. Simmers, "The Big Bang," *Peninsula*, July 1988, pp. 46–53.

220   the original McDonald's: Ray Kroc, *Grinding It Out: The Making of McDonald's* (New York, NY: Berkeley Publishing Corporation, 1977) pp. 5–13.

221   prototype of *Personal Publisher*: S. Bandura, "T/Maker: The Personal Publisher Decision," *Stanford Business School Case* #S-SB-111.

221   Tylenol: Lawrence G. Foster, *A Company That Cares: One Hundred Year Illustrated History of Johnson & Johnson* (New Brunswick, NJ: Johnson & Johnson Company, 1986) p. 123.

221   Oxydol and Lava Soap: Schisgall, *Eyes on Tomorrow: The Evolution of Procter & Gamble* (Chicago, IL: J. G. Ferguson Publishing Company, 1981) p. 112.

221   Wetordry: Minnesota Mining and Manufacturing Company, *Our Story So Far: Notes from the First 75 Years of 3M Company* (St. Paul, MN: Minnesota Mining and Manufacturing Company, 1977) pp. 64–65.

221   Xerox: Miller, "Sometimes the Biggest Mistake Is Saying No to a Future Success," p. 30.

222   Stew Leonard's: Ron Zemke and Dick Schaaf, *The Service Edge: 101 Companies That Profit from Customer Care* (Markham, Ontario: Penguin Books, 1989) pp. 317–321.

223   Walmart has a policy called *LTC*: Zemke and Schaaf, *The Service Edge*, p. 362.

223   L.L.Bean innovations came: "L. L. ean, Inc.," *Harvard Business School Case* #9-366-013.

225   The fax machine is: P. Drucker, "Marketing 101 for a Fast-Changing Decade," *Wall Street Journal*, November 20, 1990.

225   3M Post-it Notes: Nayak and Ketteringham, *Breakthroughs!*, pp. 50–74.

225   Federal Express: Nayak and Ketteringham, *Breakthroughs!*, p. 318.

225   Debbie Fields: Debbie Fields, *One Smart Cookie* (New York, NY: Simon and Schuster, 1987) pp. 56–58.

225 **David Sarnoff:** Boorstin, *The Americans: The Democratic Experience,* p. 154.

226 **Windham Hill:** Michael Ray and Rochelle Myers, *Creativity in Business* (New York, NY: Doubleday, 1986) p. 128.

226 **The first microwave oven:** Nayak and Ketteringham, *Breakthroughs!,* p. 195.

226 **Akio Morita of Sony:** Akio Morita, *Made in Japan* (New York, NY: E.P. Dutton, 1986) p. 79.

226 **"Consumers, when confronted with something new":** Jean-Pierre Vitrac, "Prospective Design," in *Design Management,* ed. Mark Oakley (Oxford, England: Basil Blackwell, 1990) p. 305.

227 **"Certainly, the search":** Nayak and Ketteringham, *Breakthroughs!,* pp. 17–18.

228 ***Personal Publisher* product:** S. Bandura, "T/Maker: The Personal Publisher Decision," *Stanford Business School Case* #S-SB-111.

229 **"Like most great ideas":** Steve Jobs, talk given at Stanford Business School, May 1980.

229 **Band-aids:** Foster, *A Company That Cares,* p. 82.

230 **"In my age group":** Nayak and Ketteringham, *Breakthroughs!,* p. 119.

230 **At L.L. Bean, for example:** J. Skow, "Using the Old Bean," *Sports Illustrated,* December 2, 1985.

231 **Johnson's Baby Powder:** Foster, *A Company That Cares,* p. 32.

231 **Ballard Medical Products:** T. Richman, "Seducing the Customer: Dale Ballard's Perfect Selling Machine," *Inc.,* April 1988, pp. 95–104.

232 **"Of course, this is a somewhat unscientific":** Paulo Viti and Pier Paride Vidari, "Design Management at Olivetti," in *Design Management,* ed. Mark Oakley (Oxford, England: Basil Blackwell, 1990) p. 305.

232 **"What's important is experimentation":** Vinod Khosla, talk given at Stanford Business School, October 1988.

233 **Edison:** J. Collins, "The Bright Side of Every Failure," *San Jose Mercury News,* March 29, 1987, p. PC 1.

233 **"Gordon the Guided Missile":** John Cleese, speech given December 9, 1987. The speech is reproduced by Video Arts of Northbrook, Illinois.

234 **"The key to the Post-it":** Nayak and Ketteringham, *Breakthroughs!,* p. 57.

234 **"It [the popcorn]":** Nayak and Ketteringham, *Breakthroughs!,* p. 185.

235 **"I see Jennifer, Bill, and me':** B. Maxwell, "Powerfood's First Year," *Powerbar News,* December, 1987, pp. 1–4.

236 **For example, Novellus Systems:** V. Rice, "A Model Company," *San Jose Mercury News,* February 21, 1991, p. B1.

237 **Ford Model B:** Robert Lacey, *FORD: The Men and the Machine* (New York, NY: Ballantine Books, 1989) p. 82

237 **Motorola product failures:** Harry Mark Petrakis, *The Founder's Touch: The Life of Paul Galvin of Motorola* (New York, NY: McGraw-Hill Book Company, 1965) pp. 102, 129, 167, 180.

240 **"People are allowed to be persistent":** R. Burgelman, "Intraorganizational Ecology of Strategy-making and Organizational Adaptation: Theory and Field Research," *Stanford Graduate School of Business Research Paper* #1122, p. 24.

240 **Intel's internal venture program:** Burgelman, "Intraorganizational Ecology," p. 17.

244 **"You have to balance the 'flakes'":** Vinod Khosla, talk given at Stanford Business School, October 1988.

244 **"If you want the best things to happen in corporate life":** G. Melloan, "Herman Miller's Secrets of Corporate Creativity," *Wall Street Journal*, May 3, 1988, p. 31.

245 **In describing Ben Franklin's:** Daniel J. Boorstin, *The Americans: The Colonial Experience* (New York, NY: Vintage Books, 1958) pp. 251–259.

246 **"in business is conventional wisdom":** Debi Coleman, Interview with authors, August 1991.

247 **Boston Celtics:** Interview on CBS Sports during the championship series, May 1988.

248 **" . . . they did the work":** John Tracy Kidder, *The Soul of a New Machine* (Boston, MA: Little, Brown and Company, 1981) pp. 272–274.

249 **Herman Miller:** Melloan, "Herman Miller's Secrets."

249 **Merck:** From a talk given by Merck CEO Roy Vagelos at Stanford Business School, February 15, 1990.

249 **Rosenberg and Birdzell:** Nathan Rosenberg and L. E. Birdzell, Jr., *How the West Grew Rich* (New York, NY: Basic Books, Inc., 1986).

250 **"You have to find a new structure for U.S. industry":** Steve Solomon, "The Thinking Man's CEO," *Inc.*, November 1988, pp. 29–42.

250 **"If you are going to have literally hundreds":** Paul Cook, talk given at Stanford Business School, April 17, 1981.

255 **Herman Miller:** Melloan, "Herman Miller's Secrets."

255 **"You win one game":** Kidder, *The Soul of a New Machine*, p. 228.

257 **Ben and Jerry's:** Paul Hawken, *Growing a Business* (New York, NY: Firside, 1988) p. 149.

257 **Federal Express:** Zemke and Schaaf, *The Service Edge*, p. 479.

258 **William McKnight:** Mildred Houghton Comfort, *William McKnight: Industrialist* (Minneapolis, MN: T. S. Dennison & Company, Inc., 1962) pp. 132, 139, 191.

259 **Regis McKenna:** Ray and Meyers, *Creativity in Business*, p. 91.

260 **founder Paul Galvin:** Petrakis, *The Founder's Touch*, p. 209.

261 **Herman Miller lets its designers:** Melloan, "Herman Miller's Secrets."

261 **Claude Rosenberg, founder of:** Talk given at Stanford Business School, November 8, 1984.

262 **explains Ted Nierenberg:** Talk given at Stanford Business School, December 5, 1984.

263 **As Gerard Tellis and Peter Golder demonstrated:** Gerard J. Tellis and Peter N. Golder, *Will and Vision: How Latecomers Grow to Dominate Markets* (New York, NY: McGraw-Hill, 2002) pp. xiii–xv, 43–46, 288–292.

CHAPTER 9: TACTICAL EXCELLENCE

265 **"God is in the details":** "Thoughts on Business of Life," *Forbes*, August 19, 1991, p. 152.

265 **Hemingway was once asked:** Theodore A. Rees Cheney, *Getting the Words Right* (Cincinnati, OH: Writer's Digest Books, 1983) p. 3.

266 **An *Inc.* magazine survey:** J. Case, "The Origins of Entrepreneurship," *Inc.*, June, 1989, p. 62.

266 **Compaq, Apple, and IBM profits per employee:** Compaq, Apple, and IBM 1990 annual reports.

266 **"The key ingredient turned out to be":** Vance H. Trimble, *Sam Walton* (New York, NY: Dutton, 1990) pp. 120–122.

273 **"The bulk of the causes":** W. Edwards Deming, *Out of the Crisis* (Cambridge, MA: Massachusetts Institute of Technology, Center for Advanced Engineering Study, 1986). This quote is repeated by Deming over and over in his seminars, and is repeated in various forms throughout his book. To gain a complete understanding of this quote, we highly recommend reading Deming's *Out of the Crisis*.

273 **A. Richard Barber:** R. Barber, "How L. L. Bean Restored My Soles—And Warmed My Soul," *Wall Street Journal,* December 18, 1990, p. A12.

275 **Airplane parts manufacturer:** Peter F. Drucker, *Concept of the Corporation* (New York, NY: The John Day Company, 1972) pp. 157–158.

276 **how Federal Express managed:** P. Ranganath Nayak and John Ketteringham, *Breakthroughs!* (New York, NY: Rawson Associates, 1986) pp. 314–322.

278 **The famous Deming Prize:** Mary Walton, *The Deming Management Method* (New York, NY: Perigee Books, 1986) pp. 3–21.

281 **Stew Leonard's:** Ron Zemke and Dick Schaaf, *The Service Edge: 101 Companies That Profit from Customer Care* (Markham, Ontario: Penguin Books, 1989) pp. 317–321.

281 **Marriott:** Zemke and Schaaf, *The Service Edge*, pp. 117–120.

282 **Whole Foods:** B. Posner, "The Best Little Handbook in Texas," *Inc.*, February, 1989, pp. 84–87.

284 **Jim Miller:** Zemke and Schaaf, *The Service Edge*, pp. 516–519.

285 **Parisan:** Zemke and Schaaf, *The Service Edge*, pp. 356–359.

285 **Domino's:** Zemke and Schaaf, *The Service Edge*, pp. 301–304.

285 **Stew Leonard's:** Zemke and Schaaf, *The Service Edge*, pp. 317–321.

285 **Home Depot:** C. Hawkins, "Will Home Depot Be 'The Wal-Mart of the '90s'?," *Business Week*, March 19, 1990, p. 124.

288 **Frederick Herzberg found:** F. Herzberg, "One More Time: How Do You Motivate Employees?," *Harvard Business Review*, September–October 1987, pp. 109–120.

288 **L.L.Bean measures the:** Zemke and Schaaf, *The Service Edge*, pp. 378–381.

289 **Marriott:** Zemke and Schaaf, *The Service Edge*, pp. 117–120.

289 **Deluxe Corporation:** Zemke and Schaaf, *The Service Edge*, pp. 446–449.

289 **Bob Evans Restaurant:** Zemke and Schaaf, *The Service Edge*, pp. 293–296.

290 **Shewhart Cycle:** Deming, *Out of the Crisis*, p. 88.

292 **the "Golden Falcon" award:** Zemke and Schaaf, *The Service Edge*, p. 479.

294 **"I don't see how we can get":** J. Skow, "Using the Old Bean," *Sports Illustrated*, December 2, 1985.

298 **Watson of IBM:** T. Watson, "The greatest Capitalist in History," *Fortune*, August 31, 1987, p. 24.

299 **Studies on worker motivation:** D. Yankelovich and J. Immerwahr, "Putting the Work Ethic to Work," *Social Science and Modern Society* 21, no. 2 (January-February, 1984): pp. 58–76.

301 **what Fred Smith said:** Nayak and Ketteringham, *Breakthroughs!*, pp. 314–322.

INDEX

Note: Page numbers in *italics* refer to illustrations.

Ford, Henry
  "ever forward" mentality of, 88
  and market demands, 227
  mission of, 116, 119
  product failures of, 237
  vision of, 132, 137
Ford Motor Company, 188, 207, 227, 237
formality, reducing, 85
Fortune 500 companies, 169
Fortune magazine, 23
Fortune Systems, 47–48
founder-entrepreneurs, 22–23
founding fathers of the United States, 101, 134, 137
foxes and hedgehogs concept of Berlin, 159
Franklin, Benjamin, 245–46
Frost, Tom, 139
fun, importance of, 262

Gallagher, Gary, 188
Galvin, Paul, 52, 88, 260–61
Gandhi, Mahatma, 40
Gardner, John W., 148, 276
Garvin, Paul, 54
Gates, Bill, 13, 23, 44–45, 142
Gathering Storm, The (Churchill), 181
Gavilan Computer Company, 129, 260
General Electric (GE), 92, 123
General Motors (GM), 59, 207, 227
generosity, Lazier on, 3–4
Genetics Institute, 73
Genius of the AND, 158–59, 162, 269
"genius with a thousand helpers" model, 14, 22,
    74, 165
Gentes, Jim
  communication of vision, 132
  and LYCRA helmet covers, 259–60
  on mission of Giro, 122
  personal conviction of, 46
  product development of, 223, 229
  tactical execution of, 266
  and woodwork factor, 230
George, King of England, 72
Gettysburg Address of Lincoln, 134
GFP, Inc., 201–2
Gifford, Dale, 19
Giro Sport Design
  communication of vision in, 132
  core values and beliefs held by, 129–30
  designers employed by, 247
  diversity at, 244
  employee motivation at, 96
  focused strategy of, 202–3
  and hiring decisions, 244, 281

LYCRA helmet covers of, 259–60
mission of, 122
product development at, 223, 229
and standards of performance, 298
statement of purpose, 110
strategic priorities of, 269
tactical execution of, 266
See also Gentes, Jim
goal setting, 280, *280*, 286–88, *288*. *See also* BHAGs
    (big, hairy, audacious goals)
Golder, Peter, 263
Goldman Sachs, 285
Goodbye, Darkness (Manchester), 35–36
Good to Great (Collins), 2, 14, 50, 149, 156
Good to Great and the Social Sectors (Collins), 156
Good-to-Great matched-pair research method,
    149–50, *150*
Good to Great Project, 273, 279, 300
"Gordon the Guided Missile" (Cleese), 233–34
Gorman, Leon, 24–25, 88, 206, 283
Graham, Katharine, 17, 23–24, 25, 44, 50
Grant, Ulysses S., 188
Great Britain, 116–17, 120–21
Great by Choice (Collins and Hansen)
  and author's relationship with Lazier, 2
  on leadership, 156
  and luck events, 143
  on pace of decision making, 61
  research question underlying, 149
  and 10x winners, 186
  on 20 Mile March discipline, 161–62
greatness, path of, 88
gross margin, 296
group decision making, 54–57
Grousbeck, H. Irving, 78
Grove, Andy, 17, 185, 187, 240
growth, pace of, 195–200, *198*
guerrilla marketing, 256
guiding philosophies, 105. *See also* vision
gut instinct, 51–53

Hadley, Greg, 129
Hamilton, Alexander, 59
handwritten notes, value of, 67
Hannemann, Bill
  and charismatic visionary stereotype, 138
  and diversity in hiring, 244
  on focused strategy, 202–3
  and standards of performance, 298
  strategic priorities of, 269
  tactical execution of, 266
Hansen, Morten, 61, 143, 149, 186, 187
hard work, 86

options, keeping open one's, 6
OPUR (One Person Ultimately Responsible), 300
organization, strategic decision making about, 173, *174*, 192
"Organizational Vision and Visionary Organizations," 103
Osborne Computer, 196, 197, 207
Out of the Crisis (Deming), 278
Outside magazine, 256

Packard, Dave
  and growth as leader, 23
  and pace of growth, 195
  and principles and objectives of HP, 94
  and respect for people, 46
Packard's Law, 157
parables, 81
paradoxes, 158
paranoia, practicing productive, 163–64, 186–88
Parisan, 285
Parker, George, 199
Parkinson, Joseph, 121–22
participative decision making, 55–56
passion, 159
Patagonia
  and conviction of leaders, 48
  coordination of leadership at, 251
  and customer experience, 228
  and customer input, 232
  designers employed by, 247
  enthusiasm of employees of, 239
  guerrilla marketing of, 256
  office culture of, 261
  purpose of, 110, 112
  quiet time observed at, 261
  See also McDivitt, Kristine
Patterson, John Henry, 220
payables period, 296
Pearl Harbor, attack on, 186
people and organization, strategic decisions about, 173, *174*, 192, 215
people skills, hard/soft, *41*, 74–79
PepsiCo, 92, 121
performance
  conditions promoting excellent, 274–77
  effect of feedback on, 75
  expectations for, 302
  measuring, 280, *280*, 288–90
  standards of, 74–75, 78–79, 298–99
persistence, 139–47
  and Caldwell's ascent of Dawn Wall, 139–42
  of Churchill, 144–45
  with companies vs. ideas, 147
  of Jobs, 142, 144

perspectives on, 146–47
  role of, in innovation, 240
Personal CAD Systems, 80
Personal History (Graham), 24
personality, 42, 45
Personal Publisher, 221, 228–29
personal responsibility, 20, 73, 274, 276, 300
personal touch of leaders, *41*, 65–71, 82, 142
Perspective on McKinsey (Brower), 131
Peters, Tom, 243–44
Peter the Great, 182
Pharriss, Bruce, 111
Pioneer Hi-Bred International, 92, 110
pioneers, 206–8, *206*
Pixar Animation Studios, 15
Porras, Jerry, 26, 123–25, 144, 149
Porter, Michael, 177, 216
positive reinforcement, 75–79
Powell, Colin, 44
Powell, John Alfred, 220
power, 43
Powerbars, 234–35
prices, controlling, 200
priorities, identifying, 62, 64–65, 192–93, 194, 215
problem solving, 228–30, 261–62
Procter, William, 88
Procter & Gamble, 91, 117–18, 221, 227, 253
productivity, 63–64, 273
products
  failures of, 236–39
  field testing, 230
  making strategic decisions about, 173, *174*, 192
profit, 107–9
progress, stimulating, 165–66
Progressive Insurance, 23, 189
public offerings, 203, 205–6
purpose
  and basic flow of vision, strategy, tactics, *91*
  and BHAGs (big, hairy, audacious goals), 166
  and confusing "rare" with "new," 113–14
  and decentralization, *252*
  definition of, 104
  DPR Construction's implementation of, 135, 137
  as element of vision, *91*, 103, *104*, 109–14
  examples of, 130, 210
  "five whys" of, 111–12
  as guiding star, 166
  role of flexibility in, 131
  statements of, 110–11

quality issues, 273
questions
  questions-to-statements ratios, 59–60
  and stimulating communication in others, 84

Strategic Software, Inc., 128
strategy, 171–216
    about, 172
    annual meetings for setting, 193–94
    basic flow of vision, strategy, tactics, *91*
    basic process for setting, 173, *174*
    and BHAGs (big, hairy, audacious goals),
        190–91, *191*
    and decision making, 173, *174*, 192–94, *193*
    defending our flanks, 185–88
    diversification vs. focused strategy, 201–3, *204*
    essence of, 183–91
    example (Hardrock Products), 209–16
    extending victories, 188–90
    and external assessment, 173, *174*, 176–82, 192,
        193, 194, 212
    four principles of setting, 172
    and internal assessment, 173–76, *174*, 192, *193*,
        194, 211
    and leading or following the market, 206–8, *206*
    and pace of growth, 195–200
    placing big bets, 183–85
    priorities in, 192–93, 194, 215
    and public offerings, 203, 205–6
    role of flexibility in, 131
    of small to mid-sized companies, 194–208
    and stages of industry evolution analysis, 216
    time frame of, 192–93
    vision as source of, 95, 97–100, 172, 173, 190–91,
        190, 192, *193*, 194
strengths, assessing, 174–75, 211
Stryker, 189
Study of Leadership at the United States Military
        Academy at West Point, 27, 42, 44, 49
suggestion boxes, 259
Summers, Harry G., 99
Swanson, Jim, 101
Syme, Duncan, 102

tactical excellence, 265–302
    and appreciating, 280, *280*, 291–93
    basic flow of vision, strategy, tactics, *91*
    and BHAGs (big, hairy, audacious goals),
        279–80
    and continual improvement, 278–79
    and deadlines, 267–69
    environments that foster, 273–77, 280, *280*
    and expectations, 277–78
    five conditions that promote, 274–77
    and goal setting, 280, *280*, 286–88, *288*
    and hiring, 280, *280*, 281–82
    and inculturating process, 280, *280*, 282–84
    and measuring performance, 280, *280*, 288–90
    and milestone management, 269–70, *270*

    role of flexibility in, 131
    and SMaC mindset, 271–73
    and standards of performance, 298–99
    and technology and information systems,
        293–98
    and training, 280, *280*, 284–85
    and trust placed in employees, 297–98
    and values, 278
    and vision, 278
    vision as context for, 95, 97–100
Tagamet, 229–30
tanks, development of, 175
"targeting" mission type, 119–20
teachers, leaders as, 77–78, 89
Teach for America, 42–43
technology and information systems, 293–98
technology trends, 177, 212
Techstars, 152
Telecare Corporation, 20–22, 106, 110, 282
telephone technology, 219
Televideo, 197
Telles, Marcel Herrmann, 29
Tellis, Gerard, 263
10x Multiplier (return on luck), 166–67, 186
tenacity, 87–88
tensions in the workplace, 85
Tensor Corporation, 205–6, 227
Thatcher, Margaret, 40
Thermo Electron Corporation, 250
Thirteen Days (Kennedy), 55, 60
threats, external, 180–82, 212
3M Company
    decentralization practiced in, 250
    encouragement promoted at, 258
    "ever forward" mentality at, 88
    innovations of, 176, 188, 221, 223
    and Post-it Notes, 223, 225, 226, 234
    vision of, 92
time management, 63–64
T/Maker Company, 221, 228–29
"T minus 3" discipline, 279–80
Tokyo Tsushin Kogyo, 119–20
Tom's of Maine, 108
"touch and feel" approach, 231–32
training, 280, *280*, 284–85
Trammell Crow (Sobel), 79
Trilogy, 197
Trimble, Vance, 266
Truman, Harry, 53, 138, 253
trust, 297–98, 302
"Trust Wager" of Lazier, 6–8
truth, placing a premium on, 180–82
Tuchman, Barbara, 41, 96
Turner, Ted, 138

20 Mile March discipline, 161–62
"Tyranny of the OR," 158

UCLA Bruins, 100, 150–51
uncertainty, chronic state of, 15
United States
    and Civil War, 123, 188
    Constitution, 101–2, 134, 165, 283
    Declaration of Independence, 101, 134
    and Pearl Harbor attack, 186
    and post-Civil War Reconstruction, 123
    and vision of founding fathers, 101, 134, 137
United States Postal Service, 225
University Games, 256
University National Bank and Trust, 199–200
UPS (United Parcel Service), 225
US Marine Corps, 36
US Military Academy at West Point, 27, 42, 44, 49,
    140–41

vacations, 261
Vadasz, Les, 185
values and beliefs
    and authenticity in leaders, 46–49
    and basic flow of vision, strategy, tactics, *91*
    and decentralization, *252*
    and diversity, 244
    DPR Construction's implementation of, 135,
        136–37
    as element of vision, 91, 103, 104–9, *104*
    employee's violation of, 19
    examples of, 129–30, 210
    and hiring decisions, 244, 281
    incentives misaligned with, 34
    and inculturating employees, 282
    Lazier on, 9–10
    reinforcing, 69–70
    role of flexibility in, 131
    and role of profit, 107–9
    standards in, 298, 302
    and tactical execution, 278
    training seminars instilling, 284
    and warm bodies syndrome, 196
Vandt, Les, 234, 235
Vanguard, 189
venture capitalists, 195, 260
Vermont Castings, 102
victories, strategic extension of, 188–90
Vietnam War, 24, 36, 99–100, 158–59, 276
Visicorp, 197, 207, 227
vision, 90–138
    basic flow of vision, strategy, tactics, *91*
    benefits of, 95–103
    and BHAGs (big, hairy, audacious goals), *124*

and charisma, 138
clear understanding of, 137–38
Collins-Porras Vision Framework, 90, 103
communicating, 80, 132–33, 137–38
components of, 91, 103, *104*
as context for strategic and tactical decisions, 95,
    97–100
core values and beliefs components of, 91, 103,
    104–9
and decentralization, 251
DPR Construction's implementation of, 133–37
and employee motivation, 96–97
as essential to greatness, 91–92, 94
examples of, 210
and focused strategy, 202–3
and inculturating employees, 282
maintaining flexibility in, 131
mission as component of, 91, 103, *104*, 114–26
purpose as component of, 91, 103, *104*, 109–14
in small companies, 94–95
strategy's reliance on, 95, 97–100, 172, 173,
    190–91, *190*, 192, *193*, 194
and tactical execution, 278
terminology associated with, 93
writing down, 131
Viti, Paulo, 232
Vitrac, Jean Pierre, 226

Walmart
    and author's research, 189
    and J.C. Penney, 122
    Low Threshold for Change policy of, 223
    mission of, 120
    tactical execution of, 266
    technology leveraged by, 294
    vision of, 92, 137
    See also Walton, Sam
Walsh, Bill, 75–76
Walt Disney, 92, 184, 189
Walton, Sam
    early rejections experienced by, 220
    "ever forward" mentality of, 88
    and growth as leader, 23
    intuitive decision making of, 52
    and J.C. Penney, 122
    knowledge of daily operations, 68–69
    mission of, 120
    as role model, 47
    tactical execution of, 266
    vision of, 137
warm bodies syndrome, 196
Warner, H. M., 220
Warner Brothers, 220
Washington, George, 59, 137